Middle School 2-2

중간고사 완벽대비

# 적중 100

영어 기출 문제집

## 중 2

동아 | 윤정미

*Best Collection*

# 구성과 특징

교과서의 주요 학습 내용을 중심으로 학습 영역별 특성에 맞춰 단계별로 다양한 학습 기회를 제공하여 단원별 학습능력 평가는 물론 중간 및 기말고사 시험 등에 완벽하게 대비할 수 있도록 내용을 구성

## Words & Expressions

**Step1**  Key Words 단원별 핵심 단어 설명 및 풀이
Key Expression 단원별 핵심 숙어 및 관용어 설명
Word Power 반대 또는 비슷한 뜻 단어 배우기
English Dictionary 영어로 배우는 영어 단어

**Step2**  실력평가 단원별 수시평가 대비 주관식, 객관식 문제풀이

**Step3**  서술형 대비 학업성취도 및 수행능력평가 대비 서술형 문제풀이

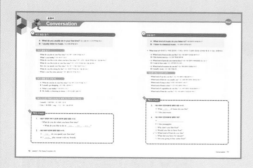

## Conversation

**Step1**  핵심 의사소통 의사소통에 필요한 주요 표현 방법 요약
핵심 Check 기본적인 표현 방법 및 활용능력 확인

**Step2**  대화문 익히기 상황에 따른 대화문 활용 및 연습

**Step3**  기본평가 시험대비 기초 학습 능력 평가

**Step4**  실력평가 단원별 수시평가 대비 주관식, 객관식 문제풀이

**Step5**  서술형 대비 학업성취도 및 수행능력평가 대비 서술형 문제풀이

## Grammar

**Step1**  주요 문법 단원별 주요 문법 사항과 예문을 알기 쉽게 설명
핵심 Check 기본 문법사항에 대한 이해 여부 확인

**Step2**  기본평가 시험대비 기초 학습 능력 평가

**Step3**  실력평가 단원별 수시평가 대비 주관식, 객관식 문제풀이

**Step4**  서술형 대비 학업성취도 및 수행능력평가 대비 서술형 문제풀이

## Reading

**Step1**  구문 분석 단원별로 제시된 문장에 대한 구문별 분석과 내용 설명
확인문제 문장에 대한 기본적인 이해와 인지능력 확인

**Step2**  확인학습A 빈칸 채우기를 통한 문장 완성 능력 확인

**Step3**  확인학습B 제시된 우리말을 영어로 완성하여 작문 능력 키우기

**Step4**  실력평가 단원별 수시평가 대비 주관식, 객관식 문제풀이

**Step5**  서술형 대비 학업성취도 및 수행능력평가 대비 서술형 문제풀이
교과서 구석구석 교과서에 나오는 기타 문장까지 완벽 학습

# Composition

## |영역별 핵심문제|

단어 및 어휘, 대화문, 문법, 독해 등 각 영역별 기출문제의 출제 유형을 분석하여 실전에 대비하고 연습할
수 있도록 문제를 배열

## |서술형 실전 및 창의사고력 문제|

학교 시험에서 점차 늘어나는 서술형 시험에 집중 대비하고 고득점을 취득하는데 만전을 기하기 위한
학습 코너

## |단원별 예상문제|

기출문제를 분석한 후 새로운 시험 출제 경향을 더하여 새롭게 출제될 수 있는 문제를 포함하여 시험에 완벽
하게 대비할 수 있도록 준비

## |단원별 모의고사|

영역별, 단계별 학습을 모두 마친 후 실전 연습을 위한 모의고사

# INSIGHT
## on the textbook

### 교과서 파헤치기

- 단어Test1~2 영어 단어 우리말 쓰기와 우리말을 영어 단어로 쓰기
- 대화문Test1~2 대화문 빈칸 완성 및 전체 대화문 쓰기
- 본문Test1~5 빈칸 완성, 우리말 쓰기, 문장 배열연습, 영어 작문하기 복습 등 단계별 반복 학습을
  통해 교과서 지문에 대한 완벽한 습득
- 구석구석지문Test1~2 지문 빈칸 완성 및 전문 영어로 쓰기

이책의 차례 # Contents

Lesson **5**  **Living Healthily and Safely**  05~58

Lesson **6**  **Different People, Different Views**  59~112

Lesson **7**  **Life in Space**  113~166

〈Insight on the textbook〉 교과서 파헤치기  01~60

〈책 속의 책〉 정답 및 해설  01~44

# Lesson 5

# Living Healthily and Safely

## 🔖 의사소통 기능

- 문제점이나 증상을 묻고 답하기
  A: What's wrong?
  B: I have a headache.

- 당부하기
  Make sure you take some medicine.

## 🔖 언어 형식

- 목적격 관계대명사
  Another problem **(which/that)** you can have is neck pain.

- call *A B*
  We **call** such people smombies.

# Words & Expressions

교과서

## Key Words

- **accident**[ǽksidənt] 명 사고
- **addiction**[ədíkʃən] 명 중독
- **advice**[ædváis] 명 충고
- **another**[ənʌ́ðər] 형 또 다른
- **around**[əráund] 부 주위에
- **author**[ɔ́:θər] 명 작가, 저자
- **back**[bæk] 명 등
- **blink**[bliŋk] 동 눈을 깜박이다
- **cause**[kɔ:z] 동 야기하다
- **celebrity**[səlébrəti] 명 유명인사, 유명인
- **delicious**[dilíʃəs] 형 맛있는
- **dentist**[déntist] 명 치과의사
- **difficult**[dífikʌlt] 형 어려운
- **dry**[drai] 형 건조한, 마른
- **during**[djúəriŋ] 전 ~ 동안
- **example**[igzǽmpl] 명 예, 사례
- **exercise**[éksərsàiz] 명 운동
- **fever**[fí:vər] 명 열, 열병
- **headache**[hédeik] 명 두통
- **health**[helθ] 명 건강
- **hole**[houl] 명 구덩이, 구멍
- **hurt**[həːrt] 동 다치다
- **increase**[inkrí:s] 동 증가하다
- **intelligent**[intélədʒənt] 형 똑똑한, 지적인
- **meal**[mi:l] 명 식사

- **medicine**[médisn] 명 약
- **nervous**[nə́rvəs] 형 초조한, 불안한
- **pain**[pein] 명 아픔, 고통
- **prevent**[privént] 동 막다, 예방하다
- **promise**[prámis] 명 약속
- **regularly**[régjulərli] 부 규칙적으로
- **safety**[séifti] 명 안전
- **sign**[sain] 명 표지판
- **simple**[símpl] 형 단순한
- **skin**[skin] 명 피부
- **smart**[smɑ:rt] 형 현명한, 말쑥한
- **sore**[sɔ:r] 형 아픈, 쓰린
- **subject**[sʌ́bdʒikt] 명 과목
- **such**[sətʃ] 형 그러한
- **terrible**[térəbl] 형 끔찍한, 무서운
- **text**[tekst] 동 문자를 보내다
- **throat**[θrout] 명 목구멍
- **thumb**[θʌm] 명 엄지손가락
- **tip**[tip] 명 조언
- **toothache**[túːθeik] 명 치통
- **unwise**[ənwáiz] 형 현명하지 않은
- **various**[véəriəs] 형 다양한
- **while**[hwail] 접 ~하는 동안
- **without**[wiðáut] 전 ~ 없이
- **zombie**[zámbi] 명 좀비, 반쯤 죽은 것 같은 사람

## Key Expressions

- **a few** 몇몇의
- **a heating pad** 찜질 패드
- **all over the world** 전 세계적으로
- **be good at ~** ~을 잘하다
- **eye level** 눈높이
- **fall asleep** 잠들다
- **for example** 예를 들어
- **from now on** 지금부터
- **get hurt** 다치다
- **get into ~** (~한 상태에) 처하다
- **have a cold** 감기에 걸리다
- **have a fever** 열이 나다
- **have a runny nose** 콧물이 흐르다

- **have a sore throat** 목이 아프다
- **Here are+복수 명사** 여기에 ~가 있다
- **instead of ~** ~ 대신에
- **look well** 건강해 보이다
- **take a rest** 휴식을 취하다, 쉬다
- **take medicine** 약을 먹다
- **talk to ~** ~에게 말하다
- **text message** 문자 메시지
- **these days** 요즈음
- **traffic light** 교통 신호등
- **try to+동사원형** ~하려고 애쓰다[노력하다]
- **turn off** ~을 끄다
- **Why don't you+동사원형 ~?** ~하는 게 어때?

## Word Power

※ 서로 반대되는 뜻을 가진 단어

- □ **wise** (현명한) ↔ **unwise** (현명하지 않은)
- □ **nervous** (초조한) ↔ **calm** (차분한)
- □ **dry** (건조한) ↔ **wet** (젖은)
- □ **without** (~ 없이) ↔ **with** (~을 가지고)
- □ **increase** (증가하다) ↔ **decrease** (감소하다)
- □ **careful** (조심하는) ↔ **careless** (부주의한)

- □ **well** (건강한) ↔ **ill** (아픈)
- □ **cheap** (싼) ↔ **expensive** (비싼)
- □ **interesting** (흥미로운) ↔ **uninteresting** (재미없는)
- □ **difficult** (어려운) ↔ **easy** (쉬운)
- □ **turn off** (끄다) ↔ **turn on** (켜다)
- □ **intelligent** (똑똑한) ↔ **stupid** (어리석은)

※ 서로 비슷한 뜻을 가진 단어

- □ **sore** : **painful** (아픈)
- □ **well** : **healthy** (건강한)
- □ **advice** : **tip** (조언, 충고)
- □ **prevent** : **inhibit** (막다)

- □ **terrible** : **awful** (끔찍한, 지독한)
- □ **nervous** : **anxious** (초조한, 불안한)
- □ **various** : **varied** (다양한)
- □ **pain** : **suffering** (고통)

## English Dictionary

- □ **addiction** 중독
  → the problem when someone cannot stop doing something, or does something too much
  어떤 일을 하는 것을 멈출 수 없거나 너무 많이 할 때의 문제

- □ **blink** 눈을 깜박이다
  → to open and close your eyes very quickly
  매우 빨리 눈을 뜨고 감다

- □ **cause** 야기하다
  → to make something happen
  어떤 일이 발생하도록 하다

- □ **medicine** 약, 약물
  → a pill or a liquid that you take when you are sick to help you get better
  아플 때 나아지도록 하기 위해 복용하는 알약 또는 액체

- □ **pad** 패드
  → a thick piece of soft material
  부드러운 소재의 두꺼운 조각

- □ **pain** 고통
  → the feeling you have when a part of your body hurts
  신체의 일부가 아플 때 가지는 느낌

- □ **prevent** 막다, 예방하다
  → to stop something from happening, or stop someone from doing
  어떤 일이 일어나거나 누군가가 하는 것을 막다

- □ **regularly** 규칙적으로
  → at the same time every day, every week, etc.
  매일, 매주 등의 같은 시간에

- □ **rest** 휴식
  → a time when you relax or sleep
  쉬거나 잠을 자는 시간

- □ **safety** 안전
  → the state of being safe and protected from danger or harm
  위험이나 해로부터 안전하고 보호받는 상태

- □ **text** 문자를 보내다
  → to send someone a written message using a cell phone
  휴대전화를 이용하여 누군가에게 문자 메시지를 보내다

- □ **throat** 목구멍
  → the passage at the back of your mouth, where you swallow
  음식을 삼키는 입의 뒤쪽에 있는 통로

- □ **thumb** 엄지손가락
  → the short thick finger on your hand that helps you hold things
  물건을 집는 데 도움이 되는 손에 있는 짧고 두꺼운 손가락

**서답형**

**01** 다음 문장의 빈칸에 주어진 영어 설명에 해당하는 말을 쓰시오.

used when one thing replaces another, or when you do a different thing

• Turn off your smartphone during meals or meetings. You can talk to people _____ _____ texting them.

➡ _____

**02** 다음 빈칸에 공통으로 들어갈 말은? (대 · 소문자 무시)

• I think you have a cold. _____ this medicine and make sure you _____ a good rest.

① take       ② get       ③ go
④ make       ⑤ look

**서답형**

**03** 다음 우리말에 맞게 빈칸에 알맞은 단어를 쓰시오.

너는 스마트폰을 볼 때 자주 눈을 깜박이지 않는다.

➡ When you look at your smartphone, you do not _____ often.

**중요**

**04** 다음 글의 흐름상 빈칸에 들어갈 가장 적절한 단어는?

Do you feel sad when you check your smartphone and there is no text message? If your answers are "yes," you may have smartphone _____.

① pain       ② author
③ addiction       ④ promise
⑤ celebrity

**[05~06]** 다음 영영풀이에 해당하는 단어를 고르시오.

**05**
the feeling you have when a part of your body hurts

① sour       ② hurt
③ pain       ④ addiction
⑤ stress

**중요**

**06**
at the same time every day, every week, etc.

① sometimes       ② always
③ carefully       ④ simply
⑤ regularly

**서답형**

**07** 다음 짝지어진 단어의 관계가 같도록 빈칸에 알맞은 말을 쓰시오.

well : healthy = anxious : _____

**08** 다음 빈칸에 들어갈 말이 알맞게 짝지어진 것은?

• Unwise or too much use of smartphones can _____ various problems.
• When you look down at your smartphone, the stress on your neck _____s.

① prevent – decrease
② prevent – increase
③ hurt – prevent
④ cause – increase
⑤ cause – decrease

**01** 다음 빈칸에 들어갈 말을 〈보기〉에서 찾아 쓰시오. (필요하면 변형하여 쓰시오.)

┌─ 보기 ┐

nervous   well   have   smombie

(1) I think he _____ a headache.

(2) You don't look _____. What's wrong?

(3) If you are a _____, you can have various safety problems.

(4) I get _____ when my smartphone is not around.

**02** 다음 영영풀이에 알맞은 단어를 〈보기〉에서 찾아 첫 번째 칸에 쓰고, 두 번째 칸에는 우리말 뜻을 쓰시오.

┌─ 보기 ┐

pad   medicine   addiction   text
blink   fever   nervous   prevent

(1) _____: to stop something from happening, or stop someone from doing: _____

(2) _____: a pill or a liquid that you take when you are sick to help you get better: _____

(3) _____: the problem when someone cannot stop doing something, or does something too much: _____

**03** 다음 빈칸에 들어갈 알맞은 단어를 주어진 철자로 시작하여 쓰시오.

┌─────────────────────────┐
• Many people like sending t_____ messages more than calling.
• Too much use of smartphones can c_____ dry eyes.
└─────────────────────────┘

**04** 다음 우리말과 같은 표현이 되도록 문장의 빈칸을 채우시오.

(1) 스마트폰 없이 사는 것은 요즘 많은 사람들에게 어렵다.
➡ Living _____ smartphones is difficult for many of us these days.

(2) 우리는 그러한 사람들을 스몸비, 즉 스마트폰 좀비라고 부른다.
➡ We call _____ people smombies, smartphone zombies.

(3) 지금부터, 나는 매일 30분 동안 걸으려고 노력할 것이다.
➡ _____ _____ _____, I will try to walk for 30 minutes every day.

(4) 잠자리에서 스마트폰을 사용하면, 쉽게 잠들지 못할 거야.
➡ If you use your smartphone in bed, you may not _____ _____ easily.

**05** 다음 빈칸에 들어갈 말을 〈보기〉에서 골라 알맞은 형태로 고쳐 쓰시오.

┌─ 보기 ┐

regular   nerve   addict   vary   text

(1) People may have smartphone _____ if they feel anxious when their smartphones are not around.

(2) Make sure you exercise _____.

(3) Unwise or too much use of smartphones can cause _____ problems.

(4) He did not notice the car because he was _____.

교과서

# Conversation

### 1 문제점이나 증상을 묻고 답하기

> **A** What's wrong? 무슨 일이니?
> **B** I have a headache. 머리가 아파요.

■ 상대방이 기분이 좋지 않거나 어딘가 아파 보일 때 What's wrong (with you)?라고 묻는다. What's the matter (with you)?라고 물을 수도 있다.

■ **문제점이나 증상을 묻는 다양한 표현들**

"무슨 일 있니?"라는 의미로 What's wrong with you? / What's the matter? / Is there anything wrong? / What happened? / What's the problem? 등을 사용한다.

■ **증상 답하기**

'나는 ~가 아프다.'는 'I have a/an+명사'로 나타내는데, 명사 자리에 아픈 증상이나 병명을 써서 어디가 아픈지를 표현한다. 아픈 증상을 나타내는 말은 주로 신체 부위 뒤에 '아픔, 통증'을 뜻하는 'ache'를 붙여 쓴다. 예를 들면 head(머리)에 ache를 붙이면 '두통'이라는 뜻의 'headache'가 된다. 이와 같은 형태로 요통 'backache', 귀앓이 'earache', 치통 'toothache' 등의 표현을 쓴다.

- A: You don't look well. 너 몸이 안 좋아 보여.
  What's wrong? 무슨 일 있니?
  B: I have a headache. 머리가 아파.

- A: What's the matter? 무슨 일 있니?
  B: My dog ate my homework. 내 개가 내 숙제를 먹어 버렸어.

- A: What's wrong, Peter? 무슨 일이니, Peter?
  B: I don't know, Ms. Kim, but my back hurts a lot. 모르겠어요, 김 선생님, 하지만 등이 매우 아파요.

### 핵심 Check

1. 다음 대화의 빈칸에 알맞은 말을 쓰시오.

   A: _____ _____ with your leg, Sam?

   B: I fell and hurt my foot while I was playing soccer.

2. 다음 주어진 문장과 같은 의미가 되도록 빈칸에 알맞은 말을 쓰시오.

   What's wrong?

   = Is there _____ _____?

**②** 당부하기

> **Make sure you take some medicine.** 약을 꼭 먹도록 하렴.

■ 상대방에게 당부하는 표현으로 '반드시 ~하도록 해라, ~을 확실히 해라'라는 의미의 'make sure ~'를 사용한다. make sure 다음에 접속사 that을 생략할 수 있고 당부하고자 하는 내용을 주어와 동사를 갖춘 문장으로 쓴다. 즉, sure 다음에는 '(that+)주어+동사'를 쓴다. 유사한 의미를 가진 표현으로 'You had better+동사원형 ~', 'Don't forget to+동사형 ~', 'Remember to+동사원형 ~' 등이 있다.

### 당부하기 표현

- A: Well, make sure you take a warm bath. 음. 꼭 따뜻하게 목욕을 하도록 하렴.
  B: OK. Thanks a lot. 알았어요. 고마워요.
- A: I think I caught a cold. 나 감기에 걸린 것 같아.
  B: That's too bad. Make sure you take some medicine and relax. 안됐구나. 꼭 약을 먹고 쉬렴.
- Remember to call me when you leave. 떠날 때 나에게 전화하는 것을 기억해라.
- Don't forget to call me when you arrive. 도착하면 나에게 전화하는 것을 잊지 마.
- You had better call me when you arrive. 너는 도착하면 나에게 전화하는 것이 좋겠다.

■ 상대방의 당부를 받아들일 때 make sure 다음에 긍정문이 오면 'OK. I will.'로 답하고, 부정문이 오면 'OK. I won't.'로 답한다.

- A: Make sure you give me a call when you get home. 집에 도착하면 내게 꼭 전화해.
  B: Okay, I will. 응. 그렇게 할게.
- A: Make sure you won't be late for the class again. 다시는 수업에 지각하지 마.
  B: Okay, I won't. 네. 안 할게요.

### 핵심 Check

3. 다음 대화의 빈칸에 들어갈 알맞은 것은?

A: Mom, can I play soccer with my friends after school?
B: Sure, but _____.

① you don't have to play soccer
② you can't
③ you had better not play soccer
④ don't forget to stay home after school
⑤ make sure you come home before dinner

**A. Listen and Talk A-1**

W: You ❶look sick. ❷What's wrong, Inho?

B: ❸I have a sore throat. I have a fever, too.

W: I think you have a cold. ❹Take this medicine and ❺make sure you take a good rest.

B: OK. Thank you.

W: 너 아파 보인다. 무슨 일이니, 인호야?
B: 목이 아파요. 열도 나요.
W: 감기에 걸린 것 같구나. 이 약을 먹고 좀 쉬도록 하렴.
B: 알겠어요. 감사합니다.

❶ 'look+형용사'는 '～처럼 보인다'는 의미이다.
❷ 문제점이나 증상을 묻는 표현으로 Is there anything wrong?, What happened?, What's the problem? 등으로 물을 수 있다.
❸ '나는 ～가 아프다.'는 표현으로 'I have a/an+명사'로 나타내는데, 명사 자리에 아픈 증상이나 병명을 써서 어디가 아픈지 표현한다.
❹ '약을 복용하다'라는 의미로 동사 take를 사용한다.
❺ 'make sure ～'는 상대방에게 당부하는 표현으로 '반드시 ～하도록 해라, ～을 확실히 해라'라는 의미다. '쉬다, 휴식을 취하다' 표현에 동사 take를 사용한다.

**Check(√) True or False**

(1) Inho has a cold.　　　　　　　　　　　　　　　　　　T ☐ F ☐

(2) The woman may be a school nurse.　　　　　　　　　T ☐ F ☐

 **B. Listen and Talk C**

W: ❶What's wrong, Andy?

B: Hello, Ms. Kim. My right thumb hurts.

W: Hmm. Do you use your smartphone a lot?

B: Yes, ❷I text a lot. Why?

W: I think you have texting thumb.

B: Texting thumb? What's texting thumb?

W: It's pain in your thumb. You can get it from ❸texting too much.

B: Oh, I didn't know that.

W: ❹Why don't you do some finger stretching exercises?

B: OK, I will.

W: And ❺make sure you don't text too much.

W: 무슨 일이니, Andy?
B: 안녕하세요, 김 선생님. 제 오른손 엄지손가락이 아파요.
W: 음. 너 스마트폰을 많이 사용하니?
B: 네, 저 문자를 많이 해요. 왜요?
W: 내 생각에 너는 texting thumb인 것 같아.
B: texting thumb이요? texting thumb이 뭐예요?
W: 엄지손가락에 통증이 있는 거야. 문자를 너무 많이 하면 생길 수 있어.
B: 오, 그건 몰랐네요.
W: 손가락 스트레칭 운동을 좀 하는 게 어떠니?
B: 네, 그럴게요.
W: 그리고 문자를 너무 많이 하지 않도록 하렴.

❶ 문제점이나 증상을 물어볼 때 사용하는 표현으로 'What's the matter?'로 바꾸어 쓸 수 있다.
❷ text는 동사로 '문자를 보내다'는 의미다.
❸ 전치사 from 뒤의 texting은 전치사의 목적어로 사용된 동명사이다.
❹ 'Why don't you+동사원형 ～?'은 '～하는 게 어때?'라는 뜻으로 제안이나 권유를 할 때 사용하는 표현이다.
❺ 상대방에게 당부하는 표현으로 '반드시 ～하도록 해라, ～을 확실히 해라'라는 의미이다.

**Check(√) True or False**

(3) Andy's right thumb hurts.　　　　　　　　　　　　　T ☐ F ☐

(4) Andy won't do any finger stretching exercises.　　　　T ☐ F ☐

### Listen and Talk A-2

W: ❶What's wrong, Peter?
B: I don't know, Ms. Kim, but ❷my back hurts a lot.
W: ❸Put a heating pad on it.
B: OK, I will.
W: And ❹make sure you do some stretching exercises.

❶ Is there anything wrong?, What happened?, What's the problem? 등과 같은 표현으로 문제점이나 증상을 물어볼 때 사용한다.
❷ 여기서 back은 명사로 '등'을 의미한다. a lot은 동사 hurts를 수식하는 부사구로 '많이'의 의미다.
❸ put A on B 형태로 'A를 B에 놓다'는 의미다.
❹ 상대방에게 당부하는 표현으로 '반드시 ~하도록 해라, ~을 확실히 해라'라는 의미다.

### Listen and Talk A-3

W: ❶What's the matter, Chris?
B: I have a terrible toothache.
W: ❷Here is some medicine. Take this.
B: Thank you.
W: And make sure you ❸go to the dentist.
B: OK, I will.

❶ 문제점이나 증상을 물어볼 때 사용하는 표현이다.
❷ 'Here is+단수 명사'로 '여기에 ~가 있다'는 의미다
❸ go to the dentist는 '치과에 가다'는 의미다.

### Listen and Talk A-4

W: What's wrong with your leg, Sam?
B: I fell and hurt my foot ❶while I was playing soccer.
W: Can you walk?
B: Yes, but it hurts a lot.
W: ❷Why don't you put some ice on it? And make sure you don't play soccer until next week.

❶ while은 접속사로 '~하는 동안'의 의미다.
❷ 'Why don't you+동사원형 ~?'은 '~하는 게 어때?'라는 의미이다.

### Listen and Talk B-1

A: You don't ❶look well. What's wrong?
B: I have a headache.
A: ❷That's too bad. Make sure you ❸take some medicine.
B: OK, I will.

❶ 'look+형용사'로 여기서 well은 형용사로 '건강한'의 의미다.
❷ 상대방의 안 좋은 일이나 소식에 대해 '안 됐다'라는 의미다.
❸ take는 '복용하다, 먹다'는 의미다.

### Listen and Talk B-2

A: You don't look well. What's wrong?
B: I have a cold.
A: That's too bad. Make sure you ❶go see a doctor.
B: OK, I will.

❶ 'go see a doctor'는 '병원에 가다'는 의미로 해석한다.

### Review 1

G: ❶What's wrong, Mike?
B: ❷I have a terrible headache.
G: I think you ❸should take some medicine.
B: OK, I will.

❶ Is there anything wrong?, What happened?, What's the problem? 등과 같은 표현으로 문제점이나 증상을 물어볼 때 사용한다.
❷ '나는 ~가 아프다.'는 표현으로 'I have a/an+명사'로 나타내는데, 명사 자리에 아픈 증상이나 병명을 써서 어디가 아픈지 표현한다.
❸ 상대방에게 조언을 할 때 조동사 should를 사용한다.

### Review 2

M: What's the matter, Mina?
G: I ❶have a sore throat. I also ❷have a runny nose.
M: I think you have a cold. Make sure you get some rest.
G: OK, I will.

❶ 'have a sore throat'는 '목이 아프다'는 의미다.
❷ 'have a runny nose'는 '콧물이 난다'는 의미다.

● 다음 우리말과 일치하도록 빈칸에 알맞은 말을 쓰시오.

### Listen and Talk A-1

W: You look sick. _____ _____, Inho?

B: I _____ _____ _____ _____ . I _____ _____ _____, too.

W: I think you _____ _____ _____. _____ this medicine and _____ _____ you _____ a good rest.

B: OK. Thank you.

해석

W: 너 아파 보인다. 무슨 일이니, 인호야?
B: 목이 아파요. 열도 나요.
W: 감기에 걸린 것 같구나. 이 약을 먹고 좀 쉬도록 하렴.
B: 알겠어요. 감사합니다.

### Listen and Talk A-2

W: What's _____, Peter?

B: I don't know, Ms. Kim, but my back _____ a lot.

W: _____ a heating pad _____ it.

B: OK, I will.

W: And _____ _____ you do some stretching exercises.

W: 무슨 일이니, Peter?
B: 모르겠어요, 김 선생님. 등이 아파요.
W: 그곳에 찜질 패드를 올려놓으렴.
B: 네, 그럴게요.
W: 그리고 스트레칭 운동을 하렴.

### Listen and Talk A-3

W: What's the _____, Chris?

B: I _____ _____ terrible toothache.

W: _____ _____ some medicine. _____ this.

B: Thank you.

W: And _____ _____ you go to the dentist.

B: OK, I will.

W: 무슨 일이니, Chris?
B: 저는 심한 치통이 있어요.
W: 여기 약이 있단다. 이것을 먹으렴.
B: 감사합니다.
W: 그리고 치과에 가도록 하렴.
B: 네, 알겠어요.

### Listen and Talk A-4

W: What's _____ _____ your leg, Sam?

B: I fell and hurt my foot _____ I was playing soccer.

W: Can you walk?

B: Yes, but it _____ a lot.

W: _____ _____ _____ put some ice on it? And _____ _____ you don't play soccer _____ next week.

W: 다리에 무슨 문제가 있니, Sam?
B: 축구를 하다가 넘어져서 발을 다쳤어요.
W: 걸을 수는 있겠니?
B: 네, 하지만 많이 아파요.
W: 얼음을 그 위에 올려놓는 게 어떠니? 그리고 다음 주까지는 축구를 하지 않도록 하렴.

## Listen and Talk B

1. **A:** You don't _____ _____. What's wrong?
   **B:** I _____ a headache.
   **A:** _____ _____ _____. Make sure you _____ some medicine.
   **B:** OK, I _____.

2. **A:** You _____ _____ _____. What's _____?
   **B:** I have a _____.
   **A:** That's too bad. _____ _____ you go see a doctor.
   **B:** OK, I will.

## Listen and Talk C

**W:** What's _____, Andy?
**B:** Hello, Ms. Kim. My right _____ hurts.
**W:** Hmm. Do you use your smartphone _____ _____?
**B:** Yes, I _____ a lot. Why?
**W:** I think you _____ texting thumb.
**B:** Texting thumb? What's texting thumb?
**W:** It's _____ in your thumb. You can _____ it from _____ too much.
**B:** Oh, I didn't know that.
**W:** _____ _____ _____ do some finger stretching exercises?
**B:** OK, I will.
**W:** And _____ _____ you don't text too much.

## Review 1

**G:** What's wrong, Mike?
**B:** I _____ _____ _____ headache.
**G:** I think you _____ _____ some medicine.
**B:** OK, I will.

## Review 2

**M:** What's _____ _____, Mina?
**G:** I _____ _____ _____ _____. I also have a _____ nose.
**M:** I think you have a cold. _____ _____ you get some rest.
**G:** OK, I will.

해석

1. A: 너 몸이 안 좋아 보여. 무슨 일 있니?
   B: 머리가 아파.
   A: 안됐다. 약을 먹으렴.
   B: 응, 그럴게.

2. A: 너 몸이 안 좋아 보여. 무슨 일 있니?
   B: 감기에 걸렸어.
   A: 안됐다. 병원에 가도록 하렴.
   B: 응, 그럴게.

W: 무슨 일이니, Andy?
B: 안녕하세요, 김 선생님. 제 오른손 엄지손가락이 아파요.
W: 음. 너 스마트폰을 많이 사용하니?
B: 네, 저 문자를 많이 해요. 왜요?
W: 내 생각에 너는 texting thumb인 것 같아.
B: texting thumb이요? texting thumb이 뭐예요?
W: 엄지손가락에 통증이 있는 거야. 문자를 너무 많이 하면 생길 수 있어.
B: 오, 그건 몰랐네요.
W: 손가락 스트레칭 운동을 좀 하는 게 어떠니?
B: 네, 그럴게요.
W: 그리고 문자를 너무 많이 하지 않도록 하렴.

G: 무슨 일 있니, Mike?
B: 머리가 너무 아파.
G: 너는 약을 먹는 것이 좋겠다.
B: 알겠어, 그럴게.

M: 무슨 일 있니, 미나야?
G: 목이 아파요. 그리고 콧물도 나요.
M: 내 생각에 네가 감기에 걸린 것 같구나. 좀 쉬도록 하렴.
G: 네, 그럴게요.

**01** 다음 우리말에 맞도록 빈칸에 들어갈 알맞은 말을 쓰시오.

> 좀 쉬도록 하렴.

➡ _____ _____ you get some rest.


**02** 다음 대화의 빈칸에 들어갈 말로 어색한 것은?

> W: _____, Sam?
> B: I fell and hurt my foot while I was playing soccer.

① What's wrong with you
② What's the matter with you
③ What happened
④ What do you mean
⑤ What's wrong with your leg


**03** 다음 대화의 빈칸에 들어갈 말로 어색한 것은?

> W: You look sick. What's wrong, Inho?
> B: I have a sore throat. I have a fever, too.
> W: I think you have a cold. _____
> B: OK. Thank you.

① Don't forget to go see a doctor.
② Make sure you take a good rest.
③ Remember to go to the dentist.
④ You should drink a lot of water.
⑤ Take this medicine.


**04** 다음 대화의 밑줄 친 우리말에 맞게 문장의 빈칸을 채우시오.

> A: You don't look well. What's wrong?
> B: 머리가 아파요.

➡ I _____ _____ headache.

[01~02] 다음 대화를 읽고 물음에 답하시오.

W: _____ (A) _____, Chris?
B: I have a terrible toothache.
W: Here is some medicine. __(B)__ this.
B: Thank you.
W: And make sure you go to the dentist.
B: OK, I will.

**01** 위 대화의 빈칸 (A)에 들어갈 말로 <u>어색한</u> 것은?

① What's wrong
② What's the problem
③ What's the matter
④ How's it going
⑤ Is there anything wrong

**02** 위 대화의 빈칸 (B)에 들어갈 말로 알맞은 것은?

① Want          ② Bring
③ Leave         ④ Make
⑤ Take

**03** 다음 대화의 순서를 바르게 배열한 것은?

> (A) I have a sore throat. I also have a runny nose.
> (B) I think you have a cold. Make sure you get some rest.
> (C) OK, I will.
> (D) What's the matter, Mina?

① (A) – (B) – (C) – (D)
② (B) – (A) – (C) – (D)
③ (B) – (C) – (A) – (D)
④ (D) – (A) – (B) – (C)
⑤ (D) – (B) – (A) – (C)

[04~06] 다음 대화를 읽고 물음에 답하시오.

G: (A)What's wrong, Mike?
B: I ___ⓐ___ a terrible headache.
G: (B)You should take some medicine.
B: OK, I will.

**04** 위 대화의 빈칸 ⓐ에 들어갈 말로 알맞은 것은?

① take          ② make
③ catch         ④ explain
⑤ have

**05** 위 대화의 밑줄 친 (A)와 같은 뜻이 되도록 다음 문장의 빈칸을 채우시오.

> = What's _____ _____ with you
> = What _____

**06** 위 대화의 밑줄 친 (B)와 바꾸어 쓸 수 <u>없는</u> 것은?

① You had better take some medicine.
② Make sure you take some medicine.
③ Don't forget to take some medicine.
④ Remember to take some medicine.
⑤ Don't remember to take some medicine.

**07** 다음 대화의 밑줄 친 부분의 의도로 알맞은 것은?

> A: You don't look well. What's wrong?
> B: I have a headache.
> A: That's too bad. <u>Make sure you take some medicine.</u>
> B: OK, I will.

① 안부 묻기          ② 의무 표현하기
③ 요청하기          ④ 당부하기
⑤ 의견 묻기

[08~10] 다음 대화를 읽고 물음에 답하시오.

> W: What's the matter, Chris?
> B: I have a terrible (A)toothache.
> W: (B)여기 약이 있단다. Take this.
> B: Thank you.
> W: And _____ (C) _____.
> B: OK, I will.

**서답형**

**08** 다음 문장은 밑줄 친 (A)에 대한 영어 설명이다. 빈칸에 알맞은 단어를 쓰시오.

> a _____ in a tooth

➡ _____

**서답형**

**09** 위 대화의 밑줄 친 (B)의 우리말에 맞게 다음 문장의 빈칸을 완성하시오.

➡ _____ _____ some medicine.

**10** 위 대화의 빈칸 (C)에 들어갈 말로 가장 적절한 것은?

① make sure you do some exercises
② don't play soccer
③ make sure you go to the dentist
④ make sure you don't text too much
⑤ you need to eat well

[11~13] 다음 대화를 읽고 물음에 답하시오.

> W: (A)무슨 일이니, Andy?
> B: Hello, Ms. Kim. My right thumb hurts.
> W: Hmm. (①) Do you use your smartphone a lot?
> B: Yes, I text a lot. Why?
> W: (②) I think you have texting thumb.
> B: Texting thumb? (③) What's texting thumb?
> W: (④) You can get it from texting too much.
> B: Oh, I didn't know that. (⑤)

> W: Why don't you do some finger stretching exercises?
> B: OK, I will.
> W: And make sure you don't text too much.

**서답형**

**11** 위 대화의 밑줄 친 (A)의 우리말에 맞게 주어진 단어를 이용하여 영어로 쓰시오.

> what, matter, with

➡ _____

**서답형**

**12** 다음 주어진 문장이 들어갈 위치로 알맞은 것은?

> It's pain in your thumb.

① ② ③ ④ ⑤

**13** 위 대화의 내용과 일치하지 <u>않는</u> 것은?

① Andy uses his smartphone a lot.
② Andy texts a lot.
③ Andy feels pain in his right thumb.
④ Ms. Kim advises Andy to do some finger stretching exercises.
⑤ Ms. Kim doesn't text too much.

**14** 다음 중 짝지어진 대화가 <u>어색한</u> 것은?

① A: What's wrong?
　 B: I have a headache.
② A: What's the matter, Chris?
　 B: I have a terrible toothache.
③ A: Here is some medicine. Take this.
　 B: Thank you.
④ A: You don't look well. Is there anything wrong?
　 B: No problem. I have a headache.
⑤ A: I have a sore throat. I have a fever, too.
　 B: I think you have a cold.

[01~02] 다음 대화를 읽고 물음에 답하시오.

W: You look sick. What's ___ⓐ___, Inho?
B: I ___ⓑ___ a sore throat. I have a fever, too.
W: I think you ___ⓒ___ a cold. (A)이 약을 먹고 꼭 충분히 쉬도록 하렴.
B: OK. Thank you.

**01** 위 대화의 흐름상 빈칸 ⓐ~ⓒ에 알맞은 말을 쓰시오.

➡ ⓐ _____ ⓑ _____ ⓒ _____

**02** 위 대화의 밑줄 친 (A)의 우리말에 맞게 주어진 어구를 이용하여 영어로 쓰시오.

> medicine, and, make, take you, a, good rest

➡ _____

**03** 다음 대화의 밑줄 친 우리말에 맞게 주어진 단어를 이용하여 빈칸을 채우시오.

> W: (A)다리에 무슨 문제가 있니, Sam?
> B: I fell and hurt my foot (B)축구를 하다가.
> W: Can you walk?
> B: Yes, but it hurts a lot.
> W: Why don't you put some ice on it? And (C)축구를 하지 않도록 하렴 until next week.

➡ (A) _____
　　(wrong, with, leg)
　　(B) _____
　　(while, was, soccer)
　　(C) _____
　　(make, sure, play)

[04~05] 다음 대화를 읽고 물음에 답하시오.

W: What's wrong, Andy?
B: Hello, Ms. Kim. My right thumb hurts.
W: Hmm. Do you use your smartphone a lot?
B: Yes, I text a lot. Why?
W: I think you have texting thumb.
B: Texting thumb? What's texting thumb?
W: _____(A)_____ You can get it from texting too much.
B: Oh, I didn't know that.
W: Why don't you do some finger stretching exercises?
B: OK, I will.
W: And _____(B)_____.

**04** 위 대화의 내용으로 보아 Andy의 질문에 대한 답으로 (A)에 들어갈 알맞은 말을 완성하시오.

➡ It's _____ in your _____.

**05** 위 대화의 빈칸 (B)에 들어갈 Ms. Kim의 충고를 완성하시오.

➡ _____ _____ you _____ _____ too much

**06** 다음 대화의 충고를 읽고, 빈칸에 들어갈 말을 주어진 단어를 이용하여 완성하시오.

> A: What's wrong, Peter?
> B: _____
> A: I think you need to eat well. Try to eat lots of fresh fruit and vegetables. And make sure you exercise regularly.
> B: OK, I will.

➡ _____ (get, tire, easily)

# Grammar

교과서

**1** 목적격 관계대명사

> • Another problem **(which/that)** you can have is neck pain.
> 네가 가질 수 있는 또 다른 문제는 목 통증이다.

■ 관계대명사절에서 관계대명사의 역할이 목적어일 때 이것을 목적격 관계대명사라고 하며, 관계대명사절의 첫머리에 위치해야 한다.

■ 목적격 관계대명사는 수식하는 선행사가 사람이면 who나 whom, that을, 사람이 아니면 which나 that을 쓴다. 목적격 관계대명사는 생략될 수 있다.

　• I know the man **(who/whom/that)** you met yesterday. 나는 네가 어제 만난 그 남자를 알아.

　• This is the book **(which/that)** I have chosen. 이것이 내가 고른 책이다.

■ 목적격 관계대명사절을 만들 때 특히 주의할 것은 동사 뒤에 목적어가 없다는 것인데, 이것은 앞에 있는 관계대명사가 동사의 목적어 역할을 하기 때문이다.

　• The person is my father. I respect **him(=the person)** the most.

　　= The person **(who/whom/that)** I respect the most is my father.

　• John is reading the book. He bought **it(=the book)** last Saturday.

　　= John is reading the book **(which/that)** he bought last Saturday.

■ 목적격 관계대명사가 전치사의 목적어인 경우 전치사는 관계대명사절의 끝에 오거나 관계대명사 앞에 올 수 있다. 전치사가 관계대명사절의 끝에 올 경우에는 관계대명사를 생략할 수 있다. 전치사가 관계대명사 앞에 올 경우에는 관계대명사 that을 쓸 수 없으며, 관계대명사를 생략하지 않는다.

　• This is the pen **(which/that)** he wrote the novel with. 이것은 그가 그 소설을 쓰는 데 썼던 펜이다.

　　= This is the pen with **which** he wrote the novel.

　　= This is the pen with that he wrote the novel. (×)

**핵심 Check**

1. 다음 우리말에 맞게 빈칸에 알맞은 말을 쓰시오.

　(1) 나는 John이 말한 그 사람을 알고 있어요.

　　➡ I know the man ＿＿＿＿＿＿＿＿＿ John mentioned.

　(2) 그는 엄마가 만들어 주는 피자를 먹는 것을 좋아한다.

　　➡ He likes to eat the pizza ＿＿＿＿＿＿＿＿＿ his mom makes.

## ② call A B

- We **call** such people smombies. 우리는 그런 사람들을 스몸비라고 부른다.
- We **elected** her chairman. 우리는 그녀를 의장으로 선출했다.

■ 'call A B'는 'A를 B라고 부르다'라는 의미로, 문법적으로는 call 다음의 명사[대명사] A를 목적어, 그리고 B에 해당하는 명사를 목적격 보어로 볼 수 있는 일종의 5형식 구문이다.

- They will **call** their daughter Sophie. 그들은 그들의 딸을 Sophie라고 부를 것이다.

■ call A B와 유사하게 목적격 보어 자리에 명사가 올 수 있는 동사로는 make, name, elect, consider 등이 있다.

| | |
|---|---|
| call A B | A를 B라고 부르다 |
| name A B | A를 B라고 이름 짓다 |
| make A B | A를 B로 만들다 |
| elect A B | A를 B로 선출하다 |
| consider A B | A를 B로 여기다[생각하다] |

- I **consider** him a friend. 나는 그를 친구로 생각한다.

■ 동사 다음에 두 개의 명사가 목적어, 목적격 보어로 쓰인다는 점에서는 consider, believe 등의 동사와 유사해 보이지만, call은 목적격 보어로 형용사나 to부정사를 취하지 않는다는 점에 유의한다.

- Can we **call** it a success? 우리가 그것을 성공이라고 부를 수 있느냐?
- We **named** her Mina. 우리는 그녀를 Mina라고 명명했다.
- She **made** her son a teacher. 그녀는 그녀의 아들을 선생님으로 만들었다.
- I **believe** him honest. 나는 그가 정직하다고 생각한다.

### 핵심 Check

**2.** 다음 우리말에 맞게 빈칸에 알맞은 말을 쓰시오.

(1) 우리는 이것을 text neck이라고 부른다.

➡ We _____ this _____ _____.

(2) 그의 발명은 그를 부자로 만들었다.

➡ His invention _____ him a _____ _____.

**01** 다음 빈칸에 들어갈 말로 알맞지 <u>않은</u> 것을 <u>모두</u> 고르시오.

> The friend _____ I met yesterday is Sue.

① who      ② whose      ③ whom
④ that      ⑤ which

**02** 다음 문장에서 어법상 어색한 부분을 바르게 고쳐 쓰시오.

(1) He showed me the photos who he had taken in Spain.

_____ ➡ _____

(2) The children which Ms. Collins is teaching are smart.

_____ ➡ _____

(3) We call the lion to be the king of beasts.

_____ ➡ _____

beast: 짐승 the king of beasts: 백수 (百獸)의 왕

**03** 다음 우리말에 맞게 괄호 안에 주어진 단어를 바르게 배열하시오.

(1) 이것이 어제 내가 산 신발들이다. (I, the shoes, yesterday, are, bought, these, which)

➡ _____

(2) 우리는 우리 물고기를 Ernie라고 불렀다. (we, Ernie, our, fish, called)

➡ _____

**04** 다음 우리말을 영어로 옮길 때, 빈칸에 알맞은 말이 순서대로 짝지어진 것은?

> 우리는 화면의 화살표를 커서라고 부른다.
> ➡ We call _____ _____.

① the arrow on the screen – a cursor
② a cursor – the arrow on the screen
③ the arrow – a cursor on the screen
④ a cursor on the screen – the arrow
⑤ on the screen a cursor – the arrow

**01** 다음 〈보기〉의 밑줄 친 부분과 다르게 쓰인 것은?

> 보기
>
> There are various things that you can do to prevent this.

① Tom bought the book that he wanted to read.
② Wayne met the girl who looked very intelligent at the party.
③ Susan is the girl who I gave some flowers yesterday.
④ The skirt which she is wearing is pretty.
⑤ I want to marry a woman that I love.

**02** 다음 빈칸에 들어갈 수 있는 말이 다른 하나는?

① Mr. Lee was my teacher _____ taught me math.
② A computer is a thing _____ people do many things with.
③ This is the pen _____ was on the table.
④ Are there any students _____ name hasn't been called?
⑤ Christina Rossetti is the poet _____ I like most.

**03** 다음 빈칸에 알맞지 않은 것은?

> We _____ him our class president.

① elected
② made
③ appointed
④ considered
⑤ took

**04** 다음 괄호 안에서 알맞은 말을 고르시오.

(1) I know the boy (which / that) everyone likes.
(2) Monica wants to see *the Mona Lisa* (who / which) Leonardo da Vinci painted.
(3) There was a program in (that / which) I really wanted to take part.
(4) Sharon wore the earrings (whom / which) I gave to her.
(5) We (call / consider) her to be a genius.

➡ (1) _____ (2) _____ (3) _____
　　(4) _____ (5) _____

**05** 다음 우리말을 주어진 어휘를 이용하여 영어로 쓰시오.

> 나는 할아버지께서 내게 해 주신 이야기들을 아직 기억한다. (the stories, still, my grandfather, tell)

➡ _____

_____

**06** 다음 중 어법상 바르지 않은 것은?

① The movie made her a star.
② Which do you consider to be the most important?
③ They elected Obama President of the USA.
④ They named their baby James.
⑤ We call such music as hip hop.

**07** 다음 중 어법상 옳은 문장은?

① This is the book who my sister bought last night.
② We sometimes have to eat side dishes whom we don't like.
③ This is the house which she lives.
④ This is something that you should bear in mind.
⑤ James is the only friend which he can trust.

**08** 다음 밑줄 친 that의 용법이 나머지 넷과 다른 것은?

① My opinion is that he really doesn't understand you.
② This is an animal that has a long nose.
③ The movie that Mike and I watched yesterday was interesting.
④ The cookies that she made were very delicious.
⑤ Jerry never touched the food that he didn't like.

**09** 다음 중 〈보기〉와 문장의 형식이 다르게 쓰인 것은?

┌─── 보기 ────┐
They called their dog Lucky.
└──────────┘

① As it is very cold outside, please keep yourself warm.
② We elected him President.
③ Jeff made his son a desk.
④ We found the boy asleep in the sofa.
⑤ Ms. Han named her cat Willow.

**10** 다음 문장에서 생략할 수 있는 것을 찾아 쓰시오.

(1) The sport that Frank can play well is basketball.
(2) The girl whom you met last night is my sister.
(3) *Annie* is the story of an 11-year-old girl who is named Annie.

➡ (1) _____ (2) _____ (3) _____

**11** 다음 두 문장을 한 문장으로 바르게 바꾼 것은?

┌────────────────────┐
• BJ is a rap singer.
• I like BJ the most.
└────────────────────┘

① BJ is whom a rap singer I like the most.
② BJ is a rap singer which I like the most.
③ BJ is a rap singer who like the most.
④ BJ is a rap singer who I like him the most.
⑤ BJ is a rap singer whom I like the most.

**12** 다음 중 밑줄 친 부분의 쓰임이 잘못된 것은?

① His success abroad has made him a national hero in Korea.
② They call it strange.
③ I consider it to be the best novel I have written in my life.
④ The students elected her as president of their class.
⑤ The town chose Mr. White as mayor.

**13** 다음 두 문장을 관계대명사를 사용하여 한 문장으로 바꾸시오.

(1) • New York is a big city.
　• Many people visit New York every year.
　➡ _____
　_____

(2) • My favorite subject is math.
　• I'm good at math.
　➡ _____
　_____

(3) • The man was my math teacher.
　• I saw the man at the mall.
　➡ _____
　_____

(4) • She is a famous movie star.
　• Many people like her.
　➡ _____
　_____

(5) • I was surprised at the speed.
　• He learned to speak with the speed.
　➡ _____
　_____
　_____

(6) • Do you know the girl?
　• Anne is talking to the girl.
　➡ _____
　_____
　_____

**14** 다음 빈칸에 자연스러운 의미가 되도록 들어갈 알맞은 것은?

> We _____ Chicago the Windy City.

① call
② want
③ give
④ regard
⑤ have

**15** 다음 밑줄 친 부분의 쓰임이 어색한 것은?

① This is the road which leads to the library.
② Fall is the season which comes after summer.
③ Philip loves the girl who I love.
④ The young boy to that Jane is talking is Alex.
⑤ The famous man lives in the town which Tom visited last year.

**16** 우리말에 맞게 괄호 안의 어휘를 바르게 배열하시오.

(1) 우리는 셰익스피어를 영국의 국민 시인이라고 부른다. (we, Shakespeare, poet, England's, call, national)
　➡ _____

(2) 나는 그를 겁쟁이라고 생각한다. (I, him, coward, be, consider, a, to)
　➡ _____

**17** 주어진 문장의 밑줄 친 부분과 용법이 같은 것을 두 개 고르시오.

> The spaghetti that Suji made for me yesterday was delicious.

① There was no hope that she would recover her health.
② The actor who I like the most is Robert.
③ I didn't know who you were talking about.
④ The movie which I want to watch is *Alita*.
⑤ They must be swallows that have come back from the south.

**01** 다음 두 문장을 관계대명사를 이용하여 한 문장으로 연결하여 쓰시오.

(1) • I bought the snack.
　• Everyone likes the snack.

　➡ _____

　_____

(2) • *Romeo and Juliet* is the movie.
　• Helen saw *Romeo and Juliet*.

　➡ _____

　_____

(3) • The person is my sister.
　• I love the person the most.

　➡ _____

　_____

(4) • The author is C. S. Lewis.
　• I like the author the most.

　➡ _____

　_____

(5) • Look at the boy.
　• Mary is talking to the boy.

　➡ _____

　_____

(6) • Look at Chris and his dog.
　• Bella is playing with them.

　➡ _____

　_____

**02** 다음 괄호 안에 주어진 말을 바르게 배열하여 문장을 완성하시오.

(1) (people / New York City / the Big Apple / call)

　➡ _____

(2) (people / hero / him / consider / may / some / a / as / not)

　➡ _____

(3) (they / her / the Boxer of the Year / named)

　➡ _____

(4) (ability / him / his / person / made / famous / a)

　➡ _____

(5) (leader / him / we / be / elected / to / a)

　➡ _____

(6) (followers / a genius / him / his / be / believed / to)

　➡ _____

(7) (they / Mike / fool / regard / as / a)

　➡ _____

**03** 다음 그림을 보고 괄호 안에 주어진 어휘를 이용하여 문장을 완성하시오.

(the park in the sky / the rooftop / call)

➡ We _____.

**04** 다음 문장에서 <u>잘못된</u> 부분을 바르게 고쳐 문장을 다시 쓰시오.

(1) Andy is the boy which Hajun met in Canada.

➡ _____

_____

(2) The table who my dad made for me is sturdy.

➡ _____

_____

(3) Hemingway is the author whom I like him the most.

➡ _____

_____

(4) The book which he wrote it is fun.

➡ _____

_____

(5) Can I borrow the book about that you told me?

➡ _____

_____

**05** 두 문장을 관계대명사를 사용하여 한 문장으로 썼을 때, 빈 칸에 해당하는 문장을 쓰시오.

(1) • I ate the chocolate cake.

＋ • _____

➡ I ate the chocolate cake which my grandmother made.

(2) • Do you remember the people?

＋ • _____

➡ Do you remember the people whom we met on the plane?

(3) • _____

＋ • He will drive the car while he stays in New York.

➡ He wants to rent a car that he will drive while he stays in New York.

(4) • _____

＋ • You can depend on the friend.

➡ Do you have a friend whom you can depend on?

**06** 다음 문장을 어법에 맞게 고쳐 쓰시오.

(1) They called him to be Mr. Long.

➡ _____

(2) They regarded him their leader.

➡ _____

**07** 괄호 안에 주어진 어휘를 이용하여 우리말에 맞게 영작하시오.

(1) 우리는 그곳에 매우 바람이 많이 불기 때문에 Chicago를 the Windy City라고 부른다. (it, there, call, windy, because, very) (we로 시작할 것)

➡ _____

_____

(2) 나는 나의 엄마가 내게 만들어 주신 과자를 좋아한다. (like, the cookies, for, make)

➡ _____

_____

(3) 내가 가장 방문하고 싶은 나라는 프랑스이다. (the country, visit, the most)

➡ _____

_____

(4) Harry는 작년에 나와 함께 일했던 파트너였다. (the partner, that, worked)

➡ _____

_____

## Be Smart with Your Smartphones!

without: '~ 없이' (전치사)

Living without smartphones is difficult for many of us these days.
동명사(주어): 단수로 취급 → 단수 동사 is를 쓴다.                                    요즈음

However, unwise or too much use of smartphones can cause various
        unwise와 too much가 or로 연결. 뒤에 나온 use를 수식

problems.

### Are you a smombie?

All over the world, people are walking around like zombies. Their
전 세계에 걸쳐                                    좀비처럼

heads are down, and their eyes are on their smartphones. We call such
                        그들의 눈은 스마트폰을 향하고 있다        call A B: A를 B라고 부르다

people smombies, smartphone zombies. If you are a smombie, you
            smombies와 smartphone zombies는 동격

can have various safety problems. You may not see a hole in the street,
                                    추측(~일지도 모른다)

so you may fall and get hurt. You may get into a car accident, too. So
그래서              다치다

what can you do to prevent these problems? It's simple. Do not look at
        to부정사의 부사적 용법(목적)        앞에 나온 다양한 안전 관련 문제들

your smartphone while you are walking!
                    ~하는 동안

### Do you have dry eyes or text neck?

Smartphones can cause various health problems. One example is dry
                                        스마트폰이 야기할 수 있는 건강 문제의 한 예

eyes. When you look at your smartphone, you do not blink often. Then
when 이하는 시간의 부사절로 '~할 때'라는 의미

your eyes will feel dry.
        feel은 감각동사로 형용사가 보어로 쓰였다.

without ~ 없이
cause 일으키다, 야기하다
various 다양한, 여러 가지의
such 그런, 그러한
zombie 좀비 (반쯤 죽은 것 같은 사람)
hole 구덩이
prevent 방지하다, 막다
simple 간단한
text neck 거북목 증후군
dry eye 안구 건조증
text 문자 메시지; (휴대 전화로) 문자를 보내다

---

### 확인문제

● 다음 문장이 본문의 내용과 일치하면 T, 일치하지 않으면 F를 쓰시오.

1  Living without smartphones is difficult for many of us these days. ☐

2  Smombies are smart zombies. ☐

3  Smombies can have various social problems. ☐

4  Smombies may not see a hole in the street, so they may fall and get hurt. ☐

Another problem you can have is neck pain. When you look down at

problem과 you 사이에 목적격 관계대명사 which/that이 생략되어 있다.　　　　　　　　　～을 내려다보다

your smartphone, the stress on your neck increases. Too much use of

형용사구

your smartphone, for example, too much texting, can cause neck pain.

Too much use of your smartphone의 한 예

We call this text neck.

call A B: A를 B라고 부르다

Here are some tips for these problems. For dry eyes, try to blink

여기 ～이 있다　　　　　　　　　　　　　　try to+동사원형: ～하려고 노력하다. cf. try+-ing: 한번 ～해 보다

often. For text neck, move your smartphone up to your eye level. You

～까지

can also do some neck stretching exercises.

**How do you feel when you don't have your smartphone with you?**

Do you feel nervous when your smartphone is not around? Do

when 이하는 시간의 부사절로 '～할 때'라는 의미　　　　　　　주위에(부사)

you feel sad when you check your smartphone and there is no text

feel은 감각동사로 형용사가 보어로 쓰였다.　　　　　　　　　　　　　　～이 없다

message? If your answers are "yes," you may have smartphone

추측(～일지도 모른다)　= smartphone addiction

things와 you 사이에는 목적격 관계대명사 that 또는 which 생략

addiction. There are various things you can do to prevent this. For

～이 있다　　　　　　　　　　to부정사의 부사적 용법(목적)

example, turn off your smartphone during meals or meetings. You can

～을 끄다　　　　　　　～ 중에

talk to people instead of texting them.

～ 하는 대신에. 뒤에 동명사가 온다.　　= people

| blink (눈을) 깜박거리다 |
| --- |
| pain 통증. 고통 |
| look down at ～을 내려다보다 |
| increase 증가하다 |
| eye level 눈높이 |
| stretch 늘이다. 뻗다 |
| nervous 초조한 |
| around 주위에 |
| addiction 중독 |
| meal 식사 |
| instead of ～ 대신에 |

---

📎 **확인문제**

● 다음 문장이 본문의 내용과 일치하면 T, 일치하지 <u>않으면</u> F를 쓰시오.

1 When you look at your smartphone, your eyes will feel dry,

and then you can't blink often. ☐

2 When you look down at your smartphone, the stress on your back increases. ☐

3 Too much texting can cause neck pain called text neck. ☐

4 If you feel nervous when your smartphone is not around, you may have smartphone

addiction. ☐

5 There are few things you can do to prevent smartphone addiction. ☐

6 You can talk to people instead of texting them to prevent smartphone addiction. ☐

● 우리말을 참고하여 빈칸에 알맞은 말을 쓰시오.

1 _____ _____ _____ Your Smartphones!

2 _____ _____ _____ is difficult for many of us these days.

3 However, _____ _____ _____ _____ _____ of smartphones can cause various problems.

4 Are you _____ _____?

5 All over the world, people are walking around _____ _____.

6 Their heads are down, and their eyes are _____ _____ _____.

7 We call _____ _____ smombies, smartphone zombies.

8 If you are a smombie, you can have _____ _____ _____.

9 You _____ _____ _____ a hole in the street, _____ you may fall and get hurt.

10 You may _____ _____ a car accident, too.

11 So what can you do _____ _____ these problems?

12 It's _____.

13 Do not look at your smartphone _____ you are _____!

14 Do you have _____ _____ or _____ _____?

15 Smartphones can cause various _____ _____.

16 One example is _____ _____.

| | |
|---|---|
| 1 | 스마트폰을 현명하게 사용하라! |
| 2 | 스마트폰 없이 사는 것은 요즘 많은 사람들에게 어렵다. |
| 3 | 하지만 스마트폰을 현명하지 않게 사용하거나 너무 과도하게 사용하는 것은 다양한 문제를 야기할 수 있다. |
| 4 | 당신은 스몸비인가요? |
| 5 | 전 세계적으로 사람들이 좀비처럼 걸어다니고 있다. |
| 6 | 그들의 머리는 아래를 향하고, 그들의 눈은 스마트폰을 향하고 있다. |
| 7 | 우리는 그런 사람들을 스몸비, 즉 스마트폰 좀비라고 부른다. |
| 8 | 만약 당신이 스몸비라면, 당신은 다양한 안전 관련 문제들을 겪을 수 있다. |
| 9 | 당신은 거리에 있는 구덩이를 보지 못할 수도 있고, 그래서 넘어져서 다칠지도 모른다. |
| 10 | 당신은 또한 교통사고를 당할지도 모른다. |
| 11 | 그렇다면 이런 문제들을 방지하기 위해 무엇을 할 수 있을까? |
| 12 | 간단하다. |
| 13 | 걷고 있는 동안에는 스마트폰을 보지 마라! |
| 14 | 당신은 안구 건조증이나 거북목 증후군이 있나요? |
| 15 | 스마트폰은 다양한 건강상의 문제를 일으킬 수 있다. |
| 16 | 한 가지 예가 안구 건조증이다. |

**17** When you _____ _____ your smartphone, you do not _____ often.

**18** Then your eyes will _____ _____.

**19** _____ _____ you can have is neck pain.

**20** When you _____ _____ _____ your smartphone, the stress _____ your neck increases.

**21** _____ _____ _____ of your smartphone, for example, _____ _____ _____, can cause neck pain.

**22** We call this _____ _____.

**23** Here are _____ _____ for these problems.

**24** For dry eyes, _____ _____ _____ often.

**25** For text neck, move your smartphone _____ _____ _____ _____.

**26** You can also do some _____ _____ _____.

**27** _____ _____ _____ _____ when you don't have your smartphone with you?

**28** Do you _____ _____ when your smartphone is not _____?

**29** Do you _____ _____ when you check your smartphone and there is _____ _____ _____?

**30** If your answers are "yes," you may have _____ _____.

**31** There are various things you can do _____ _____ _____.

**32** For example, _____ _____ your smartphone _____ meals or meetings.

**33** You can talk to people _____ _____ _____ them.

**17** 스마트폰을 볼 때, 당신은 눈을 자주 깜박거리지 않는다.

**18** 그러면 눈이 건조하다고 느낄 것이다.

**19** 일어날 수 있는 또 다른 문제는 목 통증이다.

**20** 스마트폰을 내려다볼 때, 목에 가해지는 압박이 증가한다.

**21** 스마트폰을 너무 많이 사용하는 것은, 예를 들어, 너무 많이 문자를 하는 것은 목 통증을 일으킬 수 있다.

**22** 이런 증상을 거북목 증후군이라고 부른다.

**23** 여기에 이런 문제들을 위한 몇 가지 조언이 있다.

**24** 안구 건조증에는, 눈을 자주 깜박이려고 노력해라.

**25** 거북목 증후군에는 당신의 눈높이까지 스마트폰을 위로 올려라.

**26** 목 스트레칭 운동 또한 할 수 있다.

**27** 스마트폰이 없을 때 어떤 기분이 드나요?

**28** 스마트폰이 주위에 없을 때 당신은 초조한 기분이 드는가?

**29** 스마트폰을 확인했을 때 아무런 문자 메시지가 없으면 슬픈 기분이 드는가?

**30** 만약 당신의 대답이 '그렇다'이면, 당신은 스마트폰 중독일지도 모른다.

**31** 이것을 방지하기 위해 할 수 있는 일은 여러 가지가 있다.

**32** 예를 들어, 식사나 회의 중에는 스마트폰을 꺼라.

**33** 문자를 보내는 대신에 사람들과 이야기를 할 수 있다.

● 우리말을 참고하여 본문을 영작하시오.

**1** 스마트폰을 현명하게 사용하라!

➡ _____

**2** 스마트폰 없이 사는 것은 요즘 많은 사람들에게 어렵다.

➡ _____

**3** 하지만 스마트폰을 현명하지 않게 사용하거나 너무 과도하게 사용하는 것은 다양한 문제를 야기할 수 있다.

➡ _____

**4** 당신은 스몸비인가요?

➡ _____

**5** 전 세계적으로 사람들이 좀비처럼 걸어다니고 있다.

➡ _____

**6** 그들의 머리는 아래를 향하고, 그들의 눈은 스마트폰을 향하고 있다.

➡ _____

**7** 우리는 그런 사람들을 스몸비, 즉 스마트폰 좀비라고 부른다.

➡ _____

**8** 만약 당신이 스몸비라면, 당신은 다양한 안전 관련 문제들을 겪을 수 있다.

➡ _____

**9** 당신은 거리에 있는 구덩이를 보지 못할 수도 있고, 그래서 넘어져서 다칠지도 모른다.

➡ _____

**10** 당신은 또한 교통사고를 당할지도 모른다.

➡ _____

**11** 그렇다면 이런 문제들을 방지하기 위해 무엇을 할 수 있을까?

➡ _____

**12** 간단하다.

➡ _____

**13** 걷고 있는 동안에는 스마트폰을 보지 마라!

➡ _____

**14** 당신은 안구 건조증이나 거북목 증후군이 있나요?

➡ _____

**15** 스마트폰은 다양한 건강상의 문제를 일으킬 수 있다.

➡ _____

**16** 한 가지 예가 안구 건조증이다.

➡ _____

**17** 스마트폰을 볼 때, 당신은 눈을 자주 깜박거리지 않는다.

➡ _____

**18** 그러면 눈이 건조하다고 느낄 것이다.

➡ _____

**19** 일어날 수 있는 또 다른 문제는 목 통증이다.

➡ _____

**20** 스마트폰을 내려다볼 때, 목에 가해지는 압박이 증가한다.

➡ _____

**21** 스마트폰을 너무 많이 사용하는 것은, 예를 들어, 너무 많이 문자를 하는 것은 목 통증을 일으킬 수 있다.

➡ _____

**22** 이런 증상을 거북목 증후군이라고 부른다.

➡ _____

**23** 여기에 이런 문제들을 위한 몇 가지 조언이 있다.

➡ _____

**24** 안구 건조증에는, 눈을 자주 깜박이려고 노력해라.

➡ _____

**25** 거북목 증후군에는 당신의 눈높이까지 스마트폰을 위로 올려라.

➡ _____

**26** 목 스트레칭 운동 또한 할 수 있다.

➡ _____

**27** 스마트폰이 없을 때 어떤 기분이 드나요?

➡ _____

**28** 스마트폰이 주위에 없을 때 당신은 초조한 기분이 드는가?

➡ _____

**29** 스마트폰을 확인했을 때 아무런 문자 메시지가 없으면 슬픈 기분이 드는가?

➡ _____

**30** 만약 당신의 대답이 '그렇다'이면, 당신은 스마트폰 중독일지도 모른다.

➡ _____

**31** 이것을 방지하기 위해 할 수 있는 일은 여러 가지가 있다.

➡ _____

**32** 예를 들어, 식사나 회의 중에는 스마트폰을 꺼라.

➡ _____

**33** 문자를 보내는 대신에 사람들과 이야기를 할 수 있다.

➡ _____

[01~03] 다음 글을 읽고 물음에 답하시오.

Living without smartphones is difficult for many of us these days. ⓐ , unwise or too much use of smartphones can cause various problems.

**Are you a smombie?**

All over the world, people are walking around like zombies. Their heads are down, and their eyes are on their smartphones. ⓑ We call such people smombies, smartphone zombies. If you are a smombie, you can have various safety problems. You may not see a hole in the street, so you may fall and get hurt. You may get into a car accident, too. So what can you do to prevent these problems? It's simple. Do not look at your smartphone while you are walking!

**01** 위 글의 빈칸 ⓐ에 들어갈 알맞은 것은?

① Therefore　　② However
③ In addition　　④ For example
⑤ In other words

**02** 위 글의 밑줄 친 ⓑ와 문장의 형식이 같은 것을 모두 고르시오.

① We elected him President.
② She always keeps her word.
③ He made Jane a box.
④ I found it easy.
⑤ Father bought me a camera.

**03** 위 글의 내용과 일치하지 않는 것은?

① 스마트폰 없이 사는 것은 요즘 많은 사람들에게 어렵다.
② 스마트폰을 현명하지 않게 사용하거나 너무 과도하게 사용하는 것은 다양한 문제를 야기할 수 있다.
③ 전 세계적으로 사람들이 좀비처럼 걸어다니고 있다.
④ 스몸비들은 다양한 안전 관련 문제들을 겪을 수 있다.
⑤ 안전 관련 문제들을 예방하는 것은 어렵다.

[04~07] 다음 글을 읽고 물음에 답하시오.

**Do you have dry eyes or text neck?**

Smartphones can cause various health problems. One example is dry eyes. When you look at your smartphone, you do not blink often. Then your eyes will feel dry.

ⓐOther problem you can have is neck pain. When you look down at your smartphone, the stress on your neck increases. (①) Too much use of your smartphone, for example, too much texting, can cause neck pain. (②) We call this text neck.

(③) For dry eyes, try ⓑto blink often. (④) For text neck, move your smartphone up to your eye level. (⑤) You can also do some neck stretching exercises.

**04** 위 글의 흐름으로 보아, 주어진 문장이 들어가기에 가장 적절한 곳은?

> Here are some tips for these problems.

①　　②　　③　　④　　⑤

**서답형**

**05** 위 글의 밑줄 친 ⓐ에서 어법상 틀린 부분을 찾아 고쳐 쓰시오.

_____ ➡ _____

**06** 아래 〈보기〉에서 위 글의 밑줄 친 ⓑto blink와 to부정사의 용법이 같은 것의 개수를 고르시오.

┌─── 보기 ───┐
① I found it useless to teach you math.
② She came here to have a talk with you.
③ It is dangerous to play with matches.
④ Your fault is to talk too much.
⑤ I decided to help those young children.
└───────────┘

① 1개  ② 2개  ③ 3개  ④ 4개  ⑤ 5개

**중요**

**07** 위 글의 주제로 알맞은 것은?

① the cause of dry eyes and the tips to prevent them
② health problems from smartphones and tips for them
③ some tips for avoiding text neck caused by smartphones
④ the increase of the stress due to smartphones
⑤ the importance of neck stretching for a healthy life

[08~10] 다음 글을 읽고 물음에 답하시오.

**How do you feel when you don't have your smartphone with you?**

Do you feel (A)[nervous / nervously] when your smartphone is not around? Do you feel (B)[sad / sadly] when you check your smartphone and there is no text message?

If your answers are "yes," you may have smartphone ____ⓐ____ . There are various things you can do (C)[preventing / to prevent] this. For example, turn off your smartphone during meals or meetings. You can talk to people instead of texting ⓑthem.

**서답형**

**08** 위 글의 괄호 (A)~(C)에서 어법상 알맞은 것을 골라 쓰시오.

➡ (A) _____ (B) _____ (C) _____

**서답형**

**09** 주어진 영영풀이를 참고하여 빈칸 ⓐ에 철자 a로 시작하는 단어를 쓰시오.

┌─────────────────────────────┐
│ 1. the condition of taking harmful drugs and being unable to stop taking them
│ 2. a very strong desire or need for something
└─────────────────────────────┘

➡ _____

**서답형**

**10** 위 글의 밑줄 친 ⓑthem이 가리키는 것을 본문에서 찾아 쓰시오.

➡ _____

[11~14] 다음 글을 읽고 물음에 답하시오.

ⓐLiving without smartphones is difficult for many of us these days. However, unwise or too much use of smartphones can cause various problems.

ⓑ_____

All over the world, people are walking around like zombies. Their heads are down, and their eyes are on their smartphones. We call such people smombies, smartphone zombies. If you are a smombie, you can have various safety problems. You may not see a hole in the street, so you may fall and get hurt. You may get into a car accident, too. So what can you do to prevent these problems? It's simple. Do not look at your smartphone while you are walking!

**11** 위 글의 밑줄 친 ⓐLiving과 문법적 쓰임이 같은 것을 모두 고르시오.

① The boy reading a book is my son.
② I saw you running on the ground.
③ My brother is good at dancing.
④ My hobby is watching movies.
⑤ Look at the flying bird.

**12** 위 글의 빈칸 ⓑ에 들어갈 문장으로 알맞은 것은?

① Living without smartphones is difficult.
② Are you a smombie?
③ See a hole in the street!
④ You should prevent a car accident.
⑤ A smombie isn't a troublemaker!

**13** 위 글의 내용과 일치하도록 다음 빈칸 (A)와 (B)에 알맞은 단어를 본문에서 찾아 쓰시오.

You must not look at your (A)_____ while you are walking to prevent various (B)_____ problems.

**14** 위 글을 읽고 대답할 수 없는 질문은?

① Is it easy for many of us to live without smartphones these days?
② Can too much use of smartphones cause problems?
③ What does a smombie mean?
④ What problems do smombies have?
⑤ What is the most dangerous problem that smombies may have?

[15~17] 다음 글을 읽고 물음에 답하시오.

**Do you have dry eyes or text neck?**
Smartphones can cause various health problems. One example is dry eyes. When you look ___ⓐ___ your smartphone, you do not blink often. Then your eyes will feel dry.
ⓑAnother problem you can have is neck pain. When you look down ___ⓐ___ your smartphone, the stress on your neck increases. Too much use of your smartphone, for example, too much texting, can cause neck pain. We call this text neck.
Here are some tips for these problems. ___ⓒ___ dry eyes, try to blink often. ___ⓒ___ text neck, move your smartphone ⓓup to your eye level. You can also do some neck stretching exercises.

**15** 위 글의 빈칸 ⓐ와 ⓒ에 각각 공통으로 들어갈 전치사가 바르게 짝지어진 것은?

① for – From
② at – For
③ at – From
④ for – To
⑤ on – For

서답형

**16** 위 글의 밑줄 친 문장 ⓑ에 생략된 단어를 넣어 문장을 다시 쓰시오.

➡ _____

**17** 위 글의 밑줄 친 ⓓup to와 같은 의미로 쓰인 것은?

① He's not up to the job.
② It's up to you.
③ The temperature went up to 35℃.
④ What's she up to?
⑤ She is looking up to you.

[18~21] 다음 글을 읽고 물음에 답하시오.

**How do you feel when you don't have your smartphone with you?**

ⓐDo you feel nervous when your smartphone is around? Do you feel sad when you check your smartphone and there is no text message?

If your answers are "yes," you may have smartphone addiction. There are various things you can do to prevent ⓑthis. For example, turn off your smartphone during meals or meetings. You can talk to people instead of texting them.

서답형

**18** 위 글의 밑줄 친 ⓐ에서 흐름상 어색한 부분을 찾아 고치시오.

➡ _____

서답형

**19** 위 글의 밑줄 친 ⓑthis가 가리키는 것을 본문에서 찾아 영어로 쓰시오.

➡ _____

서답형

**20** 다음 질문에 대한 알맞은 대답을 영어로 쓰시오. (두 가지)

Q: What can you do to prevent smartphone addiction?

➡ (1) _____
　　 (2) _____

**21** 위 글의 주제로 알맞은 것을 고르시오.

① living without your smartphone
② feeling sad when using a smartphone
③ how to get many text messages
④ smartphone addiction and its prevention
⑤ the danger of smartphone addiction

[22~24] 다음 글을 읽고 물음에 답하시오.

Minho: Yesterday, I fell on the street and got hurt. I was texting and I didn't see a hole.
┗ Reply: Do not use your smartphone while you are walking.

Emma: My eyes feel dry when I use my smartphone.
┗ Reply: Try to blink often.

Suji: I have neck pain ⓐwhen I text a lot.
┗ Reply: Move your smartphone up to your eye level and do some neck stretching exercises.

Eric: I think I have smartphone addiction.
┗ Reply: Turn off your smartphone during meals or meetings and talk to people instead of texting them.

**서답형**

**22** 다음 질문에 대한 알맞은 대답을 주어진 단어로 시작하여 쓰시오. (8~9 단어)

> Q: Why did Minho fall on the street and get hurt yesterday?

A: Because _____.

**23** 위 글의 밑줄 친 ⓐwhen과 같은 의미로 쓰인 것을 모두 고르시오.

① When I was a boy, I was very smart.
② I don't know when I should go.
③ Time goes very fast when I'm busy.
④ When did she promise to meet him?
⑤ When can you come?

**24** 위 글의 내용과 일치하지 않는 것은?

① 민호는 걷는 동안에는 스마트폰을 사용하지 말아야 한다.
② Emma는 스마트폰을 사용할 때 눈이 건조하다고 느낀다.
③ 수지는 문자를 많이 보낼 때 목 통증이 있다.
④ Eric은 스마트폰을 눈높이까지 들고, 목 스트레칭 운동을 해야 한다.
⑤ Eric은 식사나 회의 중에는 스마트폰을 끄고 문자를 보내는 대신에 사람들과 이야기해야 한다.

[25~27] 다음 글을 읽고 물음에 답하시오.

**How do you feel when you don't have your smartphone with you?**

Do you feel nervous when your smartphone is not around? (①) Do you feel sad when you check your smartphone and there is no text message?

(②) If your answers are "yes," you may have smartphone (A)[addition / addiction]. (③) ⓐ_____, turn (B)[on / off] your smartphone during meals or meetings. (④) You can talk to people (C)[instead of / because of] texting them. (⑤)

**25** 위 글의 ①~⑤ 중 다음 주어진 문장이 들어갈 알맞은 곳은?

> There are various things you can do to prevent this.

      ④    ⑤

**26** 위 글의 빈칸 ⓐ에 들어갈 알맞은 것은?

① For example　　② Thus
③ Moreover　　④ However
⑤ On the other hand

**서답형**

**27** 위 글의 괄호 (A)~(C)에서 문맥상 알맞은 낱말을 골라 쓰시오.

➡ (A) _____ (B) _____ (C) _____

**28** 위 글의 빈칸 (A)에 들어갈 알맞은 것은?

① health　　② mental
③ economical　　④ safety
⑤ physical

**29** 아래 〈보기〉에서 위 글의 밑줄 친 ⓐwalking과 문법적 쓰임이 <u>다른</u> 것의 개수를 고르시오.

┌─ 보기 ─┐
① Look at the boy <u>singing</u> on the street.
② Thank you for <u>helping</u> me solve it.
③ My hobby is <u>taking</u> pictures.
④ She is <u>making</u> an apple pie.
⑤ <u>Keeping</u> a diary every day is difficult.
└────────┘

① 1개　② 2개　③ 3개　④ 4개　⑤ 5개

[28~30] 다음 글을 읽고 물음에 답하시오.

Living without smartphones is difficult for many of us these days. However, unwise or too much use of smartphones can cause various problems.

**Are you a smombie?**

All over the world, people are ⓐ<u>walking</u> around like zombies. Their heads are down, and their eyes are on their smartphones. We call such people smombies, smartphone zombies. If you are a smombie, you can have various ___(A)___ problems. You may not see a hole in the street, so you may fall and get hurt. You may get into a car accident, too. So what can you do to prevent these problems? It's simple. Do not look at your smartphone while you are walking!

**30** 위 글의 주제로 알맞은 것은?

① the comfortable living by using smartphones
② the difficulty of living without using smartphones
③ the increase of people like zombies all over the world
④ a car accident which is caused by smombies
⑤ various safety problems due to unwise use of smartphones

Reading 39

[01~03] 다음 글을 읽고 물음에 답하시오.

Living without smartphones (A)[is / are] difficult for many of us these days. However, unwise or too much use of smartphones can cause various problems.

**Are you a smombie?**

All over the world, people are walking around (B)[like / alike] zombies. Their heads are down, and their eyes are on their smartphones. We call such people smombies, smartphone zombies. If you are a smombie, you can have various ⓐsafety problems. You may not see a hole in the street, so you may fall and get hurt. You may get into a car accident, too. So what can you do to prevent these problems? (C)[Its / It's] simple. Do not look at your smartphone while you are walking!

**01** 위 글의 괄호 (A)~(C)에서 어법상 알맞은 낱말을 골라 쓰시오.

➡ (A) _____ (B) _____ (C) _____

**02** 다음 빈칸 (A)~(C)에 알맞은 단어를 넣어 smombies에 대한 설명을 완성하시오.

They are people who are walking around like (A)_____ with their (B)_____ hanging down, and their (C)_____ on their smartphones.

**03** 위 글의 밑줄 친 ⓐ의 예 두 가지를 본문에서 찾아 우리말로 쓰시오.

➡ (1) _____
(2) _____

[04~06] 다음 글을 읽고 물음에 답하시오.

**Do you have dry eyes or text neck?**

Smartphones can cause various health problems. One example is dry eyes. When you look at your smartphone, you do not _____ⓐ_____ often. Then your eyes will feel dry.

Another problem you can have is neck pain. ⓑ스마트폰을 내려다볼 때, 목에 가해지는 압박이 증가한다. Too much use of your smartphone, for example, too much texting, can cause neck pain. We call this ⓒtext neck.

Here are some tips for these problems. For dry eyes, try to _____ⓓ_____ often. For text neck, move your smartphone up to your eye level. You can also do some neck stretching exercises.

**04** 주어진 영영풀이를 참고하여 빈칸 ⓐ와 ⓓ에 공통으로 들어갈 단어를 철자 b로 시작하여 쓰시오.

to shut your eyes and very quickly open them again

➡ _____

**05** 위 글의 밑줄 친 ⓑ의 우리말에 맞게 한 단어를 보충하여, 주어진 어휘를 알맞게 배열하시오. (when으로 시작할 것)

your neck / down / the stress / when / look / your smartphone / at / you / increases / ,

➡ _____
_____

**06** What does the underlined ⓒtext neck mean? Fill in the blanks with the suitable words.

> It means the neck pain which is caused by (A)_____ _____ _____ of your smartphone like too much (B)_____.

**[07~09]** 다음 글을 읽고 물음에 답하시오.

Living without smartphones is difficult for many of us these days. However, ⓐunwise or too much use of smartphones can cause various problems.

**Are you a smombie?**

All over the world, people are walking around like zombies. Their heads are down, and their eyes are on their smartphones. ⓑ우리는 그런 사람들을 스몸비, 즉 스마트폰 좀비라고 부른다. If you are a smombie, you can have various safety problems. ⓒYou may not see a hole in the street, so you may fall and get hurt. You may get into a car accident, too. So what can you do to prevent these problems? It's simple. Do not look at your smartphone while you are walking!

**07** 위 글의 밑줄 친 ⓐ의 예를 본문에서 찾아 우리말로 쓰시오. (30~35자)

➡ _____

_____

**중요**
**08** 위 글의 밑줄 친 ⓑ의 우리말에 맞게 주어진 어휘를 이용하여 7 단어로 영작하시오.

> such, smombies

➡ _____

**09** 위 글의 밑줄 친 ⓒ를 다음과 같이 바꿔 쓸 때 빈칸에 들어갈 알맞은 말을 쓰시오.

➡ _____ you may not see a hole in the street, you may fall and get hurt.

**[10~11]** 다음 글을 읽고 물음에 답하시오.

**Do you have dry eyes or text neck?**

Smartphones can cause various health problems. One example is ⓐdry eyes. When you look at your smartphone, you do not blink often. Then your eyes will feel dry.

Another problem you can have is neck pain. When you look down at your smartphone, the stress on your neck increases. Too much use of your smartphone, ⓑfor example, too much texting, can cause neck pain. We call this text neck.

Here are some tips for these problems. For dry eyes, try to blink often. For text neck, move your smartphone up to your eye level. You can also do some neck stretching exercises.

**중요**
**10** 위 글의 밑줄 친 ⓐdry eyes의 원인과 이 문제를 위한 조언을 우리말로 쓰시오.

➡ 원인: _____

조언: _____

**11** 위 글의 밑줄 친 ⓑfor example과 바꿔 쓸 수 있는 단어를 두 단어로 쓰시오.

➡ _____

### Talk and Play

A: What's wrong?
상대방이 기분이 좋지 않거나 어딘가 아파 보일 때 사용함.(= What's the matter?)

B: I have a fever.
'나는 ~가 아프다'는 표현으로 'have+a/an+병명/증상' 형태를 사용.

A: That's too bad. Make sure you get some rest.
상대방이 안 좋은 일을 당했을 때 사용하는 표현.(= I'm sorry to hear that.)

B: OK, I will.  상대방에게 당부하는 표현.(반드시 ~하도록 하다, ~을 확실히 하다)

구문해설  • fever: 열  • make sure: 확실히 ~하다  • rest: 휴식

### After You Read B

**Be Smart with Your Smartphones!**

Minho:  Yesterday, I fell on the street and got hurt. I was texting and I didn't
                                                                             현재분사
see a hole.

└, Reply: Do not use your smartphone while you are walking.

Emma:  My eyes feel dry when I use my smartphone.
               feel은 감각동사로 형용사가 보어로 쓰였다.
└, Reply: Try to blink often.
              명사적 용법(목적어)

Suji:  I have neck pain when I text a lot.
                           때(접속사)
└, Reply: Move your smartphone up to your eye level and do some
                                    ~까지
neck stretching exercises.

Eric:  I think I have smartphone addiction.
                       스마트폰 중독
└, Reply: Turn off your smartphone during meals or meetings and
          ~을 끄다 ↔ turn on
talk to people instead of texting them.
          ~ 대신에 (뒤에 명사 또는 동명사가 온다.)  = people

구문해설  • hole: 구덩이  • blink: (눈을) 깜박거리다  • text: 문자 메시지; (휴대 전화로) 문자를 보내다
• stretch: 늘이다, 뻗다  • addiction: 중독  • meal: 식사  • instead of: ~ 대신에

### Around the World

This sign says, "Be careful of using your smartphone while you are walking."
                          전치사 of의 목적어로 동명사                접속사(~하는 동안)
There are traffic lights on the ground, so people can see them while they are
                                              그래서              = traffic lights
using their smartphones.
현재분사
This sign on the ground means, "This side of the street is for people who are
                                                                    주격 관계대명사
            형용사구
texting."

구문해설  • say: (신문 · 게시 · 편지 · 책 따위가) ~라고 씌어져 있다  • mean: 의미하다

A: 무슨 일이니?
B: 나는 열이 나.
A: 안됐다. 좀 쉬도록 하렴.
B: 응, 알겠어.

스마트폰을 현명하게 사용하라!
민호: 어제, 나는 길에서 넘어져서 다쳤다. 나는 문자를 보내고 있었고 구덩이를 보지 못했다.
→ 대답: 걷는 동안에는 스마트폰을 사용하지 마라.
Emma: 나는 스마트폰을 사용할 때 눈이 건조하다고 느낀다.
→ 대답: 눈을 자주 깜박이도록 노력해라.
수지: 나는 문자를 많이 보낼 때 목 통증이 있다.
→ 대답: 스마트폰을 눈높이까지 들고, 목 스트레칭 운동을 해라.
Eric: 나는 스마트폰 중독인 것 같다.
→ 대답: 식사나 회의 중에는 스마트폰을 끄고 문자를 보내는 대신에 사람들과 이야기해라.

이 표지판은 "걷는 동안 스마트폰 사용을 주의하세요."라는 의미이다.
땅바닥에 신호등이 있어서, 사람들이 스마트폰을 사용하는 동안에도 신호등을 볼 수 있다.
땅바닥에 있는 이 표지판은 "길의 이쪽은 문자를 보내고 있는 사람들을 위한 곳입니다."라는 의미이다.

**01** 다음 주어진 두 단어의 관계가 같도록 빈칸에 알맞은 단어를 쓰시오. (주어진 철자로 시작할 것)

> expensive : cheap = stupid : i_____

**02** 다음 글의 빈칸 ⓐ와 ⓑ에 들어갈 단어가 바르게 짝지어진 것은?

> Living ___ⓐ___ smartphones is difficult for many of us these days. However, unwise or too much use of smartphones can ___ⓑ___ various problems.

① with – prevent
② with – cause
③ without – prevent
④ without – cause
⑤ without – decrease

**[03~04]** 다음 영영풀이에 해당하는 것을 고르시오.

**03**
> to spread out your arms, legs, or body as far as possible

① text        ② blink
③ stretch      ④ cause
⑤ prevent

**04**
> in the state of sleep; sleeping

① asleep       ② sour
③ intelligent    ④ various
⑤ simple

**05** 빈칸에 공통으로 들어갈 말을 주어진 철자로 시작하여 쓰시오.

> • The c_____ of the accident is not clear. The police are still looking into it.
> • Too much use of smartphones can c_____ dry eyes.

➡ _____

**06** 다음 밑줄 친 부분의 뜻이 잘못된 것은?

① Make sure you get some rest. (확실히 ~하라)
② I think you have computer game addiction! (중독)
③ My eyes are so dry. I try to blink often. (눈을 감다)
④ Do not look at your smartphone while you are walking! (~ 하는 동안)
⑤ When you look down at your smartphone, the stress on your neck increases. (압박)

**07** 다음 대화의 빈칸에 들어갈 말로 알맞지 않은 것은?

> W: _____, Chris?
> B: I have a terrible toothache.
> W: Here is some medicine. Take this.
> B: Thank you.

① What's the matter
② What's the problem
③ Is there anything wrong
④ What do you mean
⑤ What's wrong with you

**[08~10]** 다음 대화를 읽고 물음에 답하시오.

W: ⓐWhat's wrong, Andy?

B: Hello, Ms. Kim. My right thumb hurts.

W: Hmm. (①) Do you use your smartphone a lot?

B: Yes, I ⓑtext a lot. Why? (②)

W: I think you have texting thumb.

B: Texting thumb? (③)

W: It's ⓒpain in your thumb. You can get it from texting too much. (④)

B: Oh, I didn't know (A)that.

W: Why don't you ⓓdo some finger stretching exercises?

B: OK, I will. (⑤)

W: And make sure ⓔyou text too much.

**08** 주어진 문장이 들어갈 위치로 알맞은 것은?

> What's texting thumb?

① ② ③ ④ ⑤

**09** 밑줄 친 (A)that이 가리키는 것을 우리말로 쓰시오.

➡ _____

**10** 위 대화의 밑줄 친 ⓐ~ⓔ 중, 흐름상 어색한 것은?

① ⓐ ② ⓑ ③ ⓒ ④ ⓓ ⑤ ⓔ

**11** 다음 대화의 밑줄 친 부분 중 어법상 어색한 것은?

> W: What's ⓐwrong with your leg, Sam?
>
> B: I fell and hurt my foot ⓑwhile I was playing soccer.
>
> W: Can you walk?
>
> B: Yes, but it ⓒhurts a lot.
>
> W: ⓓWhy don't you put some ice on it? And ⓔmake sure don't play soccer until next week.

① ⓐ ② ⓑ ③ ⓒ ④ ⓓ ⑤ ⓔ

**12** 다음 중 짝지어진 대화가 어색한 것은?

① A: I have a headache.
   B: That's too bad.

② A: Make sure you take some medicine.
   B: OK, I will.

③ A: What's the matter, Chris?
   B: I have a terrible toothache.

④ A: I fell and hurt my foot while I was playing soccer.
   B: That sounds good.

⑤ A: Here is some medicine. Take this. And make sure you go to the dentist.
   B: OK, I will.

**13** 다음 대화의 밑줄 친 부분에 대한 설명으로 적절하지 않은 것은?

> W: ⓐWhat's the matter, Chris?
>
> B: I ⓑhave a terrible toothache.
>
> W: Here is some medicine. ⓒTake this.
>
> B: Thank you.
>
> W: And ⓓmake sure you go to the dentist.
>
> B: ⓔOK, I will.

① ⓐ: 문제점에 대해 물어볼 때 사용하는 표현이다.

② ⓑ: 이가 매우 아프다는 뜻이다.

③ ⓒ: '가져가다'라는 의미로 사용되었다.

④ ⓓ: 상대방에게 당부할 때 사용하는 표현이다.

⑤ ⓔ: 상대방의 조언에 '그렇게 하겠다'는 긍정의 표현이다.

**Grammar**

**14** 다음 밑줄 친 부분 중 어법상 어색한 것은?

> He was very ①intelligent, ②so we ③all called ④him ⑤to be Einstein.

① ② ③ ④ ⑤

**15** 다음 중 두 문장을 한 문장으로 만들 때 의미가 <u>다른</u> 하나는?

① This is the book.
   + John read the book last week.
   ➡ This is the book which John read last week.

② Grace sent an email to the boy.
   + Grace loved him.
   ➡ Grace sent an email to the boy whom she loved.

③ The card was sent to Sue.
   + I bought the card yesterday.
   ➡ Sue sent the card that I bought yesterday.

④ Remember to include all the expenses.
   + You spent the expenses.
   ➡ Remember to include all the expenses that you spent.

⑤ Those are the flowers.
   + Rachel planted them this spring.
   ➡ Those are the flowers Rachel planted this spring.

**16** 〈보기〉의 밑줄 친 which와 용법이 <u>다른</u> 하나는?

┌─ 보기 ├─
Yesterday I watched the movie <u>which</u> he recommended.
└─────

① Herold is the only person <u>that</u> I want to meet now.

② I like the dog <u>which</u> my friend gave to me.

③ I employed a young man <u>who</u> Jenny liked a lot.

④ He is wearing a jacket <u>which</u> has two pockets.

⑤ The teacher <u>whom</u> I like most teaches math.

**17** 다음 문장의 빈칸에 알맞지 <u>않은</u> 것은?

> They _____ him to be their leader.

① called                ② chose
③ considered        ④ wanted
⑤ elected

**18** 다음 밑줄 친 부분 중 생략할 수 있는 것은?

① Nick Larson is the man <u>that</u> lives in this town.

② Where did you buy <u>that</u> watch?

③ It is certain <u>that</u> he will come.

④ I like the robot <u>that</u> Kirk bought for me.

⑤ His dress is <u>that</u> of a gentleman.

**19** 괄호 안에 주어진 어휘를 사용해 다음을 영작하시오. (that 사용 금지)

(1) *Jane Eyre*는 Yumi가 어제 읽은 책이다. (the book, read)
   ➡ _____

(2) 내가 입고 있는 재킷은 나의 할머니로부터의 선물이다. (jacket, wear, a present)
   ➡ _____

(3) 사람들은 그러한 음식을 fajitas라고 부른다. (call, such, fajitas)
   ➡ _____

(4) 그 축제는 그 도시를 방문하기에 인기 있는 장소로 만들었다. (a, popular, visit)
   ➡ _____

Reading

**[20~22]** 다음 글을 읽고 물음에 답하시오.

**Are you a smombie?**

All over the world, people are walking around like zombies. Their heads are down, and their eyes are ⓐ _____ their smartphones. We call such people smombies, smartphone zombies. (①) You may not see a hole in the street, so you may fall and get hurt. (②) You may get ⓑ _____ a car accident, too. (③) So what can you do ⓒto prevent these problems? (④) It's simple. (⑤) Do not look at your smartphone while you are walking!

**20** 위 글의 흐름으로 보아, 주어진 문장이 들어가기에 가장 적절한 곳은?

> If you are a smombie, you can have various safety problems.

①      ②      ③      ④      ⑤

**21** 위 글의 빈칸 ⓐ와 ⓑ에 들어갈 전치사가 바르게 짝지어진 것은?

① from – into     ② in – at
③ on – into       ④ from – to
⑤ on – for

**22** 위 글의 밑줄 친 ⓒto prevent와 to부정사의 용법이 다른 것을 고르시오. (2개)

① She was pleased to see her son.
② He was the first man to land on the moon.
③ You are too young to understand it.
④ He is studying English to get a good job.
⑤ He promised me to come back soon.

**[23~25]** 다음 글을 읽고 물음에 답하시오.

ⓐ _____

Smartphones can cause various health problems. One example is dry eyes. When you look at your smartphone, you do not blink often. Then your eyes will feel dry.

(A)[Another / The other] problem you can have is neck pain. When you look down at your smartphone, the stress on your neck (B)[decreases / increases]. Too much use of your smartphone, ⓑ _____, too much texting, can cause neck pain. We call this text neck.

Here are some (C)[advices / tips] for these problems. For dry eyes, try to blink often. For text neck, move your smartphone up to your eye level. You can also do some neck stretching exercises.

**23** 위 글의 빈칸 ⓐ에 들어갈 문장으로 알맞은 것은?

① Blink often when using a smartphone!
② Does the stress on the neck increase?
③ What is the main reason of text neck?
④ Do you have dry eyes or text neck?
⑤ Do some neck stretching exercises!

**24** 위 글의 빈칸 ⓑ에 들어갈 알맞은 것은?

① in addition      ② for example
③ however         ④ in fact
⑤ as a result

**25** 위 글의 괄호 (A)~(C)에서 문맥이나 어법상 알맞은 낱말을 골라 쓰시오.

➡ (A) _____   (B) _____   (C) _____

[26~27] 다음 글을 읽고 물음에 답하시오.

**How do you feel when you don't have your smartphone with you?**

ⓐ스마트폰이 주위에 없을 때 당신은 초조한 기분이 드는가? Do you feel sad when you check your smartphone and there is no text message?

If your answers are "yes," you may have smartphone addiction. There are various things you can do to prevent this. ⓑFor example, turn off your smartphone while meals or meetings. You can talk to people instead of texting them.

**26** 위 글의 밑줄 친 ⓐ의 우리말에 맞게 주어진 어휘를 이용하여 10 단어로 영작하시오. (Do로 시작할 것)

| nervous, around |
| --- |

➡ _____

_____

**27** 위 글의 밑줄 친 ⓑ에서 어법상 틀린 부분을 찾아 고치시오.

_____ ➡ _____

[28~29] 다음 글을 읽고 물음에 답하시오.

Minho: Yesterday, I fell on the street and got hurt. I was texting and I didn't see a hole.
└ Reply: Do not use your smartphone while you are walking.

Emma: My eyes feel dry when I use my smartphone.
└ Reply: Try to blink often.

Suji: I have neck pain when I text a lot.
└ Reply: Move your smartphone up to your eye level and do some neck stretching exercises.

Eric: I think I have smartphone addiction.
└ Reply: Turn off your smartphone during meals or meetings and talk to people ___ⓐ___.

**28** 위 글의 빈칸 ⓐ에 들어갈 알맞은 말은?

① instead of looking at them
② besides texting them
③ through SNS
④ instead of texting them
⑤ besides emailing them

**29** Fill in the blanks with the suitable words.

| Q1: Who should try to blink often? |
| --- |
| Q2: Why should he[she] try to blink often? |

➡ Q1: _____ should try to blink often.
Q2: Because the eyes _____ _____ when he[she] uses the smartphone.

[30~31] 다음 글을 읽고 물음에 답하시오.

**How do you feel when you don't have your smartphone with you?**

Do you feel nervous when your smartphone is not around? Do you feel sad when you check your smartphone and there is no text message?

If your answers are "yes," you may have smartphone addiction. There are various things you can do to prevent this. For example, turn off your smartphone during meals or meetings. You can talk to people instead of ___ⓐ___ them.

**30** 위 글을 읽고 스마트폰 중독이라고 생각할 수 있는 경우 두 가지를 우리말로 쓰시오.

➡ (1) _____
(2) _____
_____

**31** 위 글의 빈칸 ⓐ에 text를 알맞은 형태로 쓰시오.

➡ _____

## 단원별 예상문제

**01** 다음 짝지어진 단어의 관계가 같도록 빈칸에 알맞은 말을 쓰시오.

> sore : painful = varied : _____

**02** 다음 영영풀이에 해당하는 단어는?

> a famous person

① author
② promise
③ celebrity
④ zombie
⑤ hole

**03** 다음 빈칸에 우리말에 맞게 알맞은 단어를 쓰시오. (주어진 철자로 시작하시오.)

> • 여기에 이런 문제에 대한 몇 가지 조언이 있다.
> (A) _____ _____some tips for these problems.
> • 스마트폰이 주위에 없을 때 당신은 초조한 기분이 드는가?
> (B) Do you feel n_____ when your smartphone is not around?

[04~05] 다음 대화를 읽고 물음에 답하시오.

> A: (A)너 몸이 안 좋아 보여. What's wrong?
> B: I have a headache.
> A: _____ (B) _____ Make sure you take some medicine.
> B: OK, I will.

**04** 위 대화의 밑줄 친 (A)의 우리말에 맞게 주어진 문장을 채우시오.

➡ You don't _____ _____.

**05** 위 대화의 (B)에 들어갈 말로 알맞은 것을 모두 고르시오.

① That sounds good.
② I'm sorry to hear that.
③ I'm pleased to hear that.
④ That's too bad.
⑤ How are you doing?

**06** 다음 (A)~(C)에 알맞은 말이 바르게 짝지어진 것은?

> Smartphones can cause (A)[simple / various] health problems. One example is dry eyes. When you look at your smartphone, you do not blink often. Then your eyes will feel (B)[dry / wet]. Another problem you can have is neck pain. When you look down at your smartphone, the stress on your neck [decreases / increases].

| | (A) | (B) | (C) |
|---|---|---|---|
| ① | simple | wet | increases |
| ② | simple | dry | decreases |
| ③ | various | wet | decreases |
| ④ | various | dry | increases |
| ⑤ | various | dry | decreases |

**07** 다음 대화의 밑줄 친 부분 중 어법상 어색한 것은?

> W: You ⓐlook sick. What's wrong, Inho?
> B: I ⓑhave a sore throat. I ⓒhave a fever, too.
> W: I think you ⓓhave cold. Take this medicine and ⓔmake sure you take a good rest.
> B: OK. Thank you.

① ⓐ  ② ⓑ  ③ ⓒ ④ ⓓ  ⑤ ⓔ

**[08~09] 다음 대화를 읽고 물음에 답하시오.**

W: _____(A)_____, Andy?
B: Hello, Ms. Kim. My right thumb hurts.
W: Hmm. Do you use your smartphone a lot?
B: Yes, I text a lot. Why?
W: I think you have texting thumb.
B: Texting thumb? What's texting thumb?
W: _____(B)_____. You can get it from texting too much.
B: Oh, I didn't know that.
W: ⓐ손가락 스트레칭 운동을 좀 하는 게 어떠니?
B: OK, I will.
W: And _____(C)_____.

출제율 95%

**08** 위 대화의 빈칸 (A)~(C)에 들어갈 말로 알맞은 것을 〈보기〉에서 찾아 쓰시오.

> ┤ 보기 ├
> • What can I do for you
> • What's wrong
> • It's pain in your thumb
> • don't forget to text message to me
> • make sure you don't text too much

➡ (A) _____
  (B) _____
  (C) _____

출제율 90%

**09** 위 대화의 밑줄 친 ⓐ의 우리말에 맞게 주어진 단어를 이용하여 영어로 쓰시오.

> why, you, do, some, stretching exercises

➡ _____

출제율 90%

**10** 다음 대화의 빈칸에 들어갈 말로 알맞은 것은?

> W: What's wrong, Peter?
> B: I don't know, Ms. Kim, but my back hurts a lot.
> W: Put a heating pad on it.
> B: OK, I will.
> W: And _____.

① you should not forget to lock the door
② you had better text a lot
③ make sure you do some stretching exercises
④ make sure you give me a call when you get home
⑤ make sure you get enough sleep tonight

출제율 95%

**11** 다음 문장에서 어법상 어색한 것을 바르게 고쳐 문장을 다시 쓰시오.

(1) The pizza who my dad made was really delicious.

➡ _____
_____

(2) I know the girl which you are talking about.

➡ _____
_____

(3) We elected class president Chris.

➡ _____

(4) The game that we saw it was very boring.

➡ _____

(5) He called me as Queen.

➡ _____

**12** 다음 빈칸에 들어갈 말을 <u>모두</u> 고르시오.

> Jane is the girl _____ Peter met in the park.

① who ② whose
③ whom ④ which
⑤ that

**13** 다음 중 어법상 바르지 <u>않은</u> 것은?

① Do you like the hat you bought yesterday?
② Arnold calls his daughter *My Little Princess*.
③ I met the lady with whom you had dinner last Saturday.
④ They called the ship to be Titanic.
⑤ *Yesterday* is the song that I can sing in English.

**14** 다음 우리말을 괄호 안에 주어진 어휘를 이용하여 영작하시오. (that 사용 금지)

(1) 우리는 그러한 춤을 Salsa라고 부른다. (such, call, a dance, 6 단어)

➡ _____

(2) 아무도 Nicole이 만든 스파게티를 좋아하지 않았다. (spaghetti, make, 7 단어)

➡ _____

(3) 우리는 Alex를 우리 동아리의 회장으로 선출했다. (elect, president, club, 7 단어)

➡ _____

(4) 그녀는 내가 가장 좋아하는 가수이다. (the singer, most, 8 단어)

➡ _____

[15~17] 다음 글을 읽고 물음에 답하시오.

**Are you a smombie?**

  All over the world, people are walking around ⓐlike zombies. Their heads are down, and their eyes are on their smartphones. We call such people smombies, smartphone zombies. If you are a smombie, you can have various safety problems. You may not see a hole in the street, so you may fall and get hurt. You may get into a car accident, too. So what can you do to prevent ⓑthese problems? It's simple. Do not look at your smartphone while you are ___(A)___ !

**15** 위 글의 빈칸 (A)에 들어갈 가장 알맞은 것은?

① talking ② walking
③ studying ④ eating
⑤ playing

**16** 위 글의 밑줄 친 ⓐlike와 의미가 <u>다른</u> 것은?

① He ran <u>like</u> the wind.
② You do it <u>like</u> this.
③ I had a chance to meet people of <u>like</u> mind.
④ Don't look at me <u>like</u> that.
⑤ Students were angry at being treated <u>like</u> children.

**17** 위 글의 밑줄 친 ⓑthese problems와 바꿔 쓸 수 있는 말을 본문에서 찾아 쓰시오.

➡ _____

**[18~19]** 다음 글을 읽고 물음에 답하시오.

**Do you have dry eyes or text neck?**

Smartphones can cause various ⓐ problems. One example is dry eyes. When you look at your smartphone, you do not blink often. Then your eyes will feel dry.

Another problem you can have is neck pain. When you look down at your smartphone, the stress on your neck increases. Too much use of your smartphone, for example, too much texting, can cause neck pain. We call this text neck.

Here are some tips for these problems. For dry eyes, try to blink often. For text neck, move your smartphone up to your eye level. You can also do some neck stretching exercises.

**18** 위 글의 빈칸 ⓐ에 들어갈 알맞은 것은?

① safety
② social
③ environment
④ mental
⑤ health

**19** 위 글의 내용과 일치하지 <u>않는</u> 것은?

① 스마트폰 사용은 안구 건조증을 일으킬 수 있다.
② 스마트폰 사용은 목 통증을 일으킬 수 있다.
③ 스마트폰을 내려다볼 때, 목에 가해지는 압박이 감소한다.
④ 안구 건조증에는, 눈을 자주 깜박이려고 노력해야 한다.
⑤ 거북목 증후군에는 당신의 눈높이까지 스마트폰을 위로 올려야 한다.

**[20~22]** 다음 글을 읽고 물음에 답하시오.

There are a few things I need to change to have a ⓐ life.

First, I don't exercise much. From now on, I will try to walk for 30 minutes every day.

Second, I think I eat too much fast food. I will eat fast food only once a week.

Third, I often eat at night. I will not eat after 10 o'clock.

I will try my best ⓑto keep these promises.

**20** 위 글의 빈칸 ⓐ에 healthy의 비교급을 쓰시오.

➡ _____

**21** 위 글을 읽고 더 건강한 생활을 하기 위해 필자가 바꾸어야 할 세 가지를 우리말로 쓰시오.

(1) _____
   ➡ _____
(2) _____
   ➡ _____
(3) _____
   ➡ _____

**22** 아래 〈보기〉에서 위 글의 밑줄 친 ⓑto keep과 to부정사의 용법이 <u>다른</u> 것의 개수를 고르시오. (2개)

> ┤ 보기 ├
> ① This chair seems comfortable to sit on.
> ② I have no friends to help me.
> ③ I found it difficult to persuade them.
> ④ I was shocked to hear the tragic news.
> ⑤ What a fool he is to say such a foolish thing!

① 1개   ② 2개   ③ 3개   ④ 4개   ⑤ 5개

**01** 다음 그림을 보고 아래 대화의 빈칸에 알맞은 단어를 쓰시오.

G: What's _____, Mike?
B: I _____ _____ terrible _____.
G: I think you _____ _____ some medicine.
B: OK, I _____.

**02** 다음 대화를 읽고 아래의 표를 완성하시오.

W: What's wrong, Andy?
B: Hello, Ms. Kim. My right thumb hurts.
W: Hmm. Do you use your smartphone a lot?
B: Yes, I text a lot. Why?
W: I think you have texting thumb.
B: Texting thumb? What's texting thumb?
W: It's pain in your thumb. You can get it from texting too much.
B: Oh, I didn't know that.
W: Why don't you do some finger stretching exercises?
B: OK, I will.
W: And make sure you don't text too much.

• Problem: _____ _____ (_____ in your thumb)
• Advice: (1) do some _____ _____ _____ (2) don't _____ too much

**03** 괄호 안에 주어진 단어를 이용하여 다음 대화를 완성하시오.

M: _____ (A) _____, Mina?
G: I _____ (B) _____. I also have a runny nose.
M: I think you have a cold. _____ (C) _____
G: OK, I will.

➡ (A) _____ (what, matter)
(B) _____ (a sore throat)
(C) _____ (make, you, some rest)

**04** 다음 두 문장을 관계대명사를 사용하여 한 문장으로 바꾸시오.

(1) • The book is about nature.
 • I'm reading the book.
 ➡ _____

(2) • Kenya is the country.
 • John wants to visit the country.
 ➡ _____

(3) • J. K. Rowling is a famous novelist.
 • Many people like her.
 ➡ _____
 _____

(4) • I want to know the name of the girl.
 • I met her at the party.
 ➡ _____
 _____

(5) • Start by identifying the people.
 • You want to work with the people.
 ➡ _____
 _____
 _____

(6) • The rate can be very slow.
 • Hair grows at the rate.
 ➡ _____
 _____

[05~07] 다음 글을 읽고 물음에 답하시오.

Living (A)[with / without] smartphones is difficult for many of us these days. However, unwise or too much use of smartphones can cause various problems.

**Are you a smombie?**

All over the world, people are walking around like zombies. ⓐ그들의 머리는 아래를 향하고, 그들의 눈은 스마트폰을 향하고 있다. We call such people smombies, smartphone zombies. If you are a smombie, you can have various safety problems. You may not see a (B)[hole / whole] in the street, so you may fall and get hurt. You may get into a car accident, too. So what can you do to (C)[prevent / protect] these problems? It's simple. Do not look at your smartphone while you are walking!

**05** 위 글의 괄호 (A)~(C)에서 문맥상 알맞은 낱말을 골라 쓰시오.

➡ (A) _____ (B) _____ (C) _____

**06** 위 글의 밑줄 친 ⓐ의 우리말에 맞게 한 단어를 보충하여, 주어진 어휘를 알맞게 배열하시오.

their smartphones / are / on / are / their eyes / and / their heads / ,

➡ _____

_____

**07** 다음 빈칸 (A)와 (B)에 알맞은 단어를 넣어 질문에 답하시오.

Q: Why may smombies fall and get hurt in the street?

A: Because they look at their (A)_____ while they are walking and may not see a (B)_____ in the street.

[08~10] 다음 글을 읽고 물음에 답하시오.

**Do you have dry eyes or text neck?**

Smartphones can cause various health problems. One example is dry eyes. When you look at your smartphone, you do not blink often. Then your eyes will feel dry.

Another problem you can have is neck pain. ⓐWhen you look up at your smartphone, the stress on your neck increases. Too much use of your smartphone, for example, too much texting, can cause ⓑneck pain. We call this text neck.

Here are some tips for these problems. For dry eyes, try to blink often. For text neck, move your smartphone up to your eye level. You can also do some neck stretching exercises.

**08** 위 글의 내용과 일치하도록 다음 빈칸 (A)와 (B)에 알맞은 단어를 쓰시오.

One of the health problems smartphones can cause is (A)_____ _____ and another problem is (B)_____ _____.

**09** 위 글의 밑줄 친 ⓐ에서 흐름상 어색한 부분을 찾아 고치시오.

_____ ➡ _____

**10** 위 글의 밑줄 친 ⓑneck pain의 원인과 이 문제를 위한 조언을 우리말로 쓰시오.

➡ 원인: _____

_____

조언: (1) _____

(2) _____

**01** 다음 주어진 문제점과 그에 맞는 충고를 찾아서 〈보기〉와 같이 적절한 대화를 완성하시오.

| Problem | | Advice | |
|---|---|---|---|
| • headache | • toothache | • take some medicine | • get some rest |
| • cold | • sore throat | • go see a doctor | • drink a lot of water |
| • fever | • runny nose | • go to the dentist | • take a warm bath |

┤ 보기 ├

A: You don't look well. What's wrong?

B: I have a headache.

A: That's too bad. Make sure you take some medicine.

B: OK, I will.

(1) _____

_____

(2) _____

_____

**02** 다음은 Big Ben의 사진이다. 그림을 참고하고 괄호 안에 주어진 어휘를 이용하여 문장을 완성하시오.

(the clock tower / call)

➡ People _____.

**03** 다음 내용을 바탕으로 건강한 생활을 위한 다짐을 하는 글을 쓰시오.

| **My problems are that ....** | **I'll try to ....** |
|---|---|
| e.g. I don't exercise much | e.g. walk for 30 minutes every day |

There are a few things I need (A)_____ to have a healthier life.

First, I don't exercise much. (B)_____, I will try to walk for 30 minutes every day.

Second, I think I eat too much fast food. l will eat fast food only (C)_____.

Third, I often eat at night. I will not eat (D)_____ 10 o'clock.

I will try (E)_____ to keep these promises.

## 단원별 모의고사

**01** 다음 단어에 대한 영어 설명이 <u>어색한</u> 것은?

① zombie: in stories and movies, a dead body that moves by magic

② blink: to open and close your eyes very quickly

③ prevent: to try to allow something to happen

④ simple: not difficult or complicated

⑤ traffic light: a set of colored lights at the side of the road that show when cars are allowed to move

**02** 다음 짝지어진 단어의 관계가 같도록 빈칸에 알맞은 말을 쓰시오.

well : healthy = suffering: _____

**03** 다음 영영풀이에 해당하는 단어는?

able to learn and understand things quickly

① intelligent　　② various
③ careful　　　④ dry
⑤ stupid

**04** 다음 대화의 빈칸에 공통으로 들어갈 말은?

W: You look sick. What's wrong, Inho?

B: I _____ sore throat. I _____ fever, too.

W: I think you _____ cold. Take this medicine and make sure you take a good rest.

B: OK. Thank you.

① catch　　② take a　　③ make
④ turn a　　⑤ have a

**05** 다음 대화의 순서가 바르게 배열된 것은?

(A) I fell and hurt my foot while I was playing soccer.
(B) Yes, but it hurts a lot.
(C) Can you walk?
(D) What's wrong with your leg, Sam?

① (A) – (C) – (B) – (D)
② (B) – (C) – (D) – (A)
③ (C) – (D) – (A) – (B)
④ (D) – (A) – (C) – (B)
⑤ (D) – (B) – (A) – (C)

**06** 다음 중 짝지어진 대화가 <u>어색한</u> 것은?

① A: What's wrong, Peter?
　B: I don't know, Ms. Kim, but my back hurts a lot.

② A: What's the matter with you, Jenny? You don't look well.
　B: I won first prize in the singing contest.

③ A: What's wrong with your legs, Andy?
　B: I fell and hurt them while I was playing soccer.

④ A: I have a runny nose. I have a fever, too.
　B: Take this medicine and make sure you take a good rest.

⑤ A: You don't look well. What's wrong?
　B: I couldn't sleep well last night. I'm so tired.

**07** 다음 대화의 빈칸에 들어갈 말로 <u>어색한</u> 것은?

> A: What's the matter, Inho?
> B: _____

① I have a headache.
② I have a fever.
③ I have a stomachache.
④ I hurt my back.
⑤ Make sure you take some medicine.

**[08~09]** 다음 대화를 읽고 물음에 답하시오.

> W: What's wrong, Peter?
> B: I don't know, Ms. Kim, but my back hurts a lot.
> W: Put a heating pad on ⓐit.
> B: OK, I will.
> W: And _____ (A) _____.

**08** 밑줄 친 ⓐit이 가리키는 것을 Ms. Kim의 입장에서 영어로 쓰시오.

➡ _____

**09** 위 대화의 빈칸 (A)에 들어갈 말로 <u>어색한</u> 것은?

① don't remember to do some stretching exercises
② make sure you do some stretching exercises
③ remember to do some stretching exercises
④ don't forget to do some stretching exercises
⑤ you had better do some stretching exercises

**10** 다음 대화의 빈칸 (A)에 들어갈 당부의 표현으로 가장 <u>어색한</u> 것은?

> A: You don't look well. What's wrong?
> B: I have a runny nose.
> A: That's too bad. Make sure _____(A)_____.
> B: OK, I will.

① you go see a doctor
② you take some medicine
③ you get some rest
④ you go to the dentist
⑤ you take a warm bath

**[11~12]** 다음 대화를 읽고 물음에 답하시오.

> W: What's wrong, Andy?
> B: Hello, Ms. Kim. My right thumb hurts.
> W: Hmm. Do you use your smartphone a lot?
> B: Yes, I text a lot. Why?
> W: I think you have texting thumb.
> B: Texting thumb? What's texting thumb?
> W: It's pain in your thumb. You can get (A)it from texting too much.
> B: Oh, I didn't know that.
> W: Why don't you do some finger stretching exercises?
> B: OK, I will.
> W: And make sure you don't text too much.

**11** Andy가 Ms. Kim을 만난 이유로 알맞은 것은?

① Because he texted a lot.
② Because his right thumb hurt.
③ Because he lost his smartphone.
④ To ask her what exercises to do.
⑤ To make sure he would not text too much.

**12** 위 대화의 밑줄 친 (A)it이 가리키는 것을 영어로 쓰시오.

➡ _____

**13** 괄호 안에 주어진 어휘를 이용하여 우리말을 영작하시오.

(1) Cameron은 Gillian이 가장 좋아하는 감독이다. (the director, best)

➡ _____

(2) 우리는 Jason이 우리에게 해준 이야기를 좋아했다. (the story, tell, 7단어)

➡ _____

(3) 그의 사업은 그를 백만장자로 만들었다. (business, a millionaire)

➡ _____

(4) 우리는 Bali를 신들의 섬이라고 부른다. (the Island of Gods)

➡ _____

**14** 다음 빈칸에 공통으로 들어갈 단어는?

> • Let's _____ the world a better place.
> • I will _____ him do his homework.

① call ② make
③ elect ④ consider
⑤ name

**15** 두 문장을 관계대명사를 사용하여 한 문장으로 썼을 때 빈칸의 문장을 쓰시오.

(1) • Mr. Lee is the teacher.

• _____

➡ Mr. Lee is the teacher whom every student respects.

(2) • There are various things.

• _____

➡ There are various things that you can do to prevent this.

**16** 다음 중 어법상 바르지 않은 것은?

① His music has made him a citizen of the world.
② They elected Jane club leader.
③ They considered their son to be a genius.
④ She named him after Harry Porter.
⑤ We want to call this cup as Cookie Eater.

**17** 어법상 어색한 것을 바르게 고쳐 문장을 다시 쓰시오.

(1) He is a gentleman which I built a good trust on.

➡ _____
_____

(2) These are the pants who I bought yesterday.

➡ _____
_____

(3) She doesn't consider an artist him.

➡ _____

(4) This is the issue about that we need to express our opinion.

➡ _____
_____
_____

(5) Ella received some flowers that her boy friend had sent them to her.

➡ _____
_____

(6) They call it as 'Non La'.

➡ _____

[18~20] 다음 글을 읽고 물음에 답하시오.

**Do you have dry eyes or text neck?**

Smartphones can cause various health problems. One example is dry eyes. When you look at your smartphone, you do not blink often. Then your eyes will feel (A)[dry / drily].

Another problem you can have (B)[is / are] neck pain. When you look down at your smartphone, the stress on your neck increases. Too much use of your smartphone, for example, too much texting, can cause neck pain. ⓐWe call this text neck.

Here are some tips for ⓑthese problems. For dry eyes, try to blink often. For text neck, move your smartphone up to your eye level. You can also do some neck (C)[stretching / stretched] exercises.

**18** 위 글의 괄호 (A)~(C)에서 어법상 알맞은 낱말을 골라 쓰시오.

➡ (A) _____ (B) _____ (C) _____

**19** 위 글의 밑줄 친 ⓐ와 문장의 형식이 다른 것을 모두 고르시오.

① I painted the door green.
② She sent me a long letter.
③ He found this book easily.
④ Each girl kept her love a secret.
⑤ I gave her the book.

**20** 위 글의 밑줄 친 ⓑthese problems에 해당하지 않는 것을 고르시오.

① Your eyes will feel dry.
② You often blink.
③ You can have neck pain.
④ The stress on your neck increases.
⑤ Too much texting can cause text neck.

[21~22] 다음 글을 읽고 물음에 답하시오.

**How do you feel when you don't have your smartphone with you?**

Do you feel nervous when your smartphone is not around? Do you feel sad when you check your smartphone and there is no text message?

If your answers are "yes," you may have smartphone addiction. ⓐThere are various things you can do to prevent this. For example, turn off your smartphone during meals or meetings. You can talk to people instead of texting them.

**21** 위 글의 밑줄 친 ⓐ에서 things와 you 사이에 생략된 단어를 모두 고르시오.

① which          ② who
③ what           ④ that
⑤ whom

**22** 위 글의 내용과 일치하지 않는 것은?

① 스마트폰이 주위에 없을 때 초조한 기분이 들면 스마트폰 중독일지도 모른다.
② 스마트폰을 확인했을 때 아무런 문자 메시지가 없을 경우 슬픈 기분이 들면 스마트폰 중독일지도 모른다.
③ 스마트폰 중독을 예방하기 위해 할 수 있는 일은 별로 없다.
④ 스마트폰 중독을 예방하기 위해 식사나 회의 중에는 스마트폰을 꺼야 한다.
⑤ 스마트폰 중독을 예방하기 위해 문자를 보내는 대신에 사람들과 이야기를 할 수 있다.

## Lesson 6

# Different People, Different Views

 **의사소통 기능**

- 계획 말하기
  I'm planning to see a movie this Saturday.
- 약속 정하기
  A: What time and where should we meet?
  B: How about meeting at 2:30 in front of Star Movie Theater?
  A: OK. See you then.

**언어 형식**

- 지각동사+목적어+-ing
  Daedalus **saw** birds **flying**.

- so ~ that ...
  Icarus was **so** excited **that** he forgot his father's warning.

# Words & Expressions

## Key Words

- **adventurous** [ædvéntʃərəs] 혱 모험심이 강한
- **beauty** [bjú:ti] 몡 아름다움, 미
- **brave** [breiv] 혱 용감한
- **concert** [ká:nsərt] 몡 콘서트
- **creative** [kriéitiv] 혱 창의적인
- **detail** [ditéil] 몡 세부 사항
- **different** [dífərənt] 혱 다른
- **difference** [dífərəns] 몡 차이
- **dynamic** [dainǽmik] 혱 역동적인
- **escape** [iskéip] 동 달아나다, 탈출하다
- **example** [igzǽmpl] 몡 예, 사례
- **exhibition** [èksəbíʃən] 몡 전시회
- **fall** [fɔ:l] 동 떨어지다 (-fell-fallen)
- **favorite** [féivərit] 혱 가장 좋아하는
- **feather** [féðər] 몡 (새의) 털, 깃털
- **flight** [flait] 몡 비행, 날기
- **foolish** [fú:liʃ] 혱 어리석은
- **forever** [fərévər] 분 영원히
- **forget** [fərgét] 동 잊어버리다, 잊다
- **furthermore** [fə́:rðərmɔ̀:r] 분 게다가, 더욱이
- **gather** [gǽðər] 동 모으다
- **glue** [glu:] 동 붙이다
- **Greek** [gri:k] 혱 그리스의
- **imaginative** [imǽdʒənətiv] 혱 상상력이 풍부한
- **inventor** [invéntər] 몡 발명가
- **library** [láibrèri] 몡 도서관
- **melt** [melt] 동 녹다
- **myth** [miθ] 몡 신화
- **outline** [áutlain] 몡 윤곽, 외형
- **plan** [plæn] 동 계획하다, 계획을 세우다
- **ready** [rédi] 혱 준비된
- **romantic** [roumǽntik] 혱 로맨틱한, 낭만적인
- **sci-fi movie** 공상 과학 영화
- **sentence** [séntəns] 몡 문장
- **shout** [ʃaut] 동 외치다, 소리치다
- **simple** [símpl] 혱 단순한
- **skip** [skip] 동 빼먹다, 거르다
- **special** [spéʃəl] 혱 특별한
- **subject** [sʌ́bdʒikt] 몡 주제
- **style** [stail] 몡 화풍, 스타일
- **tea** [ti:] 몡 차, 홍차
- **ticket office** 매표소
- **title** [táitl] 몡 제목
- **tower** [táuər] 몡 탑
- **violinist** [vàiəlínist] 몡 바이올린 연주자
- **warn** [wɔ:rn] 동 경고하다
- **warning** [wɔ́:rniŋ] 몡 경고, 주의
- **wax** [wæks] 몡 밀랍, 왁스
- **whole** [houl] 혱 전부의, 전체의
- **wing** [wiŋ] 몡 날개

## Key Expressions

- **be planning to+동사원형** ~할 계획이다
- **be interested in ~** ~에 관심이 있다
- **be proud of ~** ~을 자랑스러워하다
- **come from ~** ~로부터 오다
- **deal with** ~을 다루다
- **fall in love with ~** ~와 사랑에 빠지다
- **focus on ~** ~에 초점을 맞추다
- **How about -ing?** ~하는 게 어때?
- **higher and higher** 점점 더 높이
- **in addition to** ~에 더하여, ~일 뿐 아니라
- **in contrast** 그에 반해서
- **in front of ~** ~ 앞에
- **so 형용사 that ...** 너무 ~해서 …하다
- **try to+동사원형** ~하려고 시도하다
- **Why don't you+동사원형 ~?** ~하는 게 어때?

## Word Power

※ 서로 반대되는 뜻을 가진 어휘

□ **different** (다른) ↔ **same** (같은)

□ **brave** (용감한) ↔ **timid** (겁 많은, 소심한)

□ **simple** (단순한) ↔ **complicated** (복잡한)

□ **romantic** (낭만적인) ↔ **unromantic** (낭만적이지 않은)

□ **foolish** (어리석은) ↔ **wise** (현명한)

□ **interested** (관심 있는) ↔ **uninterested** (무관심한)

※ 서로 비슷한 뜻을 가진 어휘

□ **gather** : **collect** (모으다)

□ **shout** : **yell** (외치다)

□ **glue** : **paste** (붙이다)

□ **foolish** : **silly** (어리석은)

□ **melt** : **thaw** (녹다)

□ **furthermore** : **moreover** (게다가)

## English Dictionary

□ **adventurous** 모험심이 강한
→ willing to try new or exciting things
새롭고 흥미로운 일을 기꺼이 시도하려고 하는

□ **detail** 세부 사항
→ a small fact, feature, or piece of information
사소한 사실, 특징 또는 정보

□ **escape** 달아나다
→ to get away from a place or person
어떤 장소나 사람으로부터 멀리 벗어나다

□ **exhibition** 전시회
→ a public show of something
어떤 것을 공개적으로 보여주는 것

□ **feather** 깃털
→ one of the light soft things that cover a bird's body
새의 몸을 덮고 있는 가볍고 부드러운 것 중 하나

□ **flight** 비행
→ the act of flying through the air
공중을 나는 행위

□ **foolish** 어리석은
→ silly or not sensible
어리석거나 현명하지 않은

□ **furthermore** 게다가
→ used when adding another piece of information
또 다른 정보를 더할 때 사용되는

□ **gather** 모으다
→ to come together in a group
한 무리로 합치다

□ **glue** 붙이다
→ to join things together using glue
풀을 사용하여 물건을 결합하다

□ **in addition to** ~에 더하여
→ used for saying that something extra exists
추가적인 무언가가 존재한다는 것을 말하기 위해 사용되는

□ **myth** 신화
→ an old story about gods, brave people, magical creatures, etc.
신이나 용감한 사람들, 마법의 생물 등에 관한 오래된 이야기
어떤 것의 모양을 보여주는 선

□ **outline** 윤곽, 외형
→ a line that shows the shape of something

□ **romantic** 낭만적인
→ showing a strong feeling of love
강한 사랑의 감정을 드러내는

□ **shout** 소리치다
→ to say something very loudly
매우 크게 무언가를 말하다

□ **skip** 빼먹다, 거르다
→ to avoid something or not to do something
무언가를 피하거나 하지 않다

□ **tea** 차, 홍차
→ a hot drink that you make by pouring boiling water onto dried leaves
말린 잎에 끓는 물을 부어 만든 뜨거운 음료

□ **warn** 경고하다
→ to tell someone that something bad might happen, so that he or she can avoid it
그 혹은 그녀가 그것을 피할 수 있도록 누군가에게 어떤 나쁜 일이 일어날 수 있다고 말하다

□ **wax** 왁스, 밀랍
→ a substance used for making candles and crayons
양초와 크레용을 만드는 데 사용되는 물질

□ **wing** 날개
→ one of the parts of bird's or insect's body that it uses to fly
날기 위해 사용하는 새나 곤충의 몸의 한 부분

**01** 다음 빈칸에 들어갈 말로 알맞은 것은?

> We often find different paintings with the _____ subject. An example is *The Flight of Icarus* by Henri Matisse and *The Fall of Icarus* by Marc Chagall.

① different ② brave
③ foolish ④ same
⑤ fallen

**02** 다음 영어 설명을 읽고 빈칸에 알맞은 말을 쓰시오.

> In Greek _____, Icarus is the son of Daedalus, a great inventor.

> an old story about gods, brave people, magical creatures, etc.

[03~04] 다음 영어 설명에 해당하는 단어를 고르시오.

**03**
> one of the light soft things that cover a bird's body

① feature ② wing
③ feather ④ further
⑤ beak

**04**
> to say something very loudly

① escape ② gather
③ skip ④ warn
⑤ shout

서답형
**05** 다음 우리말에 맞게 빈칸에 알맞은 단어를 쓰시오.

> Matisse와 Chagall 둘 다 그들의 그림에서 같은 주제를 다루지만, 그것들은 다르다.
> ➡ Matisse and Chagall both _____ _____ the same subject in their paintings, but they are different.

중요
**06** 다음 빈칸에 들어갈 말로 알맞은 것은?

> Matisse thought that Icarus was brave and adventurous. _____, Chagall thought that Icarus was foolish.

① In addition ② In contrast
③ For example ④ Furthermore
⑤ In addition to

서답형
**07** 다음 짝지어진 단어의 관계가 같도록 빈칸에 알맞은 말을 쓰시오.

> shout – yell : collect – _____

**08** 다음 빈칸에 들어갈 말로 알맞게 짝지어진 것은?

> • Matisse's painting is very simple, but Chagall's painting has many _____.
> • Don't fly too close to the sun. The wax will _____.

① differences – freeze
② differences – melt
③ details – freeze
④ details – melt
⑤ details – gather

**01** 다음 빈칸에 들어갈 말을 〈보기〉에서 찾아 쓰시오. (필요하면 변형하여 쓰시오.)

┌──── 보기 ────┐
flight   gather   adventurous   wax
warn   detail   furthermore   outline
└─────────────┘

(1) When the wings were ready, he _____ his son, "Don't fly too close to the sun."

(2) Daedalus then _____ bird feathers and glued them together with _____.

(3) Matisse's painting is very _____. In his painting, Icarus' body has just a simple outline.

(4) Matisse thought that Icarus was brave and _____. In contrast, Chagall thought that Icarus was foolish.

**02** 영영풀이에 해당하는 단어를 〈보기〉에서 찾아 첫 번째 칸에 쓰고, 두 번째 칸에는 우리말 뜻을 쓰시오.

┌──── 보기 ────┐
adventurous   foolish   glue
skip   escape   shout
└─────────────┘

(1) _____ : silly or not sensible : _____

(2) _____ : to avoid something or not to do something : _____

(3) _____ : willing to try new or exciting things: _____

(4) _____ : to join things together using glue: _____

**03** 두 그림의 특징을 설명하는 다음 글의 빈칸에 알맞은 단어를 〈보기〉에서 골라 쓰시오. (필요하면 어형을 변화시키오.)

┌──── 보기 ────┐
detail   however   furthermore   outline
in addition to   difference   title
└─────────────┘

Matisse's painting is very simple, but Chagall's painting has many (1)_____. In Matisse's painting, there are only Icarus and some stars. (2)_____, Icarus' body has just a simple (3)_____. In contrast, Chagall painted many people and houses (4)_____ _____ _____ Icarus.

**04** 다음 우리말과 같은 표현이 되도록 문장의 빈칸을 채우시오.

(1) Daedalus는 탈출하고 싶었다.
➡ Daedalus wanted to _____.

(2) Icarus는 매우 흥분해서 아버지의 경고를 잊었다.
➡ Icarus was so excited that he forgot his father's _____.

# Conversation

**①  계획 말하기**

I'm planning to see a movie this Saturday. 나는 이번 주 토요일에 영화를 볼 계획이야.

■ 'be planning to+동사원형'은 '~할 계획이다'라는 의미로 미래의 계획을 말할 때 쓰며, '~할 예정이다' 라는 뜻의 'be going to+동사원형', 'be trying to+동사원형', 'be supposed to+동사원형' 등으로 바꿔 말할 수 있다.

■ be going to+동사원형
'be going to+동사원형' 구문은 현재 시점에서 실현 가능성을 확인할 수 있는 미래의 행위를 언급할 때 쓴다. 즉, 이미 계획했거나 결정된 일 등에 주로 쓰이며 의도한 일이거나 이미 결정된 사실임을 강조한다.

• I'm going to eat out tonight. 나는 오늘밤 외식을 할 것이다.

• We're going to buy a new car soon. 우리는 곧 새 차를 구입할 것이다.

• I'm planning to visit my grandparents this weekend. 나는 이번 주말에 조부모님을 방문할 계획이야.

■ 계획을 묻는 표현

• A: Are you planning to take a dance class? 너는 무용 수업을 받을 계획이니?
  B: Yes, I am. 응, 그래.

■ Are you planning to invite him to your birthday party?

= Are you going to invite him to your birthday party?

= Are you trying to invite him to your birthday party? 너는 너의 생일 파티에 그를 초대할 거니?

**핵심 Check**

1. 다음 대화의 빈칸에 들어갈 말로 알맞은 것은?

   A: What are you planning to do this weekend?
   B: I'm _____ a trip with my family.
   ① plan to taking        ② planning to taking
   ③ planning to take      ④ plan to take
   ⑤ go to take

## 2 약속 정하기

> **A** What time and where should we meet? 몇 시에 어디에서 만날까?
>
> **B** How about meeting at 2:30 in front of Star Movie Theater?
> Star 영화관 앞에서 2시 30분에 만나는 게 어때?
>
> **A** OK. See you then. 좋아. 그때 보자.

■ 함께 하자고 제안을 할 때는 Do you want to go with me?, How about joining me? 등으로 말한다. 약속 시간이나 장소를 정할 때는 When/Where should we meet?, Can you make it at 5?, Shall we meet at the library? 등의 표현을 사용한다.

### 약속 시간 정하기

- When should we meet?
- What time should we meet?
- Let's meet at 5.
- Can you make it at 5?
- How about five o'clock?

■ 시간 약속을 정하는 표현에 알맞은 응답

- 수락할 때
  Sure. / Okay. / Yeah. / Sounds great. / All right. 좋아.
  See you then. 그때 보자.

- 거절할 때
  I'm afraid, I can't. How about at four? 미안하지만 안 돼. 4시는 어떨까?
  I'm sorry, but I can't make it at 3. 미안하지만 3시는 안되겠어.

■ 약속 장소 정하기
- Where should we meet? 어디에서 만날까?
- Let's meet at the library. 도서실에서 만나자.

### 핵심 Check

2. 다음 대화의 빈칸에 알맞은 것은?

A: _____ should we meet at the ballpark?
B: How about meeting at two?

① What      ② How
③ Where     ④ How many
⑤ What time

**Listen and Talk A-1**

G: ❶I'm planning to go to a piano concert tomorrow. ❷Do you want to go with me, Kevin?

B: Sure. ❸What time should we meet?

G: The concert begins at 7 o'clock, so ❹let's meet at 6 at the bus stop.

B: OK. See you then.

G: 나는 내일 피아노 콘서트에 갈 예정이야. 나랑 같이 갈래, Kevin?
B: 물론이지. 몇 시에 만날까?
G: 콘서트는 7시에 시작하니까 6시에 버스 정류장에서 만나자.
B: 좋아. 그때 보자.

❶ 'be planning to+동사원형'은 '~할 계획이다'라는 의미로 미래의 계획을 말할 때 사용하는 표현이다.
❷ 함께 하자고 제안을 할 때 사용하는 표현으로 How about joining me?로 바꾸어 표현할 수 있다.
❸ 약속 시간을 정할 때 사용하는 표현으로 '몇 시에 만날까?'로 해석한다. When should we meet?으로 표현할 수 있다.
❹ 'let's+동사원형'은 '~하자'라는 제안이나 권유의 의미로 사용된다.

**Check(√) True or False**

(1) Kevin is going to go to a piano concert with the girl.   T ☐ F ☐

(2) They will meet at 7 o'clock at the bus stop.   T ☐ F ☐

**Listen and Talk A-2**

G: ❶I'm planning to go see *Cats* this Saturday. Do you want to go with me?

B: Sure. ❷What time and where should we meet?

G: The musical starts at 3 o'clock. ❸Let's meet at 2 at Dream Art Hall.

B: Great. See you on Saturday.

G: 나는 이번 주 토요일에 'Cats'를 보러 갈 계획이야. 나랑 같이 갈래?
B: 좋아. 몇 시에 어디서 만날까?
G: 뮤지컬은 3시에 시작해. 2시에 Dream 아트 홀에서 만나자.
B: 좋아. 토요일에 만나자.

❶ 'be planning to+동사원형'은 '~할 계획이다'라는 의미이며 미래의 계획을 말할 때 사용하는 표현으로, '~할 예정이다'라는 뜻의 'be going to+동사원형', 'be trying to+동사원형', 'be supposed to+동사원형' 등으로 바꿔 말할 수 있다.
❷ 약속 시간과 장소를 정할 때 사용하는 표현이다. what time은 when으로 바꾸어 쓸 수 있다.
❸ 'let's+동사원형'은 '~하자'라는 약속 시간을 제안할 때 사용된다.

**Check(√) True or False**

(3) The girl wants to go to see the musical *Cats* with the boy.   T ☐ F ☐

(4) The boy is going to meet the girl at 2 on Saturday.   T ☐ F ☐

**Listen and Talk A-3**

G: I'm planning to go see a soccer game next Friday. ❶What about joining me, Jinho?

B: That sounds great. ❷What time should we meet?

G: Let's meet at 10:30 in front of Green Stadium.

B: OK. See you then.

❶ 함께 하자고 제안하는 표현으로 How about joining me?로 바꾸어 말할 수 있다.
❷ 약속 시간을 정할 때 사용하는 표현으로 '몇 시에 만날까?'라는 의미다.

**Listen and Talk A-4**

B: ❶What are you going to do this Sunday?

G: I'm planning to go to Dream Amusement Park with my brother. ❷You can go with us if you want to.

B: ❸I'd love to. When should we meet?

G: I want to go early, so let's meet at 9 at the subway station.

B: Sounds good. I'll see you then.

❶ 미래의 계획을 물어보는 표현이다.
❷ 함께 하자고 제안하는 표현으로 if you want to 뒤에는 go with us가 생략되어 있다.
❸ 제안을 승낙하는 표현으로 I'd love to go with you.를 줄여 쓴 말이다.

**Listen and Talk B**

A: I'm planning to see a movie this Saturday. Do you want to go with me?

B: Sure. What time and where should we meet?

A: ❶How about meeting at 2:30 in front of Star Movie Theater?

B: OK. See you then.

❶ 약속 시간을 제안하는 표현으로 '~하는 게 어때?'의 뜻이다.

**Listen and Talk C**

(*Smartphone rings.*)

B: Hi, Kate. What's up?

G: Hi, Minho. ❶What are you going to do this Saturday?

B: ❷Nothing special. Why?

G: ❸I'm planning to go to the Van Gogh exhibition at the National Art Museum. Do you want to go

with me?

B: I'd love to! He's my favorite painter. ❹What time should we meet?

G: How about meeting at 11?

B: OK. ❺Where should we meet?

G: Let's meet in front of the ticket office.

B: Sounds good. I'll see you there at 11.

❶ 미래의 계획을 물어보는 표현이다.
❷ nothing은 형용사가 뒤에서 수식을 한다.
❸ '~할 계획이다'라는 의미로 미래의 계획을 말할 때 사용하는 표현이다.
❹ 시간 약속을 정하는 표현이다.
❺ 장소를 정할 때 사용하는 표현이다.

**Review 1**

G: I'm planning to go to a piano concert this Friday. ❶Why don't you join me, Kevin?

B: Sure. What time should we meet?

G: ❷Let's meet at 10:30 at the bus stop.

B: OK. See you then.

❶ 함께 하자고 제안하는 표현으로 What about joining me, Kevin?과 같은 표현이다.
❷ 약속 시간을 제안할 때 사용하는 표현이다.

**Review 2**

B: ❶I'm planning to go to a soccer game tomorrow. Do you want to go with me, Susan?

G: Sure. ❷What time should we meet?

B: The game begins at 7, so let's meet at 6 in front of Dream Stadium.

G: OK. See you then.

❶ 미래의 계획을 물어보는 표현으로, 'I'm going to go ~'와 같은 의미로 사용된다.
❷ 약속 시간을 제안할 때 사용하는 표현이다.

**Review 3**

B: Sumi, I'm planning to go shopping with Jenny this Saturday. ❶Will you join us?

G: Sounds great. ❷What time should we meet?

B: ❸How about meeting at 12:30?

G: OK. Where should we meet?

B: Let's meet in front of the shopping mall.

❶ 함께 하자고 제안하는 표현이다.
❷ 시간 약속을 정하는 표현이다.
❸ 시간을 제안할 때 사용하는 표현이다.

● 다음 우리말과 일치하도록 빈칸에 알맞은 말을 쓰시오.

### Listen and Talk A-1

G: I'm _____ _____ _____ to a piano concert tomorrow. Do you want _____ _____ _____ me, Kevin?

B: Sure. _____ _____ should we meet?

G: The concert begins at 7 o'clock, so _____ meet at 6 at the bus stop.

B: OK. _____ you then.

### Listen and Talk A-2

G: I'm _____ to go see *Cats* this Saturday. Do you _____ to go with me?

B: Sure. _____ _____ and _____ _____ we meet?

G: The musical starts at 3 o'clock. _____ _____ at 2 at Dream Art Hall.

B: Great. See you _____ Saturday.

### Listen and Talk A-3

G: I'm planning _____ _____ _____ a soccer game next Friday. _____ _____ _____ me, Jinho?

B: That _____ great. What time _____ _____ _____ _____?

G: _____ _____ at 10:30 _____ _____ _____ Green Stadium.

B: OK. See you then.

### Listen and Talk A-4

B: _____ are you _____ _____ _____ this Sunday?

G: I'm _____ _____ _____ to Dream Amusement Park with my brother. You can go with us _____ you _____ _____.

B: I'd _____ _____. _____ _____ we meet?

G: I want to go early, so _____ _____ at 9 at the subway station.

B: _____ good. I'll see you then.

### Listen and Talk B

A: I'm _____ to see a movie this Saturday. Do you _____ _____ go with me?

B: Sure. _____ _____ and _____ should we meet?

A: _____ about _____ at 2:30 in front of Star Movie Theater?

B: OK. See you then.

해석

G: 나는 내일 피아노 콘서트에 갈 예정이야. 나랑 같이 갈래, Kevin?
B: 물론이지. 몇 시에 만날까?
G: 콘서트는 7시에 시작하니까 6시에 버스 정류장에서 만나자.
B: 좋아. 그때 보자.

G: 나는 이번 주 토요일에 'Cats'를 보러 갈 계획이야. 나랑 같이 갈래?
B: 좋아. 몇 시에 어디서 만날까?
G: 뮤지컬은 3시에 시작해. 2시에 Dream 아트 홀에서 만나자.
B: 좋아. 토요일에 만나자.

G: 나는 다음 주 금요일에 축구 경기를 보러 갈 계획이야. 나랑 같이 가는 게 어떠니, 진호야?
B: 좋은 생각이다. 몇 시에 만날까?
G: Green 경기장 앞에서 10시 30분에 만나자.
B: 좋아. 그때 보자.

B: 이번 주 일요일에 무엇을 할 계획이니?
G: 나는 내 남동생과 Dream 놀이동산에 갈 예정이야. 만약 네가 원한다면 우리와 함께 가도 돼.
B: 그러고 싶어. 언제 만날까?
G: 나는 일찍 가고 싶어. 그래서 9시에 지하철역에서 만나자.
B: 좋아. 그때 보자.

A: 나는 이번 주 토요일에 영화를 볼 계획이야. 나랑 같이 갈래?
B: 물론이지. 몇 시에 어디에서 만날까?
A: Star 영화관 앞에서 2시 30분에 만나는 게 어때?
B: 좋아. 그때 보자.

### Listen and Talk C

(*Smartphone rings.*)

**B:** Hi, Kate. What's up?

**G:** Hi, Minho. What are you _____ _____ _____ this Saturday?

**B:** Nothing _____. Why?

**G:** I'm _____ _____ _____ to the Van Gogh exhibition at the National Art Museum. Do you want to go with me?

**B:** I'd _____ _____! He's my favorite painter. _____ _____ _____ we meet?

**G:** _____ _____ meeting at 11?

**B:** OK. _____ _____ we meet?

**G:** _____ meet in front _____ the ticket office.

**B:** Sounds good. I'll see you there at 11.

### Review 1

**G:** I'm planning to go to a piano concert this Friday. _____ _____ join me, Kevin?

**B:** Sure. What time _____ _____ _____?

**G:** _____ _____ at 10:30 at the bus stop.

**B:** OK. See you _____.

### Review 2

**B:** I'm planning to go to a soccer game tomorrow. _____ _____ _____ to go with me, Susan?

**G:** Sure. What time _____ we meet?

**B:** The game begins at 7, so _____ meet at 6 in _____ of Dream Stadium.

**G:** OK. See you then.

### Review 3

**B:** Sumi, _____ _____ _____ go shopping with Jenny this Saturday. Will you _____ us?

**G:** Sounds great. What time should we meet?

**B:** How about _____ at 12:30?

**G:** OK. _____ should we meet?

**B:** Let's meet _____ _____ _____ the shopping mall.

해석

(스마트폰이 울린다.)
B: 안녕, Kate. 무슨 일이야?
G: 안녕, 민호야. 이번 토요일에 뭐 할 거야?
B: 특별한 일은 없어. 왜?
G: 나는 국립 미술관에서 하는 반 고흐 전시회에 갈 계획이야. 나와 함께 갈래?
B: 그러고 싶어! 그는 내가 가장 좋아하는 화가거든. 몇 시에 만날까?
G: 11시에 만나는 게 어때?
B: 좋아. 어디에서 만날까?
G: 매표소 앞에서 만나자.
B: 좋아. 11시에 거기에서 봐.

G: 나는 이번 주 금요일에 피아노 콘서트에 갈 계획이야. 나랑 같이 가는 게 어때, Kevin?
B: 물론이지. 몇 시에 만날까?
G: 10시 30분에 버스 정류장에서 만나자.
B: 좋아. 그때 보자.

B: 나는 내일 축구 경기에 갈 계획이야. 나랑 같이 갈래, Susan?
G: 물론이지. 몇 시에 만날까?
B: 경기는 7시에 시작하니까, Dream 경기장 앞에서 6시에 만나자.
G: 좋아. 그때 보자.

B: 수미야, 나 이번 주 토요일에 Jenny와 쇼핑을 갈 계획이야. 너도 같이 갈래?
G: 좋은 생각이야. 몇 시에 만날까?
B: 12시 30분에 만나는 게 어때?
G: 좋아. 어디서 만날까?
B: 쇼핑몰 앞에서 만나자.

**01** 우리말에 맞게 주어진 단어를 이용하여 빈칸에 알맞은 말을 쓰시오.

나는 이번 주 토요일에 영화를 볼 계획이야. (plan)

➡ I'm _____ _____ _____ a movie this Saturday.

**02** 다음 대화의 빈칸에 들어갈 말이 바르게 짝지어진 것은?

A: __(A)__ should we meet?

B: How about meeting at 5:30?

A: OK. __(B)__ should we meet?

B: Let's meet in front of the library.

A: Sounds good. See you then.

① When – What time
② Why don't we – Where
③ Where – When
④ What time –Where
⑤ Why – When

**03** 다음 대화의 빈칸에 들어갈 말로 알맞은 것은?

A: _____

B: I'm planning to go to the Van Gogh exhibition at the National Art Museum.

① What are you doing now?
② Where are you going?
③ Where should we meet?
④ What were you doing last night?
⑤ What are you going to do this Saturday?

**04** 다음 대화의 빈칸에 들어갈 말로 알맞은 것은?

A: I'm planning to go to a soccer game tomorrow. Do you want to go with me, Susan?

B: Sure. _____ should we meet?

A: Let's meet at 4 after school.

① Who          ② How          ③ When
④ What         ⑤ Where

[01~02] 다음 대화를 읽고 물음에 답하시오.

Jenny: I'm planning to go to a piano concert tomorrow. _____ (A) _____
Kevin: Sure. (B)몇 시에 만날까?
Jenny: The concert begins at 7 o'clock, so let's meet at 6 at the bus stop.
Kevin: OK. See you then.

**01** 위 대화의 빈칸 (A)에 들어갈 말로 어색한 것은?

① What about joining me, Kevin?
② Can you make it around two?
③ Why don't you join me, Kevin?
④ Do you want to go with me, Kevin?
⑤ Will you join me?

서답형
**02** 위 대화의 밑줄 친 (B)의 우리말에 맞게 주어진 단어를 이용하여 영어로 쓰시오.

> time / should / what / we / meet / ?

➡ _____

서답형
**03** 자연스러운 대화가 되도록 (A)~(D)를 바르게 배열하시오.

A: I'm planning to go swimming this Wednesday. Do you want to go with me, Minsu?
(A) OK. Where should we meet?
(B) Sure. What time should we meet?
(C) How about meeting at 10:30?
(D) Let's meet at the bus stop.
B: Sounds good. See you then.

➡ _____

서답형
**04** 밑줄 친 (A)의 우리말에 맞게 주어진 어구를 이용하여 영어로 쓰시오. (어형 변화 필수)

A: (A)이번 주 일요일에 하이킹을 갈 계획이야. Do you want to go with me, Jina?
B: I'm sorry, but I have other plans.
A: OK.

> be / plan / go / hike / this Sunday

➡ _____

[05~07] 다음 대화를 읽고 물음에 답하시오.

B: What are you going to do this Sunday?
G: (A) I'm planning to go to Dream Amusement Park with my brother. You can go with us if you want to.
B: I'd love to. (B) should we meet?
G: I want to go early, so let's meet at 9 at the subway station.
B: Sounds good. I'll see you then.

중요
**05** 위 대화의 밑줄 친 (A)의 의도로 알맞은 것은?

① 시간 약속 정하기   ② 경험 말하기
③ 조언 구하기       ④ 취미 말하기
⑤ 계획 말하기

**06** 위 대화의 빈칸 (B)에 들어갈 말로 알맞은 것은?

① When       ② Who       ③ What
④ How        ⑤ Why

서답형
**07** 위 대화를 읽고 다음 물음에 대해 영어로 답하시오.

Q: When and where are the speakers going to meet?

➡ They are going _____.

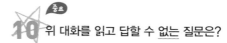

**Conversation** 시험대비 실력평가

**서답형**

**08** 다음 대화의 밑줄 친 우리말에 맞게 주어진 어구를 이용하여 영어로 쓰시오. (어형 변화 필수)

> A: I'm planning to see a movie this Saturday. Do you want to go with me?
> B: Sure. What time and where should we meet?
> A: Star 영화관 앞에서 2시 30분에 만나는 게 어때?
> B: OK. See you then.

> how / meet / 2:30 / Star Movie Theater / front / about / at / ?

➡ _____

_____

[09~10] 다음 대화를 읽고 물음에 답하시오.

> (*Smartphone rings.*)
> B: Hi, Kate. What's up?
> G: Hi, Minho. What are you going to do this Saturday?
> B: (①) Nothing special. Why?
> G: (②) I'm planning to go to the Van Gogh exhibition at the National Art Museum. Do you want to go with me?
> B: (③) What time should we meet?
> G: How about meeting at 11?
> B: (④) OK. Where should we meet?
> G: Let's meet in front of the ticket office.
> B: Sounds good. (⑤) I'll see you there at 11.

**09** 위 대화의 ①~⑤ 중 다음 문장이 들어갈 위치로 알맞은 것은?

> I'd love to! He's my favorite painter.

①     ②     ③     ④     ⑤

**중요**

**10** 위 대화를 읽고 답할 수 <u>없는</u> 질문은?

① What exhibition is Kate planning to go to this Saturday?
② What are Kate and Minho talking about?
③ When are Kate and Minho going to meet?
④ Where are Kate and Minho going to meet?
⑤ Why did Minho invite Kate to the Van Gogh exhibition?

[11~13] 다음 대화를 읽고 물음에 답하시오.

> A: I'm planning to go to the library this Monday. Do you want to go with me, Jiho?
> B: Sure. (a)몇 시에 만날까?
> A: How about ___(A)___ at 5:30?
> B: OK. Where should we meet?
> A: (b)Let's meet in front of the library.
> B: Sounds good. See you then.

**11** 위 대화의 빈칸 (A)에 들어갈 단어의 형태로 알맞은 것은?

① meet        ② to meet
③ meeting     ④ to meeting
⑤ met

**서답형**

**12** 위 대화의 밑줄 친 (a)의 우리말에 맞게 주어진 단어를 이용하여 영어로 쓰시오.

> what / should

➡ _____

**서답형**

**13** 위 대화의 밑줄 친 (b)와 같은 의미의 표현을 쓰고자 한다. 주어진 단어로 시작하여 문장을 쓰시오.

➡ Why _____?
    Shall _____?

**01** 다음 대화의 밑줄 친 (A)의 우리말에 맞게 주어진 단어를 이용하여 영작하시오.

> G: (A)나는 이번 주 금요일에 피아노 콘서트에 갈 계획이야. (plan / go / concert / this)
> Why don't you join me, Kevin?
> B: Sure. What time should we meet?
> G: Let's meet at 10:30 at the bus stop.
> B: OK. See you then.

➡ _____

 **02** 다음 대화의 빈칸 (A)와 (B)에 들어갈 문장을 주어진 〈조건〉에 맞게 완성하시오.

> A: I'm planning to go to the Picasso exhibition this Thursday. _____(A)_____, Sumi?
> B: Sure. What time should we meet?
> A: How about meeting at 4 after school?
> B: OK. _____(B)_____
> A: Let's meet at Sejong Art Hall.
> B: Sounds good. See you then.

┤ (A) 조건 ├
- 함께 하자고 제안하는 표현을 쓸 것.
- want와 with를 이용할 것

➡ _____

┤ (B) 조건 ├
- 약속 장소를 정하는 표현을 쓸 것.
- 조동사 should를 이용할 것

➡ _____

**03** 다음 대화의 빈칸에 들어갈 말로 자연스러운 것을 〈보기〉에서 찾아 쓰시오.

> B: _____(A)_____
> G: I'm planning to go to Dream Amusement Park with my brother. _____(B)_____
> B: I'd love to. _____(C)_____
> G: I want to go early, so let's meet at 9 at the subway station.
> B: Sounds good. I'll see you then.

┤ 보기 ├
- When should we meet?
- What are you going to do this Sunday?
- You can go with us if you want to.

(A) _____
(B) _____
(C) _____

**04** 다음 대화의 빈칸 (A)는 밑줄 친 말에 대한 질문이다. 주어진 〈조건〉에 맞게 문장을 완성하시오.

> G: I'm planning to go see *Cats* this Saturday. Do you want to go with me?
> B: Sure. _____(A)_____
> G: The musical starts at 3 o'clock. Let's meet at 2 at Dream Art Hall.
> B: Great. See you on Saturday.

┤ 조건 ├
- 의문사 what과 where를 이용할 것
- 접속사 and를 쓸 것
- 조동사 should를 쓸 것
  (meet)

➡ _____

# Grammar

### 1 지각동사+목적어+-ing

> • Daedalus **saw** birds **flying.** Daedalus는 새가 날고 있는 것을 보았다.
>
> • I **heard** him **sing.** 나는 그가 노래하는 소리를 들었다.

■ 지각동사는 '보다, 듣다, 느끼다'의 의미를 갖는 see, look at, watch, hear, listen to, feel 등의 동사를 말하며, 일반적으로 목적어와 함께 3형식 문장을 이루지만, 목적어와 목적격 보어가 있는 5형식 문장으로도 많이 쓰인다. 지각동사가 쓰인 5형식 문장에서 목적격 보어가 될 수 있는 말은 원형부정사와 분사(현재분사 / 과거분사)이다. 원형부정사와 현재분사의 차이는 현재분사에 진행의 의미가 들어간다는 점이다.

　• They **saw** him **cross** the street. 그들은 그가 길을 건너는 것을 보았다.

　• Did you **hear** Sally **crying**? 너는 Sally가 울고 있는 소리를 들었니?

■ '지각동사+목적어+원형부정사[현재분사]'로 쓰이는 경우, 목적어와 목적격보어는 능동 관계가 된다. '지각동사+목적어+과거분사'로 쓰이는 경우 목적어와 목적격보어의 관계는 수동이다.

　• I **felt** someone **touch** my shoulder. 나는 누군가 내 어깨를 만지는 것을 느꼈다.

　• I **heard** my name **called**. 나는 내 이름을 부르는 소리를 들었다.

■ 사역동사 make, have, let과 혼동하지 않도록 한다. 사역동사도 5형식 동사로 목적어와 목적격보어를 취하지만, 사역동사의 목적격보어로는 현재분사가 오지 않는다.

　• The teacher **made** me **do** it again. 선생님은 나에게 그것을 다시 하라고 시키셨다.

　• I **had** my bicycle **fixed** yesterday. 나는 어제 내 자전거가 수리되도록 했다.

### 핵심 Check

**1.** 다음 우리말과 일치하도록 빈칸에 알맞은 말을 쓰시오.

(1) 나는 내 동생이 숙제하고 있는 것을 보았다.

　➡ I ＿＿＿＿ my brother ＿＿＿＿ his homework.

(2) 나는 Amy가 설거지하는 소리를 들었다.

　➡ I ＿＿＿＿ Amy ＿＿＿＿ the dishes.

(3) 난 방을 청소시켜야 한다.

　➡ I must have the room ＿＿＿＿.

## 2  so ~ that ...

- Icarus was **so** excited **that** he forgot his father's warning.
  Icarus는 너무 흥분해서 아버지의 경고를 잊었다.

- It's **so** cold **that** I want to drink hot tea. 너무 추워서 나는 뜨거운 차를 마시고 싶어요.

■ 'so+형용사[부사]+that+주어+동사' 구문은 '너무 ~해서 …하다'라는 뜻으로 so 다음에는 형용사나 부사가 오고 that 다음에는 주어와 동사가 있는 절이 온다. so 다음에 나오는 말이 '원인', that 다음에 나오는 절이 그에 따른 '결과'를 나타낸다.

- It's **so** cold **that** I don't want to play outside. 너무 추워서 나는 밖에서 놀고 싶지 않다.

■ 'so ~ that …' 구문에서 that 앞에 형용사나 부사 대신 명사가 오면 so 대신 such를 쓴다.

- It gave him **such** a shock **that** his face turned white.
  그는 그것에 큰 충격을 받은 나머지 얼굴이 하얗게 질렸다.

■ 'so that+주어+동사'는 목적을 나타내어 '~하기 위해서' 혹은 '~하도록'이라는 의미로 쓰인다. 'so ~ that …'과 혼동하지 않도록 유의한다.

- He is wearing a baseball cap **so that** his face is hidden.
  그는 야구 모자를 쓰고 있어서 그의 얼굴은 가려 있었다.

■ 'so+형용사[부사]+that+주어+can ~'은 '형용사[부사]+enough+to 동사원형'으로 바꿔 쓸 수 있으며, 'so+형용사[부사]+that+주어+can't ~'는 'too+형용사[부사]+to 동사원형'으로 바꿔 쓸 수 있다.

- He is **so** rich **that** he can hire a driver.
  = He is rich **enough to** hire a driver. 그는 운전사를 고용할 수 있을 만큼 부자다.

- My sister was **so** young **that** she couldn't ride it by herself.
  = My sister was **too** young **to** ride it by herself. 제 여동생은 너무 어려서 혼자서 탈 수가 없었어요.

### 핵심 Check

**2.** 다음 우리말에 맞게 괄호 안의 단어를 바르게 배열하시오.

(1) Emma는 너무 지루해서 혼자 노래를 부르기 시작했다.
  (Emma, she, herself, singing, bored, started, was, so, that, by)
  ➡ _____

(2) 우리 팀은 경기에 이기기 위해 열심히 연습했다.
  (Our team, the game, we, could, practiced, win, so, that, hard)
  ➡ _____

(3) 나는 너무 피곤해서 일을 할 수 없었다.
  (I, I, work, was, couldn't, tired, so, that)
  ➡ _____

**01** 다음 문장에서 어법상 <u>어색한</u> 부분을 바르게 고치시오.

(1) He heard the bird sang.

_____ ➡ _____

(2) Daedalus saw birds to fly.

_____ ➡ _____

(3) She was very sick that she had to stay in bed.

_____ ➡ _____

(4) Tom was so busy what he couldn't go out.

_____ ➡ _____

**02** 주어진 단어를 어법에 맞게 빈칸에 쓰시오.

(1) They heard the baby _____. (cry)
(2) They saw the trash _____ away. (throw)
(3) People gathered to watch the house _____. (burn)
(4) She felt the rain _____ on her face. (fall)

**03** 다음 우리말을 영어로 바르게 옮긴 것은?

> 질문이 너무 쉬워서 모두가 그것에 답했다.

① The question was very easy that everybody answered it.
② The question was too easy that everybody answered it.
③ The question was enough easy that everybody answered it.
④ The question was so easy that everybody answered it.
⑤ The question was easy so that everybody answered it.

**04** 주어진 단어를 바르게 배열하여 다음 우리말을 영어로 쓰시오. 필요하다면 단어를 추가하거 나 변형하시오.

> 그는 너무 늦게 도착해서 비행기를 놓쳤다.
> (he / he / his / plane / late / missed / arrived / that)

➡ _____

**01** 다음 빈칸에 알맞은 말이 순서대로 바르게 짝지어진 것은?

> • Minsu sees some boys _____ baseball.
> • The bus was _____ late that they had to wait for a long time.

① play – too
② played – very
③ played – so
④ playing – very
⑤ playing – so

**02** 다음 빈칸에 들어갈 말로 가장 적절한 것은?

> I heard someone _____ my name on the street.

① calls
② call
③ called
④ to call
⑤ to calling

**03** 다음 빈칸에 알맞은 말이 바르게 짝지어진 것을 고르시오.

> Sujin studied _____ hard _____ she got an A on the test.

① so – that
② that – so
③ very – that
④ too – that
⑤ too – to

서답형

**04** 주어진 단어를 이용하여 다음 우리말을 영어로 쓰시오. (10 단어)

> 물고기가 너무 빨라서 나는 잡을 수가 없다.
> (the fish / catch / fast / so)

➡ _____

중요
**05** 다음 중 어법상 바르지 <u>않은</u> 것은?

① I see a person carrying a box on the street.
② We heard a girl singing on the stage.
③ She could feel somebody pulling her hair.
④ I watched him to sing in his first performance.
⑤ The students listened to Ella introduce herself.

서답형
**06** 다음 괄호 안에서 알맞은 것을 고르시오.

(1) I was surprised to see him (to touch / touching) the snake.
(2) The teacher heard Minsu (sing / sang) a song.
(3) I listened to the song (repeat / repeated) endlessly in the kitchen.
(4) Are you making her (cleaning / clean) our bathroom?
(5) Brian was (so / very) tired that he didn't go out.
(6) I got up so late (that / what) I was late for class.
(7) The boy was (too / very) small to ride a horse.

**07** 다음 중 어법상 바르지 <u>않은</u> 것은?

> I ①heard ②my name ③to call ④on the street ⑤by my neighbor.

①      ②      ③      ④      ⑤

서답형

**08** 다음 문장에서 어법상 틀린 부분을 찾아 바르게 고치시오.

> The boy was thirsty so that he drank a glass of water.

_____ ➡ _____

[09~10] 다음 우리말을 영어로 바르게 옮긴 것을 <u>모두</u> 고르시오.

**09**
> 나는 내 남동생이 강에서 수영하고 있는 것을 봤다.

① I saw my brother swam in the river.
② I saw my brother swum in the river.
③ I saw my brother swim in the river.
④ I saw my brother swimming in the river.
⑤ I saw my brother to swim in the river.

**10**
> 그는 열심히 연습해서 우승할 수 있었다.

① He practiced very hard that he could win first prize.
② He practiced hard so that he could win first prize.
③ He practiced so hard that he could win first prize.
④ He practiced too hard to win first prize.
⑤ He practiced hard enough to win first prize.

서답형

**11** 다음 대화의 빈칸에 알맞은 말을 4단어로 쓰시오.

> A: Did Mina open the window?
> B: I think so. I heard _____
> _____ .

**12** 다음 중 어법상 올바른 문장을 <u>모두</u> 고르시오.

① I heard Somi talked with Yubin.
② Minsu sees an old man reading a book.
③ He was busy so that he skipped lunch.
④ It was so a nice day that we went on a picnic.
⑤ The room is so dark that I can't see anything.

**13** 다음 중 (A)~(C)에서 어법상 옳은 것끼리 바르게 짝지은 것은?

> • Eric saw Sue (A)(painting / to paint) a picture.
> • He felt somebody (B)(touch / to touch) his hand.
> • Andrew heard his name (C)(calling / called) behind his back.

① to paint – touch – calling
② to paint – to touch – called
③ painting – touch – called
④ painting – touch – calling
⑤ painting – to touch – calling

**14** 다음 우리말을 영어로 바르게 옮기지 <u>않은</u> 것은?

> 그들은 마술이 어떻게 일어나는지를 배우기 위해 열심히 공부해야 한다.

① They must study hard so that they can learn how magic works.
② They must study so hard that they can learn how magic works.
③ They must study hard to learn how magic works.
④ They must study hard in order to learn how magic works.
⑤ They must study hard so as to learn how magic works.

**15** 다음 주어진 문장의 밑줄 친 부분과 쓰임이 같은 것은?

> I heard her <u>singing</u> in the room.

① <u>Forgetting</u> his father's warning, Icarus flew higher and higher.
② King Minos was <u>keeping</u> Daedalus and Icarus in a tall tower.
③ Mike saw a bird <u>flying</u>.
④ My plan was <u>visiting</u> Paris again.
⑤ I thought she enjoyed <u>eating</u> *bulgogi*.

서답형
**16** 다음 문장을 주어진 어휘를 이용하여 바꿔 쓰시오.

(1) My sister was very tired, so she went to bed early. (so, that)
➡ _____

(2) We had to stay at home because it rained really hard. (so, that)
➡ _____

서답형
**17** 다음 괄호 안에 주어진 어구를 이용하여 우리말을 영어로 옮기시오.

(1) 나는 정원에서 책을 읽고 있을 때, 토끼가 혼 잣말을 하고 있는 것을 들었다.
(a rabbit, a book, hear, talk, to himself)
➡ _____
_____

(2) 나는 그가 내 머리카락을 잡아당기는 것을 느낄 수 있었다. (feel, pull, my hair)
➡ _____

(3) Somin이는 Minji가 자전거를 타고 있는 것을 보았다. (a bike, see, ride)
➡ _____

(4) 그녀는 너무 천천히 걸어서 모두 그녀를 지나쳐 갔다. (everybody, walk, pass by, slowly, so, that)
➡ _____
_____

(5) 너무 배불러서 더 이상 못 먹겠어. (full, can't, so, anymore)
➡ _____

서답형
**18** 다음 문장에서 어법상 어색한 부분을 바르게 고치시오.

(1) I watched my sister to download songs from the Internet.
_____ ➡ _____

(2) The library is very big that you may get lost in it.
_____ ➡ _____

(3) She was surprised enough to say anything.
_____ ➡ _____

**01** 다음 문장에서 어법상 <u>어색한</u> 부분을 고쳐 다시 쓰시오.

(1) Eric heard Mina played the guitar.

➡ _____

(2) I saw Mike to swim in the lake.

➡ _____

(3) She felt her heart beats fast.

➡ _____

(4) Simpson won the Trophy in 2008 but saw it stealing 10 years ago.

➡ _____

_____

(5) She got up very late that she had to run all the way to school.

➡ _____

_____

(6) She speaks too quietly for me understanding.

➡ _____

(7) I left early enough arriving on time.

➡ _____

**02** 다음 두 문장을 〈보기〉와 같이 지각동사를 이용하여 한 문장으로 완성하시오.

┌─ 보기 ┤

• I went to the library.

• Sara was studying there.

➡ I saw Sara studying in the library.

• I went to the concert.

• Maryline was singing a song there.

➡ _____

**03** 다음 문장을 to부정사를 이용하여 바꿔 쓰시오.

(1) Dad was so busy that he couldn't play with us.

➡ _____

(2) The dog was so small that it could go through the hole.

➡ _____

_____

(3) The coffee is so hot that she can't drink it.

➡ _____

(4) The math problem was so easy that Laura could solve it.

➡ _____

_____

**04** 그림을 보고 주어진 어구를 바르게 배열하여 문장을 완성하시오.

Pandora, she, Zeus, the box, was, had given, opened, that, foolish, which, her, so, to

➡ _____

_____

**05** 다음 두 문장을 〈보기〉와 같이 한 문장으로 쓰시오.

> ─┤ 보기 ├─
> The boy was very kind. Everyone liked him.
> ➡ The boy was so kind that everyone liked him.

(1) • It rained really hard.
     • He couldn't play soccer.
     ➡ _____

(2) • Last night I was very tired.
     • I went to bed early.
     ➡ _____

(3) • The box was too heavy.
     • I couldn't carry it.
     ➡ _____

(4) • There were too many people.
     • We didn't get into the sea.
     ➡ _____
     _____

(5) • They had to cancel the game.
     • It rained really heavily.
     ➡ _____

**06** 〈보기〉에서 의미상 적절한 단어를 골라 빈칸에 알맞은 형태로 쓰시오.

> ─┤ 보기 ├─
> arrest / carry / take / open

(1) Sally wanted me _____ _____ the box for her.
(2) I saw Mike _____ by the police on my way home.
(3) I heard her _____ the window.
(4) Mom made me _____ the umbrella with me.

**07** 다음 문장을 so와 that을 이용하여 바꾸어 쓰시오.

(1) It was too dark for us to see anything.
     ➡ _____

(2) I want to live long enough to see you rise in the world.
     ➡ _____
     _____

**08** 다음 두 문장을 〈보기〉와 같이 한 문장으로 바꿔 쓰시오.

> ─┤ 보기 ├─
> We saw him. + He was standing still.
> = We saw him standing still.

(1) He looked at the violinist.
     + The violinist was dancing.
     ➡ _____

(2) The teacher heard Somin.
     + She was playing the piano.
     ➡ _____

**09** 다음 그림을 참고하여 단어 fall의 알맞은 형태를 빈칸에 알맞게 채우시오.

Daedalus saw Icarus _____ into the sea.

## Same Story, Different Paintings

We often find different paintings with the same subject. An example
is *The Flight of Icarus* by Henri Matisse and *The Fall of Icarus*
by Marc Chagall. They are both about the same Greek myth.

### The Greek Myth of Icarus

Daedalus was a great inventor. King Minos liked Daedalus' work so
much that he wanted to keep Daedalus with him forever. Daedalus,
however, tried to leave, so the King kept him and his son, Icarus, in a
tall tower. Daedalus wanted to escape.

One day, Daedalus saw birds flying. "Wings! I need wings!" he
shouted. Daedalus then gathered bird feathers and glued them together
with wax. When the wings were ready, he warned his son, "Don't fly
too close to the sun. The wax will melt."

Daedalus and Icarus began to fly. Icarus was so excited that he forgot
his father's warning. He flew higher and higher, and the wax began to
melt. "Oh, no! I'm falling," Icarus cried out. Icarus fell into the sea and
died.

flight 비행, 날기
myth 신화
escape 탈출하다
wing 날개
shout 외치다
gather 모으다
feather 깃털
wax 밀랍, 왁스
warn 경고하다, 주의를 주다

---

**확인문제**

● 다음 문장이 본문의 내용과 일치하면 T, 일치하지 않으면 F를 쓰시오.

1 *The Flight of Icarus* by Henri Matisse and *The Fall of Icarus* by Marc Chagall are
both about the same Greek myth. ☐

2 Icarus was a great inventor. ☐

3 Daedalus gathered bird feathers and sewed them together. ☐

4 Daedalus warned his son not to fly too close to the sun. ☐

5 Icarus was so excited that he forgot his father's warning. ☐

6 Icarus flew higher and higher, and succeeded in escaping. ☐

## Two Different Paintings

Matisse and Chagall both deal with the same subject in their
<br>Icarus 신화
paintings, but they are different. First, in Matisse's painting, you can
<br>Matisse와 Chagall의 그림
see Icarus flying, but in Chagall's painting, the boy is falling. This
<br>지각동사 see+목적어+-ing          현재진행형
difference comes from the different ideas that the two painters had.
<br>'~에서 나오다, 비롯되다'          목적격 관계대명사: the different ideas를 수식, 생략 가능
Matisse thought that Icarus was brave and adventurous. In contrast,
<br>접속사          '그에 반해서, 반면에'(앞 문장과 대조의 관계를 나타낼 때 쓰는 연결어구)
Chagall thought that Icarus was foolish.

Second, Matisse's painting is very simple, but Chagall's painting has
many details. In Matisse's painting, there are only Icarus and some
<br>there are+복수 명사: '~들이 있다'
stars. Furthermore, Icarus' body has just a simple outline. In contrast,
<br>'게다가, 더욱이'(앞 문장에 또 다른 정보를 덧붙여 제시할 때 쓰는 연결어)          '그에 반해서, 반면에'
Chagall painted many people and houses in addition to Icarus. This
<br>= besides
difference comes from the different painting styles of the two painters.
<br>'~에서 나오다, 비롯되다'
Whose painting do you like more? People will have different answers
<br>누구의'(의문형용사), 뒤의 명사 painting을 수식. more: much의 비교급
because they may see the same thing in different ways.
<br>추측을 나타내는 조동사

deal with (주제, 소재로) ~을 다루다

adventurous 모험심이 강한

in contrast 그에 반해서, 반면에

simple 단순한

detail 세부 사항

furthermore 게다가, 더욱이

outline 윤곽

in addition to ~뿐만 아니라, ~에 더하여

---

### 확인문제

- 다음 문장이 본문의 내용과 일치하면 T, 일치하지 않으면 F를 쓰시오.

1 Matisse and Chagall deal with the same subject in their paintings in different ways. ☐

2 In Matisse's painting, you can see Icarus falling. ☐

3 In Chagall's painting, Icarus is flying. ☐

4 Matisse thought that Icarus was brave and adventurous. ☐

5 Chagall thought that Icarus was foolish. ☐

6 Matisse painted many people and houses in addition to Icarus. ☐

● 우리말을 참고하여 빈칸에 알맞은 말을 쓰시오.

**1** _____ Story, _____ Paintings

**2** We often find _____ _____ with _____ _____ _____.

**3** An _____ is *The Flight of Icarus* _____ Henri Matisse and *The Fall of Icarus* _____ Marc Chagall.

**4** They are both about _____ _____ _____ _____.

**5** The _____ _____ of Icarus

**6** Daedalus was _____ _____ _____.

**7** King Minos liked Daedalus' work _____ much _____ he wanted to _____ Daedalus with him _____.

**8** Daedalus, _____, tried _____ _____, so the King _____ him and his son, Icarus, in a tall tower.

**9** Daedalus wanted _____ _____.

**10** One day, Daedalus saw birds _____.

**11** "Wings! _____ _____ _____!" he shouted.

**12** Daedalus then gathered bird feathers and _____ _____ with wax.

**13** When the wings were ready, he warned his son, "_____ _____ _____ _____ to the sun.

**14** The wax will _____."

**15** Daedalus and Icarus began _____ _____.

**16** Icarus was _____ excited _____ he forgot his father's _____.

**17** He flew _____ _____ _____, and the wax began to melt.

**18** "Oh, no! I'm falling," Icarus _____ _____.

**19** Icarus _____ _____ the sea and died.

**20** Two _____ Paintings

**21** Matisse and Chagall both _____ _____ the _____ _____ in their paintings, but they are _____.

**22** First, in Matisse's painting, you can see Icarus _____, but in Chagall's painting, the boy is _____.

**23** This difference _____ _____ the _____ _____ that the two painters had.

**24** Matisse thought that Icarus was _____ and _____.

**25** _____ _____, Chagall thought that Icarus was foolish.

**26** Second, Matisse's painting is _____ _____, but Chagall's painting has _____ _____.

**27** In Matisse's painting, there are _____ _____ and _____ _____.

**28** _____, Icarus' body has just a simple _____.

**29** _____ _____, Chagall painted many people and houses _____ _____ _____ Icarus.

**30** This _____ comes from the _____ _____ _____ of the two painters.

**31** _____ _____ do you like more?

**32** People will have different answers because they may see the _____ _____ _____ _____ _____.

20 다른 두 그림

21 Matisse와 Chagall 둘 다 그들의 그림에서 같은 주제를 다루었지만, 그것들은 다르다.

22 첫째, Matisse의 그림에서, 여러분은 Icarus가 날고 있는 것을 볼 수 있지만, Chagall의 그림에서는 그 소년이 추락하고 있다.

23 이러한 차이는 두 화가들이 갖고 있던 서로 다른 생각에서 기인한다.

24 Matisse는 Icarus가 용감하고 모험심이 강하다고 생각했다.

25 반면에 Chagall은 Icarus가 어리석다고 생각했다.

26 둘째, Matisse의 그림은 매우 단순하지만, Chagall의 그림에는 세부적인 것들이 많다.

27 Matisse의 그림에는 Icarus와 몇 개의 별들만 있다.

28 게다가 Icarus의 몸은 단지 단순한 윤곽만으로 되어 있다.

29 반면에 Chagall은 Icarus뿐만 아니라 많은 사람들과 집들을 그렸다.

30 이러한 차이는 두 화가의 서로 다른 화풍에서 기인한다.

31 여러분은 누구의 그림이 더 좋은가?

32 사람들은 같은 것을 다른 방식들로 볼 수도 있기 때문에 서로 다른 대답을 할 것이다.

● 우리말을 참고하여 본문을 영작하시오.

**1** 같은 이야기, 다른 그림
➡ _____

**2** 우리는 종종 같은 주제의 다른 그림들을 발견한다.
➡ _____

**3** 한 예가 Henri Matisse가 그린 "*The Flight of Icarus*(이카로스의 비행)"와 Marc Chagall이 그린 "*The Fall of Icarus*(이카로스의 추락)"이다.
➡ _____

**4** 그것들은 둘 다 모두 같은 그리스 신화에 관한 것이다.
➡ _____

**5** Icarus에 관한 그리스 신화
➡ _____

**6** Daedalus는 훌륭한 발명가였다.
➡ _____

**7** Minos왕은 Daedalus의 작품을 매우 좋아해서 Daedalus를 그의 곁에 영원히 두고 싶어 했다.
➡ _____

**8** 그러나 Daedalus는 떠나려고 했고, 그러자 왕은 그와 그의 아들인 Icarus를 높은 탑에 가두었다.
➡ _____

**9** Daedalus는 탈출하고 싶었다.
➡ _____

**10** 어느 날, Daedalus는 새가 날고 있는 것을 보았다.
➡ _____

**11** "날개! 날개가 필요해!" 그가 외쳤다.
➡ _____

**12** 그 다음에 Daedalus는 새의 깃털을 모아 그것들을 밀랍으로 붙였다.
➡ _____

**13** 날개가 준비되었을 때, 그는 아들에게 경고했다. "태양에 너무 가까이 날지 마라.
➡ _____

**14** 밀랍이 녹을 거야."
➡ _____

**15** Daedalus와 Icarus는 날기 시작했다.
➡ _____

**16** Icarus는 매우 흥분해서 아버지의 경고를 잊었다.
➡ _____

**17** 그는 점점 더 높이 날았고, 밀랍은 녹기 시작했다.
➡ _____

**18** "오, 안 돼! 추락하고 있어." Icarus는 비명을 질렀다.
➡ _____

**19** Icarus는 바다로 떨어져서 죽었다.
➡ _____

20 ▶ 다른 두 그림

➡ _____

21 ▶ Matisse와 Chagall 둘 다 그들의 그림에서 같은 주제를 다루었지만, 그것들은 다르다.

➡ _____

22 ▶ 첫째, Matisse의 그림에서, 여러분은 Icarus가 날고 있는 것을 볼 수 있지만, Chagall의 그림에서는 그 소년이 추락하고 있다.

➡ _____

23 ▶ 이러한 차이는 두 화가들이 갖고 있던 서로 다른 생각에서 기인한다.

➡ _____

24 ▶ Matisse는 Icarus가 용감하고 모험심이 강하다고 생각했다.

➡ _____

25 ▶ 반면에 Chagall은 Icarus가 어리석다고 생각했다.

➡ _____

26 ▶ 둘째, Matisse의 그림은 매우 단순하지만, Chagall의 그림에는 세부적인 것들이 많다.

➡ _____

27 ▶ Matisse의 그림에는 Icarus와 몇 개의 별들만 있다.

➡ _____

28 ▶ 게다가 Icarus의 몸은 단지 단순한 윤곽만으로 되어 있다.

➡ _____

29 ▶ 반면에 Chagall은 Icarus뿐만 아니라 많은 사람들과 집들을 그렸다.

➡ _____

30 ▶ 이러한 차이는 두 화가의 서로 다른 화풍에서 기인한다.

➡ _____

31 ▶ 여러분은 누구의 그림이 더 좋은가?

➡ _____

32 ▶ 사람들은 같은 것을 다른 방식들로 볼 수도 있기 때문에 서로 다른 대답을 할 것이다.

➡ _____

[01~03] 다음 글을 읽고 물음에 답하시오.

We often find ___ⓐ___ paintings with the ___ⓑ___ subject. An example is *The Flight of Icarus* by Henri Matisse and *The Fall of Icarus* by Marc Chagall. They are both about the same Greek ⓒmyth.

**The Greek Myth of Icarus**

Daedalus was a great inventor. King Minos liked Daedalus' work so much that he wanted to keep Daedalus with him forever. Daedalus, however, tried to leave, so the King kept him and his son, Icarus, in a tall tower. Daedalus wanted to escape.

One day, Daedalus saw birds flying. "Wings! I need wings!" he shouted. Daedalus then gathered bird feathers and glued them together with wax. When the wings were ready, he warned his son, "Don't fly too close to the sun. The wax will melt."

Daedalus and Icarus began to fly. Icarus was so excited that he forgot his father's warning. He flew higher and higher, and the wax began to melt. "Oh, no! I'm falling," Icarus cried out. Icarus fell into the sea and died.

**01** 위 글의 빈칸 ⓐ와 ⓑ에 들어갈 가장 알맞은 말을 고르시오.

① usual – unusual ② different – same
③ equal – unequal ④ unusual – usual
⑤ same – different

**02** 위 글의 밑줄 친 ⓒ와 같은 의미로 쓰인 것을 모두 고르시오.

① It's a myth that wolves are dangerous to people.
② I like the story of the heroes of myth and legend.
③ The common belief that Einstein was not an excellent student is a myth.
④ There is a popular myth that women are worse drivers than men.
⑤ He is famous for his study on Dangun myth.

**03** 위 글의 내용과 일치하지 않는 것은?

① King Minos wanted to keep Daedalus with him forever because he liked Daedalus' work so much.
② King Minos kept Daedalus and Icarus in a tall tower because Daedalus tried to leave.
③ Icarus gathered bird feathers and glued them together with wax.
④ Daedalus warned Icarus not to fly too close to the sun.
⑤ Icarus was excited enough to forget his father's warning.

[04~06] 다음 글을 읽고 물음에 답하시오.

**Two Different Paintings**

Matisse and Chagall both deal with the same subject in their paintings, but ⓐthey are different.

First, in Matisse's painting, you can see Icarus flying, but in Chagall's painting, the boy is falling. This difference comes from the different ideas that the two painters had. Matisse thought that Icarus was brave and adventurous. ⓑIn contrast, Chagall thought that Icarus was careful.

**04** 위 글의 주제가 되는 문장으로 알맞은 것을 고르시오.

① Both the painters deal with the same subject in their paintings.
② The paintings of Matisse and Chagall are different.
③ Different ideas of the painters made them draw the same subject differently.
④ Matisse thought that Icarus was brave and adventurous.
⑤ In Chagall's painting, Icarus is falling.

**서답형**

**05** 위 글의 밑줄 친 ⓐthey가 가리키는 것을 본문에서 찾아 쓰시오.

➡ _____

**서답형**

**06** 위 글의 밑줄 친 ⓑ에서 흐름상 어색한 부분을 찾아 고치시오.

_____ ➡ _____

[07~09] 다음 글을 읽고 물음에 답하시오.

Second, Matisse's painting is very simple, but Chagall's painting has many details. In Matisse's painting, there are only Icarus and some stars. Furthermore, Icarus' body has just a simple outline. In contrast, ⓐChagall painted many people and houses in addition to Icarus. This difference comes from the different painting styles of the two painters.

Whose painting do you like more? People will have different answers because they may see the same thing in different ways.

**중요**

**07** 위 글의 마지막 부분의 내용과 어울리는 속담을 고르시오.

① Too many cooks spoil the broth.
② So many men, so many minds.
③ A bad workman always blames his tools.
④ Do to others as you would be done by.
⑤ Two heads are better than one.

**08** 위 글의 밑줄 친 ⓐ와 의미가 다른 문장을 고르시오.

① Chagall painted not only Icarus but also many people and houses.
② Chagall painted many people and houses besides Icarus.
③ Chagall painted many people and houses as well as Icarus.
④ Chagall painted not Icarus but many people and houses.
⑤ Chagall painted not only Icarus but many people and houses as well

**서답형**

**09** 다음 문장에서 위 글의 내용과 다른 부분을 찾아서 고치시오. (두 군데)

> Because their painting styles were different, Matisse and Chagall painted the different subject in the same ways.

_____ ➡ _____

_____ ➡ _____

[10~12] 다음 글을 읽고 물음에 답하시오.

We often find different paintings ___ⓐ___ the same subject. An example is *The Flight of Icarus* ___ⓑ___ Henri Matisse and *The Fall of Icarus* ___ⓑ___ Marc Chagall. They are both about the same Greek myth.

_____ⓒ_____

Daedalus was a great inventor. King Minos liked Daedalus' work so much that he wanted to keep Daedalus with him forever. Daedalus, however, tried to leave, so the King kept him and his son, Icarus, in a tall tower. Daedalus wanted to escape.

(①) One day, Daedalus saw birds flying. (②) "Wings! I need wings!" he shouted. (③) When the wings were ready, he warned his son, "Don't fly too close to the sun. (④) The wax will melt." (⑤)

Daedalus and Icarus began to fly. Icarus was so excited that he forgot his father's warning. He flew higher and higher, and the wax began to melt. "Oh, no! I'm falling," Icarus cried out. Icarus fell into the sea and died.

**10** 위 글의 빈칸 ⓐ와 ⓑ에 들어갈 전치사가 바르게 짝지어진 것은?

① with – to　　　　② at – from

③ to – from　　　　④ with – by

⑤ at – by

**11** 위 글의 빈칸 ⓒ에 들어갈 제목으로 가장 알맞은 것을 고르시오.

① The Favorite Inventor of King Minos

② Daedalus Got Ideas from Birds

③ The Greek Myth of Daedalus

④ Look! We are Flying!

⑤ The Greek Myth of Icarus

**12** 위 글의 흐름으로 보아, 주어진 문장이 들어가기에 가장 적절한 곳은?

> Daedalus then gathered bird feathers and glued them together with wax.

①　　　②　　　③　　　④　　　⑤

[13~15] 다음 글을 읽고 물음에 답하시오.

**Two Different Paintings**

Matisse and Chagall both deal with the same subject in their paintings, but they are different.

First, in Matisse's painting, you can see Icarus flying, but in Chagall's painting, the boy is falling. This ___(A)___ comes from the different ideas ⓐthat the two painters had. Matisse thought ⓑthat Icarus was brave and adventurous. ___(B)___, Chagall thought that Icarus was foolish.

**13** 본문의 한 단어를 변형하여 위 글의 빈칸 (A)에 들어갈 알맞은 말을 쓰시오.

➡ _____

**14** 위 글의 빈칸 (B)에 들어갈 알맞은 말을 고르시오.

① Therefore　　　② In other words

③ In addition　　　④ In contrast

⑤ Moreover

**15** 다음 〈보기〉에서 위 글의 밑줄 친 ⓐ와 ⓑ의 that과 문법적 쓰임이 같은 것을 각각 고르시오.

> ① She told me that she was busy.
> ② I hope that I'll pass the test.
> ③ This is the book that he was reading.
> ④ I believe that you'll succeed.
> ⑤ The watch that you gave me keeps perfect time.

ⓐ _____　ⓑ _____

[16~18] 다음 글을 읽고 물음에 답하시오.

Second, Matisse's painting is very (A) [complex / simple], but Chagall's painting has many details. In Matisse's painting, there are only Icarus and some stars. Furthermore, Icarus' body has just a simple outline. In contrast, Chagall painted many people and houses in addition to Icarus. This difference comes from the different painting styles of the two painters.

Whose painting do you like more? People will have different answers because they may see (B)[different / the same] thing in (C) [different / the same] ways.

**서답형**

**16** 위 글의 괄호 (A)~(C)에서 문맥이나 어법상 알맞은 낱말을 골라 쓰시오.

(A) _____ (B) _____ (C) _____

**17** 위 글의 서술 방식으로 알맞은 것을 고르시오.

① 비유      ② 비교와 대조
③ 분류와 구분      ④ 정의와 지정
⑤ 인과적 분석

**18** 위 글을 읽고 대답할 수 없는 질문은?

① Whose painting is simple, Matisse's or Chagall's?
② In Matisse's painting, what can you see?
③ Why did Matisse and Chagall paint Icarus?
④ In Chagall's painting, what can you see besides Icarus?
⑤ Why did Matisse and Chagall paint the same subject differently?

[19~22] 다음 글을 읽고 물음에 답하시오.

The two paintings, *The Green Violinist* by Marc Chagall and *The Violinist at the Window* by Henri Matisse, both deal with a violinist. In both paintings, we see a man ⓐ(play) the violin. The two paintings, however, have (A)some differences. First, in Chagall's painting, we can see the man's face, but in Matisse's painting, we cannot see it. Second, in Chagall's painting, we see the violinist ⓑ(dance) while in Matisse's painting, we see him ⓒ(stand) (B)still. (C)Finally, another difference between the two paintings is that Chagall's painting is more dynamic.

**서답형**

**19** 위 글의 괄호 ⓐ~ⓒ에 주어진 단어를 각각 알맞은 형태로 쓰시오.

(A) _____
(B) _____
(C) _____

**서답형**

**20** 위 글의 밑줄 친 (A)some differences의 예를 우리말로 쓰시오. (세 가지)

(1) _____
_____
(2) _____
_____
(3) _____

**21** 위 글의 밑줄 친 (B)still과 같은 의미로 쓰인 것을 고르시오.

① Can you sit still there?
② I'm still hungry!
③ She had a still better idea.
④ The weather was cold and wet. Still, we had a great time.
⑤ Do you still live at the same address?

**서답형**

**22** 위 글의 밑줄 친 문장 (C)의 맨 뒤에 생략된 말을 쓰시오.

➡ _____

[23~25] 다음 글을 읽고 물음에 답하시오.

Second, Matisse's painting is ⓐvery simple, but Chagall's painting has many details. In Matisse's painting, there are only Icarus and some stars. Furthermore, Icarus' body has just a simple outline. In contrast, Chagall painted many people and houses in addition to Icarus. This difference comes from the different painting styles of the two painters.

Whose painting do you like more? People will have different answers because they may see the same thing in different ways.

서답형

**23** 위 글에서 Matisse의 그림을 밑줄 친 ⓐ처럼 말한 이유를 우리말로 쓰시오.

➡ _____

_____

서답형

**24** 다음 영영풀이에 해당하는 단어를 본문에서 찾아 쓰시오.

> the main shape or edge of something, without any details

➡ _____

중요

**25** 다음 빈칸 (A)와 (B)에 알맞은 단어를 넣어 Matisse와 Chagall의 화풍에 대한 소개를 완성하시오.

> Matisse painted in a very (A)_____ way, but Chagall painted (B)_____ _____ in his painting.

[26~28] 다음 글을 읽고 물음에 답하시오.

**Two Different Paintings**

Matisse and Chagall both deal with the same subject in their paintings, but they are different.

First, in Matisse's painting, you can see Icarus flying, but in Chagall's painting, the boy is falling. ⓐThis difference comes from the different ideas that the two painters had. Matisse thought that Icarus was brave and adventurous. ____ⓑ____ contrast, Chagall thought that Icarus was foolish.

서답형

**26** 다음 빈칸 (A)와 (B)에 알맞은 단어를 넣어 ⓐThis difference 에 대한 설명을 완성하시오.

> Icarus is (A)_____ in Matisse's painting, but he is (B)_____ in Chagall's painting.

중요

**27** 위 글의 빈칸 ⓑ에 알맞은 것은?

① To          ② Of          ③ In
④ For         ⑤ With

**28** 위 글을 읽고 대답할 수 없는 질문은?

① Do Matisse and Chagall both deal with the same subject in their paintings?
② What is Icarus doing in Matisse's painting?
③ What is Icarus doing in Chagall's painting?
④ Why did Matisse think that Icarus was brave and adventurous?
⑤ Did Chagall also think that Icarus was brave and adventurous?

[29~30] 다음 글을 읽고 물음에 답하시오.

Second, Matisse's painting is very ___ⓐ___, but Chagall's painting has many details. In Matisse's painting, there are only Icarus and some stars. ___ⓑ___, Icarus' body has just a simple outline. ___ⓒ___, Chagall painted many people and houses in addition to Icarus. This difference comes from the different painting styles of the two painters.

Whose painting do you like more? People will have different answers because they may see the same thing in different ways.

**29** 위 글의 빈칸 ⓐ에 알맞은 것은?

① clean ② difficult
③ bright ④ complex
⑤ simple

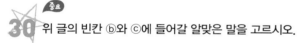

**30** 위 글의 빈칸 ⓑ와 ⓒ에 들어갈 알맞은 말을 고르시오.

① Therefore – On the other hand
② Furthermore – In contrast
③ For example – Likewise
④ In other words – In contrast
⑤ Moreover – In addition

**31** 위 글의 내용과 일치하도록 다음 빈칸 (A)와 (B)에 알맞은 단어를 쓰시오.

Because of their (A)___ ___
___, Matisse and Chagall painted the same (B)___ in different ways.

**32** 다음 미술 작품 설명서와 일치하도록 〈보기〉에서 알맞은 단어를 골라 두 화가가 그린 그림을 비교·대조하는 벤 다이어그램(Venn Diagram)에 그 번호를 쓰시오.

Title: The Flight of Icarus
Painter: Henri Matisse
In Matisse's painting, Icarus is flying. He thought Icarus was brave and adventurous. His painting is very simple. He drew only Icarus and some stars.

Title: The Fall of Icarus
Painter: Marc Chagall
In Chagall's painting, Icarus is falling. He thought Icarus was foolish. His painting has many details. He painted many people and houses in addition to Icarus.

┤ 보기 ├
① many details, ② Icarus, ③ falling,
④ brave and adventurous, ⑤ very simple,
⑥ foolish, ⑦ flying

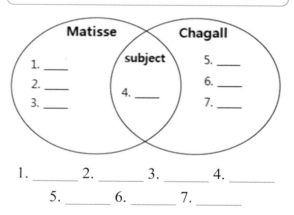

1. ___ 2. ___ 3. ___ 4. ___
5. ___ 6. ___ 7. ___

Reading **93**

**[01~03]** 다음 글을 읽고 물음에 답하시오.

We often find different paintings with the same (A)[object / subject]. An example is *The Flight of Icarus* by Henri Matisse and *The Fall of Icarus* by Marc Chagall. ⓐThey are both about the same Greek myth.

**The Greek Myth of Icarus**

Daedalus was a great inventor. King Minos liked Daedalus' work so much that he wanted to keep Daedalus with him (B)[forever / temporarily]. Daedalus, however, tried to leave, so the King kept him and his son, Icarus, in a tall tower. Daedalus wanted to escape.

One day, Daedalus saw birds flying. "Wings! I need wings!" he shouted. Daedalus then gathered bird feathers and glued ⓑthem together with wax. When the wings were ready, he warned his son, "Don't fly too close to the sun. The wax will melt."

Daedalus and Icarus began to fly. Icarus was so (C)[exciting / excited] that he forgot his father's ⓐ . He flew higher and higher, and the wax began to melt. "Oh, no! I'm falling," Icarus cried out. Icarus fell into the sea and died.

**01** 본문의 한 단어를 변형하여 위 글의 빈칸 ⓐ에 들어갈 알맞은 말을 쓰시오.

➡ _____

**02** 위 글의 밑줄 친 ⓐThey와 ⓑthem이 가리키는 것을 본문에서 찾아 쓰시오.

ⓐ _____

ⓑ _____

**03** 위 글의 괄호 (A)~(C)에서 문맥이나 어법상 알맞은 낱말을 골라 쓰시오.

(A) _____ (B) _____ (C) _____

**[04~06]** 다음 글을 읽고 물음에 답하시오.

**Two Different Paintings**

Matisse and Chagall both deal with ⓐthe same subject in their paintings, but they are different.

First, in Matisse's painting, you can see Icarus flying, but in Chagall's painting, the boy is falling. This difference comes from ⓑ the different ideas that the two painters had them. Matisse thought that Icarus was brave and adventurous. In contrast, Chagall thought that Icarus was foolish.

**04** 위 글의 밑줄 친 ⓐthe same subject가 가리키는 것을 영어로 쓰시오.

➡ _____

**05** 위 글의 밑줄 친 ⓑ에서 어법상 틀린 부분을 찾아 고치시오.

_____ ➡ _____

**06** 본문의 내용과 일치하도록 다음 빈칸 (A)~(D)에 알맞은 단어를 쓰시오.

Matisse thought that Icarus was (A)_____ _____ _____, so in his painting Icarus is (B)_____. But as Chagall thought that Icarus was (C)_____, you can see Icarus (D)_____ in his painting.

[07~09] 다음 글을 읽고 물음에 답하시오.

ⓐSecond, Matisse's painting has many details, but Chagall's painting is very simple. In Matisse's painting, there are only Icarus and some stars. Furthermore, Icarus' body has just a simple outline. In contrast, Chagall painted many people and houses in addition to Icarus. This difference comes from the different painting styles of the two painters.

Whose painting do you like more? People will have different answers ⓑ같은 것을 다른 방식들로 볼 수도 있기 때문에.

**07** 위 글의 밑줄 친 ⓐ에서 흐름상 어색한 부분을 찾아 고치시오. (두 군데)

➡ _____

_____

_____

**08** 위 글의 밑줄 친 ⓑ의 우리말에 맞게 주어진 어휘를 이용하여 10 단어로 영작하시오.

| because, may see, different ways |
| --- |

➡ _____

**09** 다음 빈칸 (A)와 (B)에 알맞은 단어를 넣어 Matisse와 Chagall의 그림에 대한 소개를 완성하시오.

In Matisse's painting, you can see only (A)_____ and (B)_____ _____. Moreover, Icarus' body has just (C)_____ _____ _____. On the other hand, in Chagall's painting, you can see many people and houses as well as (D)_____.

[10~12] 다음 글을 읽고 물음에 답하시오.

We often find different paintings with the same subject. An example is *The Flight of Icarus* by Henri Matisse and *The Fall of Icarus* by Marc Chagall. They are both about the same Greek myth.

**The Greek Myth of Icarus**

Daedalus was a great inventor. King Minos liked Daedalus' work __(A)__ much __(B)__ he wanted to keep Daedalus with him forever. Daedalus, however, tried to leave, so the King kept him and his son, Icarus, in a tall tower. Daedalus wanted to escape.

ⓐOne day, Daedalus saw birds to fly. "Wings! I need wings!" he shouted. Daedalus then gathered bird feathers and glued them together with wax. When the wings were ready, he warned his son, "Don't fly too close to the sun. The wax will melt."

Daedalus and Icarus began to fly. Icarus was __(A)__ excited __(B)__ he forgot his father's warning. He flew higher and higher, and the wax began to melt. "Oh, no! I'm falling," Icarus cried out. Icarus fell into the sea and died.

**10** 위 글의 빈칸 (A)와 (B)에 들어갈 알맞은 말을 쓰시오.

(A) _____ (B) _____

**11** 위 글의 밑줄 친 ⓐ에서 어법상 틀린 부분을 찾아 고치시오.

_____ ➡ _____

**12** 다음 문장에서 위 글의 내용과 다른 부분을 찾아서 고치시오.

*The Flight of Icarus* and *The Fall of Icarus* are different paintings but have the different subject.

_____ ➡ _____

## Talk and Play

**A:** I'm planning to go to the library this Monday. Do you want to go with me, Jiho?
~할 계획이다 　　　　　　　　　　　　　　　　함께 가자고 제안하기

**B:** Sure. What time should we meet?
약속 시간 정하는 표현

**A:** How about meeting at 5:30?
How about+-ing?: ~하는 게 어때?

**B:** OK. Where should we meet?
약속 장소 정하는 표현

**A:** Let's meet in front of the library.

**B:** Sounds good. See you then.

구문해설 · How about ~?: ~은 어때?　　· in front of ~: ~ 앞에

## Around the World

### Narcissus

Narcissus was proud of his beauty. One day, he saw his face in the water and
~을 자랑스러워했다　　　　(과거의) 어느 날
fell in love with himself.
~와 사랑에 빠졌다　　주어와 같은 대상이므로 재귀대명사 사용

### Pandora

There was a box that had all the bad things in the world inside. Pandora
주격 관계대명사(= which)　　　　　　　　　　　　　　안에
opened it, and they all came out.
= the box　= all the bad things in the world

### Orpheus

Orpheus was a great musician. When his wife died, he met Hades and told
시간의 부사절을 이끄는 접속사　　　　하데스(죽음과 지하 세계를 관장하는 신)
him, "Please return my wife to me."

구문해설 · inside: 내부에[로], 안쪽에[으로]　· return: 돌려주다, 도로 보내다

## After You Read D Reading Project

Title: *The Flight of Icarus*

Painter: Henri Matisse

In Matisse's painting, Icarus is flying. He thought Icarus was brave and
현재진행시제
adventurous. His painting is very simple. He drew only Icarus and some stars.
Matisse's　　　　　　　　　　draw–drew–drawn

Title: T*he Fall of Icarus*

Painter: Marc Chagall

In Chagall's painting, Icarus is falling. He thought Icarus was foolish. His
현재진행시제
painting has many details. He painted many people and houses in addition to
Chagall's
Icarus.
= besides

구문해설 · adventurous: 모험심이 강한　· simple: 단순한　· drew: draw의 과거
· detail: 세부 사항　· in addition to: ~뿐만 아니라, ~에 더하여

**Words & Expressions**

**01** 다음 두 단어의 관계가 같도록 빈칸에 알맞은 단어를 주어진 철자로 시작하여 쓰시오.

> melt : thaw = moreover : f_____

**02** 다음 글의 빈칸 ⓐ와 ⓑ에 들어갈 단어로 바르게 짝지어진 것은?

> • The house is beautiful. ⓐ_____ it's in a great location.
> • Minsu and his brother are very different. Minsu is funny. _____, his brother is very serious.

① However – In addition
② However – In contrast
③ Furthermore – In addition
④ Furthermore – In contrast
⑤ Similarly – However

[03~04] 다음 영영 풀이에 해당하는 것을 고르시오.

**03**

> a hot drink that you make by pouring boiling water onto dried leaves

① juice       ② beverage       ③ tea
④ coffee      ⑤ milk

**04**

> the act of flying through the air

① flight       ② float       ③ wing
④ feather      ⑤ form

**05** 다음 빈칸에 공통으로 들어갈 말을 쓰시오.

> • This week, let's learn how to _____ _____ your anger.
> • The book _____s _____ the subject of love.
> • A: Can you handle the situation by yourself?
>   B: Of course, I can. I can _____ _____ it without any help.

**06** 다음 중 밑줄 친 부분의 뜻이 잘못된 것은?

① Icarus was so excited that he forgot his father's warning. (경고)
② Daedalus tried to think of ways to escape. (달아나다)
③ I'm planning to go to the Van Gogh exhibition. (전시회)
④ Daedalus then gathered bird feathers and glued them together with wax. (붙이다)
⑤ Chagall painted many people and houses in addition to Icarus. (게다가)

**Conversation**

**07** 다음 대화를 순서에 맞게 바르게 배열하시오.

> (A) Let's meet at 10:30 in front of Green Stadium.
> (B) That sounds great. What time should we meet?
> (C) I'm planning to go see a soccer game next Friday. What about joining me, Jinho?
> (D) OK. See you then.

➡ _____

[08~10] 다음 대화를 읽고 물음에 답하시오.

(*Smartphone rings.*)
B: Hi, Kate. What's up?
G: Hi, Minho. What are you going to do this Saturday?
B: Nothing special. Why? (①)
G: I'm planning to go to the Van Gogh exhibition at the National Art Museum. Do you want to go with me? (②)
B: I'd love to! He's my favorite painter. What time should we meet? (③)
G: How about meeting at 11? (④)
B: OK. (⑤)
G: Let's meet in front of the ticket office.
B: Sounds good. I'll see you there at 11.

**08** 주어진 문장이 들어갈 위치로 알맞은 것은?

> Where should we meet?

①      ②      ③      ④      ⑤

**09** 다음 질문에 대한 답을 위 대화에서 찾아 쓰시오.

> Q: What are the speakers going to do this Saturday?

➡ _____

**10** 위 대화의 내용과 일치하지 <u>않는</u> 것은?

① Kate is planning to go to the Van Gogh exhibition.
② Minho will be busy on Saturday.
③ Van Gogh is Minho's favorite painter.
④ Kate and Minho are going to meet at 11.
⑤ Kate and Minho are going to meet in front of the ticket office.

**11** 다음에 제시된 〈조건〉에 맞게 아래 대화의 빈칸을 완성하시오.

┌─── 조건 ───
(1) 수영을 갈 계획을 말하는 표현을 쓸 것. 'plan'을 이용하여 진행형으로 쓸 것.
(2) 'how'를 이용하여 만날 시간을 제안하는 표현을 쓸 것.
(3) 'should'를 이용하여 만날 장소를 묻는 표현을 쓸 것.

A: (1) _____
   this Wednesday. Do you want to go with me, Minsu?
B: Sure. What time should we meet?
A: (2) _____ at 10:30?
B: OK. (3) _____
A: Let's meet at the bus stop.
B: Sounds good. See you then.

**12** 다음 대화의 밑줄 친 부분에 대한 설명으로 적절하지 <u>않은</u> 것은?

B: Sumi, ⓐI'm planning to go shopping with Jenny this Saturday. ⓑWill you join us?
G: Sounds great. ⓒWhat time should we meet?
B: ⓓHow about meeting at 12:30?
G: OK. ⓔWhere should we meet?
B: Let's meet in front of the shopping mall.

① ⓐ: 미래의 계획을 말하는 것으로 'I'm going to go shopping with Jenny this Saturday.'와 같은 표현이다.
② ⓑ: 함께 하자고 제안하는 말로 'How about joining us?'와 같은 표현이다.
③ ⓒ: 약속 시간을 정하는 표현으로 'When should we meet?'으로 바꾸어 쓸 수 있다.
④ ⓓ: 약속 시간을 제안하는 말로 'Can you make it at 12:30?'으로 바꾸어 쓸 수 있다.
⑤ ⓔ: 약속 장소를 정하는 말로 'Do you want to go with me?'와 바꾸어 쓸 수 있다.

**13** 다음 빈칸에 알맞은 말이 순서대로 짝지어진 것은?

> • Stella smelled something _____ in the kitchen.
> • He saw his mom _____ dinner in the kitchen.

① burn – to make    ② burns – making

③ burnt – made    ④ to burn – makes

⑤ burning – make

**14** 다음 그림을 보고 괄호 안에 주어진 어휘를 이용하여 빈칸에 알맞은 말을 쓰시오.

(1)    (2)    (3)

(1) I saw a person _____ the guitar. (play)

(2) I saw a person _____ his bag. (carry)

(3) I saw a person _____ the wall. (paint)

**15** 다음 중 어법상 바르지 <u>않은</u> 것은?

① The weather was so nice that I went for a walk.

② I was very hungry that I ate a whole pizza.

③ It was such a shock that her face turned white.

④ The music is too loud for me to sleep.

⑤ The water is cold enough to kill an ordinary person.

**16** 다음 중 어법상 바르지 <u>않은</u> 것은?

① I often watch them talking on the phone.

② He ran so fast that nobody could follow him.

③ I was so busy that I forgot Mia's birthday.

④ Did you see the man walked his dog?

⑤ She had me cook the curry and rice yesterday.

**17** 괄호 안에 주어진 어휘를 이용하여 다음을 영작하시오.

(1) 나는 누군가가 내 이름을 반복하는 것을 들었다. (someone, repeat)

➡ _____

(2) 소녀는 소년이 물고기에게 먹이를 주고 있는 것을 보았다. (see, feed)

➡ _____

(3) 너는 그가 그 소식을 말하는 것을 들었니? (listen, tell, the news)

➡ _____

(4) 그는 너무 배가 고파서 피자 세 조각을 먹었다. (eat, piece, that)

➡ _____

(5) 음식이 너무 맛이 없어서 우리는 그것을 먹지 않았다. (the food, awful, so, eat)

➡ _____

(6) 이 상자는 너무 무거워서 제가 들 수가 없어요. (this box, carry, to)

➡ _____

Reading

**[18~21]** 다음 글을 읽고 물음에 답하시오.

We often find different paintings with the same (a)subject. An example is *The ___ⓐ___ of Icarus* by Henri Matisse and *The Fall of Icarus* by Marc Chagall. They are both about the same Greek myth.

**The Greek Myth of Icarus**

Daedalus was a great inventor. King Minos liked Daedalus' work so much that he wanted to keep Daedalus with him forever. Daedalus, however, tried to leave, so the King kept him and his son, Icarus, in a tall tower. Daedalus wanted to escape.

One day, Daedalus saw birds ___ⓑ___. "Wings! I need wings!" he shouted. Daedalus then gathered bird feathers and glued them together with wax. When the wings were ready, he warned his son, "Don't ___ⓒ___ too close to the sun. _____(A)_____ "

Daedalus and Icarus began ___ⓓ___. Icarus was so excited that he forgot his father's warning. He ___ⓔ___ higher and higher, and the wax began to melt. "Oh, no! I'm falling," Icarus cried out. Icarus fell into the sea and died.

**18** 위 글의 빈칸 ⓐ~ⓔ에 fly를 알맞은 형태로 쓰시오.

ⓐ _____ ⓑ _____ ⓒ _____

ⓓ _____ ⓔ _____

**19** 위 글의 빈칸 (A)에 들어갈 알맞은 말을 고르시오.

① It will follow you.
② The wax will melt.
③ I won't be able to follow you.
④ You'll become blind.
⑤ You won't be able to fly fast.

**20** 위 글의 밑줄 친 (a)subject와 같은 의미로 쓰인 것을 고르시오.

① Biology is my favourite subject.
② Children are subject to their parents.
③ We need a male subject between the ages of 18 and 25 for the experiment.
④ What is the subject of this sentence?
⑤ The landscape was a popular subject with many 18th century painters.

**21** 위 글의 마지막 부분에서 알 수 있는 Icarus의 성격으로 가장 알맞은 것을 고르시오.

① wise          ② patient
③ careless       ④ reasonable
⑤ curious

**[22~24]** 다음 글을 읽고 물음에 답하시오.

**Two Different Paintings**

Matisse and Chagall both ⓐdeal with the same subject in their paintings, but ⓑthey are different.

First, in Matisse's painting, you can see Icarus flying, but in Chagall's painting, the boy is falling. This difference comes from the different ideas that the two painters had. Matisse thought that Icarus was brave and adventurous. In contrast, Chagall thought that Icarus was foolish.

**22** 위 글의 밑줄 친 ⓐdeal with와 바꿔 쓸 수 있는 단어를 모두 고르시오.

① control        ② treat
③ trade          ④ prepare
⑤ handle

**23** 위 글의 밑줄 친 ⓑthey are different의 구체적인 내용을 우리말로 설명하시오.

➡ _____

_____

**24** 위 글의 내용과 일치하지 <u>않는</u> 것은?

① Matisse와 Chagall 둘 다 그들의 그림에서 같은 주제를 다루었다.
② Matisse와 Chagall은 같은 주제를 서로 다르게 그렸다.
③ 두 그림의 차이는 두 화가들의 서로 다른 생활에서 기인한다.
④ Matisse는 Icarus가 용감하고 모험심이 강하다고 생각했다.
⑤ Chagall은 Icarus가 어리석다고 생각했다.

**[25~27]** 다음 글을 읽고 물음에 답하시오.

(①) Second, Matisse's painting is very simple, but Chagall's painting has many details. (②) In Matisse's painting, there are only Icarus and some stars. (③) Furthermore, Icarus' body has just a simple outline. (④) In contrast, Chagall painted many people and houses in addition to Icarus. (⑤)

Whose painting do you like more? People will have different answers because they may see the same thing in different ways.

**25** 위 글의 흐름으로 보아, 주어진 문장이 들어가기에 가장 적절한 곳은?

This difference comes from the different painting styles of the two painters.

① ② ③ ④ ⑤

**26** 위 글의 앞에 나왔을 내용으로 가장 알맞은 것을 고르시오.

① Matisse와 Chagall이 같은 주제를 고르게 된 첫 번째 배경
② Matisse의 화풍 설명
③ Chagall의 화풍 설명
④ Matisse와 Chagall이 같은 주제를 다르게 다룬 것에 관한 첫 번째 설명
⑤ Matisse와 Chagall의 그림에 대한 사람들의 선호도

**27** 다음 중 위 글의 내용과 어울리지 <u>않는</u> 말을 하는 사람을 고르시오.

동명: I like Matisse's painting because I like a simple style.
창수: I don't like Matisse's painting because there aren't many details in his painting.
희진: Chagall's painting looks good to me because I like a painting with many details.
준규: I think Matisse and Chagall chose the same subject because they had the same painting style.
민지: I like Matisse's painting, but I think there may be someone who doesn't like it.

① 동명 ② 창수 ③ 희진
④ 준규 ⑤ 민지

**01** 출제율 85%

다음 짝지어진 단어의 관계가 같도록 빈칸에 알맞은 단어를 주어진 철자로 시작하여 쓰시오.

> shout : yell = silly : f_____

**02** 출제율 90%

다음 영영 풀이에 해당하는 단어는?

> to tell someone that something bad might happen, so that he or she can avoid it

① escape  ② shout  ③ warn
④ gather  ⑤ skip

**03** 출제율 95%

다음 글의 빈칸 (A)~(C)에 들어갈 말로 알맞은 것은?

> Daedalus, however, tried to leave, so the King kept him and his son, Icarus, in a tall tower. Daedalus wanted to escape. One day, Daedalus saw birds flying. "Wings! I need wings!" he ___(A)___. Daedalus then ___(B)___ bird feathers and glued them together with wax. When the wings were ready, he warned his son, "Don't fly too close to the sun. The ___(C)___ will melt."

① skipped – collected – feathers
② skipped – gathered – wax
③ shouted – gathered – feathers
④ shouted – escaped – feathers
⑤ shouted – gathered – wax

**04** 출제율 100%

대화의 밑줄 친 ⓐ~ⓔ 중 어법상 어색한 것은?

> B: What are you going to do this Sunday?
> G: I'm ⓐplanning to go to Dream Amusement Park with my brother. You can go with us ⓑif you want to.
> B: ⓒI'd love to. ⓓWhen should we meet?
> G: I want to go early, so ⓔlet's to meet at 9 at the subway station.
> B: Sounds good. I'll see you then.

① ⓐ  ② ⓑ  ③ ⓒ  ④ ⓓ  ⑤ ⓔ

**05** 출제율 95%

다음 글의 밑줄 친 (A)~(E)의 해석으로 틀린 것은?

> First, in Matisse's painting, you can see Icarus flying, but in Chagall's painting, the boy is falling. This (A)difference comes from the different ideas that the two painters had. Matisse thought that Icarus was (B)brave and adventurous. (C)In contrast, Chagall thought that Icarus was foolish. Second, Matisse's painting is very simple, but Chagall's painting has many (D)details. In Matisse's painting, there are only Icarus and some stars. Furthermore, Icarus' body has just a simple (E)outline.

① (A) 차이  ② (B) 용감한
③ (C) 게다가  ④ (D) 세부 사항
⑤ (E) 윤곽

**[06~07]** 다음 대화를 읽고 물음에 답하시오.

> G: (A)나는 이번 주 금요일에 피아노 콘서트에 갈 계획이야. Why don't you join me, Kevin?
> B: Sure. _____(B)_____
> G: Let's meet at 10:30.
> B: OK. See you then.

## 06 위 대화의 밑줄 친 (A)의 우리말에 맞게 주어진 문장의 빈칸을 채우시오.

> I'm _____ _____ _____ _____
> a piano concert this Friday.

## 07 위 대화의 빈칸 (B)에 들어갈 말로 알맞은 것을 고르시오.

① Will you join us?
② What time should we meet?
③ Where should we meet?
④ Do you want to go with me?
⑤ Do you have time?

**[08~10]** 다음 대화를 읽고 물음에 답하시오.

> (*Smartphone rings.*)
> B: Hi, Kate. What's up?
> G: Hi, Minho. (A)이번 토요일에 뭐 할 거야?
> B: Nothing special. Why?
> G: I'm planning to go to the Van Gogh exhibition at the National Art Museum. Do you want to go with me?
> B: (B)I'd love to! He's my favorite painter. ⓐ should we meet?
> G: ⓑ meeting at 11?
> B: OK. ⓒ should we meet?
> G: Let's meet in front of the ticket office.
> B: Sounds good. I'll see you there at 11.

## 08 위 대화의 빈칸 ⓐ~ⓒ에 들어갈 말로 알맞은 것은?

① When – How – Where
② When – How about – Why
③ What time – How about – Where
④ What time – What about – When
⑤ Where – What about – What time

## 09 위 대화의 밑줄 친 (A)의 우리말에 맞게 주어진 어휘를 배열하여 대화를 완성하시오.

> are / going / what / you / to / this / do / Saturday

➡ _____

## 10 위 대화의 밑줄 친 (B)를 생략되지 않은 문장으로 쓰시오.

➡ _____

## 11 다음 빈칸에 들어갈 말이 바르게 짝지어진 것은?

> • I saw the moon _____ above the horizon.
> • This problem is easy _____ for everybody to solve.

① rising – too        ② rising – enough
③ rose – too          ④ rose – enough
⑤ rise – too

**[12~13]** 어법상 올바른 문장을 모두 고르시오.

## 12
① I saw Junho taking a picture.
② The teacher saw Hoyeong to dance.
③ I felt somebody watched me.
④ He was looking at the monkey ate bananas.
⑤ I heard two men fight with each other.

## 13
① It was too sad that I cried a lot.
② The cake was delicious so that I ate it all.
③ Tom was so nervous that he made a big mistake.
④ He was too hungry to get to sleep last night.
⑤ The man is rich enough that he can buy anything he wants.

## 14 다음 중 어법상 틀린 문장의 개수는?

출제율 95%

ⓐ We saw the spider spinning its web.
ⓑ We heard her played the piano.
ⓒ Gabriel listened to her telling him what she did.
ⓓ Jocelyn felt him held her hand.
ⓔ He was so nervous that he made some mistakes on the test.
ⓕ The dog ran too quickly for me to catch it.
ⓖ The sky was enough clear to see stars very well.

① 1개  ② 2개  ③ 3개  ④ 4개  ⑤ 5개

**[15~17] 다음 글을 읽고 물음에 답하시오.**

We often find different paintings with the same subject. An example is *The Flight of Icarus* by Henri Matisse and *The Fall of Icarus* by Marc Chagall. They are both about the same Greek myth.

**The Greek Myth of Icarus**

Daedalus was a great inventor. King Minos liked Daedalus' work so much that he wanted to keep Daedalus with him forever. Daedalus, ____ⓐ____, tried to leave, so the King kept him and his son, Icarus, in a tall tower. Daedalus wanted to escape.

One day, Daedalus saw birds flying. "Wings! I need wings!" he shouted. Daedalus then gathered bird feathers and glued them together with wax. When the wings were ready, he warned his son, "Don't fly too close to the sun. The wax will melt."

Daedalus and Icarus began ⓑto fly. Icarus was so excited that he forgot his father's warning. He flew higher and higher, and the wax began to melt. "Oh, no! I'm falling," Icarus cried out. Icarus fell into the sea and died.

## 15 위 글의 빈칸 ⓐ에 들어갈 알맞은 말을 고르시오.

출제율 90%

① therefore  ② however
③ in addition  ④ for example
⑤ as a result

## 16 위 글의 밑줄 친 ⓑto fly와 to부정사의 용법이 다른 것을 모두 고르시오.

출제율 90%

① When did you make the decision to leave here?
② She decided to leave right now.
③ It was the best decision to leave immediately.
④ To leave as soon as possible, he made a quick decision.
⑤ My decision was to leave at once.

## 17 위 글을 읽고 대답할 수 없는 질문은?

출제율 100%

① Are the subjects of *The Flight of Icarus* and *The Fall of Icarus* different?
② What's the subject of *The Flight of Icarus*?
③ Why did King Minos keep Daedalus and Icarus in a tall tower?
④ How did Daedalus gather bird feathers?
⑤ Why did Icarus fly higher and higher?

**[18~21] 다음 글을 읽고 물음에 답하시오.**

**Two Different Paintings**

ⓐMatisse와 Chagall 둘 다 그들의 그림에서 같은 주제를 다루었지만, 그것들은 다르다.

ⓑFirst, in Matisse's painting, you can see Icarus falling, but in Chagall's painting, the boy is flying. This difference ⓒcomes from the ⓓdifferent ideas that the two painters had. Matisse thought that Icarus was brave and adventurous. In contrast, Chagall thought that Icarus was foolish.

*출제율 95%*

**18** 위 글의 밑줄 친 ⓐ의 우리말에 맞게 한 단어를 보충하여, 주어진 어휘를 알맞게 배열하시오.

> different / are / but / the same subject / deal / they / Matisse and Chagall both / in their paintings

➡ _____

_____

*출제율 100%*

**19** 위 글의 밑줄 친 ⓑ에서 흐름상 어색한 부분을 찾아 고치시오. (두 군데)

_____ ➡ _____

_____ ➡ _____

*출제율 85%*

**20** 위 글의 밑줄 친 ⓒcomes from과 바꿔 쓸 수 없는 말을 모두 고르시오.

① is due to
② results from
③ causes
④ arises from
⑤ results in

*출제율 90%*

**21** 위 글의 밑줄 친 ⓓdifferent ideas의 구체적인 내용을 우리말로 설명하시오.

➡ _____

_____

**[22~24]** 다음 글을 읽고 물음에 답하시오.

Second, Matisse's painting is very simple, but Chagall's painting has many details. In Matisse's painting, there are only Icarus and some stars. ⓐFurthermore, Icarus' body has just a simple outline. In contrast, Chagall painted many people and houses in addition to Icarus. ⓑThis difference comes from the ___(A)___ painting styles of the two painters.

Whose painting do you like more? People will have ___(B)___ answers because they may see the same thing in ___(C)___ ways.

*출제율 100%*

**22** 위 글의 한 단어를 변형하여 위 글의 빈칸 (A)~(C)에 공통으로 들어갈 알맞은 단어를 쓰시오.

➡ _____

*출제율 95%*

**23** 위 글의 밑줄 친 ⓐFurthermore와 바꿔 쓸 수 없는 말을 고르시오.

① Additionally
② Moreover
③ Beside
④ In addition
⑤ Besides

*출제율 90%*

**24** 다음 빈칸 (A)와 (B)에 알맞은 단어를 넣어 ⓑThis difference에 대한 소개를 완성하시오.

> Matisse painted only Icarus whose body has just (A)_____ _____ _____ and some stars. But Chagall painted not only Icarus but also (B)_____ _____ like many people and houses.

**01** 아래 〈조건〉에 맞게 주어진 단어를 이용하여 대화의 빈칸을 완성하시오.

> B: What are you going to do this Sunday?
> G: I'm planning to go to Dream Amusement Park with my brother.     (A)     .
> B: I'd love to. When should we meet?
> G: I want to go early, so     (B)     .
> B: Sounds good. I'll see you then.

┤ 조건 ├

(A) • 함께 가자고 제안하는 표현을 쓸 것.
　　• you를 주어로 하는 평서문으로 문장을 시작하고, if절을 쓸 것.
　　• 'go with'와 'want to'를 이용할 것
(B) • 지하철역에서 9시에 만나자고 제안하는 표현을 쓸 것.
　　• let's로 문장을 시작할 것.

(A) _____

(B) _____

**02** 다음 대화의 밑줄 친 우리말을 주어진 어휘를 배열하여 완성하시오.

> A: I'm planning to go hiking this Sunday. 나와 함께 갈래(you / want / do / to / with / go / me), Jina?
> B: I'm sorry, but I have other plans.
> A: OK.

➡ _____

**03** 다음 대화를 읽고 아래의 물음에 영어로 답하시오.

> A: I'm planning to go to the library this Monday. Do you want to go with me, Jiho?
> B: Sure. What time should we meet?
> A: How about meeting at 5:30?
> B: OK. Where should we meet?
> A: Let's meet in front of the library.
> B: Sounds good. See you then.

(1) Where are they going to go this Monday?

➡ _____

(2) When are they going to meet?

➡ _____

**04** 다음 문장을 to부정사를 이용하여 다시 쓰시오.

(1) The room was so noisy that we couldn't hear him speak.

➡ _____

(2) She speaks so fast that I can't understand her.

➡ _____

(3) The math problem is so easy that anyone can solve it.

➡ _____

★ 중요

**05** 다음 두 문장을 하나의 문장으로 쓰시오.

(1) • Minsu played soccer.
    • Did you see him?
  ➡ _____

(2) • Sophia opened the window.
    • Did you hear it?
  ➡ _____

(3) • Your mom touched you on the shoulder.
    • Did you feel it?
  ➡ _____
_____

**06** 그림을 보고 괄호 안에 주어진 어구들을 바르게 배열하여 문장을 완성하시오.

(Orpheus, Hades, musician, his wife, him, a, was, returned, great, that, such, to)

➡ _____
_____

**[07~09]** 다음 글을 읽고 물음에 답하시오.

   ⓐ우리는 종종 같은 주제의 다른 그림들을 발견한다. An example is *The Flight of Icarus* by Henri Matisse and *The Fall of Icarus* by Marc Chagall. They are both about ⓑthe same Greek myth.

**The Greek Myth of Icarus**

   Daedalus was a great inventor. ⓒKing Minos liked Daedalus' work so much that he wanted to keep Daedalus with him forever. Daedalus, however, tried to leave, so the King kept him and his son, Icarus, in a tall tower. Daedalus wanted to escape.

   One day, Daedalus saw birds flying. "Wings! I need wings!" he shouted. Daedalus then gathered bird feathers and glued them together with wax. When the wings were ready, he warned his son, "Don't fly too close to the sun. The wax will melt."

   Daedalus and Icarus began to fly. Icarus was so excited that he forgot ⓓhis father's warning. He flew higher and higher, and the wax began to melt. "Oh, no! I'm falling," Icarus cried out. Icarus fell into the sea and died.

**07** 위 글의 밑줄 친 ⓐ의 우리말에 맞게 주어진 어휘를 이용하여 9 단어로 영작하시오.

| often, paintings, with |
|---|

➡ _____
_____

★ 중요

**08** 위 글의 밑줄 친 ⓑ와 ⓓ가 가리키는 것을 본문에서 찾아 쓰시오.

ⓑ _____
ⓓ _____

**09** 위 글의 밑줄 친 문장 ⓒ를 다음과 같이 바꿔 쓸 때 빈칸에 들어갈 알맞은 말을 쓰시오.

| King Minos wanted to keep Daedalus with him forever _____ he liked Daedalus' work so much. |
|---|

**01** 다음 주어진 정보를 이용하여 대화의 빈칸을 완성하시오.

> plan: go see a soccer game / what time: at 10:00 / where: at the bus stop

> **A:** _____ see a soccer game. Do you want to go with me?
> **B:** Sure. _____?
> **A:** How _____ at 10:00 at the bus stop?
> **B:** OK. See you then.

**02** 〈보기〉에 주어진 어휘와 so와 that을 이용하여 3 문장 이상 쓰시오.

> 보기
>
> | very nervous | very happy | very tired | really sad |
> | play well | danced | fell asleep on the floor | everybody cried |

(1) _____

(2) _____

(3) _____

(4) _____

**03** 다음 내용을 바탕으로 두 그림을 비교 · 대조하는 글을 쓰시오.

> • **subject:** a violinist
> *The Green Violinist* **by Marc Chagall**
> • We can see the man's face.
> • We see the violinist dancing.
> • Chagall's painting is more dynamic.
> *The Violinist at the Window* **by Henri Matisse**
> • We cannot see the man's face.
> • We see the violinist standing still.

> The two paintings, *The Green Violinist* by Marc Chagall and *The Violinist at the Window* by Henri Matisse, both deal with (A) _____. In both paintings, we see a man playing the violin. The two paintings, however, have some differences. First, in Chagall's painting, we (B)_____ the man's face, but in Matisse's painting, we cannot see it. Second, in Chagall's painting, we see the violinist (C)_____ while in Matisse's painting, we see him (D)_____. Finally, another difference between the two paintings is that Chagall's painting is (E)_____.

## 단원별 모의고사

**01** 다음 단어에 대한 영어 설명이 <u>어색한</u> 것은?

① in contrast: used when you are comparing two things or people and saying that the second one is very different from the first

② forever: for all of the time in the future

③ wax: a substance used for making candles and crayons

④ skip: to get away from a place or person

⑤ in addition to: used for saying that something extra exists

**02** 다음 짝지어진 단어의 관계가 같도록 빈칸에 알맞은 말을 쓰시오.

different : same = complicated : _____

**[03~04]** 다음 대화의 빈칸에 들어갈 말로 알맞은 것을 고르시오.

**03**

G: I'm planning to go to a piano concert this Friday. Why don't you join me, Kevin?

B: Sure. What time should we meet?

G: _____

B: OK. See you then.

① I'd like to, but I have to take care of my younger brother.

② Did you know Mars has its moons?

③ Let's meet at 10:30 at the bus stop.

④ Let's meet at the bus stop.

⑤ I'm afraid I can't. I'm going on a family trip.

**04**

B: What are you going to do this Sunday?

G: I'm planning to go to Dream Amusement Park with my brother. You can go with us if you want to.

B: I'd love to. _____

G: I want to go early, so let's meet at 9.

B: Sounds good. I'll see you then.

① How about meeting at the park?

② What is going on?

③ When does it begin?

④ Where should we meet?

⑤ When should we meet?

**05** 다음 영영풀이에 해당하는 단어를 고르시오.

a small fact, feature, or piece of information

① detail      ② myth      ③ title
④ tea         ⑤ wax

**06** 다음 중 짝지어진 대화가 <u>어색한</u> 것은?

① A: What time should we meet?
   B: How about meeting at 5:30?

② A: Where should we meet?
   B: Let's meet in front of the library.

③ A: Do you want to go with me?
   B: I'd love to!

④ A: What are you going to do this Saturday?
   B: Nothing special. Why?

⑤ A: What time and where should we meet?
   B: Sounds good. See you then.

**[07~09]** 다음 대화를 읽고 물음에 답하시오.

> (*Smartphone rings.*)
> B: Hi, Kate. What's up?
> G: Hi, Minho. What are you going to do this Saturday?
> B: Nothing special. Why?
> G: I'm planning to go to the Van Gogh exhibition at the National Art Museum. Do you want to go with me?
> B: I'd love to! He's my favorite painter.
> _____(A)_____
> G: How about meeting at 11?
> B: OK. Where should we meet?
> G: Let's meet in front of the ticket office.
> B: Sounds good. I'll see you there at 11.

**07** 위 대화의 빈칸 (A)에 들어갈 말로 알맞은 것은?

① What time does the museum open?
② What time should we meet?
③ Where should we meet?
④ Where is the museum?
⑤ How about you?

**08** Where are Kate and Minho going to meet? (be going to 를 이용하여 쓸 것)

➡ _____

**09** 위 대화를 읽고, Kate가 Minho에게 보내는 메시지를 완성하시오.

> Minho, don't forget our _____ for this Saturday. I'll see you at 11 _____ _____ _____ the _____ _____ of the National Art Museum.

**10** 다음 대화의 내용과 일치하면 T, 일치하지 않으면 F에 표시하시오.

> Minho: Sumi, I'm planning to go shopping with Jenny this Saturday. Will you join us?
> Sumi: Sounds great. What time should we meet?
> Minho: How about meeting at 12:30?
> Sumi: OK. Where should we meet?
> Minho: Let's meet in front of the shopping mall.

(1) Miho is planning to go shopping by himself. (T / F)
(2) Minho and Sumi are going to meet at 12:30 in front of the shopping mall. (T / F)

**11** 다음 대화의 빈칸에 알맞은 것은?

> B: I'm planning to go to a soccer game tomorrow. Do you want to go with me, Susan?
> G: Sure. What time should we meet?
> B: The game begins at 7, so _____
> G: OK. See you then.

① why don't we go to a soccer game?
② I want to meet you tomorrow.
③ let's meet at 6 in front of Dream Stadium.
④ where should we meet?
⑤ we have to make haste.

**12** 다음 대화를 순서대로 배열하시오.

> (A) The musical starts at 3 o'clock. Let's meet at 2 at Dream Art Hall.
> (B) Sure. What time and where should we meet?
> (C) I'm planning to go see *Cats* this Saturday. Do you want to go with me?
> (D) Great. See you on Saturday.

➡ _____

**13** 주어진 단어를 이용하여 다음 우리말을 영어로 쓰시오.

(1) 나는 나의 삼촌이 기타를 치는 것을 들었다.
(hear, play, guitar)

➡ _____

(2) 나는 그들이 집안에서 운동화를 신고 있는 것을 보았다. (see, wear, their sneakers)

➡ _____

(3) 나는 한 여왕이 장미의 향기를 맡고 있는 것을 보았다. (see, smell, a rose)

➡ _____

(4) 그 영화가 너무 좋아서 그들은 그것을 두 번 보았다. (good, that, watch, twice)

➡ _____

(5) 날씨가 너무 나빠서 그들은 집에 있었다.
(the weather, bad, that, stay home)

➡ _____

(6) John은 너무 아파서 학교에 갈 수 없다. (too, sick)

➡ _____

**14** 다음 두 문장을 'so ~ that' 구문을 사용하여 한 문장으로 연결하여 쓰시오.

(1) • This problem is really easy.
　　• So, everybody can solve it.

➡ _____

(2) • We decided to have dinner at the restaurant once again.
　　• Because the meal was very good.

➡ _____
_____

**15** 다음 중 어법상 바르지 <u>않은</u> 것은?

① We heard Joy to talk on the phone.
② Mr. Kim was so full that he couldn't eat anymore.
③ It is interesting to watch her dance to the music.
④ Eric saw Minsu playing soccer.
⑤ The girl was so happy that she jumped up and down.

**16** 다음 두 문장이 서로 <u>다른</u> 의미를 갖는 것은?

① We felt the ground shaking for a few seconds.
= We felt the ground shake for a few seconds.
② She studied so hard that she could pass the exam.
= She studied hard so that she could pass the exam.
③ We watched the woman getting into the car.
= We watched the woman get into the car.
④ The students were very tired. So, they fell asleep during the movie.
= The students were so tired that they fell asleep during the movie.
⑤ I want to take a nap because I'm very tired.
= I'm so tired that I want to take a nap.

**17** 다음 문장에서 어법상 어색한 부분을 바르게 고치시오.

(1) I heard him ran down the stairs.

_____ ➡ _____

(2) I felt my heart to beat fast.

_____ ➡ _____

(3) Can you smell something burns?

_____ ➡ _____

(4) The kids were too tired at the end of the race that they just walked.

_____ ➡ _____

(5) The floor was slippery so that I almost fell.

_____ ➡ _____

(6) The box was light enough for the man to carry it.

_____ ➡ _____

**[18~21]** 다음 글을 읽고 물음에 답하시오.

We often find different paintings with the same subject. An example is *The Flight of Icarus* by Henri Matisse and *The Fall of Icarus* by Marc Chagall. They are both about the same Greek myth.

**The Greek Myth of Icarus**

Daedalus was a great inventor. King Minos liked Daedalus' work so much that he wanted to keep Daedalus with ⓐhim forever. Daedalus, however, tried to leave, so the King kept him and ⓑhis son, Icarus, in a tall tower. Daedalus wanted to escape.

One day, Daedalus saw birds (A)flying. "Wings! ⓒI need wings!" he shouted. Daedalus then gathered bird feathers and glued them together with wax. When the wings were ready, he warned his son, "Don't fly too close to the sun. The wax will melt."

Daedalus and Icarus began to fly. Icarus was so excited that he forgot ⓓhis father's warning. (B)그는 점점 더 높이 날았고, 밀랍은 녹기 시작했다. "Oh, no! ⓔI'm falling," Icarus cried out. Icarus fell into the sea and died.

**18** 아래 〈보기〉에서 위 글의 밑줄 친 (A)flying과 문법적 쓰임이 같은 것의 개수를 고르시오.

① They were on a plane flying from London to New York.
② I'm flying to Hong Kong tomorrow.
③ The Wright Brothers dreamed of flying in the sky.
④ Look at the children flying kites there.
⑤ The pilot finished flying the large passenger plane.

① 1개  ② 2개  ③ 3개  ④ 4개  ⑤ 5개

**19** 위 글의 밑줄 친 ⓐ~ⓔ 중 가리키는 대상이 같은 것끼리 짝 지어진 것은?

① ⓐ와 ⓑ  ② ⓐ와 ⓒ  ③ ⓑ와 ⓓ
④ ⓒ와 ⓓ  ⑤ ⓓ와 ⓔ

**20** 위 글의 내용과 일치하도록 다음 빈칸 (A)와 (B)에 알맞은 단어를 쓰시오.

Matisse and Chagall drew different paintings with the (A)_____ _____, the Greek Myth of Icarus, who fell into the sea and died because he forgot his father's (B)_____.

**21** 위 글의 밑줄 친 (B)의 우리말에 맞게 주어진 어휘를 이용하여 11 단어로 영작하시오.

flew, and, the wax

➡ _____

# Lesson 7

# Life in Space

## 의사소통 기능

- 알고 있는지 묻기
  A: Did you hear about the new musical?
  B: Yes, I did. / No, I didn't.

- 궁금증 표현하기
  I'm really curious about it.

## 언어 형식

- 현재완료
  I**'ve** never **seen** a blue sky.

- It ~ to부정사
  **It**'s difficult **to walk on Earth**.

# Words & Expressions

## Key Words

- **adventure** [ædvéntʃər] 몡 모험
- **air** [ɛər] 몡 공기
- **amazing** [əméiziŋ] 혱 놀라운
- **arrive** [əráiv] 동 도착하다
- **balloon** [bəlúːn] 몡 풍선
- **container** [kəntéinər] 몡 그릇, 용기
- **curious** [kjúəriəs] 혱 궁금한, 호기심이 많은
- **dessert** [dizə́ːrt] 몡 디저트
- **different** [dífərənt] 혱 다른
- **difficult** [dífikʌlt] 혱 어려운
- **ever** [évər] 뷔 줄곧, 내내
- **everywhere** [évriwὲər] 뷔 모든 곳에
- **excited** [iksáitid] 혱 신난, 흥분한
- **exciting** [iksáitiŋ] 혱 흥미진진한
- **exploration** [èkspləréiʃən] 몡 탐험, 탐사
- **finally** [fáinəli] 뷔 마침내
- **fix** [fiks] 동 고치다
- **foreign** [fɔ́ːrən] 혱 외국의
- **float** [flout] 동 뜨다, 떠가다
- **form** [fɔːrm] 동 형성하다, 만들어 내다
- **French** [frentʃ] 혱 프랑스의
- **grass** [græs] 몡 풀, 잔디
- **hear** [hiər] 동 듣다 (-heard-heard)
- **hill** [hil] 몡 언덕
- **interesting** [íntərəstiŋ] 혱 재미있는, 흥미로운
- **land** [lænd] 동 착륙하다
- **laugh** [læf] 동 웃다
- **lie** [lai] 동 눕다 (-lay-lain)
- **little** [litl] 혱 작은
- **marathon** [mǽrəθὰn] 몡 마라톤
- **musical** [mjúːzikəl] 몡 뮤지컬
- **nearest** [níərist] (near의 최상급) 가장 가까운
- **other** [ʌ́ðər] 혱 다른
- **poster** [póustər] 몡 포스터
- **recently** [ríːsntli] 뷔 최근에
- **ride** [raid] 동 타다 (-rode-ridden)
- **save** [seiv] 동 구하다, 절약하다
- **secret** [síːkrit] 몡 비밀, 기밀
- **shake** [ʃeik] 동 흔들다 (-shook-shaken)
- **shout** [ʃaut] 동 외치다
- **since** [sins] 접 ～한 이래로
- **soft** [sɔːft] 혱 부드러운
- **spaceship** [spéisʃip] 몡 우주선
- **space station** 우주 정거장
- **space suit** 우주복
- **swallow** [swálou] 동 삼키다
- **taste** [teist] 몡 맛
- **thirsty** [θə́ːrsti] 혱 목마른
- **thrilling** [θríliŋ] 혱 아주 신나는
- **type** [taip] 몡 종류, 유형
- **towards** [tɔ́ːrdz] 전 ～쪽으로, ～을 향하여
- **vegetable** [védʒətəbl] 몡 야채, 채소
- **wet** [wet] 혱 젖은
- **wind** [wind] 몡 바람

## Key Expressions

- **all night** 하룻밤 내내, 밤새도록
- **be born** 태어나다
- **be covered with** ～으로 뒤덮이다
- **be curious about ～** ～에 관해 궁금해 하다
- **don't have to+동사원형** ～할 필요 없다
- **each other** (둘 사이의) 서로
- **for example** 예를 들어
- **get on** ～에 타다
- **get wet** 젖다
- **here it is** (물건을 건네줄 때) 여기 있어
- **in surprise** 놀라서
- **in the air** 공중에
- **lie down** 눕다
- **not ～ anymore** 더 이상 ～ 않다
- **pull down** 아래로 끌어내리다
- **roll down** 굴러 내려가다
- **run up to ～** ～으로 달려가다
- **sound+형용사** ～처럼 들리다
- **take a walk** 산책하다
- **talk about ～** ～에 관해 말하다
- **try to+동사원형** ～하려고 시도하다

## Word Power

※ 서로 반대되는 뜻을 가진 어휘

- [ ] **different** (다른) ↔ **same** (같은)
- [ ] **arrive** (도착하다) ↔ **depart** (출발하다)
- [ ] **difficult** (어려운) ↔ **easy** (쉬운)
- [ ] **excited** (신나는) ↔ **bored** (지루한)
- [ ] **land** (착륙하다) ↔ **take off** (이륙하다)
- [ ] **interesting** (흥미로운) ↔ **uninteresting** (재미없는)

- [ ] **little** (작은) ↔ **big** (큰)
- [ ] **near** (가까운) ↔ **far** (먼)
- [ ] **soft** (부드러운) ↔ **hard** (딱딱한)
- [ ] **wet** (젖은) ↔ **dry** (마른)
- [ ] **get on** (타다) ↔ **get off** (내리다)
- [ ] **intelligent** (똑똑한) ↔ **stupid** (어리석은)

※ 서로 비슷한 뜻을 가진 어휘

- [ ] **amazing** : **surprising** (놀라운)
- [ ] **fix** : **repair** (고치다, 수리하다)
- [ ] **form** : **build** (형성하다)
- [ ] **recently** : **lately** (최근에)

- [ ] **save** : **rescue** (구하다)
- [ ] **shout** : **yell** (외치다)
- [ ] **exciting** : **thrilling** (신나는)
- [ ] **land** : **touch down**(착륙하다)

## English Dictionary

- [ ] **adventure** 모험
  - → an unusual, exciting, and possibly dangerous activity, such as a trip
  - 여행과 같이 특이하고, 흥미진진하며, 위험할 수도 있는 활동

- [ ] **amazing** 놀라운
  - → extremely surprising
  - 매우 놀라운

- [ ] **arrive** 도착하다
  - → to reach a place, especially at the end of a journey
  - 특히 여행이 끝날 때, 어떤 장소에 도착하다

- [ ] **curious** 호기심 많은
  - → interested in learning about people or things around you
  - 주변 사람 또는 사물을 알고자 하는 데 관심이 있는

- [ ] **exploration** 탐험, 탐사
  - → the activity of searching and finding out about something
  - 무언가를 찾고 알아내는 활동

- [ ] **foreign** 외국의
  - → belonging or connected to a country that is not your own
  - 자신의 나라가 아닌 나라와 관련되어 있거나 속해 있는

- [ ] **float** 뜨다
  - → to stay on the surface of a liquid and not sink
  - 액체의 표면에 머무르고 가라앉지 않다

- [ ] **form** 형성하다, 만들다
  - → to make something into a particular shape
  - 어떤 것을 특정한 모양으로 만들다

- [ ] **land** 착륙하다
  - → to arrive on the ground or other surface after moving down through the air
  - 공중에서 아래로 이동한 후 땅이나 다른 표면에 도착하다

- [ ] **swallow** 삼키다
  - → to cause food, drink, pills, etc. to move from your mouth into your stomach by using the muscles of your throat
  - 목의 근육을 사용함으로써 음식, 음료, 약 등을 입에서 배 속으로 움직이도록 하다

- [ ] **secret** 비밀
  - → a piece of information that is only known by one person or a few people and should not be told to others
  - 한 사람이나 몇 사람만 알고 다른 사람에게는 말하지 말아야 하는 정보

- [ ] **spaceship** 우주선
  - → a vehicle used for travel in space
  - 우주에서 여행하기 위해 사용되는 운송 수단

- [ ] **space station** 우주 정거장
  - → a place or vehicle in space where people can stay
  - 사람들이 머물 수 있는 우주에 있는 장소나 탈것

- [ ] **towards** ~을 향해
  - → in the direction of, or closer to someone or something
  - 누군가나 어떤 것의 방향으로 또는 더 가까이

 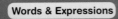
서답형
**01** 다음 문장의 빈칸에 주어진 영어 설명에 해당하는 말을 쓰시오.

> Rada and Jonny thought about it all night and didn't tell Mom and Dad about it. It was their _____.

> a piece of information that is only known by one person or a few people and should not be told to others

중요
**02** 다음 빈칸에 들어갈 말로 가장 적절한 것은?

> Jonny opened a milk container and shook it. The milk _____ed in the air and formed balls.

① float          ② reach
③ swallow          ④ fix
⑤ look

[03~04] 다음 영영풀이에 해당하는 단어를 고르시오.

**03**
> to move something down, using your hands

① roll down          ② be born
③ in surprise          ④ pull down
⑤ each other

중요
**04**
> covered in or full of water or another liquid

① soft          ② dry
③ near          ④ simple
⑤ wet

서답형
**05** 다음 우리말에 맞게 빈칸에 알맞은 단어를 쓰시오.

> 언덕들이 있어. 그리고 언덕들은 부드러운 초록색의 잔디로 덮여 있지.
> ➡ There are hills, and they _____ _____ _____ soft green grass.

**06** 다음 빈칸에 공통으로 들어갈 말로 알맞은 것은?

> • He put a grape into his mouth and _____ed it.
> • One _____ doesn't make a summer.

① plan          ② land
③ swallow          ④ throw
⑤ laugh

서답형
**07** 다음 짝지어진 단어의 관계가 같도록 빈칸에 알맞은 말을 쓰시오.

> amazing : surprising = lately : _____

중요
**08** 다음 빈칸에 들어갈 말로 알맞게 짝지어진 것은?

> • They looked at _____ other and laughed.
> • Rada and Jonny _____ down on the soft green grass and rolled down the hill.

① one – laid          ② each – rolled
③ every – lied          ④ each – lay
⑤ one – pulled

**01** 다음 빈칸에 들어갈 말을 〈보기〉에서 찾아 쓰시오. (필요하면 변형하여 쓰시오.)

┤ 보기 ├
curious   excite   pull   cover

(1) It's also hard to jump there because Earth _____ you down.

(2) Hills are _____ with soft green grass.

(3) It was _____ to think about all the new things they were going to see and do.

(4) I'm really _____ about the space marathon.

**02** 다음 그림에 맞게 〈보기〉에서 단어를 골라 알맞은 표현을 쓰시오. (어형 변화 필수)

┤ 보기 ├
cover   pull   roll down   shake   land

(1)   (2)   (3)

(1) A girl is _____ a bottle.

(2) A ball is _____ the hill.

(3) An airplane is _____.

**03** 다음 빈칸에 공통으로 알맞은 단어를 주어진 철자로 시작하여 쓰시오.

(1) • You have to fill out a f_____ on their website.
  • The milk floated in the air and f_____ed balls. Jonny swallowed the balls.

(2) • The sailors saw l_____ in the distance.
  • The plane l_____ed safely at last.

**04** 다음 우리말과 같은 표현이 되도록 문장의 빈칸을 채우시오.

(1) 그들은 우주에서 태어났다.
  ➡ They _____ _____ in space.

(2) Rada와 Jonny는 깜짝 놀라 아빠를 보았고, 그에게 둥둥 떠서 갔다.
  ➡ Rada and Jonny looked at Dad in _____ and floated towards him.

(3) 모든 곳에 공기가 있기 때문에 너는 크고 무거운 우주복을 입을 필요가 없어.
  ➡ You _____ _____ _____ wear your big heavy _____ _____ because there is air _____.

**05** 다음 영영풀이에 해당하는 단어를 〈보기〉에서 찾아 첫 번째 칸에 쓰고, 두 번째 칸에는 우리말 뜻을 쓰시오.

┤ 보기 ├
space station   exploration   secret
air   space suit   adventure

(1) _____: the gases around you, which you breathe: _____

(2) _____: a piece of information that is only known by one person or a few people and should not be told to others _____

(3) _____: a special piece of clothing that astronauts wear in space: _____

# Conversation

교과서

## 1 알고 있는지 묻기

A  Did you hear about the new musical? 새로운 뮤지컬에 대해 들어 봤니?
B  Yes, I did. / No, I didn't. 응. 들어 봤어. / 아니. 못 들어 봤어.

■ 'Did you hear about ~?'은 '~에 대해서 들어 봤니?'라는 의미로 새로운 정보에 대해서 알고 있는지 묻는 표현이다. 비슷한 표현으로 'Do you know (about) ~?', 'Are you aware (of) ~?'와 현재완료를 사용해 'Have you heard about ~?'으로 들어 본 적이 있는지 물을 수도 있다.

- A: Did you hear about the new store on Main Street? Main가에 있는 새 가게에 대해 들어 봤니?
  B: Yes, I did. / No, I didn't. 응. 들어 봤어. / 아니. 못 들어 봤어.

- A: Are you aware that ice cream is from China? 너는 아이스크림이 중국에서 왔다는 것을 알고 있니?
  B: No. That's interesting. 아니. 그거 참 흥미롭구나.

- A: Have you heard about the new waffle shop? 새 와플 가게에 대해 들어 본 적 있니?
  B: Yeah. I saw an ad about it on a poster. 응. 포스터에서 그것에 대한 광고를 봤어.

■ 알고 있음을 표현할 때
- I'm aware of the situation. / I've been told about it. / I've heard about it.

### 핵심 Check

1. 다음 대화의 밑줄 친 ⓐ의 의도로 알맞은 것은?

   G: Hojin, ⓐdid you hear about the speaking contest?
   B: No, I didn't. Where did you hear about it?
   G: From the school newspaper.

   ① 놀람 표현하기      ② 확신하는지 묻기
   ③ 알고 있는지 묻기      ④ 도움이 필요한지 묻기
   ⑤ 대안 묻기

2. 다음 주어진 문장과 같은 의미가 되도록 빈칸에 알맞은 말을 쓰시오.

   Did you hear about the accident?
   = _____ you _____ _____ the accident?

## ② 궁금증 표현하기

> **I'm really curious about it.** 나는 그것에 대해 정말 궁금해.

- 'I'm really curious about ~.'은 '나는 ~에 대해서 정말 궁금해.'라는 의미로 새로운 정보에 대하여 궁금증을 표현하거나 보다 많은 정보를 알고 싶을 때 사용하는 표현이다. 'I'd like to know more about ~.', 'I'm interested in ~, I want to know ~.' 등으로도 표현할 수 있다.

  - The cat was naturally curious about its new surroundings. 그 고양이는 원래 새로운 환경에 호기심이 있었다.
  - We are curious about why you never called us. 우리는 왜 네가 우리에게 전화를 하지 않았는지가 궁금하다.

- '~하고 싶다, 궁금해지다'라는 의미는 'be[become] curious to+동사원형'으로 나타낼 수 있다.

  - They were curious to find out who won the game. 그들은 누가 게임을 이겼는지 알고 싶다.
  - I'm curious to know more about her. 나는 그녀에 관하여 더 알고 싶다.

### 핵심 Check

**3.** 다음 대화의 빈칸에 들어갈 알맞은 것은?

A: Why did you borrow the book about Mars?

B: It's because I'm curious _____ the universe.

① in       ② to       ③ for

④ with       ⑤ about

**4.** 다음 문장과 같은 의미로 사용될 수 있는 것을 <u>모두</u> 고르시오.

I am curious about this movie.

① I'd like to know more about this movie.

② I want to know about this movie.

③ I can tell you about this movie.

④ I don't know much about this movie.

⑤ I'm curious to know more about this movie.

**Conversation** 교과서 대화문 익히기

### Listen and Talk A-1

B: ❶Did you hear about the first spaceship ❷that went into space?

G: No, I didn't. ❸I'm curious about it.

B: This is a poster of the spaceship.

G: Really? I want to buy it.

B: 너는 우주에 간 첫 번째 우주선에 대해 들어 봤니?
G: 아니, 못 들어 봤어. 궁금하다.
B: 이것이 그 우주선 포스터야.
G: 정말? 그것을 사고 싶다.

❶ '~에 대해서 들어 봤니?'라는 의미로 새로운 정보에 대해서 알고 있는지 묻는 표현이다.

❷ that went into space는 주격 관계대명사절로 선행사인 the first spaceship을 꾸며주는 역할을 한다.

❸ 궁금증을 표현하거나 보다 많은 정보를 알고 싶을 때 사용하는 표현이다. 'I'd like to know more about ~.', 'I'm interested in ~, I want to know ~' 등으로 표현할 수도 있다.

**Check(√) True or False**

(1) G didn't know about the first spaceship that went into space.   T ☐ F ☐

(2) G has an interest in the spaceship.   T ☐ F ☐

### Listen and Talk A-2

G: ❶Did you hear about the new book about Mars?

B: No, I didn't. ❷I'm really curious about Mars.

G: Look. It's ❸right here. ❹It's about Mars and its moons.

B: Great. I think I'll buy the book.

G: 너는 화성에 관한 새로운 책에 관해 들어 봤니?
B: 아니, 못 들어 봤어. 나는 화성에 관해 정말 궁금해.
G: 봐. 바로 여기 있어. 그것은 화성과 그것의 위성들에 관한 내용이야.
B: 멋지다. 이 책을 사야겠어.

❶ '~에 대해서 들어 봤니?'라는 의미로 새로운 정보에 대해서 알고 있는지 묻는 표현으로 'Do you know (about) ~?', 'Are you aware (of) ~?' 등으로 바꾸어 쓸 수 있다.

❷ 궁금증을 표현하거나 보다 많은 정보를 알고 싶을 때 사용하는 표현이다. 'I'd like to know more about ~.', 'I'm interested in ~, I want to know ~' 등으로 표현할 수도 있다.

❸ 여기서 right는 부사로 '바로'라는 뜻이다.

❹ be about은 '~에 관한 것이다'로 해석한다.

**Check(√) True or False**

(3) B knew about the book about Mars.   T ☐ F ☐

(4) B is going to buy the book about Mars.   T ☐ F ☐

### Listen and Talk A-3

**G:** ❶Did you hear about the space marathon?
**B:** No, I didn't.
**G:** It's a marathon on a space station. Look at this video.
**B:** OK. ❷I'm really curious about it.

❶ '~에 대해서 들어 봤니?'라는 의미로 새로운 정보에 대해서 알고 있는지 묻는 표현으로 'Do you know (about) ~?', 'Are you aware (of) ~?' 등으로 바꾸어 쓸 수 있다.
❷ 궁금증을 표현하거나 보다 많은 정보를 알고 싶을 때 사용하는 표현이다.

### Listen and Talk A-4

**G:** Did you hear about the new space food?
**B:** Yes, I did. It's ❶a type of ice cream.
**G:** Yes, and ❷here it is. It looks good.
**B:** I'm really curious about the taste.

❶ a type of: ~의 일종
❷ 상대방에게 물건을 건네줄 때 사용하는 표현으로 '여기 있다'는 의미이다.

### Listen and Talk B

**A:** Look at this. ❶Did you hear about the new musical?
**B:** Yes, I did. I heard it has great songs.
**A:** Oh, I'm really curious about it.

❶ Have you heard about the new musical?로 바꾸어 표현할 수 있다.

### Listen and Talk B

**A:** Look at this. Did you hear about the new musical?
**B:** No, I didn't.
**A:** I heard it has great songs.
**B:** Oh, ❶I'm really curious about it.

❶ 'I'd like to know more about it.'으로 바꾸어 표현할 수 있다.

### Listen and Talk C

**B:** Subin, ❶did you hear about the new movie, *Life on the Moon?*
**G:** No, I didn't.
**B:** I heard it's really good.
**G:** ❷I'm really curious about the movie. What's it about?
**B:** It's about a man ❸who is trying to live on the moon.
**G:** ❹That sounds interesting.
**B:** Look. The movie is playing at the Space Theater here.
**G:** What time is the movie?
**B:** It begins at 2:30.
**G:** Let's eat lunch first and then see the movie.
**B:** OK. I'm hungry. Let's go!

❶ are you aware of the new movie로 바꾸어 쓸 수 있다.
❷ 궁금증을 표현하거나 보다 많은 정보를 알고 싶을 때 사용하는 표현이다. I'd like to know more about the movie.로 바꾸어 쓸 수 있다.
❸ who 이하의 문장은 선행사 a man을 수식하는 주격 관계대명사절이다.
❹ 'sound+형용사' 형태로 '그거 재미있겠다.'는 뜻이다.

### Review 1

**G:** Tony, ❶did you hear about the movie, *My Hero*?
**B:** No, I didn't.
**G:** Well, I heard it's really good.
**B:** I'm really curious about the movie. What's it about?
**G:** ❷It's about a father who saves his son.

❶ '~에 대해서 들어 봤니?'라는 의미로 새로운 정보에 대해서 알고 있는지 묻는 표현으로 'Do you know (about) ~?', 'Are you aware (of) ~?' 등으로 바꾸어 쓸 수 있다.
❷ be about은 '~에 관한 것이다'로 해석하고, who saves his son은 선행사 a father를 수식하는 주격 관계대명사절이다.

### Review 2

**G:** Did you hear about the new book, *Living in a Foreign Country*?
**B:** No, I didn't.
**G:** Look. It's right here. ❶It's about living in New York.
**B:** Great. I'm really curious about this book.
**G:** ❷Me, too.

❶ be about은 '~에 관한 것[내용]이다'는 뜻이고, 전치사 about 뒤에 동명사 living 형태를 사용한다.
❷ '나도 그래.'의 뜻으로 So am I.로 바꿔 쓸 수 있다.

● 다음 우리말과 일치하도록 빈칸에 알맞은 말을 쓰시오.

### Listen and Talk A-1

**B:** Did you _____ _____ the first spaceship _____ went into space?

**G:** No, I didn't. I'm _____ _____ it.

**B:** This is a poster of the spaceship.

**G:** Really? I want _____ _____ it.

**B:** 너는 우주에 간 첫 번째 우주선에 대해 들어 봤니?
**G:** 아니, 못 들어 봤어. 궁금하다.
**B:** 이것이 그 우주선 포스터야.
**G:** 정말? 그것을 사고 싶다.

### Listen and Talk A-2

**G:** _____ you _____ _____ the new book about Mars?

**B:** No, I didn't. _____ _____ _____ _____ Mars.

**G:** Look. It's _____ _____. It's _____ Mars and its moons.

**B:** Great. I think I'll buy the book.

**G:** 너는 화성에 관한 새로운 책에 관해 들어 봤니?
**B:** 아니, 못 들어 봤어. 나는 화성에 관해 정말 궁금해.
**G:** 봐. 바로 여기 있어. 그것은 화성과 그것의 위성들에 관한 내용이야.
**B:** 멋지다. 이 책을 사야겠어.

### Listen and Talk A-3

**G:** _____ _____ _____ _____ the space marathon?

**B:** No, _____ _____.

**G:** It's a marathon on a space station. _____ _____ this video.

**B:** OK. _____ _____ _____ _____ it.

**G:** 너는 우주 마라톤에 대해 들어 봤니?
**B:** 아니, 못 들어 봤어.
**G:** 그것은 우주 정거장에서 하는 마라톤이야. 이 비디오를 봐.
**B:** 알겠어. 정말 궁금하다.

### Listen and Talk A-4

**G:** Did you hear _____ the new space food?

**B:** Yes, I did. It's _____ _____ of ice cream.

**G:** Yes, and _____ _____ _____. It looks good.

**B:** I'm really _____ _____ the taste.

**G:** 너는 새로운 우주 음식에 대해 들어 봤니?
**B:** 응, 들어 봤어. 그건 일종의 아이스크림이야.
**G:** 응, 여기 있어. 맛있어 보인다.
**B:** 그 맛이 참 궁금하다.

### Listen and Talk B

1. **A:** Look at this. Did you hear _____ the new musical?

   **B:** Yes, I did. I _____ it has great songs.

   **A:** Oh, I'm really _____ _____ it.

2. **A:** _____ _____ this. Did you _____ _____ the new musical?

   **B:** No, I didn't.

   **A:** I heard _____ _____ _____ _____.

   **B:** Oh, I'm really _____ about it.

1. **A:** 이것 봐. 새 뮤지컬에 대해 들어 봤니?
   **B:** 응, 들어 봤어. 좋은 노래들이 나온다고 들었어.
   **A:** 오, 정말 궁금하다.

2. **A:** 이것 봐. 새 뮤지컬에 대해 들어 봤니?
   **B:** 아니, 못 들어 봤어.
   **A:** 좋은 노래들이 나온다고 들었어.
   **B:** 오, 정말 궁금하다.

## Listen and Talk C

B: Subin, did you hear _____ the new movie, *Life on the Moon*?

G: No, I didn't.

B: I heard it's really _____.

G: I'm really _____ _____ the movie. What's it _____?

B: It's _____ a man _____ is trying _____ _____ on the moon.

G: That sounds _____.

B: Look. The movie _____ _____ at the Space Theater here.

G: _____ _____ is the movie?

B: It _____ at 2:30.

G: _____ eat lunch first _____ _____ see the movie.

B: OK. I'm _____. Let's go!

## Review 1

G: Tony, _____ _____ hear about the movie, *My Hero*?

B: No, I didn't.

G: Well, I _____ it's really good.

B: I'm really _____ about the movie. What's it _____?

G: It's _____ a father _____ saves his son.

## Review 2

G: Did you hear _____ the new book, *Living in a Foreign Country*?

B: No, I didn't.

G: Look. It's _____ here. It's about _____ in New York.

B: Great. I'm really _____ _____ this book.

G: Me, too.

해석

B: 수빈아, "달에서의 생활"이라는 새 영화에 대해서 들어 봤니?
G: 아니.
B: 굉장히 좋다고 들었거든.
G: 그 영화가 정말 궁금하네. 뭐에 관한 거야?
B: 달에서 살기 위해 노력하는 한 남자에 관한 영화래.
G: 그거 재미있겠다.
B: 봐. 그 영화가 여기 우주 극장에서 상영되고 있어.
G: 영화가 몇 시에 상영되는데?
B: 2시 30분에 시작해.
G: 우선 점심부터 먹고 영화를 보자.
B: 좋아. 나 배고파. 가자!

G: Tony, 영화 My Hero에 대해 들어 봤니?
B: 아니, 못 들어 봤어.
G: 음, 정말 좋다고 들었어.
B: 그 영화에 대해 정말 궁금하다. 무엇에 대한 것이니?
G: 그것은 아들을 구하는 아빠에 관한 거야.

G: 새 책인 "Living in a Foreign Country"에 대해 들어 봤니?
B: 아니, 못 들어 봤어.
G: 봐. 바로 여기 있어. 그것은 뉴욕에서의 삶에 관한 거야.
B: 멋지다. 이 책이 정말 궁금해.
G: 나도 그래.

**01** 다음 우리말에 맞도록 빈칸에 들어갈 알맞은 말을 쓰시오.

나는 화성에 관해 정말 궁금해.
➡ I'm really _____ _____ Mars.

**02** 다음 대화의 빈칸에 들어갈 말로 알맞은 것은?

A: _____ the new movie, *My Father*?
B: No, I didn't, but I'm curious about it.

① Are you curious about    ② Why don't we see
③ Tell me about            ④ Did you hear about
⑤ Are you interested in

**03** 다음 대화의 빈칸에 들어갈 말로 알맞은 것은? (2개)

A: What are you looking at?
B: I'm looking at this poster. _____
A: It's Mars.

① I'd like to know where this place is.
② I know where this place is.
③ I want to know where this place is.
④ I have heard where this place is.
⑤ I'm amazed about this place.

**04** 다음 대화의 밑줄 친 우리말에 맞게 문장의 빈칸을 채우시오.

A: 새 영화 New Moon에 대해 들어 봤니?
B: No, I didn't, but I'm really curious about it.

➡ Did you _____ _____ the new movie, *New Moon*?

[01~02] 다음 대화를 읽고 물음에 답하시오.

B: _____(A)_____ the spaceship that went into space?

G: No, I didn't. I _____(B)_____ it.

B: This is a poster of the spaceship.

G: Really? I want to buy it.

**01** 위 대화의 빈칸 (A)에 들어갈 말로 알맞은 것은?

① Have you bought
② Have you seen the poster of
③ What do you think of
④ Did you hear about
⑤ Did you want to know about

**02** 위 대화의 빈칸 (B)에 들어갈 말로 알맞은 것을 <u>모두</u> 고르시오.

① am tired of
② am surprised at
③ am full of
④ am curious about
⑤ want to know about

**03** 다음 대화의 순서를 알맞게 배열한 것은?

(A) OK. I'm really curious about it.

(B) It's a marathon on a space station. Look at this video.

(C) No, I didn't.

(D) Did you hear about the space marathon?

① (A) – (B) – (C) – (D)
② (B) – (A) – (C) – (D)
③ (B) – (C) – (A) – (D)
④ (C) – (B) – (D) – (A)
⑤ (D) – (C) – (B) – (A)

[04~05] 다음 대화를 읽고 물음에 답하시오.

G: Did you hear ___(A)___ the new space food?

B: Yes, I did. It's a type of ice cream.

G: Yes, and (B)여기 있어. It looks good.

B: I'm really curious ___(A)___ the taste.

**04** 위 대화의 빈칸 (A)에 공통으로 들어갈 말로 알맞은 것은?

① with
② about
③ in
④ for
⑤ at

**서답형**

**05** 위 대화의 밑줄 친 (B)의 우리말에 해당하는 표현을 주어진 단어를 포함하여 세 단어로 쓰시오.

➡ _____ (here)

**06** 다음 두 사람의 대화가 <u>어색한</u> 것은?

① A: What are you looking at?
   B: This picture. I want to know who the painter is.

② A: Did you hear about the new movie star, William Black?
   B: No, I didn't, but I'm curious about him.

③ A: Did you hear about the new TV show, *Hip Hop*?
   B: No, I didn't, but I'm curious about it.

④ A: Look at this. Did you hear about the new musical?
   B: No, I didn't. I heard it has great songs.

⑤ A: I'm really curious about the movie. What's it about?
   B: It's about a man who is trying to live on the moon.

**서답형**

**07** 다음 대화의 밑줄 친 우리말에 맞게 주어진 단어를 이용하여 영어로 쓰시오. (어형 변화 필수)

> G: Tony, did you hear about the movie, *My Hero*?
> B: No, I didn't.
> G: Well, I heard it's really good.
> B: I'm really curious about the movie. What's it about?
> G: 그것은 아들을 구하는 아버지에 관한 거야.

> it / about / a father / who / save / son

➡ _____

**중요**

**08** 다음 대화의 밑줄 친 부분의 의도로 알맞은 것은?

> G: Did you hear about the new book about Mars?
> B: No, I didn't. I'm really curious about Mars.

① 알고 있는지 묻기　② 의무 표현하기
③ 확신 표현하기　④ 궁금증 표현하기
⑤ 의견 묻기

[09~10] 다음 대화를 읽고 물음에 답하시오.

> Bin: Subin, ⓐdid you hear about the new movie, *Life on the Moon*?
> Subin: No, I didn't.
> Bin: I heard it's really good.
> Subin: I'm really ⓑcurious about the movie. What's it about?
> Bin: It's about a man ⓒwho are trying to live on the moon.
> Subin: That sounds ⓓinteresting.
> Bin: Look. The movie is playing at the Space Theater here.
> Subin: What time is the movie?
> Bin: It ⓔbegins at 2:30.
> Subin: Let's eat lunch first and then see the movie.

> Bin: OK. I'm hungry. Let's go!

**09** 위 대화의 밑줄 친 ⓐ~ⓔ 중 어법상 어색한 것은?

① ⓐ　② ⓑ　③ ⓒ　④ ⓓ　⑤ ⓔ

**중요**

**10** 위 대화를 읽고 답할 수 없는 질문은?

① What are they talking about?
② Is Subin interested in the new movie?
③ What is the movie, *Life on the Moon*, about?
④ What time does the movie begin?
⑤ What are they going to do after seeing the movie?

[11~12] 다음 대화를 읽고 물음에 답하시오.

> D: Did you hear about the new space food?
> B: _____(A)_____ It's a type of ice cream.
> G: Yes, and here it is. It looks good.
> B: I'm really ___(B)___ about the taste.

**11** 위 대화의 빈칸 (A)에 들어갈 말로 알맞은 것은?

① Yes, I am.　② Yes, I did.
③ No, I don't.　④ No, I haven't.
⑤ Of course not.

**서답형**

**12** 위 대화의 빈칸 (B)에 들어갈 말에 대한 영어 풀이를 보고 주어진 철자로 시작하여 쓰시오.

> wanting to know something, or to learn about the world

➡ c_____

[01~02] 다음 대화를 읽고 물음에 답하시오.

G: (A)새 책인 "Living in a Foreign Country"에 대해 들어 봤니?
B: No, I didn't.
G: Look. It's right here. It's about living in New York.
B: Great. (B)이 책이 정말 궁금해.
G: Me, too.

**01** 위 대화의 밑줄 친 (A)의 우리말에 맞게 주어진 단어를 이용하여 영작하시오.

hear, the new book, *Living in a Foreign Country*

➡ _____

_____

**02** 위 대화의 밑줄 친 (B)의 우리말에 맞게 'curious'와 'really'를 이용하여 영작하시오.

➡ _____

**03** 다음 대화의 빈칸에 들어갈 말로 자연스러운 것을 〈보기〉에서 찾아 문장을 쓰시오.

A: _____ (A)
B: No, I didn't. _____ (B)
A: They are comfortable and not that expensive.
B: Oh, _____ (C)

┤ 보기 ├
• What about them?
• I'm curious about them.
• Did you hear about the new running shoes, *Speed*?

(A) _____
(B) _____
(C) _____

**04** 다음 대화의 밑줄 친 질문에 대한 답을 주어진 단어를 활용하여 조건에 맞게 영작하시오.

G: Tony, did you hear about the movie, *My Hero*?
B: No, I didn't.
G: Well, I heard it's really good.
B: I'm really curious about the movie. (A) What's it about?
G: _____

┤ 조건 ├
• 전치사를 사용할 것
• 관계대명사를 사용할 것
• 현재시제를 사용할 것

(a father, save, his son)

➡ It's _____.

**05** 다음 대화들을 순서대로 배열했을 때, 제일 마지막에 오는 문장을 쓰시오.

(A) I heard it's really good.
(B) Subin, did you hear about the new movie, *Life on the Moon*?
(C) I'm really curious about the movie. What's it about?
(D) It's about a man who is trying to live on the moon.
(E) That sounds interesting.
(F) No, I didn't.

➡ _____

# Grammar

**① 현재완료**

> • I**'ve** never **seen** a blue sky. 전 한 번도 파란 하늘을 본 적이 없어요.
> • **Have** you ever **thought** about becoming a teacher?
> 선생님이 되는 것에 대해 생각해 본 적이 있어요?

■ 현재완료는 'have[has]+과거분사'의 형태로 과거에 시작된 동작과 그 동작의 현재 상태를 동시에 표현한다.

■ 의문문은 'Have[Has]+주어+과거분사 ~?'이며, 부정문은 'have[has]+not[never]+과거분사'로 나타낸다.

  • I **haven't smoked** for ten years. 나는 10년 동안 담배를 안 피우고 있어요.
  • **Have** you **done** your homework already? 숙제를 벌써 했니?

■ 현재완료는 '계속(~해 왔다), 경험(~한 적이 있다), 완료(막[벌써] ~했다), 결과(~해 버렸다)'의 네 가지 용법으로 쓰인다. 계속적 용법은 보통 'for(~ 동안)+기간 명사'나 'since(~부터, ~ 이래로)+시간 명사'와 함께 쓰이며, 경험은 'once(한 번), twice(두 번), three times(세 번), ever(이제껏), never(한 번도 ~않다), before(전에)' 등과 같은 부사(구)와 쓰인다. 완료 용법은 보통 'already(이미, 벌써), just(막, 방금), yet(아직, 벌써)' 등과 같은 부사와 쓰이고, 결과 용법은 과거에 발생한 사건이 현재 미치고 있는 결과를 포함한다.

  • Mary **has studied** French for 5 years. 〈계속〉 Mary는 5년 동안 불어를 공부해 오고 있다.
  • I **have** never **heard** such a sad story. 〈경험〉 나는 그런 슬픈 이야기를 들어 본 적이 없다.
  • He **has** already **spent** all his money. 〈완료〉 그는 이미 자신의 돈을 다 써버렸다.
  • The girl **has lost** her dog at the park. 〈결과〉
    그 소녀는 공원에서 그녀의 개를 잃어버렸다. (그 결과 (그녀의 개가) 지금 없다.)

■ 현재완료는 과거에 시작된 동작과 그 동작의 현재 상태를 동시에 표현하므로 명백한 과거를 나타내는 yesterday, ~ ago, last week 등의 부사(구)나 의문사 when과는 함께 쓰이지 않는다.

  • He wasn't present at the meeting last week. (○)

    He hasn't been present at the meeting last week. (✕) 그는 지난 주 모임에 참석하지 않았다.

  ※ have[has] been to vs. have[has] gone to
    have[has] been to는 '~에 가 본 적이 있다'는 경험을 나타내고, have[has] gone to는 '~에 가고 없다'는 결과를 나타낸다. 그러므로 have[has] gone to는 3인칭만 주어로 쓸 수 있다.

**핵심 Check**

**1.** 다음 주어진 동사를 빈칸에 어법에 맞게 쓰시오.

(1) He _____ _____ English for ten years. (study)

(2) I have not _____ from her for six years. (hear)

(3) _____ you _____ a famous person before? (meet)

## ② It ~ to부정사

> - **It**'s difficult **to walk** on Earth. 지구에서는 걷는 것이 어려워요.
> - **It** is good **to know** how to say hello. 인사하는 법을 아는 것이 좋다.

■ 비교적 긴 to부정사 부분이 문장의 주어로 쓰일 때 그 to부정사 부분을 일반적인 주어의 자리인 문장의 맨 앞에 두지 않고 문장 제일 뒤에 둔다. 대신 주어 자리에는 it을 넣어주는데 그것을 가주어 it이라고 부르고 문장 뒤로 간 to부정사 부분은 진주어라고 부른다. 이때 쓰인 it은 가주어이므로 구체적인 뜻이 없으며, '…하는 것은 ~하다'로 해석한다.

- **It** is easy **to play** the piano. 피아노를 치는 것은 쉽다.
  = **To play** the piano is easy.

- **It** is interesting **to watch** birds. 조류 관찰은 재미있다.
  = **To watch** birds is interesting.

■ It ~ to부정사의 의미상 주어
to부정사의 동작을 실제로 하는 사람을 to부정사의 의미상 주어라고 한다. to부정사의 의미상 주어는 to부정사 바로 앞에 'for+명사의 목적격'의 형태로 쓴다. It ~ to부정사 구문에서 to부정사의 의미상 주어가 없는 경우는 특별한 사람이 아니라 일반적인 사람이기 때문이다. 문장에 쓰인 형용사가 nice, kind, smart, wise 등과 같이 사람의 성향, 성격을 나타내는 말일 때는 'of+목적격'을 쓴다. 또한 to부정사의 부정은 to부정사 앞에 not[never]을 써서 'not[never]+to V'로 나타내며 '…하지 않는 것은 ~하다'로 해석한다.

- **It** is important for you **to choose** good friends. 네가 좋은 친구를 고르는 것은 중요하다.

- **It** is nice of you **to show** me the way. 길을 가르쳐 주셔서 감사합니다.

- **It** is easy **not to think** outside the box. 새로운 사고를 하지 않는 것은 쉽다.

### 핵심 Check

**2.** 다음 우리말과 일치하도록 빈칸에 알맞은 말을 쓰시오.

(1) 운동을 하는 것이 왜 중요할까요?

➡ Why _____ _____ _____ _____ exercise?

(2) 구명 조끼를 입는 것이 안전하다.

➡ _____ is safe _____ wear a life jacket.

(3) 내가 피아노를 치는 것은 쉽다.

➡ It's easy _____ _____ _____ _____ the piano.

**Grammar** 시험대비 기본평가

**01** 다음 빈칸에 알맞은 것을 고르시오.

> **A:** Isn't it good _____ with friends?
> **B:** Yes, of course.

① to travel in Korea
② travels in Korea
③ to traveling in Korea
④ of you to travel in Korea
⑤ your travel in Korea

**02** 다음 중 어법상 어색한 문장은?

① Have you ever seen a koala?
② The plane has just left for Seoul.
③ I have gone to Hong Kong.
④ Marianne has played the piano for 10 years.
⑤ I have already washed my hands.

**03** 다음 문장에서 어법상 어색한 부분을 바르게 고치시오.

(1) My parents have just return from the trip.

_____ ➡ _____

(2) Rada has eaten dinner with Jonny last weekend.

_____ ➡ _____

(3) How long do you have been in Canada?

_____ ➡ _____

(4) They've worked here for last year.

_____ ➡ _____

(5) That is nervous to sing in front of the class.

_____ ➡ _____

(6) It will be helpful reads the book.

_____ ➡ _____

**01** 다음 중 어법상 바르지 <u>않은</u> 것은?

① Emily has caught a big fish and she is very excited.
② I've never heard her use bad language before.
③ They have lived in that house for more than 20 years.
④ When have you watched the new movie?
⑤ Hermionne has gone back to her country already.

**02** 다음 중 어법상 바른 것은?

① It isn't easy studies English every day.
② It is so kind for you to lend me the book.
③ That's necessary to wear a helmet.
④ It's better run your own business if you can.
⑤ It has become common practice to chat online.

**03** 다음 빈칸에 알맞은 말이 바르게 짝지어진 것은?

• _____ the team won ten games this year?
• It was hard _____ a science experiment.

① Is – to do          ② Is – done
③ Has – to do        ④ Has – done
⑤ Was – doing

**04** 다음 문장의 빈칸에 들어갈 알맞은 것은?

| _____ is easy to play musical instruments. |

① It          ② This          ③ That
④ What       ⑤ One

**05** 다음 대화의 빈칸에 들어갈 말로 알맞은 것은?

M: Where's your homework, Peter?
W: I'm sorry, but I have not finished it _____.

① just        ② already        ③ yet
④ for         ⑤ since

서답형
**06** 다음 괄호 안에서 알맞은 말을 고르시오.

(1) Alex (have / has) decided to visit an art museum in London.
(2) I (don't have / haven't) seen David today.
(3) Jane is not here now. She has (been / gone) to Stockholm to find work.
(4) Bella (has been / went) to the United States in 2011.
(5) It is always exciting (sleeps / to sleep) in a tent.
(6) It is impossible (of / for) them to get lost.

**07** 다음 중 어법상 옳은 것은?

① Angie has bought a new smartphone yesterday.
② Have she told you the good news yet?
③ I have gone to England once.
④ I have already seen the movie.
⑤ I've been learning English since ten years.

**중요**

**08** 다음 중 밑줄 친 부분의 쓰임이 다른 하나는?

① It is impossible to live without air and water.
② It was not accepted in old days.
③ It's important for the students to do the project in three days.
④ It is dangerous to be in the street after dark.
⑤ It is better to be safe than sorry.

**09** 다음 질문에 대한 응답으로 알맞은 것은?

Has he had any serious problems with ear in the past?

① Yes, he has.　② Yes, he is.
③ Yes, he does.　④ No, he isn't.
⑤ No, he doesn't.

**서답형**

**10** 주어진 어휘를 이용하여 다음 우리말을 영작하시오.

규칙적으로 휴식을 취할 필요가 있다.
(it, a break, regularly, take, necessary, to)

➡ _____

**11** 다음 두 문장을 한 문장으로 바르게 연결한 것은?

• Jack went back to his home.
• And he is not here now.

① Jack went to his home.
② Jack went to his home already.
③ Jack hasn't been to his home.
④ Jack hasn't come back to his home yet.
⑤ Jack has gone to his home.

**중요**

**12** 다음 우리말과 일치하도록 빈칸에 알맞은 단어로 묶은 것은?

비행기를 조종하는 것은 내 꿈 중 한 가지이다.
➡ _____ is a dream of mine _____ an airplane.

① It – fly　② It – to fly
③ That – fly　④ That – to fly
⑤ This – flying

**13** 다음 〈보기〉의 밑줄 친 부분과 용법이 같은 것은?

보기

He has worked for the company for more than 10 years.

① My mom has been sick since last week.
② She has gone to Japan.
③ Judy has been to America five times.
④ Kevin has already heard about the party at school.
⑤ Megan has lost her wallet on the train.

**서답형**

## 14 다음 문장에서 어법상 어색한 것을 바르게 고쳐 다시 쓰시오.

(1) It is difficult for me guess the ending of the story.

➡ _____

(2) This is boring to read a science book.

➡ _____

(3) It is important read for an hour every day.

➡ _____

(4) I have worked in the hospital snack bar then.

➡ _____

(5) Jim has had a cat since three years.

➡ _____

(6) Garry has been to New York on business and he stays there now.

➡ _____

**서답형**

## 15 다음 두 문장을 비슷한 뜻을 가진 한 문장으로 바꿔 쓰시오.

(1) Josh lost his smartphone. So, he doesn't have any smartphone now.

➡ _____

(2) Sophia started to live in Georgia five years ago. And she still lives there.

➡ _____

## [16~17] 다음 우리말에 맞게 영작한 것을 고르시오.

## 16
> 너는 작년 이후로 아주 키가 컸다.

① You grew very tall since last year.
② You have grown very tall last year.
③ You have grown very tall for last year.
④ You have grown very tall as last year.
⑤ You have grown very tall since last year.

## 17
> 기말고사 후에 친구들과 어울리는 것은 정말 신이 나.

① It is very exciting hang out with my friends after finals.
② It is very exciting hangs out with my friends after finals.
③ It is very exciting to hang out with my friends after finals.
④ That is very exciting to hang out with my friends after finals.
⑤ That is very exciting hanging out with my friends after finals.

## 18 다음 중 어법상 어색한 것을 고르시오. (2개)

① It is necessary for Daniel to talk to his parents.
② It's nice for her to take care of her young sister.
③ It is fun to swim in the lake.
④ When have you watched the movie with her?
⑤ We have lived here since I was born.

**01** 다음 우리말에 맞게 주어진 어구를 바르게 배열하시오.

(1) Kelly는 10살 이후로 LA에서 살고 있다.
(Kelly, she, years, LA, has, was, lived, 10, old, since, in)

➡ _____

(2) 정부는 교육에 더 관심을 가지게 되었다.
(education, the government, interested, become, has, more, in)

➡ _____
_____

(3) 그는 그 소문에 대해 들은 적이 있어.
(the rumor, heard, he, has, about)

➡ _____

(4) 다른 나라들을 여행하는 것은 멋지다.
(countries, it, wonderful, travel, is, other, to, to)

➡ _____

(5) 그가 그 경기의 표를 구하는 것이 가능하니?
(the game, it, tickets, him, possible, get, is, for, for, to)

➡ _____

**02** 다음 우리말을 (1) to부정사 주어를 써서, (2) 가주어를 써서 영작하시오.

• 밤에 운전하는 것은 위험하다.
(1) _____
(2) _____

• 물건을 훔치는 것은 잘못이다.
(1) _____
(2) _____

**03** 그림을 보고, 주어진 어휘를 이용하여 자신의 경험에 대해 쓰시오. (현재완료 시제로 주어와 동사를 갖춘 완전한 문장으로 쓸 것.)

(1) (eat, nacho)

➡ _____
_____

(2) (have, to)

➡ _____
_____

**04** 다음 주어진 두 문장을 한 문장으로 바꿔 쓰시오.

(1) • Sonya visited New York again.
• It is her third visit.

➡ _____

(2) • I ate dinner a moment ago.
• So I am full now.

➡ _____

**05** 다음 문장을 It으로 시작하여 다시 쓰시오.

(1) To think about all the new things was exciting.

➡ _____

(2) To swim in the cool blue sea was great.

➡ _____

(3) To eat a lot of vegetables is good.

➡ _____

(4) That the pen is mightier than the sword is true.

➡ _____

**06** 다음 우리말을 괄호 안에 주어진 어휘를 이용하여 영작하시오.

(1) 나는 한 번도 일출을 본 적이 없다.
    (a sunrise, see, never, 6 단어)

➡ _____

(2) 그는 영어를 20년 동안 가르쳐 왔다.
    (teach, 7 단어)

➡ _____

(3) 이 물을 마셔도 안전한가요?
    (this water, safe, drink, 7 단어)

➡ _____

(4) 내가 그 팀에서 축구를 하게 되어 운이 좋다.
    (the team, lucky, me, 10 단어)

➡ _____

(5) 이를 매일 닦는 것은 중요하다.
    (brush your teeth, important, 9 단어)

➡ _____

**07** 다음 문장에서 어법상 어색한 것을 고쳐 문장을 다시 쓰시오.

(1) When have you heard from Susan?

➡ _____

(2) Mr. Brown has lived in Jeju-do for 2010.

➡ _____

(3) Have you gone to Canada before?

➡ _____

(4) Use a ticket machine in the theater is easy.

➡ _____

(5) It's important for her understands him.

➡ _____

**08** 다음 문장을 부정문과 의문문으로 각각 바꿔 쓰시오.

> They have already finished their project.

부정문 _____

의문문 _____

**09** 다음 두 문장의 의미가 같도록 빈칸에 알맞은 말을 쓰시오.

(1) It started raining last Saturday. It is still raining.

➡ It _____ last Saturday.

(2) Aiko went back to Tokyo. She is in Tokyo now.

➡ Aiko _____ to Tokyo.

## The Best New Thing

Rada lived on a little world, far out in space. She lived there with
　　　　　　　　　　　　　　　　　　멀리　　　우주에서
her father, mother, and brother Jonny. Rada's father and other people
worked on spaceships. Only Rada and Jonny were children, and they
우주선에서 일했다
were born in space. One day, Dad told Rada and Jonny, "We're going
태어났다　　　(과거의) 어느 날.　　　　are going: 현재진행의 의미가 아니라 가까운 미래를 나타냄
back to Earth tomorrow." Rada and Jonny looked at Dad in surprise
돌아가다　　　　　　　　　　　　　　　　　　　　　　　놀라서
and floated towards him. Rada asked Dad, "What's it like on Earth?"

"Everything is different there. For example, the sky is blue," answered
　　　　　　　　　　= on Earth  인용문을 먼저 쓰고 '~가 말했다'를 뒤에 쓸 때: 주어와 동사의 순서를 바꾸어 쓸 수 있음
Dad. "I've never seen a blue sky," said Jonny. "The sky is always black
현재완료(경험). never: have와 과거분사 사이에 not 대신에 부정의 의미를 강조　　　　빈도부사: be동사 뒤에 위치.
here," said Rada. "You don't have to wear your big heavy space suits
　　　　　　　　　　　　　~할 필요가 없다
because there is air everywhere. It's also hard to jump there because
　　　　　　　　　　　　　　　It은 가주어로서 진주어인 to jump there를 대신한다.
Earth pulls you down," said Dad. "What else?" asked Rada. "There are
너를 끌어당긴다　　　　　　　　　　그 밖에
hills, and they are covered with soft green grass. You can roll down the
　　　　　= hills.　　~으로 뒤덮여 있다
hills," answered Mom. "Dad, have you ever rolled down a hill?" asked
　　　　　　　　　　　　　　　　현재완료(경험)　　　roll down: 굴러 내려가다
Rada. "Yes, it's really amazing!" answered Dad. Jonny was thirsty, so
　　　　　　　　　　　　　　　　　　　　　　　　　　결과를 나타내는 접속사.
he opened a milk container and shook it. The milk floated in the air and
　　　　　　　　　　　　　　　　　a milk container
formed balls. Jonny swallowed the balls. "Jonny, if you drink milk that
　　　　　　　　　　　　　　　　　　'우유를 먹기 위해 우유 용기를 열어 흔들어서 우유 방울을 만들어 먹는 것'
way on Earth, you'll get wet," said Mom.
젖다

be born 태어나다
in surprise 놀라서
towards ~을 향하여, ~ 쪽으로
space suit 우주복
pull down ~을 끌어내리다
be covered with ~으로 덮여 있다
ever 언젠가, 줄곧
container 그릇, 용기
swallow 삼키다

---

✐ **확인문제**

● 다음 문장이 본문의 내용과 일치하면 T, 일치하지 않으면 F를 쓰시오.

1  Rada and Jonny were born in space. ☐

2  The sky is always black in space. ☐

3  You don't have to wear your big heavy space suits because Earth pulls you down. ☐

4  You can roll down the hills which are covered with soft green grass. ☐

Later that night, Rada and Jonny talked a long time about Earth. It
늦게 =for a long time: 오랫동안 It: 가주어
was exciting to think about all the new things they were going to see
진주어 things와 they 사이에 목적격 관계대명사 which/that이 생략
and do. There was one new thing Rada and Jonny really wanted to do.
thing과 Rada 사이에 목적격 관계대명사 which/that이 생략
They thought about it all night and didn't tell Mom and Dad about it. It
one new thing
was their secret. The next day, Rada's family got on a spaceship. "It's
(교통수단을) 타다
going to be a long trip," said Mom. "That's alright. I'm so excited!"
going to+동사원형: 미래의 구체적인 계획을 통해 곧 일어날 것이라고 판단할 수 있는 일에 사용  = all right  excited는 과거분사지만 완전히 형용사화되어 so로 수식할 수 있음.
said Rada. The spaceship finally landed. "Dad, it's difficult to walk
가주어 진주어
on Earth," said Rada. "I know. Earth is pulling you down," said Dad.
pull down: 끌어당기다. 지구에 중력이 있음을 의미
Rada and Jonny couldn't float anymore. That was the first new thing.
우주에서는 공중에 떠다녔지만, 지구에서는 중력 때문에 더 이상 떠다닐 수 없음을 의미. 앞 문장 전체
"What's that sound?" asked Rada. "A bird is singing," said Mom. "I've
be동사 현재형+-ing: 현재진행형, 현재 하고 있는 동작을 나타낸다.
never heard a bird sing," said Rada. "And I've never felt the wind,"
현재완료(경험), '결코 들어 본 적이 없다' 지각동사 hear+목적어+동사원형/-ing  현재완료(경험), '바람을 한 번도 느껴 본 적이 없다'
said Jonny. These were all new things. Rada and Jonny ran up the
near의 최상급, '가장 가까운'
nearest hill. At the top, they looked at each other and laughed. Then
laughed 앞에 주어인 they가 중복되어 생략
they lay down on the soft green grass and rolled down the hill. That
다)의 과거형. lie-lay-lain / lay-laid-laid: 놓다, 눕히다
was their secret! "This is the best new thing of all!" shouted Rada and
good의 최상급
Jonny. And they ran up to the top of the hill again.
~으로 뛰어 올라갔다

secret 비밀

all night 밤새도록

get on ~에 타다. ~에 오르다

each other 서로

lie 눕다

---

📎 **확인문제**

● 다음 문장이 본문의 내용과 일치하면 T, 일치하지 <u>않으면</u> F를 쓰시오.

1  It was exciting for Rada and Jonny to think about all the new things they were
   going to see and do on Earth. ☐

2  Rada and Jonny thought about one new thing they really wanted to do on Earth and
   told Mom and Dad about it. ☐

3  Rada has ever heard a bird sing. ☐

4  Rada and Jonny's secret was to lie down on the grass and roll down the hill. ☐

● 우리말을 참고하여 빈칸에 알맞은 말을 쓰시오.

**1** The _____ New Thing

**2** Rada lived on a little world, _____ _____ _____.

**3** She _____ _____ _____ her father, mother, and brother Jonny.

**4** Rada's father and other people _____ _____ spaceships.

**5** _____ Rada and Jonny were children, and they _____ _____ in space.

**6** One day, Dad told Rada and Jonny, "We're _____ _____ _____ Earth tomorrow."

**7** Rada and Jonny looked at Dad _____ _____ and floated towards him.

**8** Rada asked Dad, "_____ _____ _____ on Earth?"

**9** "Everything _____ _____ there.

**10** _____ _____, the sky is blue," answered Dad.

**11** "_____ _____ _____ a blue sky," said Jonny.

**12** "The sky _____ _____ _____ here," said Rada.

**13** "You _____ _____ _____ wear your big heavy space suits because _____ _____ _____ everywhere.

**14** It's also hard to jump there because Earth _____ _____ _____," said Dad.

**15** "_____ _____?" asked Rada.

**16** "There are hills, and they _____ _____ _____ soft green grass.

**17** You can _____ _____ the hills," answered Mom.

**18** "Dad, _____ _____ _____ _____ _____ a hill?" asked Rada.

**19** "Yes, it's really _____!" answered Dad.

**20** Jonny was thirsty, so he _____ a milk container and _____ it.

**21** The milk _____ in the air and _____ balls.

**22** Jonny _____ the balls.

**23** "Jonny, if you drink milk that way on Earth, you'll _____ _____," said Mom.

---

**1** 최고의 새로운 것

**2** Rada는 먼 우주의 작은 세계에 살고 있었다.

**3** 그녀는 아빠, 엄마 그리고 남동생 Jonny와 함께 그곳에서 살고 있었다.

**4** Rada의 아빠와 다른 사람들은 우주선에서 일했다.

**5** Rada와 Jonny만이 아이들이었고, 그들은 우주에서 태어났다.

**6** 어느 날, 아빠가 Rada와 Jonny에게, "우리는 내일 지구로 돌아갈 거야."라고 말했다.

**7** Rada와 Jonny는 깜짝 놀라 아빠를 바라보았고, 그에게 둥둥 떠서 갔다.

**8** Rada가 아빠에게, "지구는 어떤 곳인가요?"라고 물었다.

**9** "그곳에선 모든 것이 다르단다.

**10** 예를 들어, 하늘은 파란색이지."라고 아빠가 대답했다.

**11** "전 한 번도 파란 하늘을 본 적이 없어요."라고 Jonny가 말했다.

**12** "여기는 하늘이 항상 검은색이잖아요."라고 Rada가 말했다.

**13** "그곳에는 모든 곳에 공기가 있기 때문에 크고 무거운 우주복을 입을 필요가 없단다.

**14** 또한 지구가 너희들을 끌어당기기 때문에 거기에서는 점프하는 것도 어렵단다." 아빠가 말했다.

**15** "그 밖에 또 뭐가 있어요?" Rada가 물었다.

**16** "언덕들이 있는데 그것들은 부드러운 초록색의 잔디로 뒤덮여 있단다.

**17** 언덕을 굴러 내려갈 수도 있어." 엄마가 대답했다.

**18** "아빠, 언덕을 굴러 내려가 본 적 있어요?" Rada가 물었다.

**19** "그럼, 정말 놀라워!" 아빠가 대답했다.

**20** Jonny는 목이 말라서 우유 용기를 열어 그것을 흔들었다.

**21** 우유가 공기 중으로 떠서 방울을 형성했다.

**22** Jonny는 그 우유 방울을 삼켰다.

**23** "Jonny, 만약 네가 지구에서 그런 식으로 우유를 마신다면, 다 젖을 거야." 엄마가 말했다.

**24** _____ _____ _____, Rada and Jonny talked a long time about Earth.

**25** It was _____ to think about _____ _____ _____ they were going to see and do.

**26** There was _____ _____ _____ Rada and Jonny really wanted to do.

**27** They thought about it _____ _____ and didn't tell Mom and Dad about it.

**28** It was _____ _____.

**29** The next day, Rada's family _____ _____ a spaceship.

**30** "_____ _____ _____ _____ a long trip," said Mom.

**31** "That's alright. I'm _____ _____!" said Rada.

**32** The spaceship _____ landed.

**33** "Dad, it's difficult _____ _____ on Earth," said Rada.

**34** "I know. Earth is _____ _____ _____," said Dad.

**35** Rada and Jonny _____ _____ _____.

**36** That was _____ _____ _____ _____.

**37** "_____ that sound?" asked Rada.

**38** "A bird _____ _____," said Mom.

**39** "_____ _____ _____ a bird sing," said Rada.

**40** "And _____ _____ _____ the wind," said Jonny.

**41** _____ were all new things.

**42** Rada and Jonny ran up _____ _____ hill.

**43** At the top, they looked at _____ _____ and laughed.

**44** Then they _____ _____ on the soft green grass and _____ _____ the hill.

**45** That was _____ _____!

**46** "This is the _____ _____ _____ of all!" shouted Rada and Jonny.

**47** And they ran _____ _____ _____ _____ of the hill again.

---

**24** 그날 밤 늦게, Rada와 Jonny는 지구에 대해서 오랜 시간 이야기했다.

**25** 그들이 보고, 하게 될 모든 새로운 것들을 생각하는 것은 흥미로웠다.

**26** Rada와 Jonny가 정말로 하고 싶었던 한 가지 새로운 것이 있었다.

**27** 그들은 밤새 그것에 대해서 생각했고 엄마와 아빠에게는 그것을 말하지 않았다.

**28** 그것은 그들의 비밀이었다.

**29** 다음날, Rada의 가족은 우주선에 올랐다.

**30** "긴 여행이 될 거야." 엄마가 말했다.

**31** "괜찮아요. 정말 신나요!" Rada가 말했다.

**32** 우주선이 마침내 착륙했다.

**33** "아빠, 지구에서는 걷는 것이 어려워요." Rada가 말했다.

**34** "그래. 지구가 너를 끌어당기고 있거든." 아빠가 말했다.

**35** Rada와 Jonny는 더 이상 떠다닐 수 없었다.

**36** 그것이 첫 번째 새로운 것이었다.

**37** "저건 무슨 소리죠?"라고 Rada가 물었다.

**38** "새가 노래하는 거야." 엄마가 말했다.

**39** "새가 노래하는 것을 들어 본 적이 없어요."라고 Rada가 말했다.

**40** "그리고 저는 바람을 느껴 본 적도 없어요."라고 Jonny가 말했다.

**41** 이러한 것들이 모두 새로운 것들이었다.

**42** Rada와 Jonny는 가장 가까운 언덕으로 뛰어 올라갔다.

**43** 꼭대기에서, 그들은 서로를 쳐다보고 웃었다.

**44** 그리고 나서 그들은 부드러운 초록 잔디에 누워서 언덕 아래로 굴러 내려갔다.

**45** 그것이 그들의 비밀이었다!

**46** "이것이 모든 것들 중에서 최고의 새로운 것이에요!" Rada와 Jonny는 외쳤다.

**47** 그리고 그들은 언덕 꼭대기로 다시 뛰어 올라갔다.

● 우리말을 참고하여 본문을 영작하시오.

**1** 최고의 새로운 것
➡ _____

**2** Rada는 먼 우주의 작은 세계에 살고 있었다.
➡ _____

**3** 그녀는 아빠, 엄마 그리고 남동생 Jonny와 함께 그곳에서 살고 있었다.
➡ _____

**4** Rada의 아빠와 다른 사람들은 우주선에서 일했다.
➡ _____

**5** Rada와 Jonny만이 아이들이었고, 그들은 우주에서 태어났다.
➡ _____

**6** 어느 날, 아빠가 Rada와 Jonny에게, "우리는 내일 지구로 돌아갈 거야."라고 말했다.
➡ _____

**7** Rada와 Jonny는 깜짝 놀라 아빠를 바라보았고, 그에게 둥둥 떠서 갔다.
➡ _____

**8** Rada가 아빠에게, "지구는 어떤 곳인가요?"라고 물었다.
➡ _____

**9** "그곳에선 모든 것이 다르단다.
➡ _____

**10** 예를 들어, 하늘은 파란색이지."라고 아빠가 대답했다.
➡ _____

**11** "전 한 번도 파란 하늘을 본 적이 없어요."라고 Jonny가 말했다.
➡ _____

**12** "여기는 하늘이 항상 검은색이잖아요."라고 Rada가 말했다.
➡ _____

**13** "그곳에는 모든 곳에 공기가 있기 때문에 크고 무거운 우주복을 입을 필요가 없단다.
➡ _____

**14** 또한 지구가 너희들을 끌어당기기 때문에 거기에서는 점프하는 것도 어렵단다." 아빠가 말했다.
➡ _____

**15** "그 밖에 또 뭐가 있어요?" Rada가 물었다.
➡ _____

**16** "언덕들이 있는데 그것들은 부드러운 초록색의 잔디로 뒤덮여 있단다.
➡ _____

**17** 언덕을 굴러 내려갈 수도 있어." 엄마가 대답했다.
➡ _____

**18** "아빠, 언덕을 굴러 내려가 본 적 있어요?" Rada가 물었다.
➡ _____

**19** "그럼, 정말 놀라워!" 아빠가 대답했다.
➡ _____

**20** Jonny는 목이 말라서 우유 용기를 열어 그것을 흔들었다.
➡ _____

**21** 우유가 공기 중으로 떠서 방울을 형성했다.
➡ _____

**22** Jonny는 그 우유 방울을 삼켰다.
➡ _____

**23** "Jonny, 만약 네가 지구에서 그런 식으로 우유를 마신다면, 다 젖을 거야." 엄마가 말했다.
➡ _____

**24** 그날 밤 늦게, Rada와 Jonny는 지구에 대해서 오랜 시간 이야기했다.
➡ _____

**25** 그들이 보고, 하게 될 모든 새로운 것들을 생각하는 것은 흥미로웠다.
➡ _____

**26** Rada와 Jonny가 정말로 하고 싶었던 한 가지 새로운 것이 있었다.
➡ _____

**27** 그들은 밤새 그것에 대해서 생각했고 엄마와 아빠에게는 그것을 말하지 않았다.
➡ _____

**28** 그것은 그들의 비밀이었다.
➡ _____

**29** 다음날, Rada의 가족은 우주선에 올랐다.
➡ _____

**30** "긴 여행이 될 거야." 엄마가 말했다.
➡ _____

**31** "괜찮아요. 정말 신나요!" Rada가 말했다.
➡ _____

**32** 우주선이 마침내 착륙했다.
➡ _____

**33** "아빠, 지구에서는 걷는 것이 어려워요." Rada가 말했다.
➡ _____

**34** "그래. 지구가 너를 끌어당기고 있거든." 아빠가 말했다.
➡ _____

**35** Rada와 Jonny는 더 이상 떠다닐 수 없었다.
➡ _____

**36** 그것이 첫 번째 새로운 것이었다.
➡ _____

**37** "저건 무슨 소리죠?"라고 Rada가 물었다.
➡ _____

**38** "새가 노래하는 거야." 엄마가 말했다.
➡ _____

**39** "새가 노래하는 것을 들어 본 적이 없어요."라고 Rada가 말했다.
➡ _____

**40** "그리고 저는 바람을 느껴 본 적도 없어요."라고 Jonny가 말했다.
➡ _____

**41** 이러한 것들이 모두 새로운 것들이었다.
➡ _____

**42** Rada와 Jonny는 가장 가까운 언덕으로 뛰어 올라갔다.
➡ _____

**43** 꼭대기에서, 그들은 서로를 쳐다보고 웃었다.
➡ _____

**44** 그러고 나서 그들은 부드러운 초록 잔디에 누워서 언덕 아래로 굴러 내려갔다.
➡ _____

**45** 그것이 그들의 비밀이었다!
➡ _____

**46** "이것이 모든 것들 중에서 최고의 새로운 것이에요!" Rada와 Jonny는 외쳤다.
➡ _____

**47** 그리고 그들은 언덕 꼭대기로 다시 뛰어 올라갔다.
➡ _____

[01~04] 다음 글을 읽고 물음에 답하시오.

Rada lived on a little world, far out ⓐ_____ space. She lived there with her father, mother, and brother Jonny. Rada's father and other people worked on spaceships. Only Rada and Jonny were children, and they were born in space.

One day, Dad told Rada and Jonny, "We're going back to Earth tomorrow."

Rada and Jonny looked at Dad in surprise and floated towards him.

Rada asked Dad, "What's (A)it like ⓑ_____ Earth?"

"Everything is different there. For example, the sky is blue," answered Dad.

"I've never seen a blue sky," said Jonny.

"The sky is always black here," said Rada.

**01** 위 글의 빈칸 ⓐ와 ⓑ에 들어갈 전치사가 바르게 짝지어진 것은?

① for – to
② in – for
③ in – on
④ from – to
⑤ for – on

**02** 위 글의 밑줄 친 (A)it과 문법적 쓰임이 같은 것을 모두 고르시오.

① I think it strange that she wants them.
② How's it going with you?
③ It was wine, not water, that you drank.
④ It is impossible to get there in time.
⑤ As it happened, I left the book at home.

**03** 위 글의 종류로 알맞은 것을 고르시오.

① book report
② article
③ biography
④ essay
⑤ science fiction

**04** 위 글의 내용과 일치하지 않는 것은?

① Rada lived far out in space with her family.
② Rada and Jonny were born in space.
③ When Rada and Jonny heard they were returning to space, they were surprised.
④ Dad said everything was different on Earth.
⑤ The sky was always black in space.

[05~08] 다음 글을 읽고 물음에 답하시오.

"You don't have to wear your big heavy space suits because there is air everywhere. It's also hard to jump there because Earth pulls you down," said Dad.

"What else?" asked Rada.

"There are hills, and they are covered with soft green grass. You can roll down the hills," answered Mom.

"Dad, ⓐhave you ever rolled down a hill?" asked Rada.

"Yes, it's really amazing!" answered Dad.

Jonny was thirsty, so he opened a milk container and _____(A)_____ it. The milk floated in the air and formed balls. Jonny swallowed the balls.

"Jonny, ⓑ만약 네가 지구에서 그런 식으로 우유를 마신다면, 다 젖을 거야," said Mom.

**서답형**

**05** 위 글의 빈칸 (A)에 shake를 알맞은 형태로 쓰시오.

➡ _____

**06** 아래 〈보기〉에서 위 글의 밑줄 친 ⓐ의 현재완료와 용법이 같은 것의 개수를 고르시오.

① He has lost his pen.
② We have visited Paris before.
③ I have learned English since 2015.
④ She hasn't cleaned her room yet.
⑤ How many times have you seen it?

① 1개　② 2개　③ 3개　④ 4개　⑤ 5개

**서답형**

**07** 위 글의 밑줄 친 ⓑ의 우리말에 맞게 주어진 어휘를 이용하여 11 단어로 영작하시오.

drink, that way, get wet

➡ _____

**중요**

**08** 다음 중 Rada와 Jonny가 지구에서 처음 경험하게 될 일이 아닌 것을 고르시오.

① 우주복을 입을 필요가 없는 것
② 점프를 쉽게 할 수 있는 것
③ 부드러운 초록색의 잔디로 뒤덮여 있는 언덕을 보는 것
④ 언덕을 굴러 내려가는 것
⑤ 우유 방울을 삼키는 대신 마시는 것

[09~11] 다음 글을 읽고 물음에 답하시오.

Later that night, Rada and Jonny talked a long time about Earth. ⓐIt was (A)[exciting / excited] to think about all the new things they were going to see and do. There was one new thing Rada and Jonny really wanted to do. They thought about ⓑit all (B)[night / nights] and didn't tell Mom and Dad about ⓒ it. It was their secret.

The next day, Rada's family got (C)[on / off] a spaceship.

"It's going to be a long trip," said Mom.

"That's alright. I'm so excited!" said Rada.

**서답형**

**09** 위 글의 밑줄 친 ⓐIt, ⓑit, ⓒit이 가리키는 것을 본문에서 찾아 영어로 쓰시오.

(A) _____
_____
(B) _____
(C) _____

**서답형**

**10** 위 글의 괄호 (A)~(C)에서 문맥이나 어법상 알맞은 낱말을 골라 쓰시오.

(A) _____ (B) _____ (C) _____

**11** 위 글에서 알 수 있는 Rada와 Jonny의 심경으로 가장 알맞은 것을 고르시오.

① upset　　　　② confused
③ worried　　　④ disappointed
⑤ expectant

[12~15] 다음 글을 읽고 물음에 답하시오.

The spaceship finally (A)[landed / took off]. "Dad, it's difficult to walk on Earth," said Rada.

"I know. Earth is (B)[pulling / pushing] you down," said Dad.

Rada and Jonny couldn't float anymore. That was the first new thing.

"What's that sound?" asked Rada.

"A bird is singing," said Mom.

"I've never heard a bird sing," said Rada.

"And I've never felt the wind," said Jonny.

These were all new things.

Rada and Jonny ran up to the nearest hill. At the top, they looked at each other and laughed. ⓐThen they lie down on the soft green grass and rolled down the hill. That was their secret!

"This is the best (C)[familiar / new] thing of all!" shouted Rada and Jonny.

And they ran up to the top of the hill again.

**서답형**

**12** 위 글의 괄호 (A)~(C)에서 문맥상 알맞은 낱말을 골라 쓰시오.

(A) _____ (B) _____ (C) _____

**서답형**

**13** 위 글의 밑줄 친 ⓐ에서 어법상 **틀린** 부분을 찾아 고치시오.

_____ ➡ _____

**14** 위 글의 제목으로 알맞은 것을 고르시오.

① Oh, It's Difficult to Walk on Earth!
② Be Careful! Earth Is Pulling You Down!
③ Guess What? I Can't Float Anymore!
④ New Things They Experienced on Earth
⑤ How to Roll Down the Hill

**중요**

**15** 위 글의 내용과 일치하지 **않는** 것은?

① 지구에서는 걷는 것이 어렵다고 Rada가 아빠에게 말했다.
② 지구에서 Rada와 Jonny는 더 이상 떠다닐 수 없었다.
③ Rada는 새가 노래하는 것을 들어 본 적이 있다.
④ Jonny는 바람을 느껴 본 적이 없다.
⑤ Rada와 Jonny는 부드러운 초록 잔디에 누워서 언덕 아래로 굴러 내려갔다.

[16~18] 다음 글을 읽고 물음에 답하시오.

"You don't have to wear your big heavy space suits because there is air everywhere. (①) It's also hard to jump there because Earth pulls you down," said Dad.

(②) "There are hills, and they are covered with soft green grass. (③) You can roll down the hills," answered Mom.

(④) "Dad, have you ever rolled down a hill?" asked Rada.

(⑤) "Yes, it's really amazing!" answered Dad.

Jonny was thirsty, so he opened a milk container and shook it. The milk floated in the air and formed balls. Jonny swallowed the balls.

"Jonny, if you drink milk that way on Earth, you'll get wet," said Mom.

위 글의 흐름으로 보아, 주어진 문장이 들어가기에 가장 적절한 곳은?

> "What else?" asked Rada.

①      ②      ③      ④      ⑤

**서답형**

**17** 다음 빈칸 (A)~(C)에 알맞은 단어를 넣어 우주에서 우유 먹는 법을 완성하시오.

> In space, you can't drink milk in the same way as people do on Earth. First, you open a milk container and ____(A)____ it. Then, the milk floats in the air and forms ____(B)____ . Finally, you can ____(C)____ the balls.

(A) _____ (B) _____ (C) _____

**중요**

**18** 위 글을 읽고 대답할 수 <u>없는</u> 질문은?

① Why is there no need to wear your big heavy space suits on Earth?
② Why is it difficult to jump on Earth?
③ What can you do on the hills that are covered with soft green grass?
④ When did Dad roll down a hill?
⑤ When Jonny was thirsty, what did he do?

---

[19~21] 다음 글을 읽고 물음에 답하시오.

The spaceship finally landed.
"Dad, it's difficult to walk on Earth," said Rada.
"I know. Earth is pulling you down," said Dad.
Rada and Jonny couldn't float anymore. That was the first new thing.
"What's that sound?" asked Rada.
"A bird is singing," said Mom.
"I've never heard a bird sing," said Rada.
"And I've never felt the wind," said Jonny.
ⓐThese were all <u>familiar</u> things.
Rada and Jonny ran up the nearest hill. At the top, they looked at each other and laughed. Then ⓑ그들은 부드러운 초록 잔디에 누워서 언덕 아래로 굴러 내려갔다. That was their secret!
"This is the best new thing of all!" shouted Rada and Jonny.
And they ran up to the top of the hill again.

**서답형**

**19** What was the first new thing to Rada and Jonny? Fill in the blanks with the suitable words. (6 words)

➡ It was that _____.

**서답형**

**20** 위 글의 밑줄 친 ⓐ에서 흐름상 <u>어색한</u> 부분을 찾아 고치시오.

_____ ➡ _____

**서답형**

**21** 위 글의 밑줄 친 ⓑ의 우리말에 맞게 주어진 어휘를 이용하여 13 단어로 영작하시오.

> on the soft green grass

➡ _____

_____

**[22~24]** 다음 글을 읽고 물음에 답하시오.

The next morning, Rada's family went to a park. Rada said to Dad, "Dad, I've never ___ⓐ___ a bike before." "Let's ___ⓑ___ bikes, then," said Dad. They then ___ⓒ___ bikes together. The weather was great, and it was so fun.

In the afternoon, Rada's family went to the beach. Jonny said to Mom, "I've never swum before." "Let's swim, then," said Mom. It was great to swim in the cool blue sea.

At night, Rada and Jonny talked about living on Earth. "It's wonderful to live on Earth," Rada said to Jonny. "Yes. It's great to be here," Jonny said.

**서답형**

**22** 위 글의 빈칸 ⓐ~ⓒ에 ride를 알맞은 형태로 쓰시오.

ⓐ _____  ⓑ _____  ⓒ _____

**서답형**

**23** 위 글을 읽고 Rada의 가족이 한 일을 우리말로 쓰시오.

오전: _____

오후: _____

밤: _____

**서답형**

**24** What did Rada and Jonny think about living on Earth? Answer in English in a full sentence.

➡ _____

_____

**[25~27]** 다음 글을 읽고 물음에 답하시오.

Later that night, Rada and Jonny talked a long time about Earth. ⓐIt was exciting ⓑto think about all the new things they were going to see and do them. There was one new thing Rada and Jonny really wanted to do. They thought about it all night and didn't tell Mom and Dad about it. It was their secret.

The next day, Rada's family got on a spaceship. "It's going to be a long trip," said Mom. "That's alright. I'm so excited!" said Rada.

**25** 아래 〈보기〉에서 위 글의 밑줄 친 ⓐIt과 문법적 쓰임이 같은 것의 개수를 고르시오.

① It is warmer than yesterday.
② It is important to choose good friends.
③ Look! It's going up that tree.
④ It is impossible to master English in a month or two.
⑤ I think it necessary that you should do it at once.

① 1개  ② 2개  ③ 3개  ④ 4개  ⑤ 5개

**서답형**

**26** 위 글의 밑줄 친 ⓑ에서 어법상 틀린 부분을 찾아 고치시오.

_____ ➡ _____

**서답형**

**27** What was Rada and Jonny's secret? Answer in English. (8 words)

➡ _____

[28~30] 다음 글을 읽고 물음에 답하시오.

The spaceship finally landed.
"Dad, it's difficult to walk on Earth," said Rada.
"I know. Earth is pulling you down," said Dad.
Rada and Jonny couldn't float anymore. That was the first new thing.
"What's that sound?" asked Rada.
"A bird is singing," said Mom.
"ⓐI've never heard a bird to sing," said Rada.
"And I've never felt the wind," said Jonny.
These were all new things.

Rada and Jonny ran up to the nearest hill. At the top, they looked at each other and laughed. Then they lay down on the soft green grass and rolled down the hill. That was their secret!
"This is the best new thing of all!" shouted Rada and Jonny.
And they ran up to the top of the hill again.

**28** 위 글의 주제로 알맞은 것을 고르시오.

① final landing of the spaceship
② new things Rada and Jonny experienced on Earth
③ the gravity of the Earth
④ the way Rada heard a bird sing and Jonny felt the wind
⑤ Rada and Jonny who enjoyed rolling down the hill

**서답형**

**29** 위 글의 밑줄 친 ⓐ에서 어법상 틀린 부분을 찾아 고치시오.

_____ ➡ _____

**30** 위 글을 읽고 대답할 수 없는 질문은?

① Why is it difficult to walk on Earth?
② Was it possible for Rada and Jonny to float on Earth?
③ Has Jonny ever felt the wind?
④ What did Rada and Jonny do at the top of the hill?
⑤ How many times did Rada and Jonny run up to the top of the hill?

[01~03] 다음 글을 읽고 물음에 답하시오.

Rada lived on a little world, far out in space. She lived there with her father, mother, and brother Jonny. Rada's father and other people worked on spaceships. Only Rada and Jonny were children, and they were born in space.

One day, Dad told Rada and Jonny, "We're going back to Earth tomorrow."

ⓐRada와 Jonny는 깜짝 놀라 아빠를 바라보았고, 그에게 둥둥 떠서 갔다.

Rada asked Dad, "What's it like on Earth?"

"Everything is different there. For example, the sky is blue," answered Dad.

"I've never seen a blue sky," said Jonny.

"The sky is always black here," said Rada.

**01** 위 글의 내용과 일치하도록 다음 빈칸 (A)와 (B)에 알맞은 단어를 쓰시오.

> In space, there were no (A)_____ except Rada and Jonny (B)_____ were born there.

**02** 위 글의 밑줄 친 ⓐ의 우리말에 맞게 한 단어를 보충하여, 주어진 어휘를 알맞게 배열하시오.

> surprise/ towards / looked / him / and / Rada and Jonny / floated / Dad / at

➡ _____

_____

**03** 다음 빈칸에 알맞은 단어를 넣어 우주와 지구의 차이점을 완성하시오.

> The _____ of the sky in space is different from that on Earth.

[04~06] 다음 글을 읽고 물음에 답하시오.

"You don't have to wear your big heavy space suits because there is air everywhere. It's also hard to jump there because Earth pulls you down," said Dad.

"What else?" asked Rada.

"There are hills, and they are covered with soft green grass. You can roll down the hills," answered Mom.

"Dad, have you ever rolled down a hill?" asked Rada.

"ⓐYes, it's really amazing!" answered Dad.

Jonny was thirsty, so he opened a milk container and shook it. The milk floated in the air and formed balls. Jonny swallowed the balls.

ⓑ"Jonny, if you will drink milk that way on Earth, you'll get wet," said Mom.

**04** 위 글의 내용과 일치하도록 다음 빈칸 (A)~(D)에 알맞은 말을 쓰시오.

| | in space | on Earth |
|---|---|---|
| wear your big heavy space suits | (A) _____ | (A) need not |
| to jump | easy | (B)_____ |
| how to have milk | swallow the milk (C)_____ | drink milk |

**05** 위 글의 밑줄 친 ⓐYes, 뒤에 생략된 말을 쓰시오. (2 단어)

➡ _____

**06** 위 글의 밑줄 친 ⓑ에서 어법상 틀린 부분을 찾아 고치시오.

_____ ➡ _____

**[07~09]** 다음 글을 읽고 물음에 답하시오.

The spaceship finally landed.
"Dad, it's difficult to walk on Earth," said Rada.
"I know. Earth is pulling you down," said Dad.
ⓐRada and Jonny couldn't float anymore. That was the first new thing.
"What's that sound?" asked Rada.
"A bird is singing," said Mom.
"(A)I've (_____) heard a bird sing," said Rada.
"And (B)I've (_____) felt the wind," said Jonny.
These were all new things.
Rada and Jonny ran up the nearest hill. At the top, they looked at each other and laughed. Then they lay down on the soft green grass and rolled down the hill. That was their secret!

**07** 위 글의 밑줄 친 (A)와 (B)가 각각 다음 문장과 같은 뜻이 되도록 빈칸에 공통으로 들어갈 알맞은 한 단어를 쓰시오.

(A): This is the first time I've ever heard a bird sing,
(B): This is the first time I've ever felt the wind,

➡ _____

**08** 위 글의 밑줄 친 ⓐ를 다음과 같이 바꿔 쓸 때 빈칸에 들어갈 알맞은 말을 쓰시오.

Rada and Jonny could _____ _____ float.

**09** What was Rada and Jonny's secret? Fill in the blanks with the suitable words.

It was that they _____ _____ on the soft green grass and _____ _____ the hill.

**[10~12]** 다음 글을 읽고 물음에 답하시오.

Rada lived on a little world, far out in space. She lived there with her father, mother, and brother Jonny. Rada's father and (A)[another / other] people worked on spaceships. Only Rada and Jonny were children, and they were born in space.
One day, Dad told Rada and Jonny, "We're going back to Earth tomorrow."
ⓐRada and Jonny looked at Dad in surprise and ran towards him.
Rada asked Dad, "(B)[How / What] is it like on Earth?"
"Everything is (C)[different / similar] ⓑthere. For example, the sky is blue," answered Dad.
"I've never seen a blue sky," said Jonny.
"The sky is always black ⓒhere," said Rada.

**10** 위 글의 괄호 (A)~(C)에서 문맥이나 어법상 알맞은 낱말을 골라 쓰시오.

(A) _____ (B) _____ (C) _____

**11** 위 글의 밑줄 친 ⓐ에서 흐름상 어색한 부분을 찾아 고치시오.

_____ ➡ _____

**12** 위 글의 밑줄 친 ⓑthere와 ⓒhere가 가리키는 것을 본문에서 찾아 쓰시오.

ⓑ _____ ⓒ _____

# 구석구석

 해석

## One Minute Speech

Did you hear about the new book, *Dave's Adventures*?
상대방이 알고 있는지 물어보는 표현이다
This book is about Dave and his adventures in the woods.
～에 관한 것이다
The main characters are Dave and a big bear. The story is fun.

Are you curious about the book?
be curious about ～: ～에 관해 궁금해하다
Then you should read it!

구문해설 · adventure 모험  · be about ～에 관한 것이다  · main character 주인공
· curious 궁금한, 호기심 있는

새 책인 Dave의 모험에 관해 들어 봤니? 이 책은 Dave와 숲에서의 그의 모험에 관한 거야. 주인공은 Dave와 큰 곰이야. 이야기가 재미있어. 그 책에 관해 궁금하니? 그러면 그것을 꼭 읽어 봐야 해!

## Read and Complete

1. Rada's family lived in space. One day, they decided to go back to Earth.
   decide는 to부정사를 목적어로 취한다
2. Rada's family talked about life on Earth. They talked about the blue sky and

   hills which are covered with green grass.
   주격 관계대명사+be동사: 생략 가능
3. The next day, Rada's family got on a spaceship. It was a long trip to Earth.
   get on: 타다, 오르다, get off: 내리다
4. When they arrived on Earth, Rada and Jonny ran up the nearest hill and
   arrive on: ～에 도착하다                                          형용사 near의 최상급
   rolled down it. That was the best new thing to them.
   the hill

구문해설 · in space: 우주에서  · decide: ～을 결정하다  · be covered with: ～으로 뒤덮여 있다
· roll down: 굴러 내려가다

1. Rada의 가족은 우주에서 살고 있었다. 어느 날, 그들은 지구로 돌아가기로 결정했다.
2. Rada의 가족은 지구의 생활에 대해 이야기했다. 그들은 파란 하늘과 초록색 잔디로 뒤덮인 언덕에 대해 이야기했다.
3. 다음날, Rada의 가족은 우주선에 올랐다. 그것은 지구로의 긴 여행이었다.
4. 그들이 지구에 도착했을 때, Rada와 Jonny는 가장 가까운 언덕으로 뛰어 올라가 아래로 굴러 내려 갔다. 그것은 그들에게 최고의 새로운 것이었다.

## Around the World

1. Russia sent the first dog into space. It was small, and its name was Laika.
   the+서수: 최초의                                            the dog's
2. Yuri Gagarin went into space for the first time.
   처음으로, 최초로
3. The USA sent the first human to the moon. His name was Neil Armstrong.
   ～을 …로 보냈다
4. Russia built the first space station. It flew around the Earth almost 3,000
   날아다녔다, 선회했다      지구
   times.

구문해설 · space station: 우주 정거장  · almost: 거의  · times: ～ 번, ～ 배

1. 러시아는 우주에 최초의 개를 보냈다. 그것은 작았고, 이름은 Laika였다.
2. Yuri Gagarin이 최초로 우주에 갔다.
3. 미국은 달에 최초의 인간을 보냈다. 그의 이름은 Neil Armstrong이었다.
4. 러시아가 최초의 우주 정거장을 건설하였다. 그것은 거의 3천 번 지구 주변을 돌았다.

**01** 다음 주어진 두 단어의 관계가 같도록 빈칸에 알맞은 단어를 쓰시오.

> excited : bored = take off : _____

**02** 다음 글의 빈칸 ⓐ와 ⓑ에 들어갈 단어로 바르게 짝지어진 것은?

> • You ⓐ_____ wear your big heavy space suits because there is air everywhere.
> • It's also hard to jump there because Earth ⓑ_____.

① have to – rolls you down
② must not – pulls down you
③ don't need to – pulls you up
④ don't have to – pulls you down
⑤ cannot – pulls down you

[03~04] 다음 영영풀이에 해당하는 것을 고르시오.

**03**
> to come out of a mother's body

① be curious about   ② roll down
③ be born          ④ swallow
⑤ get on

**04**
> to arrive on the ground or other surface after moving down through the air

① land      ② float
③ take off   ④ get on
⑤ form

**05** 다음 빈칸에 공통으로 들어갈 말을 쓰시오.

> • That desk takes up too much _____.
>   *take up: 차지하다
> • There are 90 parking _____s in this parking lot.
> • On June 18, China sent its first spacewoman into _____.
>   *spacewoman: 여성 우주비행사

**06** 다음 밑줄 친 부분의 뜻이 잘못된 것은?

① This is a poster of the spaceship. (우주선)
② It's a type of ice cream. (종류)
③ Rada and Jonny looked at Dad in surprise. (놀라서)
④ They were born in space. (태어났다)
⑤ On sunny days, people go to parks and lie down on the grass. (구르다)

**07** 다음 대화를 순서에 맞게 바르게 배열한 것은?

> (A) Yes, and here it is. It looks good.
> (B) Yes, I did. It's a type of ice cream.
> (C) Did you hear about the new space food?
> (D) I'm really curious about the taste.

① (A) – (B) – (D) – (C)
② (B) – (A) – (C) – (D)
③ (C) – (A) – (B) – (D)
④ (C) – (B) – (A) – (D)
⑤ (D) – (B) – (C) – (A)

[08~10] 다음 대화를 읽고 물음에 답하시오.

B: Subin, did you hear about the new movie, *Life on the Moon*?
G: No, I didn't.
B: I heard it's really good. (①)
G: I'm really curious about the movie. (②)
B: It's about a man who is trying to live on the moon. (③)
G: That sounds interesting.
B: Look. The movie is playing at the Space Theater here. (④)
G: What time is the movie?
B: It begins at 2:30. (⑤)
G: Let's eat lunch first and then see the movie.
B: OK. I'm hungry. Let's go!

**08** 주어진 문장이 들어갈 위치로 알맞은 것은?

> What's it about?

①      ②      ③      ④      ⑤

**09** 다음 질문에 대한 답을 위 대화에서 찾아 쓰시오.

> Q: What is the movie, *Life on the Moon*, about?

➡ _____

**10** 위 대화의 내용과 일치하지 <u>않는</u> 것은?

① Subin heard the new movie is really good.
② Subin has an interest in the new movie.
③ The new movie is playing now.
④ They are going to see the movie after eating lunch.
⑤ The movie is about a man trying to live on the moon.

**11** 다음 그림을 보고 제시된 〈조건〉에 맞게 아래 대화의 빈칸을 완성하시오.

┌─── 조건 ├─
(1) 'hear'를 사용할 것.
(2) 'really'와 'curious'를 사용하여 새로운 정보에 관심을 나타내는 표현을 쓸 것.
(3) 축약형을 사용하여 세 단어로 쓸 것
└─────────────┘

A: (1) _____ the new book, *The Best New Thing*?
B: No, I didn't.
A: I heard it's really interesting.
B: (2) _____
   (3) _____
A: It's about a family who lives in space.
B: That sounds interesting.

**12** 다음 대화의 밑줄 친 부분에 대한 설명으로 적절하지 <u>않은</u> 것은?

G: ⓐ<u>Did you hear about the new book, *Living in a Foreign Country*?</u>
B: No, I didn't.
G: Look. It's ⓑ<u>right</u> here. ⓒ<u>It's about living in New York.</u>
B: Great. ⓓ<u>I'm really curious about this book.</u>
G: ⓔ<u>Me, too.</u>

① ⓐ: 상대방이 어떤 정보를 알고 있는지를 묻는 말이다.
② ⓑ: 형용사로 '올바른'의 의미다.
③ ⓒ: 새 책의 내용에 관해 설명하는 말이다.
④ ⓓ: 새로운 정보에 대해 궁금증을 표현하는 말이다.
⑤ ⓔ: 상대방의 말에 자신도 그렇다고 동의하는 표현이다.

**Grammar**

**13** 다음 빈칸에 들어갈 말이 나머지와 다른 하나는?

① It was easy _____ me to find his new house.

② It was foolish _____ you to believe him.

③ It's difficult _____ me to play the piano well.

④ It was exciting _____ him to play soccer with his friends.

⑤ It can be dangerous _____ her to drive fast.

**14** 다음 빈칸에 들어갈 표현이 순서대로 바르게 짝지어진 것을 고르시오.

I _____ him since I _____ a child.

① have known – was
② have known – has been
③ have known – had been
④ knew – was
⑤ knew – has been

**15** 다음 밑줄 친 부분의 쓰임이 나머지 넷과 다른 것은?

① I <u>have eaten</u> French food before.
② Jane <u>has been</u> to Jeju-do many times.
③ She <u>has</u> never <u>met</u> a movie star.
④ <u>Have</u> you <u>tried</u> to protect the environment?
⑤ My English <u>has improved</u> since I moved to Australia.

**16** 다음 문장을 주어진 말로 시작하여 다시 쓰시오.

(1) Tony must hand in his report by tomorrow.

➡ It is necessary _____

_____.

(2) You should be careful when you cross the street.

➡ It is necessary _____

_____.

**17** 다음 ⓐ~ⓗ 중 옳은 것을 모두 고르면?

ⓐ Has Daniel found his wallet yesterday?
ⓑ I have lost my backpack.
ⓒ I've never gone to Egypt before.
ⓓ How long has Mr. Williams worked for this company?
ⓔ I have taught English since 10 years.
ⓕ It's important follows the rules.
ⓖ That is a pity that you cannot come to my party.
ⓗ It's fun to ride a horse.

① ⓐ, ⓒ
② ⓑ, ⓒ, ⓓ
③ ⓑ, ⓓ, ⓗ
④ ⓓ, ⓔ, ⓗ
⑤ ⓓ, ⓔ, ⓖ

**18** 다음 밑줄 친 부분의 쓰임이 다른 하나는?

① It's hard <u>to fix</u> a bike.
② It's nice <u>to take</u> a walk in the park.
③ It's necessary <u>to learn</u> English.
④ He has gone never <u>to return</u>.
⑤ It is exciting <u>to cook</u>.

**19** 다음 중 어법상 어색한 문장은?

① It is bad for your teeth to drink too much soda.

② It was exciting to watch the baseball game.

③ It is important for you to be careful all the time.

④ James has eaten too much and he is sick now.

⑤ Peter, have you finished your project yesterday?

**Reading**

**[20~22]** 다음 글을 읽고 물음에 답하시오.

One day, Dad told Rada and Jonny, "We ⓐ are going back to Earth tomorrow."

Rada and Jonny looked at Dad in surprise and floated towards him.

Rada asked Dad, "ⓑ지구는 어떤 곳인가요?"

"Everything is different there.      (A)      , the sky is blue," answered Dad.

"I've never seen a blue sky," said Jonny.

"The sky is always black here," said Rada.

**20** 위 글의 빈칸 (A)에 들어갈 알맞은 말을 고르시오.

① However        ② Therefore

③ In addition     ④ For example

⑤ That is

**21** 위 글의 밑줄 친 ⓐare going과 문법적 쓰임이 같은 것을 모두 고르시오.

① He is studying English in his room.

② What is she doing now?

③ She is leaving Seoul tonight.

④ Who is singing a song there?

⑤ He is coming here next week.

**22** 위 글의 밑줄 친 ⓑ의 우리말에 맞게 5 단어로 영작하시오.

➡ _____

**[23~24]** 다음 글을 읽고 물음에 답하시오.

"You don't have to wear your big heavy space suits (A)[because / though] there is air everywhere. It's also hard to jump there because Earth pulls you down," said Dad.

"(B)[How / What] else?" asked Rada.

"There are hills, and they are covered with soft green grass. You can roll down the hills," answered Mom.

"Dad, have you ever rolled down a hill?" asked Rada.

"Yes, it's really amazing!" answered Dad.

Jonny was thirsty, so he opened a milk container and shook it. The milk floated in the air and formed balls. Jonny swallowed the balls.

"Jonny, (C)[if / unless] you drink milk that way on Earth, you'll get wet," said Mom.

**23** 위 글의 괄호 (A)~(C)에서 문맥상 알맞은 낱말을 골라 쓰시오.

(A) _____ (B) _____ (C) _____

**24** 위 글의 내용과 일치하지 <u>않는</u> 것은?

① 지구에서는 크고 무거운 우주복을 입을 필요가 없다.

② 지구에서는 점프하는 것이 어렵다.

③ 지구에서는 언덕을 굴러 내려갈 수도 있다.

④ 아빠는 언덕을 굴러 내려가 본 적이 있다.

⑤ Jonny는 목이 말라서 우유 용기를 열고 그것을 마셨다.

[25~27] 다음 글을 읽고 물음에 답하시오.

Later that night, Rada and Jonny talked a long time about Earth. It was exciting @to think about all the new things they were going to see and do. ⓑThere was one new thing Rada and Jonny really wanted to do. They thought about it all night and didn't tell Mom and Dad about it. It was their secret.

The next day, Rada's family got on a spaceship.

"It's going to be a long trip," said Mom.

"ⓒThat's alright. I'm so excited!" said Rada.

**25** 위 글의 밑줄 친 @to think와 to부정사의 용법이 다른 것을 모두 고르시오.

① He opened the door, only to find the room empty.

② It is difficult to know oneself.

③ He has many children to look after.

④ She was very happy to get the birthday present.

⑤ To see is to believe.

**26** 위 글의 밑줄 친 문장 ⓑ에 생략된 한 단어를 넣어 문장을 다시 쓰시오.

➡ _____

_____

**27** 위 글의 밑줄 친 ⓒThat이 가리키는 것을 본문에서 찾아 쓰시오.

➡ _____

[28~30] 다음 글을 읽고 물음에 답하시오.

The spaceship finally landed.

"Dad, it's difficult to walk on Earth," said Rada.

"I know. Earth is pulling you down," said Dad.

Rada and Jonny couldn't float anymore. That was the first new thing.

"What's that sound?" asked Rada.

"A bird is singing," said Mom.

"I've never heard a bird sing," said Rada.

"And I've never felt the wind," said Jonny. (①) Rada and Jonny ran up the nearest hill. (②) At the top, they looked at each other and laughed. (③) Then they lay down on the soft green grass and rolled down the hill. (④) That was their secret! (⑤)

"This is the best new thing of all!" shouted Rada and Jonny.

And they ran up to the top of the hill again.

**28** 위 글의 흐름으로 보아, 주어진 문장이 들어가기에 가장 적절한 곳은?

These were all new things.

①      ②      ③      ④      ⑤

**29** 다음 문장에서 위 글의 내용과 다른 부분을 찾아서 고치시오.

Rada has ever heard a bird sing and Jonny has ever felt the wind.

_____ ➡ _____

_____ ➡ _____

**30** 본문의 내용과 일치하도록 다음 빈칸에 알맞은 단어를 쓰시오.

To Rada and Jonny, the _____ _____ _____ of all was to lie down on the soft green grass and roll down the hill.

**01** 출제율 95%

다음 짝지어진 단어의 관계가 같도록 빈칸에 알맞은 말을 쓰시오.

> intelligent : stupid = rough : _____

**02** 출제율 90%

다음 영영 풀이에 해당하는 단어는?

> in the direction of, or closer to someone or something

① along   ② out   ③ towards
④ into   ⑤ across

**03** 출제율 85%

다음 대화의 밑줄 친 (A)와 같은 의미의 문장을 주어진 단어를 활용하여 쓰시오.

> G: Did you hear about the space marathon?
> B: No, I didn't.
> G: It's a marathon on a space station. Look at this video.
> B: OK. (A)I'm really curious about it.

➡ _____ (interest)

**04** 출제율 95%

다음 대화의 밑줄 친 부분 중 어법상 어색한 것은?

> G: ⓐDid you hear about the new book, *Living in a Foreign Country*?
> B: ⓑNo, I didn't.
> G: Look. It's right here. It's about ⓒto live in New York.
> B: Great. ⓓI'm really curious about this book.
> G: ⓔMe, too.

① ⓐ   ② ⓑ   ③ ⓒ   ④ ⓓ   ⑤ ⓔ

**05** 출제율 100%

다음 글의 밑줄 친 (A)~(E)의 해석으로 틀린 것은?

> Later that night, Rada and Jonny (A)talked a long time about Earth. It was (B)exciting to think about all the new things they were going to see and do. There was one new thing Rada and Jonny really wanted to do. They thought about it (C)all night and didn't tell Mom and Dad about it. It was their (D)secret. The next day, Rada's family (E)got on a spaceship.

① (A) 오랜 시간 이야기했다
② (B) 흥미진진한
③ (C) 밤새
④ (D) 비밀
⑤ (E) 우주선에서 내렸다

**[06~07]** 다음 대화를 읽고 물음에 답하시오.

> B: (A)너는 우주로 간 첫 번째 우주선에 대해 들어봤니?
> G: No, I didn't. I'm curious about it.
> B: This is a poster of the spaceship.
> G: Really? _____ (B)

**06** 출제율 85%

위 대화의 밑줄 친 (A)의 우리말에 맞게 주어진 문장의 빈칸을 채우시오.

> Did you _____ _____ the first spaceship _____ went _____ space?

**07** 출제율 95%

위 대화의 (B)에 들어갈 말로 알맞은 것을 고르시오.

① What about you?
② I want to buy it.
③ I'm sorry to hear that.
④ I haven't heard about it.
⑤ I'm very interested in fashion.

**[08~10]** 다음 대화를 읽고 물음에 답하시오.

B: Subin, (A)did you hear about the new movie, *Life on the Moon*?

G: No, I didn't.

B: I heard it's really good.

G: (B)그 영화가 정말 궁금해. What's it about?

B: It's about a man _____ ⓐ _____

G: That sounds interesting.

B: Look. The movie is playing at the Space Theater here.

G: What time is the movie?

B: It begins at 2:30.

G: Let's eat lunch first and then see the movie.

B: OK. I'm hungry. Let's go!

**08** 위 대화의 빈칸 ⓐ에 들어갈 말을 주어진 단어를 배열하여 의미가 통하도록 문장을 완성하시오.

> is / to / live / the / trying / who / on / moon

➡ _____

**09** 위 대화의 밑줄 친 (A)와 같은 의미가 되도록 '현재완료'를 사용하여 문장을 쓰시오.

➡ _____

**10** 위 대화의 밑줄 친 (B)의 우리말에 맞게 주어진 어휘를 배열하여 대화를 완성하시오.

> really / about / I'm / curious / the / movie

➡ _____

**11** 다음 빈칸에 알맞은 말이 순서대로 짝지어진 것은?

> • I have known her _____ 10 years.
> • I have known her _____ 2010.

① for – during
② during – for
③ for – since
④ since – for
⑤ as – for

**12** 다음 우리말을 주어진 어휘를 이용하여 영작하시오.

(1) 그는 삼십 분째 잠들어 있다. (sleep)

➡ _____

(2) 그 유명 인사는 방금 공항에 도착했어.
(the celebrity, the airport, arrive)

➡ _____

(3) Sue는 전에 프랑스에 가 본 적이 없다.
(be, never, to)

➡ _____

(4) 나는 새로 온 그 학생의 이름을 잊어버렸다.
(그래서 지금 생각나지 않는다.)
(forget, the new student)

➡ _____

(5) 다양한 의견을 나누는 것이 중요해.
(share, various, important, to)

➡ _____

(6) 네가 내 생일을 기억해 줘서 고마워.
(nice, remember, to)

➡ _____

**13** 다음 중 어법상 적절한 문장은?

① It's great to is here.
② It's fun to playing with friends.
③ It is boring fish in the lake.
④ It's exciting for us having you here.
⑤ It is better to drink ice tea in summer.

**14** 다음 중 어법상 바르지 않은 것은?

① I have known him since I was young.
② Have you gone to London before?
③ It has been cold and cloudy for the last three days.
④ The banana has not turned brown yet.
⑤ How long have you known her?

**15** 다음 두 문장이 같도록 할 때 빈칸에 알맞은 것은?

> To predict the future is impossible.
> ➡ It is impossible _____ the future.

① predict
② predicts
③ to predicting
④ predicting
⑤ to predict

**[16~17]** 다음 글을 읽고 물음에 답하시오.

One day, Dad told Rada and Jonny, "We're going back ⓐ_____ Earth tomorrow."
Rada and Jonny looked ⓑ_____ Dad ⓒ_____ surprise and floated ⓓ_____ him.
Rada asked Dad, "What's it (A)like ⓔ_____ Earth?"
"Everything is different there. For example, the sky is blue," answered Dad.
"I've never seen a blue sky," said Jonny.
"The sky is always black here," said Rada.

**16** 위 글의 빈칸 ⓐ~ⓔ에 알맞지 않은 전치사를 고르시오.

① to     ② at     ③ with
④ towards     ⑤ on

**17** 위 글의 밑줄 친 (A)like와 같은 의미로 쓰인 것을 고르시오.

① Does he like to go there?
② She was like a daughter to me.
③ I like playing the piano.
④ There are many things of like shape.
⑤ How did you like it?

**[18~20]** 다음 글을 읽고 물음에 답하시오.

"You don't have to wear your big heavy space suits _____ⓐ_____. ⓑIt's also hard to jump there because Earth pulls you down," said Dad.
"What else?" asked Rada.
"There are hills, and ⓒthey are covered with soft green grass. You can roll down the hills," answered Mom.
"Dad, have you ever rolled down a hill?" asked Rada.
"Yes, ⓓit's really amazing!" answered Dad.
Jonny was thirsty, so he opened a milk container and shook ⓔit. The milk floated in the air and formed balls. Jonny swallowed the balls.
"Jonny, if you drink milk that way on Earth, you'll get wet," said Mom.

**18** 위 글의 빈칸 ⓐ에 들어갈 알맞은 말을 고르시오.

① because they are so heavy
② so that you can jump easily
③ because there is air everywhere
④ because Earth pulls you down
⑤ so that you can roll down the hills

**19** 위 글의 밑줄 친 ⓑ와 바꿔 쓸 수 <u>없는</u> 말을 <u>모두</u> 고르시오.

① To jump there is also hard
② That's also hard jumping there
③ It's also hard for you to jump there
④ Jumping there is also hard
⑤ That's also hard to jump there

**20** 위 글의 밑줄 친 ⓒthey, ⓓit, ⓔit이 가리키는 것을 각각 영어로 쓰시오.

ⓒ _____

ⓓ _____

ⓔ _____

[21~23] 다음 글을 읽고 물음에 답하시오.

Later that night, Rada and Jonny talked a long time about Earth. ⓐIt was exciting to think about all the new things they were going to see and do. There was one new thing Rada and Jonny really wanted to do. They thought about it all night and didn't tell Mom and Dad about it. It was their secret.

The next day, Rada's family got on a spaceship.

"It's going to be a long trip," said Mom.

"That's alright. I'm so ___(A)___ !" said Rada.

**21** 위 글의 빈칸 (A)에 들어갈 알맞은 말을 고르시오.

① bored
② interesting
③ pleasant
④ excited
⑤ surprised

**22** 위 글의 밑줄 친 문장 ⓐ에서 all the new things와 they 사이에 들어갈 수 있는 말을 <u>모두</u> 고르시오.

① which ② who ③ that
④ what ⑤ whom

**23** 위 글의 내용과 일치하지 <u>않는</u> 것은?

① 밤 늦게, Rada와 Jonny는 지구에 대해서 오랜 시간 이야기했다.
② Rada와 Jonny는 지구에서 그들이 보고, 그리고 하게 될 모든 새로운 것들을 생각했다.
③ Rada와 Jonny는 정말로 하고 싶었던 한 가지 새로운 것이 있었다.
④ 부모님은 Rada와 Jonny가 정말로 하고 싶어하는 한 가지 새로운 것에 대해 듣고서 흥미로워하셨다.
⑤ "긴 여행이 될 거야."라고 엄마가 말했다.

[24~25] 다음 글을 읽고 물음에 답하시오.

The spaceship ⓐfinally landed.

"Dad, it's difficult to walk on Earth," said Rada.

"I know. Earth is pulling you down," said Dad.

Rada and Jonny couldn't float anymore. That was the first new thing.

"What's that sound?" asked Rada.

"A bird is singing," said Mom.

"I've never heard a bird sing," said Rada.

"And I've never felt the wind," said Jonny.

ⓑThese were all new things.

**24** 위 글의 밑줄 친 ⓐfinally와 바꿔 쓸 수 <u>없는</u> 말을 고르시오.

① at last
② consequently
③ after all
④ in the end
⑤ in the long run

**25** 위 글의 밑줄 친 ⓑThese가 가리키는 것 세 가지를 본문에서 찾아 우리말로 쓰시오.

(1) _____

(2) _____

(3) _____

01 다음 그림을 보고 아래 〈조건〉에 따라 대화를 완성하시오.

Gimchi
Snack
new snack

It tastes like Gimchi.

┤ 조건 ├

(A) new snack에 대한 정보를 알고 있는 지 묻는 말을 hear를 사용하여 쓸 것.

(B) 새로운 정보에 대하여 궁금증을 표현할 때 사용하는 표현을 전치사 about을 이용하여 쓸 것.

A: (A) _____

B: No, I didn't.

A: It tastes like Gimchi.

B: Oh, (B) _____

02 다음 대화의 밑줄 친 우리말을 주어진 어휘를 배열하여 완성하시오.

A: Did you hear about the new game, *MVP*?

B: No, I didn't, but I'm curious about it.

A: It's a baseball game. 네가 좋아하는 선수를 선택하고 경기할 수 있어.

you / a player / can / who / choose / you / and / like / play

➡ _____

03 다음 빈칸에 알맞은 단어를 〈보기〉에서 골라 쓰시오.

┤ 보기 ├

before    ago    since    for

(1) I caught a cold two weeks ago. I have caught a cold _____ two weeks.

(2) Yesterday I adopted a pet. I have never had a pet _____.

(3) Joe started to live in Seoul from 2010. Joe has lived in Seoul _____ 2010.

04 다음 대화를 읽고 아래 물음에 영어로 답하시오.

Andy: Subin, did you hear about the new movie, *Life on the Moon*?

Subin: No, I didn't.

Andy: I heard it's really good.

Subin: I'm really curious about the movie. What's it about?

Andy: It's about a man who is trying to live on the moon.

Subin: That sounds interesting.

Andy: Look. The movie is playing at the Space Theater here.

Subin: What time is the movie?

Andy: It begins at 2:30.

Subin: Let's eat lunch first and then see the movie.

Andy: OK. I'm hungry. Let's go!

(1) What are Subin and Andy talking about?

➡ _____

(2) What will Subin and Andy do before they see the movie? (4 단어로 쓸 것)

➡ _____

**05** 가주어 It을 사용하여 주어진 문장과 같은 의미가 되도록 쓰시오.

(1) To answer his questions was easy.

➡ _____

(2) Camping food is easy to cook.

➡ _____

(3) Seoul is safe and comfortable to live in.

➡ _____

(4) She was very wise to say so.

➡ _____

**06** 다음 두 문장의 의미가 같도록 문장의 빈칸을 완성하시오.

(1) He was born in Busan and he still lives in Busan.

➡ He _____ _____ in Busan _____ he was born.

(2) I read the book twice and I read it again today.

➡ I _____ _____ the book _____ _____.

(3) Somebody took my umbrella, so I don't have my umbrella now.

➡ Somebody _____ _____ my umbrella.

[07~09] 다음 글을 읽고 물음에 답하시오.

"You (A)[have to / don't have to] wear your big heavy space suits because there is air everywhere. It's also (B)[easy / hard] to jump there ⓐbecause Earth pulls down you," said Dad.

"What else?" asked Rada.

"There are hills, and they are covered with soft green grass. You can roll down the hills," answered Mom.

"Dad, have you ever rolled down a hill?" asked Rada.

"Yes, it's really (C)[amazing / amazed]!" answered Dad.

Jonny was thirsty, so he opened a milk container and shook it. The milk floated in the air and formed balls. Jonny swallowed the balls.

ⓑ"Jonny, if you drink milk that way on Earth, you'll get wet," said Mom.

**07** 위 글의 괄호 (A)~(C)에서 문맥이나 어법상 알맞은 낱말을 골라 쓰시오.

(A) _____ (B) _____ (C) _____

**08** 위 글의 밑줄 친 ⓐ에서 어법상 틀린 부분을 찾아 고치시오.

_____ ➡ _____

**09** 다음 빈칸 (A)와 (B)에 알맞은 단어를 넣어 엄마가 밑줄 친 ⓑ처럼 말한 이유를 완성하시오.

It's because milk will spill out of the container and make you (A)_____ _____ if you open a milk container and (B)_____ it on Earth.

*spill: (액체가) 흐르다, 쏟아지다; 쏟다

**01** 주어진 어휘와 가주어 It을 이용하여 3 문장 이상을 쓰시오.

┌─ 보기 ─────────────────────────────────────────────┐

| learn a new language | see a doctor | exercise regularly |
| learn Chinese | go to the beach | search information |

└──────────────────────────────────────────────────┘

(1) _____

(2) _____

(3) _____

(4) _____

(5) _____

**02** 다음 내용을 바탕으로 Rada와 Jonny가 지구에 도착한 다음 날 했을 새로운 경험에 대한 글을 쓰시오.

┌──────────────────────────────────────────────────┐

The next morning, Rada's family went to a park.

Dad, I've never ridden a bike before.

OK. Let's ride bikes.

In the afternoon, they went to the beach.

Mom, I've never swum before.

Let's swim, then.

At night, Rada and Jonny talked about living on Earth.

It's wonderful to live on Earth.

Yes. It's great to be here.

└──────────────────────────────────────────────────┘

┌──────────────────────────────────────────────────┐

The next morning, Rada's family went to a park. Rada said to Dad, "Dad, I've never (A) _____ before." "Let's ride bikes, then," said Dad. They then (B)_____ together. The weather was great, and it was so fun.

In the afternoon, Rada's family went to the beach. Jonny said to Mom, "I've never (C)_____." "Let's swim, then," said Mom. It was great (D)_____ in the cool blue sea.

At night, Rada and Jonny talked about (E)_____. "It's wonderful to live on Earth," Rada said to Jonny. "Yes. It's great to be here," Jonny said.

└──────────────────────────────────────────────────┘

**단원별 모의고사**

**01** 다음 단어에 대한 영어 설명이 <u>어색한</u> 것은?

① in surprise: feeling or showing surprise because of something unexpected

② container: something that you keep things in

③ lie: to be or to get into a position with your body flat on something

④ roll down: to move something down, using your hands

⑤ thrilling: exciting and interesting

**02** 다음 짝지어진 단어의 관계가 같도록 빈칸에 알맞은 말을 쓰시오.

different : same = _____ : depart

**03** 다음 영영풀이에 해당하는 단어를 고르시오.

to stay on the surface of a liquid and not sink

① float     ② swallow     ③ lie
④ roll      ⑤ arrive

**04** 다음 중 짝지어진 대화가 <u>어색한</u> 것은?

① A: Did you hear about the new running shoes, *Speed*?
  B: No, I didn't. What about them?

② A: Did you hear about the new restaurant, *Rose*?
  B: Yes, I did. It has good service.

③ A: The new snack tastes like Gimchi.
  B: Oh, I'm curious about it.

④ A: Did you hear about the new song, *Loving You*?
  B: No, I didn't. It's a Korean pop song.

⑤ A: Did you hear about the new TV show?
  B: No, I didn't.

**[05~06]** 다음 대화의 빈칸에 들어갈 말로 알맞은 것을 고르시오.

**05**

G: _____
B: No, I didn't. I'm really curious about Mars.
G: Look. It's right here. It's about Mars and its moons.
B: Great. I think I'll buy the book.

① Have you ever been to Mars?
② Did you know Mars has its moons?
③ Did you hear about the new book about Mars?
④ Do you want to know about Mars?
⑤ Did you buy the book about Mars?

**06**

G: Tony, did you hear about the movie, *My Hero*?
B: No, I didn't.
G: Well, I heard it's really good.
B: I'm really curious about the movie.
_____
G: It's about a father who saves his son.

① What about you?
② What is going on?
③ Is it good?
④ Look at this video.
⑤ What's the movie about?

**[07~09]** 다음 대화를 읽고 물음에 답하시오.

Andy: Subin, did you hear about the new movie, *Life on the Moon*?

Subin: No, I didn't.

Andy: I heard it's really good.

Subin: _____(A)_____ What's it about?

Andy: It's about a man who is trying to live on the moon.

Subin: That sounds interesting.

Andy: Look. The movie is playing at the Space Theater here.

Subin: What time is the movie?

Andy: It begins at 2:30.

Subin: Let's eat lunch first and then see the movie.

Andy: OK. I'm hungry. Let's go!

**07** 위 대화의 빈칸 (A)에 들어갈 말로 알맞은 것은?

① I want to know more about the man.
② I'm really curious about the movie.
③ I'm not interested in the movie.
④ What do you want to know about the movie?
⑤ I'm not really curious about it.

**08** What are they going to do after this dialogue? (6 단어로 답할 것)

➡ _____

**09** 위 대화를 요약한 글이다. 빈칸에 들어갈 알맞은 말을 쓰시오.

Andy and Subin are talking about the movie, *Life on the Moon*. It is _____ a man _____ is trying to live on the moon.

**10** 다음 대화의 내용과 일치하면 T, 일치하지 않으면 F에 표시하시오.

Girl: Did you hear about the new book, *Living in a Foreign Country*?

Boy: No, I didn't.

Girl: Look. It's right here. It's about living in New York.

Boy: Great. I'm really curious about this book.

Girl: Me, too.

(1) They are talking about living in New York. (T / F)
(2) The boy is interested in the new book. (T / F)

**11** 다음 대화의 빈칸에 들어갈 말은?

G: Tony, did you hear about the movie, *My Hero*?

B: No, I didn't.

G: _____

B: I'm really curious about the movie. What's it about?

G: It's about a father who saves his son.

① I don't know about the movie, either.
② I want to know what the movie is about.
③ Why don't we see the movie?
④ What time does the movie begin?
⑤ Well, I heard it's really good.

**12** 다음 대화의 마지막 말 앞에 올 순서가 바르게 배열된 것은?

> (A) No, I didn't.
> (B) Great. I'm really curious about this book.
> (C) Look. It's right here. It's about living in New York.
> (D) Did you hear about the new book, *Living in a Foreign Country*?

> G: Me, too.

① (A) – (C) – (B) – (D)
② (B) – (C) – (D) – (A)
③ (C) – (D) – (A) – (B)
④ (D) – (A) – (C) – (B)
⑤ (D) – (B) – (A) – (C)

**13** 다음 중 어법상 어색한 것을 고르시오.

① I've never swum before.
② When have you visited Italy?
③ She has lost her notebook in the classroom.
④ I have just finished my project.
⑤ Have you ever been to Spain before?

**14** 다음 주어진 문장의 밑줄 친 부분과 쓰임이 같은 것은?

> It was interesting to watch sci-fi movies.

① How long does it take to go to the station?
② It was Mike that we visited yesterday.
③ It was difficult for me to answer the question.
④ Start a new file and put this letter in it.
⑤ It will take time to get to the new city hall.

**15** 다음 문장에서 어법상 어색한 것을 바르게 고치시오.

(1) Have you found your umbrella an hour ago?
　_____ ➡ _____

(2) I started to play the piano long time ago. And I still enjoy playing it. So, I played the piano since a long time.
　_____ ➡ _____

(3) I have never gone to London.
　_____ ➡ _____

(4) Search information using the Internet is easy.
　_____ ➡ _____

(5) It's necessary of you to wear a helmet.
　_____ ➡ _____

**16** 다음 우리말을 주어진 어휘를 이용하여 영작하시오.

(1) 그는 10살 때부터 그녀를 알았다.
　(know, since, ten years old)
　➡ _____

(2) 그는 아직 숙제를 끝마치지 못했다. (finish)
　➡ _____

(3) 그들은 그 영화를 네 번 보았다.
　(see the movie)
　➡ _____

(4) 그녀는 파리로 가 버렸다. (현재 여기에 없다.)
　(have)
　➡ _____

(5) 이 웹사이트를 방문한 것이 도움이 되었다.
　(helpful, this web site)
　➡ _____

(6) 아이가 큰 개를 목욕시키기는 힘들다.
　(a child, wash, hard, to)
　➡ _____

**[17~18]** 다음 글을 읽고 물음에 답하시오.

> One day, Dad told Rada and Jonny, "We're going back to Earth tomorrow."
> Rada and Jonny looked at Dad in surprise and floated towards him.
> Rada asked Dad, "What's it like on Earth?"
> "Everything is different there. For example, the sky is blue," answered Dad.
> "ⓐI've never seen a blue sky," said Jonny.
> "The sky is always black here," said Rada.

**17** 다음 빈칸 (A)와 (B)에 알맞은 단어를 넣어 지구와 우주의 하늘의 색깔에 대한 설명을 완성하시오.

> On Earth, the color of the sky is (A)_____ from that in space. It's (B)_____, not black.

**18** 위 글의 밑줄 친 ⓐ의 현재완료와 용법이 <u>다른</u> 것을 <u>모두</u> 고르시오.

① How long <u>have</u> you <u>known</u> Mr. Green?
② I <u>have</u> just <u>finished</u> my work.
③ I <u>have visited</u> New York three times.
④ She <u>has been</u> ill for a week.
⑤ <u>Have</u> you ever <u>written</u> a letter in English?

**[19~21]** 다음 글을 읽고 물음에 답하시오.

> "You don't have to wear your big heavy space suits because there is air everywhere. It's also hard to jump there because Earth pulls you down," said Dad.
> "What ___ⓐ___ ?" asked Rada.

> "There are hills, and they are covered with soft green grass. You can roll down the hills," answered Mom.
> "Dad, ⓑ언덕을 굴러 내려가 본 적 있어요?" asked Rada.
> "Yes, it's really amazing!" answered Dad.
> Jonny was thirsty, so he opened a milk container and shook it. The milk floated in the air and formed balls. Jonny swallowed the balls.
> "Jonny, if you drink milk that way on Earth, you'll get wet," said Mom.

**19** 주어진 영영풀이를 참고하여 빈칸 ⓐ에 철자 e로 시작하는 단어를 쓰시오.

> in addition; besides

➡ e_____

**20** 위 글의 밑줄 친 ⓑ의 우리말에 맞게 한 단어를 보충하여, 주어진 어휘를 알맞게 배열하시오.

> a hill / ever / you / rolled / have / ?

➡ _____

**21** 다음 중 위 글의 내용을 올바르게 이해하지 <u>못한</u> 사람을 고르시오.

> 혜수: It's not necessary for Rada and Jonny to wear their big heavy space suits on Earth.
> 정미: Unlike in space, there is air everywhere on Earth and there is gravity, too.
> 수민: It's not easy to jump on Earth because of gravity.
> 규식: It will be easy to jump on Earth if Rada and Jonny wear their space suits.
> 나윤: Rada and Jonny will be able to roll down the hills.

① 혜수     ② 정미     ③ 수민
④ 규식     ⑤ 나윤

# INSIGHT
## on the textbook

교과서 파헤치기

Lesson **5** **Living Healthily and Safely**

Lesson **6** **Different People, Different Views**

Lesson **7** **Life in Space**

※ 다음 영어를 우리말로 쓰시오.

| | | | |
|---|---|---|---|
| 01 | advice | 22 | intelligent |
| 02 | celebrity | 23 | difficult |
| 03 | during | 24 | hurt |
| 04 | unwise | 25 | promise |
| 05 | sore | 26 | accident |
| 06 | fever | 27 | safety |
| 07 | simple | 28 | example |
| 08 | blink | 29 | increase |
| 09 | thumb | 30 | author |
| 10 | prevent | 31 | terrible |
| 11 | throat | 32 | addiction |
| 12 | health | 33 | cause |
| 13 | skin | 34 | pain |
| 14 | nervous | 35 | from now on |
| 15 | various | 36 | all over the world |
| 16 | hole | 37 | fall asleep |
| 17 | subject | 38 | instead of ~ |
| 18 | dry | 39 | get into ~ |
| 19 | meal | 40 | take a rest |
| 20 | medicine | 41 | have a sore throat |
| 21 | regularly | 42 | for example |
| | | 43 | look well |

※ 다음 우리말을 영어로 쓰시오.

| | | |
|---|---|---|
| 01 | 엄지손가락 | |
| 02 | 구덩이, 구멍 | |
| 03 | 건강 | |
| 04 | 어려운 | |
| 05 | 약속 | |
| 06 | 규칙적으로 | |
| 07 | 단순한 | |
| 08 | 초조한, 불안한 | |
| 09 | 충고 | |
| 10 | 막다, 예방하다 | |
| 11 | 다치다 | |
| 12 | ~ 동안 | |
| 13 | 피부 | |
| 14 | 눈을 깜박이다 | |
| 15 | 다양한 | |
| 16 | 유명인사, 유명인 | |
| 17 | 아픈, 쓰린 | |
| 18 | 현명하지 않은 | |
| 19 | 과목 | |
| 20 | 약 | |
| 21 | 열, 열병 | |

| | | |
|---|---|---|
| 22 | 건조한, 마른 | |
| 23 | 똑똑한, 지적인 | |
| 24 | 목구멍 | |
| 25 | 식사 | |
| 26 | 증가하다 | |
| 27 | 치과의사 | |
| 28 | 현명한, 말쑥한 | |
| 29 | 운동 | |
| 30 | 중독 | |
| 31 | ~ 없이 | |
| 32 | 치통 | |
| 33 | 안전 | |
| 34 | 작가, 저자 | |
| 35 | ~ 대신에 | |
| 36 | 몇몇의 | |
| 37 | 요즈음 | |
| 38 | 콧물이 흐르다 | |
| 39 | 예를 들어 | |
| 40 | 휴식을 취하다, 쉬다 | |
| 41 | ~하려고 애쓰다[노력하다] | |
| 42 | 잠들다 | |
| 43 | 지금부터 | |

※ 다음 영영풀이에 알맞은 단어를 <보기>에서 골라 쓴 후, 우리말 뜻을 쓰시오.

1 _____ : a time when you relax or sleep: _____

2 _____ : a thick piece of soft material: _____

3 _____ : to make something happen: _____

4 _____ : a hollow place in something solid or in the surface of something: _____

5 _____ : to open and close your eyes very quickly: _____

6 _____ : at the same time every day, every week, etc.: _____

7 _____ : the feeling you have when a part of your body hurts: _____

8 _____ : to send someone a written message using a cell phone: _____

9 _____ : the passage at the back of your mouth, where you swallow: _____

10 _____ : to become larger or greater in size, amount, number, etc.: _____

11 _____ : a pill or a liquid that you take when you are sick to help you get better: _____

12 _____ : to stop something from happening, or stop someone from doing: _____

13 _____ : the state of being safe and protected from danger or harm: _____

14 _____ : the short thick finger on your hand that helps you hold things: _____

15 _____ : physical activity that is done in order to become stronger and healthier: _____

16 _____ : the problem when someone cannot stop doing something, or does something too much: _____

| 보기 | | | |
|---|---|---|---|
| throat | medicine | exercise | cause |
| prevent | addiction | rest | text |
| hole | thumb | blink | increase |
| pad | pain | regularly | safety |

※ 다음 우리말과 일치하도록 빈칸에 알맞은 말을 쓰시오.

### Listen and Talk A-1

W: You _____ _____. _____ _____, Inho?

B: I _____ _____ _____ _____. I _____ _____ _____, too.

W: I think you _____ _____ _____. _____ this _____ and _____ _____ you _____ a good _____.

B: OK. _____ _____.

W: 너 아파 보인다. 무슨 일이니, 인호야?
B: 목이 아파요. 열도 나요.
W: 감기에 걸린 것 같구나. 이 약을 먹고 좀 쉬도록 하렴.
B: 알겠어요. 감사합니다.

### Listen and Talk A-2

W: What's _____, Peter?

B: I don't know, Ms. Kim, but my _____ _____ _____ _____.

W: _____ a heating pad _____ it.

B: OK, _____ _____.

W: And _____ _____ you do some _____ _____.

W: 무슨 일이니, Peter?
B: 모르겠어요, 김 선생님, 등이 아파요.
W: 그곳에 찜질 패드를 올려놓으렴.
B: 네, 그럴게요.
W: 그리고 스트레칭 운동을 하렴.

### Listen and Talk A-3

W: What's the _____, Chris?

B: I _____ _____ terrible _____.

W: _____ _____ some _____. _____ this.

B: Thank you.

W: And _____ _____ you go to the _____.

B: OK, _____ _____.

W: 무슨 일이니, Chris?
B: 저는 심한 치통이 있어요.
W: 여기 약이 있단다. 이것을 먹으렴.
B: 감사합니다.
W: 그리고 치과에 가도록 하렴.
B: 네, 알겠어요.

### Listen and Talk A-4

W: What's _____ _____ your leg, Sam?

B: I _____ and _____ my foot _____ I was playing soccer.

W: _____ you _____?

B: Yes, but it _____ a lot.

W: _____ _____ _____ put some ice on it? And _____ _____ you _____ _____ soccer _____ next week.

W: 다리에 무슨 문제가 있니, Sam?
B: 축구를 하다가 넘어져서 발을 다쳤어요.
W: 걸을 수는 있겠니?
B: 네, 하지만 많이 아파요.
W: 얼음을 그 위에 올려놓는 게 어떠니? 그리고 다음 주까지는 축구를 하지 않도록 하렴.

## Listen and Talk B

1. **A:** You _____ _____ _____. What's _____?

   **B:** I _____ _____ _____.

   **A:** _____ _____ _____. _____ _____ you _____ some medicine.

   **B:** OK, I _____.

2. **A:** You _____ _____ _____. What's _____?

   **B:** I _____ _____ _____.

   **A:** That's too bad. _____ _____ you go see a _____.

   **B:** OK, _____ _____.

## Listen and Talk C

**W:** What's _____, Andy?

**B:** Hello, Ms. Kim. My right _____ _____.

**W:** Hmm. Do you _____ your smartphone _____ _____?

**B:** Yes, I _____ _____ _____. Why?

**W:** I think you _____ _____ _____.

**B:** Texting thumb? What's texting thumb?

**W:** It's _____ in _____ _____. You can _____ it _____ _____ too much.

**B:** Oh, I _____ _____ that.

**W:** _____ _____ _____ do some finger stretching exercises?

**B:** OK, I will.

**W:** And _____ _____ _____ _____ _____ too much.

## Review 1

**G:** What's _____, Mike?

**B:** I _____ _____ _____ _____.

**G:** I think you _____ _____ _____ _____.

**B:** OK, _____ _____.

## Review 2

**M:** What's _____ _____, Mina?

**G:** I _____ _____ _____ _____. I also _____ _____ _____ _____.

**M:** I think you have a _____. _____ _____ you _____ _____ _____.

**G:** OK, _____.

1. **A:** 너 몸이 안 좋아 보여. 무슨 일 있니?
   **B:** 머리가 아파.
   **A:** 안됐다. 약을 먹으렴.
   **B:** 응, 그럴게.

2. **A:** 너 몸이 안 좋아 보여. 무슨 일 있니?
   **B:** 감기에 걸렸어.
   **A:** 안됐다. 병원에 가도록 하렴.
   **B:** 응, 그럴게.

**W:** 무슨 일이니, Andy?
**B:** 안녕하세요, 김 선생님. 제 오른손 엄지손가락이 아파요.
**W:** 음. 너 스마트폰을 많이 사용하니?
**B:** 네, 저 문자를 많이 해요. 왜요?
**W:** 내 생각에 너는 texting thumb인 것 같아.
**B:** texting thumb이요? texting thumb이 뭐예요?
**W:** 엄지손가락에 통증이 있는 거야. 문자를 너무 많이 하면 생길 수 있어.
**B:** 오, 그건 몰랐네요.
**W:** 손가락 스트레칭 운동을 좀 하는 게 어떠니?
**B:** 네, 그럴게요.
**W:** 그리고 문자를 너무 많이 하지 않도록 하렴.

**G:** 무슨 일 있니, Mike?
**B:** 머리가 너무 아파.
**G:** 너는 약을 먹는 것이 좋겠다.
**B:** 알겠어, 그럴게.

**M:** 무슨 일 있니, 미나야?
**G:** 목이 아파요. 그리고 콧물도 나요.
**M:** 내 생각에 네가 감기에 걸린 것 같구나. 좀 쉬도록 하렴.
**G:** 네, 그럴게요.

※ 다음 우리말에 맞도록 대화를 영어로 쓰시오.

### Listen and Talk A-1

W: _____

B: _____

W: _____

B: _____

W: 너 아파 보인다. 무슨 일이니, 인호야?
B: 목이 아파요. 열도 나요.
W: 감기에 걸린 것 같구나. 이 약을 먹고 좀 쉬도록 하렴.
B: 알겠어요. 감사합니다.

### Listen and Talk A-2

W: _____

B: _____

W: _____

B: _____

W: _____

W: 무슨 일이니, Peter?
B: 모르겠어요, 김 선생님. 등이 아파요.
W: 그곳에 찜질 패드를 올려놓으렴.
B: 네, 그럴게요.
W: 그리고 스트레칭 운동을 하렴.

### Listen and Talk A-3

W: _____

B: _____

W: _____

B: _____

W: _____

B: _____

W: 무슨 일이니, Chris?
B: 저는 심한 치통이 있어요.
W: 여기 약이 있단다. 이것을 먹으렴.
B: 감사합니다.
W: 그리고 치과에 가도록 하렴.
B: 네, 알겠어요.

### Listen and Talk A-4

W: _____

B: _____

W: _____

B: _____

W: _____

W: 다리에 무슨 문제가 있니, Sam?
B: 축구를 하다가 넘어져서 발을 다쳤어요.
W: 걸을 수는 있겠니?
B: 네, 하지만 많이 아파요.
W: 얼음을 그 위에 올려놓는 게 어떠니? 그리고 다음 주까지는 축구를 하지 않도록 하렴.

## Listen and Talk B

1. A: _____
   B: _____
   A: _____
   B: _____

2. A: _____
   B: _____
   A: _____
   B: _____

## Listen and Talk C

W: _____
B: _____
W: _____
B: _____
W: _____
B: _____
W: _____
B: _____
W: _____
B: _____
W: _____

## Review 1

G: _____
B: _____
G: _____
B: _____

## Review 2

M: _____
G: _____
M: _____
G: _____

1. A: 너 몸이 안 좋아 보여. 무슨 일 있니?
   B: 머리가 아파.
   A: 안됐다. 약을 먹으렴.
   B: 응, 그럴게.

2. A: 너 몸이 안 좋아 보여. 무슨 일 있니?
   B: 감기에 걸렸어.
   A: 안됐다. 병원에 가도록 하렴.
   B: 응, 그럴게.

W: 무슨 일이니, Andy?
B: 안녕하세요, 김 선생님. 제 오른손 엄지손가락이 아파요.
W: 음. 너 스마트폰을 많이 사용하니?
B: 네, 저 문자를 많이 해요. 왜요?
W: 내 생각에 너는 texting thumb인 것 같아.
B: texting thumb이요? texting thumb이 뭐예요?
W: 엄지손가락에 통증이 있는 거야. 문자를 너무 많이 하면 생길 수 있어.
B: 오, 그건 몰랐네요.
W: 손가락 스트레칭 운동을 좀 하는 게 어떠니?
B: 네, 그럴게요.
W: 그리고 문자를 너무 많이 하지 않도록 하렴.

G: 무슨 일 있니, Mike?
B: 머리가 너무 아파.
G: 너는 약을 먹는 것이 좋겠다.
B: 알겠어, 그럴게.

M: 무슨 일 있니, 미나야?
G: 목이 아파요. 그리고 콧물도 나요.
M: 내 생각에 네가 감기에 걸린 것 같구나. 좀 쉬도록 하렴.
G: 네, 그럴게요.

※ 다음 우리말과 일치하도록 빈칸에 알맞은 것을 골라 쓰시오.

1 _____ _____ _____ Your Smartphones!
    A. with         B. Smart        C. Be

2 _____ _____ smartphones is _____ for many of us these _____.
    A. days        B. living      C. difficult    D. without

3 However, _____ or too much _____ of smartphones can _____ various problems.
    A. use         B. cause      C. unwise

4 _____ you a _____?
    A. smombie     B. are

5 All _____ the world, people are walking _____ _____ zombies.
    A. like         B. over      C. around

6 Their heads are _____, and their _____ are _____ their smartphones.
    A. on          B. down      C. eyes

7 We _____ _____ _____ smombies, smartphone zombies.
    A. such        B. people    C. call

8 _____ you are a smombie, you can have _____ _____ problems.
    A. safety      B. if        C. various

9 You _____ not see a hole in the street, _____ you may _____ and get _____.
    A. so          B. hurt      C. may     D. fall

10 You may _____ _____ a car accident, _____.
    A. get         B. too       C. into

11 So _____ can you do _____ _____ these problems?
    A. to          B. what     C. prevent

12 _____ _____.
    A. simple      B. it's

13 Do not look _____ your smartphone _____ you are _____!
    A. while      B. at       C. walking

14 Do you have _____ eyes or _____ _____?
    A. text        B. dry       C. neck

15 Smartphones can _____ various _____ _____.
    A. health     B. cause     C. problems

16 One _____ is _____ _____.
    A. example    B. eyes     C. dry

---

1 스마트폰을 현명하게 사용하라!

2 스마트폰 없이 사는 것은 요즘 많은 사람들에게 어렵다.

3 하지만 스마트폰을 현명하지 않게 사용하거나 너무 과도하게 사용하는 것은 다양한 문제를 야기할 수 있다.

4 당신은 스몸비인가요?

5 전 세계적으로 사람들이 좀비처럼 걸어다니고 있다.

6 그들의 머리는 아래를 향하고, 그들의 눈은 스마트폰을 향하고 있다.

7 우리는 그런 사람들을 스몸비, 즉 스마트폰 좀비라고 부른다.

8 만약 당신이 스몸비라면, 당신은 다양한 안전 관련 문제들을 겪을 수 있다.

9 당신은 거리에 있는 구덩이를 보지 못할 수도 있고, 그래서 넘어져서 다칠지도 모른다.

10 당신은 또한 교통사고를 당할지도 모른다.

11 그렇다면 이런 문제들을 방지하기 위해 무엇을 할 수 있을까?

12 간단하다.

13 걷고 있는 동안에는 스마트폰을 보지 마라!

14 당신은 안구 건조증이나 거북목 증후군이 있나요?

15 스마트폰은 다양한 건강상의 문제를 일으킬 수 있다.

16 한 가지 예가 안구 건조증이다.

**17** _____ you _____ _____ your smartphone, you do not _____ often.
A. blink          B. look          C. when          D. at

**18** Then _____ eyes will _____ _____.
A. dry          B. feel          C. your

**19** _____ problem you can _____ is neck _____.
A. have          B. pain          C. another

**20** When you look _____ _____ your smartphone, the stress _____ your neck _____.
A. at          B. increases          C. on          D. down

**21** Too much _____ of your smartphone, _____ example, too much _____, can _____ neck pain.
A. texting          B. for          C. use          D. cause

**22** We _____ this _____ neck.
A. text          B. call

**23** _____ are some _____ for these _____.
A. tips          B. problems          C. here

**24** For _____ eyes, _____ to _____ often.
A. blink          B. try          C. dry

**25** For text neck, _____ your smartphone _____ to your eye _____.
A. level          B. up          C. move

**26** You can _____ do some neck _____.
A. stretching          B. also          C. exercises

**27** _____ do you _____ when you _____ have your smartphone with you?
A. feel          B. how          C. don't

**28** Do you _____ _____ when your smartphone is not _____?
A. nervous          B. around          C. feel

**29** Do you _____ _____ when you _____ your smartphone and there is no _____ message?
A. sad          B. text          C. feel          D. check

**30** If your _____ are "yes," you _____ have smartphone _____.
A. may          B. answers          C. addiction

**31** _____ are _____ things you can do to _____ this.
A. prevent          B. there          C. various

**32** For example, _____ _____ your smartphone _____ meals or meetings.
A. off          B. turn          C. during

**33** You can talk to people _____ _____ _____ them.
A. texting          B. instead          C. of

17 스마트폰을 볼 때, 당신은 눈을 자주 깜박거리지 않는다.

18 그러면 눈이 건조하다고 느낄 것이다.

19 일어날 수 있는 또 다른 문제는 목 통증이다.

20 스마트폰을 내려다볼 때, 목에 가해지는 압박이 증가한다.

21 스마트폰을 너무 많이 사용하는 것은, 예를 들어, 너무 많이 문자를 하는 것은 목 통증을 일으킬 수 있다.

22 이런 증상을 거북목 증후군이라고 부른다.

23 여기에 이런 문제들을 위한 몇 가지 조언이 있다.

24 안구 건조증에는, 눈을 자주 깜박이려고 노력해라.

25 거북목 증후군에는 당신의 눈높이까지 스마트폰을 위로 올려라.

26 목 스트레칭 운동 또한 할 수 있다.

27 스마트폰이 없을 때 어떤 기분이 드나요?

28 스마트폰이 주위에 없을 때 당신은 초조한 기분이 드는가?

29 스마트폰을 확인했을 때 아무런 문자 메시지가 없으면 슬픈 기분이 드는가?

30 만약 당신의 대답이 '그렇다'이면, 당신은 스마트폰 중독일지도 모른다.

31 이것을 방지하기 위해 할 수 있는 일은 여러 가지가 있다.

32 예를 들어, 식사나 회의 중에는 스마트폰을 꺼라.

33 문자를 보내는 대신에 사람들과 이야기를 할 수 있다.

※ 다음 우리말과 일치하도록 빈칸에 알맞은 말을 쓰시오.

1 _____ _____ _____ Your Smartphones!

2 _____ _____ _____ is difficult for many of us _____

_____.

3 However, _____ _____ _____ _____ _____ of

smartphones _____ _____ various problems.

4 _____ you _____ _____?

5 _____ _____ _____ _____, people are _____

_____ _____ _____.

6 Their heads are _____, and their eyes are _____ _____

_____.

7 We _____ _____ _____ _____, smartphone zombies.

8 If you are a smombie, you can have _____ _____ _____.

9 You _____ _____ _____ a hole in the street, _____

you _____ _____ and _____ _____.

10 You _____ _____ _____ a car accident, _____.

11 So what can you do _____ _____ _____ _____?

12 It's _____.

13 _____ _____ _____ your smartphone _____

you are _____!

14 Do you have _____ _____ or _____ _____?

15 Smartphones can cause _____ _____ _____.

16 _____ _____ is _____ _____.

1 스마트폰을 현명하게 사용하라!

2 스마트폰 없이 사는 것은 요즘 많은 사람들에게 어렵다.

3 하지만 스마트폰을 현명하지 않게 사용하거나 너무 과도하게 사용하는 것은 다양한 문제를 야기할 수 있다.

4 당신은 스몸비인가요?

5 전 세계적으로 사람들이 좀비처럼 걸어다니고 있다.

6 그들의 머리는 아래를 향하고, 그들의 눈은 스마트폰을 향하고 있다.

7 우리는 그런 사람들을 스몸비, 즉 스마트폰 좀비라고 부른다.

8 만약 당신이 스몸비라면, 당신은 다양한 안전 관련 문제들을 겪을 수 있다.

9 당신은 거리에 있는 구덩이를 보지 못할 수도 있고, 그래서 넘어져서 다칠지도 모른다.

10 당신은 또한 교통사고를 당할지도 모른다.

11 그렇다면 이런 문제들을 방지하기 위해 무엇을 할 수 있을까?

12 간단하다.

13 걷고 있는 동안에는 스마트폰을 보지 마라!

14 당신은 안구 건조증이나 거북목 증후군이 있나요?

15 스마트폰은 다양한 건강상의 문제를 일으킬 수 있다.

16 한 가지 예가 안구 건조증이다.

**17** When you _____ _____ your smartphone, you do not _____ _____.

**18** Then your eyes _____ _____ _____.

**19** _____ _____ you can have _____ _____ _____.

**20** When you _____ _____ _____ your smartphone, the _____ _____ your neck _____.

**21** _____ _____ _____ of your smartphone, for example, _____ _____ _____, can cause _____ _____.

**22** We _____ this _____ _____.

**23** _____ _____ _____ _____ for these problems.

**24** For _____ _____, _____ _____ _____ often.

**25** For text neck, _____ your smartphone _____ _____ _____ _____.

**26** You _____ _____ do some _____ _____.

**27** _____ _____ _____ _____ when you don't have your smartphone with you?

**28** Do you _____ _____ when your smartphone is not _____?

**29** Do you _____ _____ when you check your smartphone and there is _____ _____ _____?

**30** If your _____ are "yes," you may have _____ _____.

**31** There are various things you can do _____ _____ _____.

**32** _____ _____, _____ _____ your smartphone _____ meals or meetings.

**33** You _____ talk to people _____ _____ _____ them.

| | |
|---|---|
| **17** | 스마트폰을 볼 때, 당신은 눈을 자주 깜박거리지 않는다. |
| **18** | 그러면 눈이 건조하다고 느낄 것이다. |
| **19** | 일어날 수 있는 또 다른 문제는 목 통증이다. |
| **20** | 스마트폰을 내려다볼 때, 목에 가해지는 압박이 증가한다. |
| **21** | 스마트폰을 너무 많이 사용하는 것은, 예를 들어, 너무 많이 문자를 하는 것은 목 통증을 일으킬 수 있다. |
| **22** | 이런 증상을 거북목 증후군이라고 부른다. |
| **23** | 여기에 이런 문제들을 위한 몇 가지 조언이 있다. |
| **24** | 안구 건조증에는, 눈을 자주 깜박이려고 노력해라. |
| **25** | 거북목 증후군에는 당신의 눈높이까지 스마트폰을 위로 올려라. |
| **26** | 목 스트레칭 운동 또한 할 수 있다. |
| **27** | 스마트폰이 없을 때 어떤 기분이 드나요? |
| **28** | 스마트폰이 주위에 없을 때 당신은 초조한 기분이 드는가? |
| **29** | 스마트폰을 확인했을 때 아무런 문자 메시지가 없으면 슬픈 기분이 드는가? |
| **30** | 만약 당신의 대답이 '그렇다'이면, 당신은 스마트폰 중독일지도 모른다. |
| **31** | 이것을 방지하기 위해 할 수 있는 일은 여러 가지가 있다. |
| **32** | 예를 들어, 식사나 회의 중에는 스마트폰을 꺼라. |
| **33** | 문자를 보내는 대신에 사람들과 이야기를 할 수 있다. |

※ 다음 문장을 우리말로 쓰시오.

**1** Be Smart with Your Smartphones!

➡ _____

**2** Living without smartphones is difficult for many of us these days.

➡ _____

**3** However, unwise or too much use of smartphones can cause various problems.

➡ _____

**4** Are you a smombie?

➡ _____

**5** All over the world, people are walking around like zombies.

➡ _____

**6** Their heads are down, and their eyes are on their smartphones.

➡ _____

**7** We call such people smombies, smartphone zombies.

➡ _____

**8** If you are a smombie, you can have various safety problems.

➡ _____

**9** You may not see a hole in the street, so you may fall and get hurt.

➡ _____

**10** You may get into a car accident, too.

➡ _____

**11** So what can you do to prevent these problems?

➡ _____

**12** It's simple.

➡ _____

**13** Do not look at your smartphone while you are walking!

➡ _____

**14** Do you have dry eyes or text neck?

➡ _____

**15** Smartphones can cause various health problems.

➡ _____

**16** One example is dry eyes.

➡ _____

**17** ➤ When you look at your smartphone, you do not blink often.

➡ _____

**18** ➤ Then your eyes will feel dry.

➡ _____

**19** ➤ Another problem you can have is neck pain.

➡ _____

**20** ➤ When you look down at your smartphone, the stress on your neck increases.

➡ _____

**21** ➤ Too much use of your smartphone, for example, too much texting, can cause neck pain.

➡ _____

**22** ➤ We call this text neck.

➡ _____

**23** ➤ Here are some tips for these problems.

➡ _____

**24** ➤ For dry eyes, try to blink often.

➡ _____

**25** ➤ For text neck, move your smartphone up to your eye level.

➡ _____

**26** ➤ You can also do some neck stretching exercises.

➡ _____

**27** ➤ How do you feel when you don't have your smartphone with you?

➡ _____

**28** ➤ Do you feel nervous when your smartphone is not around?

➡ _____

**29** ➤ Do you feel sad when you check your smartphone and there is no text message?

➡ _____

**30** ➤ If your answers are "yes," you may have smartphone addiction.

➡ _____

**31** ➤ There are various things you can do to prevent this.

➡ _____

**32** ➤ For example, turn off your smartphone during meals or meetings.

➡ _____

**33** ➤ You can talk to people instead of texting them.

➡ _____

※ 다음 괄호 안의 단어들을 우리말에 맞도록 바르게 배열하시오.

**1** (Smart / Be / with / Smartphones! / Your)
➡ _____

**2** (without / living / is / smartphones / for / difficult / of / many / us / days. / these)
➡ _____

**3** (unwise / however, / or / much / too / of / use / can / smartphones / problems. / various / cause)
➡ _____

**4** (you / are / smombie? / a)
➡ _____

**5** (over / all / world, / the / are / people / around / walking / zombies. / like)
➡ _____

**6** (heads / their / down, / are / and / eyes / their / are / smartphones. / their / on)
➡ _____

**7** (call / we / people / such / smombies, / zombies. / smartphone)
➡ _____

**8** (you / if / a / are / smombie, / can / you / various / have / problems. / safety)
➡ _____

**9** (may / you / see / not / hole / a / the / in / street, / you / so / fall / may / hurt. / get / and)
➡ _____

**10** (may / you / into / get / car / a / too. / accident,)
➡ _____

**11** (what / so / you / can / to / do / problems? / these / prevent)
➡ _____

**12** (simple. / it's)
➡ _____

**13** (not / do / at / look / smartphone / your / you / while / walking! / are)
➡ _____

**14** (you / do / dry / have / or / eyes / neck? / text)
➡ _____

**15** (can / smartphones / cause / problems. / health / various)
➡ _____

**16** (example / one / eyes. / dry / is)
➡ _____

1 스마트폰을 현명하게 사용하라!

2 스마트폰 없이 사는 것은 요즘 많은 사람들에게 어렵다.

3 하지만 스마트폰을 현명하지 않게 사용하거나 너무 과도하게 사용하는 것은 다양한 문제를 야기할 수 있다.

4 당신은 스몸비인가요?

5 전 세계적으로 사람들이 좀비처럼 걸어다니고 있다.

6 그들의 머리는 아래를 향하고, 그들의 눈은 스마트폰을 향하고 있다.

7 우리는 그런 사람들을 스몸비, 즉 스마트폰 좀비라고 부른다.

8 만약 당신이 스몸비라면, 당신은 다양한 안전 관련 문제들을 겪을 수 있다.

9 당신은 거리에 있는 구덩이를 보지 못할 수도 있고, 그래서 넘어져서 다칠지도 모른다.

10 당신은 또한 교통사고를 당할지도 모른다.

11 그렇다면 이런 문제들을 방지하기 위해 무엇을 할 수 있을까?

12 간단하다.

13 걷고 있는 동안에는 스마트폰을 보지 마라!

14 당신은 안구 건조증이나 거북목 증후군이 있나요?

15 스마트폰은 다양한 건강상의 문제를 일으킬 수 있다.

16 한 가지 예가 안구 건조증이다.

**17** (you / when / at / look / smartphone, / your / do / you / not / often. / blink)
➡ _____

**18** (your / then / will / eyes / dry. / feel)
➡ _____

**19** (problem / another / can / you / is / have / pain. / neck)
➡ _____

**20** (you / when / down / look / your / at / smartphone, / stress / the / on / increases. / neck / your)
➡ _____

**21** (much / too / of / use / smartphone, / your / example,/ for / much / too / texting, / cause / can / pain. / neck)
➡ _____

**22** (call / we / neck. / text / this)
➡ _____

**23** (are / here / tips / some / for / problems. / these)
➡ _____

**24** (dry / for / eyes, / to / try / often. / blink)
➡ _____

**25** (text / for / neck, / your / move / smartphone / to / up / level. / eye / your)
➡ _____

**26** (can / you / do / also / neck / some / exercises. / stretching)
➡ _____

**27** (do / how / feel / you / you / when / have / don't / smartphone / you? / with / your)
➡ _____

**28** (you / do / nervous / feel / when / smartphone / your / around? / not / is)
➡ _____

**29** (you / do / sad / feel / you / when / check / smartphone / your / and / is / there / text / message? / no)
➡ _____

**30** (your / if / answers / "yes," / are / may / you / addiction. / smartphone / have)
➡ _____

**31** (are / there / things / various / can / you / to / do / this. / prevent)
➡ _____

**32** (example, / for / off / turn / smartphone / your / meals / meetings. / during / or)
➡ _____

**33** (can / you / talk / people / to / of / instead / them. / texting)
➡ _____

---

**17** 스마트폰을 볼 때, 당신은 눈을 자주 깜박거리지 않는다.

**18** 그러면 눈이 건조하다고 느낄 것이다.

**19** 일어날 수 있는 또 다른 문제는 목 통증이다.

**20** 스마트폰을 내려다볼 때, 목에 가해지는 압박이 증가한다.

**21** 스마트폰을 너무 많이 사용하는 것은, 예를 들어, 너무 많이 문자를 하는 것은 목 통증을 일으킬 수 있다.

**22** 이런 증상을 거북목 증후군이라고 부른다.

**23** 여기에 이런 문제들을 위한 몇 가지 조언이 있다.

**24** 안구 건조증에는, 눈을 자주 깜박이려고 노력해라.

**25** 거북목 증후군에는 당신의 눈높이까지 스마트폰을 위로 올려라.

**26** 목 스트레칭 운동 또한 할 수 있다.

**27** 스마트폰이 없을 때 어떤 기분이 드나요?

**28** 스마트폰이 주위에 없을 때 당신은 초조한 기분이 드는가?

**29** 스마트폰을 확인했을 때 아무런 문자 메시지가 없으면 슬픈 기분이 드는가?

**30** 만약 당신의 대답이 '그렇다'이면, 당신은 스마트폰 중독일지도 모른다.

**31** 이것을 방지하기 위해 할 수 있는 일은 여러 가지가 있다.

**32** 예를 들어, 식사나 회의 중에는 스마트폰을 꺼라.

**33** 문자를 보내는 대신에 사람들과 이야기를 할 수 있다.

※ 다음 우리말을 영어로 쓰시오.

**1** 스마트폰을 현명하게 사용하라!

➡ _____

**2** 스마트폰 없이 사는 것은 요즘 많은 사람들에게 어렵다.

➡ _____

**3** 하지만 스마트폰을 현명하지 않게 사용하거나 너무 과도하게 사용하는 것은 다양한 문제를 야기할 수 있다.

➡ _____

**4** 당신은 스몸비인가요?

➡ _____

**5** 전 세계적으로 사람들이 좀비처럼 걸어다니고 있다.

➡ _____

**6** 그들의 머리는 아래를 향하고, 그들의 눈은 스마트폰을 향하고 있다.

➡ _____

**7** 우리는 그런 사람들을 스몸비, 즉 스마트폰 좀비라고 부른다.

➡ _____

**8** 만약 당신이 스몸비라면, 당신은 다양한 안전 관련 문제들을 겪을 수 있다.

➡ _____

**9** 당신은 거리에 있는 구덩이를 보지 못할 수도 있고, 그래서 넘어져서 다칠지도 모른다.

➡ _____

**10** 당신은 또한 교통사고를 당할지도 모른다.

➡ _____

**11** 그렇다면 이런 문제들을 방지하기 위해 무엇을 할 수 있을까?

➡ _____

**12** 간단하다.

➡ _____

**13** 걷고 있는 동안에는 스마트폰을 보지 마라!

➡ _____

**14** 당신은 안구 건조증이나 거북목 증후군이 있나요?

➡ _____

**15** 스마트폰은 다양한 건강상의 문제를 일으킬 수 있다.

➡ _____

**16** 한 가지 예가 안구 건조증이다.

➡ _____

**17** 스마트폰을 볼 때, 당신은 눈을 자주 깜박거리지 않는다.

➡️ _____

**18** 그러면 눈이 건조하다고 느낄 것이다.

➡️ _____

**19** 일어날 수 있는 또 다른 문제는 목 통증이다.

➡️ _____

**20** 스마트폰을 내려다볼 때, 목에 가해지는 압박이 증가한다.

➡️ _____

**21** 스마트폰을 너무 많이 사용하는 것은, 예를 들어, 너무 많이 문자를 하는 것은 목 통증을 일으킬 수 있다.

➡️ _____

**22** 이런 증상을 거북목 증후군이라고 부른다.

➡️ _____

**23** 여기에 이런 문제들을 위한 몇 가지 조언이 있다.

➡️ _____

**24** 안구 건조증에는, 눈을 자주 깜박이려고 노력해라.

➡️ _____

**25** 거북목 증후군에는 당신의 눈높이까지 스마트폰을 위로 올려라.

➡️ _____

**26** 목 스트레칭 운동 또한 할 수 있다.

➡️ _____

**27** 스마트폰이 없을 때 어떤 기분이 드나요?

➡️ _____

**28** 스마트폰이 주위에 없을 때 당신은 초조한 기분이 드는가?

➡️ _____

**29** 스마트폰을 확인했을 때 아무런 문자 메시지가 없으면 슬픈 기분이 드는가?

➡️ _____

**30** 만약 당신의 대답이 '그렇다'이면, 당신은 스마트폰 중독일지도 모른다.

➡️ _____

**31** 이것을 방지하기 위해 할 수 있는 일은 여러 가지가 있다.

➡️ _____

**32** 예를 들어, 식사나 회의 중에는 스마트폰을 꺼라.

➡️ _____

**33** 문자를 보내는 대신에 사람들과 이야기를 할 수 있다.

➡️ _____

※ 다음 우리말과 일치하도록 빈칸에 알맞은 말을 쓰시오.

## Talk and Play

1. A: What's _____?

2. B: I _____ _____ _____.

3. A: That's too bad. _____ _____ you get _____ _____.

4. B: OK, _____ _____.

## After You Read B

1. _____ _____ _____ Your Smartphones!

2. Minho: Yesterday, I _____ on the street and _____ _____.

3. I _____ _____ and I _____ _____ a hole.

4. Reply: _____ _____ use your smartphone _____ you _____ _____.

5. Emma: My eyes _____ _____ when I use my smartphone.

6. Reply: _____ _____ _____ often.

7. Suji: I have neck pain _____ I _____ _____ _____.

8. Reply: Move your smartphone _____ _____ your _____ _____ and do some neck _____ _____.

9. Eric: I think I _____ _____ _____.

10. Reply: _____ _____ your smartphone _____ meals or meetings and talk to people _____ _____ _____ them.

## Around the World

1. This sign says, "_____ _____ of _____ your smartphone _____ you are walking."

2. _____ _____ traffic lights on the ground, _____ people can see them _____ they _____ _____ their smartphones.

3. This sign on the ground _____, "This _____ of the street is for people _____ _____ _____."

## 구석구석 지문 Test

※ 다음 우리말을 영어로 쓰시오.

### Talk and Play

1. A: 무슨 일이니?
➡ _____

2. B: 나는 열이 나.
➡ _____

3. A: 안됐다. 좀 쉬도록 하렴.
➡ _____

4. B: 응, 알겠어.
➡ _____

### After You Read B

1. 스마트폰을 현명하게 사용하라!
➡ _____

2. 민호: 어제, 나는 길에서 넘어져서 다쳤다.
➡ _____

3. 나는 문자를 보내고 있었고 구덩이를 보지 못했다.
➡ _____

4. 대답: 걷는 동안에는 스마트폰을 사용하지 마라.
➡ _____

5. Emma: 나는 스마트폰을 사용할 때 눈이 건조하다고 느낀다.
➡ _____

6. 대답: 눈을 자주 깜박이도록 노력해라.
➡ _____

7. 수지: 나는 문자를 많이 보낼 때 목 통증이 있다.
➡ _____

8. 대답: 스마트폰을 눈높이까지 들고, 목 스트레칭 운동을 해라.
➡ _____

9. Eric: 나는 스마트폰 중독인 것 같다.
➡ _____

10. 대답: 식사나 회의 중에는 스마트폰을 끄고 문자를 보내는 대신에 사람들과 이야기해라.
➡ _____

### Around the World

1. 이 표지판은 "걷는 동안 스마트폰 사용을 주의하세요."라는 의미이다.
➡ _____

2. 바닥에 신호등이 있어서, 사람들이 스마트폰을 사용하는 동안에도 신호등을 볼 수 있다.
➡ _____

3. 바닥에 있는 이 표지판은 "길의 이쪽 편은 문자를 보내고 있는 사람들을 위한 곳입니다."라는 의미이다.
➡ _____

※ 다음 영어를 우리말로 쓰시오.

| | | | |
|---|---|---|---|
| 01 | special | 22 | imaginative |
| 02 | brave | 23 | feather |
| 03 | creative | 24 | different |
| 04 | simple | 25 | sentence |
| 05 | detail | 26 | forget |
| 06 | adventurous | 27 | inventor |
| 07 | whole | 28 | example |
| 08 | beauty | 29 | foolish |
| 09 | subject | 30 | outline |
| 10 | warning | 31 | furthermore |
| 11 | melt | 32 | ready |
| 12 | dynamic | 33 | myth |
| 13 | escape | 34 | warn |
| 14 | flight | 35 | fall in love with ~ |
| 15 | exhibition | 36 | be interested in ~ |
| 16 | romantic | 37 | deal with |
| 17 | difference | 38 | in addition to |
| 18 | skip | 39 | be proud of ~ |
| 19 | forever | 40 | in contrast |
| 20 | gather | 41 | focus on ~ |
| 21 | glue | 42 | Why don't you+동사원형~? |
| | | 43 | try to+동사원형 |

※ 다음 우리말을 영어로 쓰시오.

| 01 | 주제 | | 22 | 다른 | |
|---|---|---|---|---|---|
| 02 | 전부의, 전체의 | | 23 | 어리석은 | |
| 03 | 역동적인 | | 24 | 문장 | |
| 04 | 경고하다 | | 25 | 영원히 | |
| 05 | 달아나다, 탈출하다 | | 26 | 상상력이 풍부한 | |
| 06 | 전시회 | | 27 | 잊어버리다, 잊다 | |
| 07 | 단순한 | | 28 | 발명가 | |
| 08 | 신화 | | 29 | 준비된 | |
| 09 | 아름다움, 미 | | 30 | 게다가, 더욱이 | |
| 10 | 특별한 | | 31 | 예, 사례 | |
| 11 | 모으다 | | 32 | 세부 사항 | |
| 12 | 로맨틱한, 낭만적인 | | 33 | 빼먹다, 거르다 | |
| 13 | 공상 과학 영화 | | 34 | 경고, 주의 | |
| 14 | 모험심이 강한 | | 35 | ~을 다루다 | |
| 15 | (새의) 털, 깃털 | | 36 | 점점 더 높이 | |
| 16 | 차이 | | 37 | ~와 사랑에 빠지다 | |
| 17 | 용감한 | | 38 | ~ 앞에 | |
| 18 | 녹다 | | 39 | ~에 더하여 | |
| 19 | 창의적인 | | 40 | ~하려고 시도하다 | |
| 20 | 비행, 날기 | | 41 | ~에 관심이 있다 | |
| 21 | 윤곽, 외형 | | 42 | ~을 자랑스러워하다 | |
| | | | 43 | ~에 초점을 맞추다 | |

※ 다음 영영풀이에 알맞은 단어를 <보기>에서 골라 쓴 후, 우리말 뜻을 쓰시오.

1 _____ : a public show of something: _____

2 _____ : to say something very loudly: _____

3 _____ : silly or not sensible: _____

4 _____ : the act of flying through the air: _____

5 _____ : showing a strong feeling of love: _____

6 _____ : to get away from a place or person: _____

7 _____ : to come together in a group: _____

8 _____ : a small fact, feature, or piece of information: _____

9 _____ : willing to try new or exciting things: _____

10 _____ : a line that shows the shape of something: _____

11 _____ : to avoid something or not to do something: _____

12 _____ : one of the light soft things that cover a bird's body: _____

13 _____ : one of the parts of bird's or insect's body that it uses to fly: _____

14 _____ : used when adding another piece of information: _____

15 _____ : an old story about gods, brave people, magical creatures, etc.: _____

16 _____ : to tell someone that something bad might happen, so that he or she can avoid it: _____

보기

| | | | |
|---|---|---|---|
| warn | feather | gather | adventurous |
| exhibition | escape | myth | foolish |
| romantic | wing | flight | furthermore |
| skip | shout | detail | outline |

※ 다음 우리말과 일치하도록 빈칸에 알맞은 말을 쓰시오.

### Listen and Talk A-1

G: I'm _____ _____ _____ to a piano concert tomorrow. Do you want _____ _____ _____ me, Kevin?

B: Sure. _____ _____ _____ we _____?

G: The concert _____ _____ 7 o'clock, so _____ _____ at 6 at the bus stop.

B: OK. _____ you _____.

G: 나는 내일 피아노 콘서트에 갈 예정이야. 나랑 같이 갈래, Kevin?
B: 물론이지. 몇 시에 만날까?
G: 콘서트는 7시에 시작하니까 6시에 버스 정류장에서 만나자.
B: 좋아. 그때 보자.

### Listen and Talk A-2

G: I'm _____ _____ _____ _____ Cats this Saturday. Do you _____ _____ _____ _____ with me?

B: Sure. _____ _____ and _____ _____ we meet?

G: The musical starts _____ _____ _____. _____ _____ at 2 at Dream Art Hall.

B: Great. _____ you _____ _____.

G: 나는 이번 주 토요일에 'Cats'를 보러 갈 계획이야. 나랑 같이 갈래?
B: 좋아. 몇 시에 어디서 만날까?
G: 뮤지컬은 3시에 시작해. 2시에 Dream 아트 홀에서 만나자.
B: 좋아. 토요일에 만나자.

### Listen and Talk A-3

G: I'm _____ _____ _____ _____ a soccer game next Friday. _____ _____ _____ me, Jinho?

B: That _____ great. What time _____ _____ _____?

G: _____ _____ at 10:30 _____ _____ _____ Green Stadium.

B: OK. See you then.

G: 나는 다음 주 금요일에 축구 경기를 보러 갈 계획이야. 나랑 같이 가는 게 어떠니, 진호야?
B: 좋은 생각이다. 몇 시에 만날까?
G: Green 경기장 앞에서 10시 30분에 만나자.
B: 좋아. 그때 보자.

### Listen and Talk A-4

B: _____ are you _____ _____ _____ this Sunday?

G: I'm _____ _____ _____ to Dream Amusement Park with my brother. You can go with us _____ you _____ _____.

B: I'd _____ _____. _____ _____ we meet?

G: I want to go early, so _____ _____ at 9 at the subway station.

B: _____ good. I'll see you then.

B: 이번 주 일요일에 무엇을 할 계획이니?
G: 나는 내 남동생과 Dream 놀이동산에 갈 예정이야. 만약 네가 원한다면 우리와 함께 가도 돼.
B: 그러고 싶어. 언제 만날까?
G: 나는 일찍 가고 싶어, 그래서 9시에 지하철역에서 만나자.
B: 좋아. 그때 보자.

### Listen and Talk B

A: I'm _____ _____ _____ a movie this Saturday. Do you _____ _____ go with me?

B: Sure. _____ _____ and _____ should we _____?

A: _____ about _____ at 2:30 in front of Star Movie Theater?

B: OK. _____ _____.

A: 나는 이번 주 토요일에 영화를 볼 계획이야. 나랑 같이 갈래?
B: 물론이지. 몇 시에 어디에서 만날까?
A: Star 영화관 앞에서 2시 30분에 만나는 게 어때?
B: 좋아. 그때 보자.

### Listen and Talk C

(*Smartphone rings.*)

B: Hi, Kate. What's _____?

G: Hi, Minho. What are you _____ _____ _____ this Saturday?

B: _____ _____. Why?

G: I'm _____ _____ _____ to the Van Gogh exhibition at the National Art Museum. Do you _____ _____ _____ with me?

B: I'd _____ _____! He's my favorite painter. _____ _____ _____ we _____?

G: _____ _____ _____ at 11?

B: OK. _____ _____ we meet?

G: _____ meet _____ _____ _____ the ticket office.

B: Sounds good. I'll _____ _____ _____ at 11.

### Review 1

G: I'm _____ _____ go to a piano concert this Friday. _____ _____ _____ _____ me, Kevin?

B: Sure. What time _____ _____ _____ _____?

G: _____ _____ at 10:30 _____ _____ _____ _____ _____.

B: OK. See you _____.

### Review 2

B: I'm _____ _____ _____ to a soccer game tomorrow. _____ _____ _____ to go with me, Susan?

G: Sure. _____ _____ _____ we _____?

B: The game begins at 7, so _____ _____ at 6 _____ _____ _____ Dream Stadium.

G: OK. See you then.

### Review 3

B: Sumi, _____ _____ _____ _____ _____ _____ with Jenny this Saturday. Will you _____ us?

G: Sounds great. _____ time should we _____?

B: How _____ _____ at 12:30?

G: OK. _____ _____ we _____?

B: Let's _____ _____ _____ _____ the shopping mall.

(스마트폰이 울린다.)

B: 안녕, Kate. 무슨 일이야?

G: 안녕, 민호야. 이번 토요일에 뭐 할 거야?

B: 특별한 일은 없어. 왜?

G: 나는 국립 미술관에서 하는 반 고흐 전시회에 갈 계획이야. 나와 함께 갈 래?

B: 그러고 싶어! 그는 내가 가장 좋아하 는 화가거든. 몇 시에 만날까?

G: 11시에 만나는 게 어때?

B: 좋아. 어디에서 만날까?

G: 매표소 앞에서 만나자.

B: 좋아. 11시에 거기에서 봐.

G: 나는 이번 주 금요일에 피아노 콘서 트에 갈 계획이야. 나랑 같이 가는 게 어때, Kevin?

B: 물론이지. 몇 시에 만날까?

G: 10시 30분에 버스 정류장에서 만나자.

B: 좋아. 그때 보자.

B: 나는 내일 축구 경기에 갈 계획이야. 나랑 같이 갈래, Susan?

G: 물론이지. 몇 시에 만날까?

B: 경기는 7시에 시작하니까, Dream 경 기장 앞에서 6시에 만나자.

G: 좋아. 그때 보자.

B: 수미야, 나 이번 주 토요일에 Jenny 와 쇼핑을 갈 계획이야. 너도 같이 갈래?

G: 좋은 생각이야. 몇 시에 만날까?

B: 12시 30분에 만나는 게 어때?

G: 좋아. 어디서 만날까?

B: 쇼핑몰 앞에서 만나자.

※ 다음 우리말에 맞도록 대화를 영어로 쓰시오.

### Listen and Talk A-1

G: _____

_____

B: _____

G: _____

B: _____

G: 나는 내일 피아노 콘서트에 갈 예정이야. 나랑 같이 갈래, Kevin?
B: 물론이지. 몇 시에 만날까?
G: 콘서트는 7시에 시작하니까 6시에 버스 정류장에서 만나자.
B: 좋아. 그때 보자.

### Listen and Talk A-2

G: _____

B: _____

G: _____

B: _____

G: 나는 이번 주 토요일에 'Cats'를 보러 갈 계획이야. 나랑 같이 갈래?
B: 좋아. 몇 시에 어디서 만날까?
G: 뮤지컬은 3시에 시작해. 2시에 Dream 아트 홀에서 만나자.
B: 좋아. 토요일에 만나자.

### Listen and Talk A-3

G: _____

_____

B: _____

G: _____

B: _____

G: 나는 다음 주 금요일에 축구 경기를 보러 갈 계획이야. 나랑 같이 가는 게 어떠니, 진호야?
B: 좋은 생각이다. 몇 시에 만날까?
G: Green 경기장 앞에서 10시 30분에 만나자.
B: 좋아. 그때 보자.

### Listen and Talk A-4

B: _____

G: _____

_____

B: _____

G: _____

B: _____

B: 이번 주 일요일에 무엇을 할 계획이니?
G: 나는 내 남동생과 Dream 놀이동산에 갈 예정이야. 만약 네가 원한다면 우리와 함께 가도 돼.
B: 그러고 싶어. 언제 만날까?
G: 나는 일찍 가고 싶어, 그래서 9시에 지하철역에서 만나자.
B: 좋아. 그때 보자.

### Listen and Talk B

A: _____

B: _____

A: _____

B: _____

A: 나는 이번 주 토요일에 영화를 볼 계획이야. 나랑 같이 갈래?
B: 물론이지. 몇 시에 어디에서 만날까?
A: Star 영화관 앞에서 2시 30분에 만나는 게 어때?
B: 좋아. 그때 보자.

## Listen and Talk C

(*Smartphone rings.*)

B: _____

G: _____

B: _____

G: _____

_____

B: _____

G: _____

B: _____

G: _____

B: _____

---

### Review 1

G: _____

_____

B: _____

G: _____

B: _____

---

### Review 2

B: _____

_____

G: _____

B: _____

G: _____

---

### Review 3

B: _____

G: _____

B: _____

G: _____

B: _____

---

(스마트폰이 울린다.)
B: 안녕, Kate. 무슨 일이야?
G: 안녕, 민호야. 이번 토요일에 뭐 할 거야?
B: 특별한 일은 없어. 왜?
G: 나는 국립 미술관에서 하는 반 고흐 전시회에 갈 계획이야. 나와 함께 갈래?
B: 그러고 싶어! 그는 내가 가장 좋아하는 화가거든. 몇 시에 만날까?
G: 11시에 만나는 게 어때?
B: 좋아. 어디에서 만날까?
G: 매표소 앞에서 만나자.
B: 좋아. 11시에 거기에서 봐.

G: 나는 이번 주 금요일에 피아노 콘서트에 갈 계획이야. 나랑 같이 가는 게 어때, Kevin?
B: 물론이지. 몇 시에 만날까?
G: 10시 30분에 버스 정류장에서 만나자.
B: 좋아. 그때 보자.

B: 나는 내일 축구 경기에 갈 계획이야. 나랑 같이 갈래, Susan?
G: 물론이지. 몇 시에 만날까?
B: 경기는 7시에 시작하니까, Dream 경기장 앞에서 6시에 만나자.
G: 좋아. 그때 보자.

B: 수미야, 나 이번 주 토요일에 Jenny와 쇼핑을 갈 계획이야. 너도 같이 갈래?
G: 좋은 생각이야. 몇 시에 만날까?
B: 12시 30분에 만나는 게 어때?
G: 좋아. 어디서 만날까?
B: 쇼핑몰 앞에서 만나자.

※ 다음 우리말과 일치하도록 빈칸에 알맞은 것을 골라 쓰시오.

**1** _____ Story, _____ Paintings
A. Different      B. Same

**2** We often find _____ _____ with the _____ _____.
A. subject      B. paintings      C. same      D. different

**3** An _____ is *The Flight of Icarus* by Henri Matisse _____ *The Fall of Icarus* _____ Marc Chagall.
A. by      B. and      C. example

**4** They are _____ about the _____ Greek _____.
A. both      B. myth      C. same

**5** The _____ _____ of Icarus
A. Myth      B. Greek

**6** Daedalus was _____ _____ _____.
A. great      B. a      C. inventor

**7** King Minos liked Daedalus' work _____ much _____ he wanted to _____ Daedalus with him _____.
A. that      B. keep      C. forever      D. so

**8** Daedalus, _____, _____ to leave, _____ the King _____ him and his son, Icarus, in a tall tower.
A. so      B. however      C. kept      D. tried

**9** Daedalus _____ _____ _____.
A. to      B. escape      C. wanted

**10** _____ day, Daedalus _____ birds _____.
A. saw      B. one      C. flying

**11** "Wings! I _____ _____!" he _____.
A. shouted      B. need      C. wings

**12** Daedalus then _____ bird _____ and _____ them together with _____.
A. wax      B. feathers      C. gathered      D. glued

**13** When the wings were _____, he _____ his son, "_____ fly too _____ to the sun.
A. warned      B. close      C. don't      D ready

**14** The _____ will _____."
A. melt      B. wax

**15** Daedalus and Icarus _____ _____ _____.
A. to      B. began      C. fly

**16** Icarus was _____ excited _____ he _____ his father's _____.
A. warning      B. that      C. forgot      D. so

**17** He _____ higher and _____, and the wax began to _____.
A. melt      B. flew      C. higher

**18** "Oh, no! I'm _____," Icarus _____.
A. cried      B. falling      C. out

**19** Icarus _____ the sea and _____.
A. into      B. died      C. fell

---

**1** 같은 이야기, 다른 그림

**2** 우리는 종종 같은 주제의 다른 그림들을 발견한다.

**3** 한 예가 Henri Matisse가 그린 "The Flight of Icarus(이카로스의 비행)"와 Marc Chagall이 그린 "The Fall of Icarus(이카로스의 추락)"이다.

**4** 그것들은 둘 다 같은 그리스 신화에 관한 것이다.

**5** Icarus에 관한 그리스 신화

**6** Daedalus는 훌륭한 발명가였다.

**7** Minos왕은 Daedalus의 작품을 매우 좋아해서 Daedalus를 그의 곁에 영원히 두고 싶어 했다.

**8** 그러나 Daedalus는 떠나려고 했고, 그러자 왕은 그와 그의 아들인 Icarus를 높은 탑에 가두었다.

**9** Daedalus는 탈출하고 싶었다.

**10** 어느 날, Daedalus는 새가 날고 있는 것을 보았다.

**11** "날개! 날개가 필요해!" 그가 외쳤다.

**12** 그 다음에 Daedalus는 새의 깃털을 모아 그것들을 밀랍으로 붙였다.

**13** 날개가 준비되었을 때, 그는 아들에게 경고했다. "태양에 너무 가까이 날지 마라.

**14** 밀랍이 녹을 거야."

**15** Daedalus와 Icarus는 날기 시작했다.

**16** Icarus는 매우 흥분해서 아버지의 경고를 잊었다.

**17** 그는 점점 더 높이 날았고, 밀랍은 녹기 시작했다.

**18** "오, 안 돼! 추락하고 있어." Icarus는 비명을 질렀다.

**19** Icarus는 바다로 떨어져서 죽었다.

**20** Two _____ _____

A. Paintings    B. Different

**21** Matisse and Chagall both _____ _____ the same _____ in their paintings, but they are _____.

A. with    B. different    C. subject    D. deal

**22** First, in Matisse's _____, you can _____ Icarus _____, but in Chagall's painting, the boy is _____.

A. painting    B. flying    C. falling    D. see

**23** This difference _____ _____ the _____ _____ that the two painters had.

A. different    B. from    C. comes    D. ideas

**24** Matisse _____ that Icarus was _____ and _____.

A. adventurous    B. thought    C. brave

**25** In _____, Chagall _____ that Icarus was _____.

A. contrast    B. foolish    C. thought

**26** Second, Matisse's painting is very _____, _____ Chagall's painting has many _____.

A. but    B. details    C. simple

**27** In Matisse's painting, _____ are _____ Icarus and _____ _____.

A. only    B. stars    C. there    D. some

**28** _____, Icarus' body has _____ a simple _____.

A. outline    B. furthermore    C. just

**29** _____ _____, Chagall painted many people and houses in _____ _____ Icarus.

A. addition    B. contrast    C. to    D. in

**30** This _____ comes from the _____ painting _____ of the two painters.

A. styles    B. different    C. difference

**31** _____ _____ do you like _____?

A. more    B. painting    C. whose

**32** People will have different answers _____ they may see the _____ thing in _____ _____.

A. because    B. different    C. same    D. ways

**20** 다른 두 그림

**21** Matisse와 Chagall 둘 다 그들의 그림에서 같은 주제를 다루었지만, 그것들은 다르다.

**22** 첫째, Matisse의 그림에서, 여러분은 Icarus가 날고 있는 것을 볼 수 있지만, Chagall의 그림에서는 그 소년이 추락하고 있다.

**23** 이러한 차이는 두 화가들이 갖고 있던 서로 다른 생각에서 기인한다.

**24** Matisse는 Icarus가 용감하고 모험심이 강하다고 생각했다.

**25** 반면에 Chagall은 Icarus가 어리석다고 생각했다.

**26** 둘째, Matisse의 그림은 매우 단순하지만, Chagall의 그림에는 세부적인 것들이 많다.

**27** Matisse의 그림에는 Icarus와 몇 개의 별들만 있다.

**28** 게다가 Icarus의 몸은 단지 단순한 윤곽만으로 되어 있다.

**29** 반면에 Chagall은 Icarus뿐만 아니라 많은 사람들과 집들을 그렸다.

**30** 이러한 차이는 두 화가의 서로 다른 화풍에서 기인한다.

**31** 여러분은 누구의 그림이 더 좋은가?

**32** 사람들은 같은 것을 다른 방식들로 볼 수도 있기 때문에 서로 다른 대답을 할 것이다.

※ 다음 우리말과 일치하도록 빈칸에 알맞은 말을 쓰시오.

**1** _____ Story, _____ _____

**2** We often find _____ _____ with _____ _____ _____.

**3** An _____ is *The Flight of Icarus* _____ Henri Matisse and *The Fall of Icarus* _____ Marc Chagall.

**4** They are _____ about _____ _____ _____ _____.

**5** The _____ _____ of Icarus

**6** Daedalus was _____ _____ _____.

**7** King Minos liked Daedalus' _____ _____ much _____ he _____ _____ _____ Daedalus with him _____.

**8** Daedalus, _____, _____ _____ _____, _____ the King _____ him and his son, Icarus, in a tall tower.

**9** Daedalus _____ _____ _____.

**10** One day, Daedalus _____ _____ _____.

**11** "Wings! _____ _____ _____!" he _____.

**12** Daedalus then _____ bird feathers and _____ _____ _____ _____ _____.

**13** When the wings were _____, he _____ his son, "_____ _____ _____ _____ to the sun.

**14** The wax _____ _____."

**15** Daedalus and Icarus _____ _____ _____ _____.

**16** Icarus was _____ excited _____ he forgot his father's _____.

**17** He flew _____ _____ _____, and the wax began to melt.

**18** "Oh, no! I'm _____," Icarus _____ _____.

**19** Icarus _____ _____ the sea and _____.

---

**1** 같은 이야기, 다른 그림

**2** 우리는 종종 같은 주제의 다른 그림들을 발견한다.

**3** 한 예가 Henri Matisse가 그린 "The Flight of Icarus(이카로스의 비행)"와 Marc Chagall이 그린 "The Fall of Icarus(이카로스의 추락)"이다.

**4** 그것들은 둘 다 같은 그리스 신화에 관한 것이다.

**5** Icarus에 관한 그리스 신화

**6** Daedalus는 훌륭한 발명가였다.

**7** Minos왕은 Daedalus의 작품을 매우 좋아해서 Daedalus를 그의 곁에 영원히 두고 싶어 했다.

**8** 그러나 Daedalus는 떠나려고 했고, 그러자 왕은 그와 그의 아들인 Icarus를 높은 탑에 가두었다.

**9** Daedalus는 탈출하고 싶었다.

**10** 어느 날, Daedalus는 새가 날고 있는 것을 보았다.

**11** "날개! 날개가 필요해!" 그가 외쳤다.

**12** 그 다음에 Daedalus는 새의 깃털을 모아 그것들을 밀랍으로 붙였다.

**13** 날개가 준비되었을 때, 그는 아들에게 경고했다. "태양에 너무 가까이 날지 마라.

**14** 밀랍이 녹을 거야."

**15** Daedalus와 Icarus는 날기 시작했다.

**16** Icarus는 매우 흥분해서 아버지의 경고를 잊었다.

**17** 그는 점점 더 높이 날았고, 밀랍은 녹기 시작했다.

**18** "오, 안 돼! 추락하고 있어." Icarus는 비명을 질렀다.

**19** Icarus는 바다로 떨어져서 죽었다.

20 Two _____ _____

21 Matisse and Chagall _____ _____ _____ the _____ _____ in their paintings, but they are _____.

22 First, in Matisse's painting, you can _____ _____ _____ , but in Chagall's painting, the boy is _____.

23 This difference _____ _____ the _____ _____ that the two painters had.

24 Matisse _____ that Icarus was _____ and _____.

25 _____ _____, Chagall thought that Icarus was _____.

26 Second, Matisse's painting is _____ _____, but Chagall's painting has _____ _____.

27 In Matisse's painting, there are _____ _____ and _____ _____.

28 _____, Icarus' body has just a _____ _____.

29 _____ _____, Chagall painted many people and houses _____ _____ _____ Icarus.

30 This _____ _____ _____ the _____ _____ _____ of the two painters.

31 _____ _____ do you _____ _____?

32 People will have different answers _____ they may see the _____ _____ _____ _____ _____.

20 다른 두 그림

21 Matisse와 Chagall 둘 다 그들의 그림에서 같은 주제를 다루었지만, 그것들은 다르다.

22 첫째, Matisse의 그림에서, 여러분은 Icarus가 날고 있는 것을 볼 수 있지만, Chagall의 그림에서는 그 소년이 추락하고 있다.

23 이러한 차이는 두 화가들이 갖고 있던 서로 다른 생각에서 기인한다.

24 Matisse는 Icarus가 용감하고 모험심이 강하다고 생각했다.

25 반면에 Chagall은 Icarus가 어리석다고 생각했다.

26 둘째, Matisse의 그림은 매우 단순하지만, Chagall의 그림에는 세부적인 것들이 많다.

27 Matisse의 그림에는 Icarus와 몇 개의 별들만 있다.

28 게다가 Icarus의 몸은 단지 단순한 윤곽만으로 되어 있다.

29 반면에 Chagall은 Icarus뿐만 아니라 많은 사람들과 집들을 그렸다.

30 이러한 차이는 두 화가의 서로 다른 화풍에서 기인한다.

31 여러분은 누구의 그림이 더 좋은가?

32 사람들은 같은 것을 다른 방식들로 볼 수도 있기 때문에 서로 다른 대답을 할 것이다.

※ 다음 문장을 우리말로 쓰시오.

**1** Same Story, Different Paintings
➡ _____

**2** We often find different paintings with the same subject.
➡ _____

**3** An example is *The Flight of Icarus* by Henri Matisse and *The Fall of Icarus* by Marc Chagall.
➡ _____

**4** They are both about the same Greek myth.
➡ _____

**5** The Greek Myth of Icarus
➡ _____

**6** Daedalus was a great inventor.
➡ _____

**7** King Minos liked Daedalus' work so much that he wanted to keep Daedalus with him forever.
➡ _____

**8** Daedalus, however, tried to leave, so the King kept him and his son, Icarus, in a tall tower.
➡ _____

**9** Daedalus wanted to escape.
➡ _____

**10** One day, Daedalus saw birds flying.
➡ _____

**11** "Wings! I need wings!" he shouted.
➡ _____

**12** Daedalus then gathered bird feathers and glued them together with wax.
➡ _____

**13** When the wings were ready, he warned his son, "Don't fly too close to the sun.
➡ _____

**14** The wax will melt."
➡ _____

**15** Daedalus and Icarus began to fly.
➡ _____

**16** Icarus was so excited that he forgot his father's warning.
➡ _____

**17** He flew higher and higher, and the wax began to melt.
➡ _____

**18** "Oh, no! I'm falling," Icarus cried out.
➡ _____

**19** Icarus fell into the sea and died.
➡ _____

**20** Two Different Paintings

➡ _____

**21** Matisse and Chagall both deal with the same subject in their paintings, but they are different.

➡ _____

**22** First, in Matisse's painting, you can see Icarus flying, but in Chagall's painting, the boy is falling.

➡ _____

_____

**23** This difference comes from the different ideas that the two painters had.

➡ _____

**24** Matisse thought that Icarus was brave and adventurous.

➡ _____

**25** In contrast, Chagall thought that Icarus was foolish.

➡ _____

**26** Second, Matisse's painting is very simple, but Chagall's painting has many details.

➡ _____

**27** In Matisse's painting, there are only Icarus and some stars.

➡ _____

**28** Furthermore, Icarus' body has just a simple outline.

➡ _____

**29** In contrast, Chagall painted many people and houses in addition to Icarus.

➡ _____

**30** This difference comes from the different painting styles of the two painters.

➡ _____

**31** Whose painting do you like more?

➡ _____

**32** People will have different answers because they may see the same thing in different ways.

➡ _____

## 본문 Test

※ 다음 괄호 안의 단어들을 우리말에 맞도록 바르게 배열하시오.

**1** (Story, / Paintings / Same / Different)
➡ _____

**2** (often / we / different / find / with / paintings / same / subject. / the)
➡ _____

**3** (example / an / is *Icarus* / of / *Flight* / *The* / Henri / by / Matisse / and / *of* / *The* / *Icarus* / *Fall* / Marc / by / Chagall.)
➡ _____

**4** (are / they / about / both / the / Greek / same / myth.)
➡ _____

**5** (Greek / The / Icarus / of / Myth)
➡ _____

**6** (was / Daedalus / a / inventor. / great)
➡ _____

**7** (Minos / King / Daedalus' / liked / so / work / much / that / wanted / he / keep / to / Daedalus / forever. / him / with)
➡ _____

**8** (however, / Daedalus, / to / tried / leave, / the / so / King / him / kept / and / son, / his / Icarus, / a / in / tower. / tall)
➡ _____

**9** (wanted / Daedalus / escape. / to)
➡ _____

**10** (day, / one / saw / Daedalus / flying. / birds)
➡ _____

**11** ("wings! / need / I / wings!" / shouted. / he)
➡ _____

**12** (then / Daedalus / gathered / feathers / bird / and / them / glued / wax. / with / together)
➡ _____

**13** (the / when / wings / ready, / were / warned / he / son, / his / "don't / too / fly / close / sun. / the / to)
➡ _____

**14** (wax / the / melt." / will)
➡ _____

**15** (Icarus / and / Daedalus / began / fly. / to)
➡ _____

**16** (was / Icarus / excited / so / that / forgot / he / warning. / father's / his)
➡ _____

**17** (flew / he / higher, / and / higher / and / wax / the / melt. / to / began)
➡ _____

**18** ("oh, / I'm / no! / falling," / cried / Icarus / out.)
➡ _____

**19** (fell / Icarus / into / sea / the / died. / and)
➡ _____

1 같은 이야기, 다른 그림
2 우리는 종종 같은 주제의 다른 그림들을 발견한다.
3 한 예가 Henri Matisse가 그린 "The Flight of Icarus(이카로스의 비행)"와 Marc Chagall이 그린 "The Fall of Icarus(이카로스의 추락)"이다.
4 그것들은 둘 다 같은 그리스 신화에 관한 것이다.
5 Icarus에 관한 그리스 신화
6 Daedalus는 훌륭한 발명가였다.
7 Minos왕은 Daedalus의 작품을 매우 좋아해서 Daedalus를 그의 곁에 영원히 두고 싶어 했다.
8 그러나 Daedalus는 떠나려고 했고, 그러자 왕은 그와 그의 아들인 Icarus를 높은 탑에 가두었다.
9 Daedalus는 탈출하고 싶었다.
10 어느 날, Daedalus는 새가 날고 있는 것을 보았다.
11 "날개! 날개가 필요해!" 그가 외쳤다.
12 그 다음에 Daedalus는 새의 깃털을 모아 그것들을 밀랍으로 붙였다.
13 날개가 준비되었을 때, 그는 아들에게 경고했다. "태양에 너무 가까이 날지 마라.
14 밀랍이 녹을 거야."
15 Daedalus와 Icarus는 날기 시작했다.
16 Icarus는 매우 흥분해서 아버지의 경고를 잊었다.
17 그는 점점 더 높이 날았고, 밀랍은 녹기 시작했다.
18 "오, 안 돼! 추락하고 있어." Icarus는 비명을 질렀다.
19 Icarus는 바다로 떨어져서 죽었다.

**20** (Different / Two / Paintings)

➡ _____

**21** (Chagall / and / Matisse / deal / both / with / same / the / subject / their / in / paintings, / they / but / different. / are)

➡ _____

**22** (in / first, / painting, / Matisse's / can / you / see / flying, / Icarus / in / but / painting, / Chagall's / boy / falling. / is / the)

➡ _____

_____

**23** (difference / this / from / comes / different / the / ideas / that / two / the / had. / painters)

➡ _____

**24** (thought / Matisse / that / was / Icarus / adventurous. / and / brave)

➡ _____

**25** (contrast, / in / thought / Chagall / Icarus / that / foolish. / was)

➡ _____

**26** (Matisse's / second, / is / painting / simple, / very / Chagall's / but / has / painting / details. / many)

➡ _____

_____

**27** (Matisse's / in / painting, / are / there / Icarus / only / and / stars. / some)

➡ _____

**28** (Icarus' / furthermore, / body / just / has / a / outline. / simple)

➡ _____

**29** (contrast, / in / painted / Chagall / people / many / and / houses / addition / in / Icarus. / to)

➡ _____

**30** (difference / this / from / comes / different / the / styles / painting / the / of / painters. / two)

➡ _____

**31** (painting / whose / like / you / more? / do)

➡ _____

**32** (will / people / different / have / because / answers / they / see / may / same / the / in / thing / ways. / different)

➡ _____

_____

**20** 다른 두 그림

**21** Matisse와 Chagall 둘 다 그들의 그림에서 같은 주제를 다루었지만, 그것들은 다르다.

**22** 첫째, Matisse의 그림에서, 여러분은 Icarus가 날고 있는 것을 볼 수 있지만, Chagall의 그림에서는 그 소년이 추락하고 있다.

**23** 이러한 차이는 두 화가들이 갖고 있던 서로 다른 생각에서 기인한다.

**24** Matisse는 Icarus가 용감하고 모험심이 강하다고 생각했다.

**25** 반면에 Chagall은 Icarus가 어리석다고 생각했다.

**26** 둘째, Matisse의 그림은 매우 단순하지만, Chagall의 그림에는 세부적인 것들이 많다.

**27** Matisse의 그림에는 Icarus와 몇 개의 별들만 있다.

**28** 게다가 Icarus의 몸은 단지 단순한 윤곽만으로 되어 있다.

**29** 반면에 Chagall은 Icarus뿐만 아니라 많은 사람들과 집들을 그렸다.

**30** 이러한 차이는 두 화가의 서로 다른 화풍에서 기인한다.

**31** 여러분은 누구의 그림이 더 좋은가?

**32** 사람들은 같은 것을 다른 방식들로 볼 수도 있기 때문에 서로 다른 대답을 할 것이다.

※ 다음 우리말을 영어로 쓰시오.

1 ▸ 같은 이야기, 다른 그림
➡ _____

2 ▸ 우리는 종종 같은 주제의 다른 그림들을 발견한다.
➡ _____

3 ▸ 한 예가 Henri Matisse가 그린 "*The Flight of Icarus*(이카로스의 비행)"와 Marc Chagall이 그린 "*The Fall of Icarus*(이카로스의 추락)"이다.
➡ _____

4 ▸ 그것들은 둘 다 모두 같은 그리스 신화에 관한 것이다.
➡ _____

5 ▸ Icarus에 관한 그리스 신화
➡ _____

6 ▸ Daedalus는 훌륭한 발명가였다.
➡ _____

7 ▸ Minos왕은 Daedalus의 작품을 매우 좋아해서 Daedalus를 그의 곁에 영원히 두고 싶어 했다.
➡ _____

8 ▸ 그러나 Daedalus는 떠나려고 했고, 그러자 왕은 그와 그의 아들인 Icarus를 높은 탑에 가두었다.
➡ _____

9 ▸ Daedalus는 탈출하고 싶었다.
➡ _____

10 ▸ 어느 날, Daedalus는 새가 날고 있는 것을 보았다.
➡ _____

11 ▸ "날개! 날개가 필요해!" 그가 외쳤다.
➡ _____

12 ▸ 그 다음에 Daedalus는 새의 깃털을 모아 그것들을 밀랍으로 붙였다.
➡ _____

13 ▸ 날개가 준비되었을 때, 그는 아들에게 경고했다. "태양에 너무 가까이 날지 마라.
➡ _____

14 ▸ 밀랍이 녹을 거야."
➡ _____

15 ▸ Daedalus와 Icarus는 날기 시작했다.
➡ _____

16 ▸ Icarus는 매우 흥분해서 아버지의 경고를 잊었다.
➡ _____

17 ▸ 그는 점점 더 높이 날았고, 밀랍은 녹기 시작했다.
➡ _____

18 ▸ "오, 안 돼! 추락하고 있어." Icarus는 비명을 질렀다.
➡ _____

19 ▸ Icarus는 바다로 떨어져서 죽었다.
➡ _____

**20** 다른 두 그림

➡ _____

**21** Matisse와 Chagall 둘 다 그들의 그림에서 같은 주제를 다루었지만, 그것들은 다르다.

➡ _____

**22** 첫째, Matisse의 그림에서, 여러분은 Icarus가 날고 있는 것을 볼 수 있지만, Chagall의 그림에서는 그 소년이 추락하고 있다.

➡ _____

**23** 이러한 차이는 두 화가들이 갖고 있던 서로 다른 생각에서 기인한다.

➡ _____

**24** Matisse는 Icarus가 용감하고 모험심이 강하다고 생각했다.

➡ _____

**25** 반면에 Chagall은 Icarus가 어리석다고 생각했다.

➡ _____

**26** 둘째, Matisse의 그림은 매우 단순하지만, Chagall의 그림에는 세부적인 것들이 많다.

➡ _____

**27** Matisse의 그림에는 Icarus와 몇 개의 별들만 있다.

➡ _____

**28** 게다가 Icarus의 몸은 단지 단순한 윤곽만으로 되어 있다.

➡ _____

**29** 반면에 Chagall은 Icarus뿐만 아니라 많은 사람들과 집들을 그렸다.

➡ _____

**30** 이러한 차이는 두 화가의 서로 다른 화풍에서 기인한다.

➡ _____

**31** 여러분은 누구의 그림이 더 좋은가?

➡ _____

**32** 사람들은 같은 것을 다른 방식들로 볼 수도 있기 때문에 서로 다른 대답을 할 것이다.

➡ _____

※ 다음 우리말과 일치하도록 빈칸에 알맞은 말을 쓰시오.

## Talk and Play

1. A: _____ _____ _____ go to the library this Monday. Do you _____ _____ _____ _____ me, Jiho?

2. B: Sure. _____ _____ should we _____?

3. A: _____ _____ _____ at 5:30?

4. B: OK. _____ should we _____?

5. A: _____ _____ _____ _____ _____ _____ the library.

6. B: _____ good. _____ you _____.

## Around the World

1. Narcissus: Narcissus _____ _____ _____ his beauty.

2. _____ _____, he saw his face in the water and _____ _____ _____ _____ _____.

3. Pandora: There was a box _____ had _____ _____ _____ in the world inside.

4. Pandora opened it, and _____ _____ _____ _____.

5. Orpheus: Orpheus was _____ _____ _____.

6. When his wife died, he _____ Hades and told him, "Please _____ _____ _____ to me."

## After You Read D Reading Project

1. _____: *The Flight of Icarus*

2. _____: Henri Matisse

3. _____ Matisse's _____, Icarus _____ _____.

4. He _____ Icarus was _____ and _____.

5. His painting is very _____. He _____ _____ Icarus and _____ _____.

6. _____: *The Fall of Icarus*

7. _____: Marc Chagall

8. In Chagall's painting, Icarus _____ _____. He _____ Icarus _____ _____.

9. His painting has _____ _____. He painted many people and houses _____ _____ _____ Icarus.

1. A: 나는 이번 주 월요일에 도서관에 갈 예정이야. 나랑 같이 갈래, 지호야?
2. B: 물론이지. 몇 시에 만날까?
3. A: 5시 30분에 만나는 게 어때?
4. B: 좋아. 어디서 만날까?
5. A: 도서관 앞에서 만나자.
6. B: 좋은 생각이야. 그때 보자.

1. Narcissus: Narcissus는 그의 아름다움을 자랑스러워했다.
2. 어느 날, 그는 물에 비친 그의 얼굴을 봤고 자신과 사랑에 빠졌다.
3. 판도라: 세상의 온갖 나쁜 것들이 들어 있는 상자가 하나 있었다.
4. 판도라는 그 상자를 열었고, 그것들이 모두 밖으로 나왔다.
5. 오르페우스: 오르페우스는 훌륭한 음악가였다.
6. 그는 아내가 죽었을 때 하데스를 만나, "제발 제 아내를 제게 돌려보내 주세요."라고 말했다.

1. 제목: The Flight of Icarus(이카로스의 비행)
2. 화가: Henri Matisse
3. Matisse의 그림에서, Icarus는 날고 있다.
4. 그는 Icarus가 용감하고 모험심이 강하다고 생각했다.
5. 그의 그림은 매우 단순하다. 그는 Icarus와 몇 개의 별들만 그렸다.
6. 제목: The Fall of Icarus(이카로스의 추락)
7. 화가: Marc Chagall
8. Chagall의 그림에서, Icarus는 추락하고 있다. 그는 Icarus가 어리석다고 생각했다.
9. 그의 그림에는 세부적인 것들이 많다. 그는 Icarus뿐만 아니라 많은 사람들과 집들을 그렸다.

## 구석구석 지문 Test

※ 다음 우리말을 영어로 쓰시오.

### Talk and Play

1. A: 나는 이번 주 월요일에 도서관에 갈 예정이야. 나랑 같이 갈래, 지호야?
➡

2. B: 물론이지. 몇 시에 만날까?
➡

3. A: 5시 30분에 만나는 게 어때?
➡

4. B: 좋아. 어디서 만날까?
➡

5. A: 도서관 앞에서 만나자.
➡

6. B: 좋은 생각이야. 그때 보자.
➡

### Around the World

1. Narcissus: Narcissus는 그의 아름다움을 자랑스러워했다.
➡

2. 어느 날, 그는 물에 비친 그의 얼굴을 봤고 자신과 사랑에 빠졌다.
➡

3. 판도라: 세상의 온갖 나쁜 것들이 들어 있는 상자가 하나 있었다.
➡

4. 판도라는 그 상자를 열었고, 그것들이 모두 밖으로 나왔다.
➡

5. 오르페우스: 오르페우스는 훌륭한 음악가였다.
➡

6. 그는 아내가 죽었을 때 하데스를 만나, "제발 제 아내를 제게 돌려보내 주세요."라고 말했다.
➡

### After You Read D Reading Project

1. 제목: 이카로스의 비행
➡

2. 화가: Henri Matisse
➡

3. Matisse의 그림에서, Icarus는 날고 있다.
➡

4. 그는 Icarus가 용감하고 모험심이 강하다고 생각했다.
➡

5. 그의 그림은 매우 단순하다. 그는 Icarus와 몇 개의 별들만 그렸다.
➡

6. 제목: 이카로스의 추락
➡

7. 화가: Marc Chagall
➡

8 Chagall의 그림에서, Icarus는 추락하고 있다. 그는 Icarus가 어리석다고 생각했다.
➡

9. 그의 그림에는 세부적인 것들이 많다. 그는 Icarus뿐만 아니라 많은 사람들과 집들을 그렸다.
➡

※ 다음 영어를 우리말로 쓰시오.

| | | |
|---|---|---|
| 01 | arrive | |
| 02 | adventure | |
| 03 | taste | |
| 04 | amazing | |
| 05 | difficult | |
| 06 | float | |
| 07 | shout | |
| 08 | balloon | |
| 09 | container | |
| 10 | different | |
| 11 | curious | |
| 12 | thirsty | |
| 13 | everywhere | |
| 14 | space station | |
| 15 | exploration | |
| 16 | finally | |
| 17 | since | |
| 18 | foreign | |
| 19 | excited | |
| 20 | lie | |
| 21 | swallow | |

| | | |
|---|---|---|
| 22 | shake | |
| 23 | towards | |
| 24 | spaceship | |
| 25 | fix | |
| 26 | wet | |
| 27 | laugh | |
| 28 | save | |
| 29 | recently | |
| 30 | space suit | |
| 31 | form | |
| 32 | secret | |
| 33 | soft | |
| 34 | thrilling | |
| 35 | don't have to+동사원형 | |
| 36 | each other | |
| 37 | be covered with | |
| 38 | pull down | |
| 39 | lie down | |
| 40 | for example | |
| 41 | be curious about ~ | |
| 42 | run up to ~ | |
| 43 | not ~ anymore | |

※ 다음 우리말을 영어로 쓰시오.

| 01 | 모험 | |
| 02 | 풍선 | |
| 03 | 어려운 | |
| 04 | 떠가다 | |
| 05 | 신난, 흥분한 | |
| 06 | 다른 | |
| 07 | 탐험, 탐사 | |
| 08 | 부드러운 | |
| 09 | 놀라운 | |
| 10 | 마침내 | |
| 11 | ~한 이래로 | |
| 12 | 고치다 | |
| 13 | 외국의 | |
| 14 | 우주선 | |
| 15 | 비밀, 기밀 | |
| 16 | 모든 곳에 | |
| 17 | 바람 | |
| 18 | 외치다 | |
| 19 | 흔들다 | |
| 20 | 궁금한, 호기심이 많은 | |
| 21 | ~쪽으로, ~을 향하여 | |

| 22 | 우주복 | |
| 23 | 목마른 | |
| 24 | 그릇, 용기 | |
| 25 | 삼키다 | |
| 26 | 언덕 | |
| 27 | 눕다 | |
| 28 | 아주 신나는 | |
| 29 | 웃다 | |
| 30 | 젖은 | |
| 31 | 풀, 잔디 | |
| 32 | 최근에 | |
| 33 | 구하다 | |
| 34 | 맛 | |
| 35 | ~에 관해 궁금해 하다 | |
| 36 | ~하려고 시도하다 | |
| 37 | 놀라서 | |
| 38 | 더 이상 ~ 않다 | |
| 39 | ~으로 뒤덮이다 | |
| 40 | ~에 타다 | |
| 41 | 예를 들어 | |
| 42 | (둘 사이의) 서로 | |
| 43 | 굴러 내려가다 | |

※ 다음 영영풀이에 알맞은 단어를 <보기>에서 골라 쓴 후, 우리말 뜻을 쓰시오.

1 _____ : extremely surprising: _____

2 _____ : to stay on the surface of a liquid and not sink: _____

3 _____ : a vehicle used for travel in space: _____

4 _____ : to make something into a particular shape: _____

5 _____ : to reach a place, especially at the end of a journey: _____

6 _____ : to keep someone or something safe from death, harm, loss, etc.:

_____

7 _____ : interested in learning about people or things around you: _____

8 _____ : covered with or containing liquid, especially water: _____

9 _____ : the activity of searching and finding out about something: _____

10 _____ : belonging or connected to a country that is not your own: _____

11 _____ : in the direction of, or closer to someone or something: _____

12 _____ : a place or vehicle in space where people can stay: _____

13 _____ : an unusual, exciting, and possibly dangerous activity, such as a trip:

_____

14 _____ : to cause food, drink, pills, etc. to move from your mouth into your

stomach by using the muscles of your throat: _____

15 _____ : to arrive on the ground or other surface after moving down through the

air: _____

16 _____ : a piece of information that is only known by one person or a few people

and should not be told to others: _____

| 보기 | | | |
|---|---|---|---|
| land | foreign | amazing | spaceship |
| form | arrive | towards | secret |
| adventure | float | wet | save |
| swallow | space station | curious | exploration |

※ 다음 우리말과 일치하도록 빈칸에 알맞은 말을 쓰시오.

### Listen and Talk A-1

B: Did you _____ _____ the first spaceship _____ _____ _____ _____?

G: No, I didn't. I'm _____ _____ it.

B: This is a poster of the _____.

G: Really? I _____ _____ _____ it.

B: 너는 우주에 간 첫 번째 우주선에 대해 들어 봤니?
G: 아니, 못 들어 봤어. 궁금하다.
B: 이것이 그 우주선 포스터야.
G: 정말? 그것을 사고 싶다.

### Listen and Talk A-2

G: _____ you _____ _____ the new book about Mars?

B: No, I didn't. _____ _____ _____ _____ Mars.

G: Look. It's _____ _____. It's _____ Mars and its moons.

B: Great. I think I'll _____ the book.

G: 너는 화성에 관한 새로운 책에 관해 들어 봤니?
B: 아니, 못 들어 봤어. 나는 화성에 관해 정말 궁금해.
G: 봐. 바로 여기 있어. 그것은 화성과 그것의 위성들에 관한 내용이야.
B: 멋지다. 이 책을 사야겠어.

### Listen and Talk A-3

G: _____ _____ _____ _____ _____ the space marathon?

B: No, _____ _____.

G: It's a marathon on a _____. _____ _____ this video.

B: OK. _____ _____ _____ _____ it.

G: 너는 우주 마라톤에 대해 들어 봤니?
B: 아니, 못 들어 봤어.
G: 그것은 우주 정거장에서 하는 마라톤이야. 이 비디오를 봐.
B: 알겠어. 정말 궁금하다.

### Listen and Talk A-4

G: Did you hear _____ the new _____ _____?

B: Yes, I did. It's _____ _____ _____ ice cream.

G: Yes, and _____ _____ _____. It _____ _____.

B: I'm really _____ _____ _____ _____.

G: 너는 새로운 우주 음식에 대해 들어 봤니?
B: 응, 들어 봤어. 그건 일종의 아이스크림이야.
G: 응, 여기 있어. 맛있어 보인다.
B: 그 맛이 참 궁금하다.

### Listen and Talk B

1. A: Look at this. Did you hear _____ the new musical?

   B: Yes, I did. I _____ it has great songs.

   A: Oh, I'm really _____ _____ it.

2. A: _____ _____ this. Did you _____ _____ the new musical?

   B: _____, I _____.

   A: I heard _____ _____ _____ _____ _____.

   B: Oh, I'm _____ _____ _____ it.

1. A: 이것 봐. 새 뮤지컬에 대해 들어 봤니?
   B: 응, 들어 봤어. 좋은 노래들이 나온다고 들었어.
   A: 오, 정말 궁금하다.

2. A: 이것 봐. 새 뮤지컬에 대해 들어 봤니?
   B: 아니, 못 들어 봤어.
   A: 좋은 노래들이 나온다고 들었어.
   B: 오, 정말 궁금하다.

### Listen and Talk C

**B:** Subin, did you _____ _____ the new movie, *Life on the Moon*?

**G:** No, I _____.

**B:** I _____ it's really _____.

**G:** I'm really _____ _____ the movie. What's it _____?

**B:** It's _____ a man _____ is _____ _____ _____ on the moon.

**G:** That _____ _____.

**B:** Look. The movie _____ _____ at the Space Theater here.

**G:** _____ _____ is the movie?

**B:** It _____ _____ 2:30.

**G:** _____ _____ _____ first _____ _____ see the movie.

**B:** OK. I'm _____. _____ _____!

**B:** 수빈아, "달에서의 생활"이라는 새 영화에 대해서 들어 봤니?
**G:** 아니.
**B:** 굉장히 좋다고 들었거든.
**G:** 그 영화가 정말 궁금하네. 뭐에 관한 거야?
**B:** 달에서 살기 위해 노력하는 한 남자에 관한 영화래.
**G:** 그거 재미있겠다.
**B:** 봐. 그 영화가 여기 우주 극장에서 상영되고 있어.
**G:** 영화가 몇 시에 상영되는데?
**B:** 2시 30분에 시작해.
**G:** 우선 점심부터 먹고 영화를 보자.
**B:** 좋아. 나 배고파. 가자!

### Review 1

**G:** Tony, _____ _____ _____ _____ the movie, *My Hero*?

**B:** _____, I _____.

**G:** Well, I _____ it's really good.

**B:** I'm really _____ _____ the movie. What's it _____?

**G:** It's _____ a father _____ _____ _____ _____.

**G:** Tony, 영화 My Hero에 대해 들어 봤니?
**B:** 아니, 못 들어 봤어.
**G:** 음, 정말 좋다고 들었어.
**B:** 그 영화에 대해 정말 궁금하다. 무엇에 대한 것이니?
**G:** 그것은 아들을 구하는 아빠에 관한 거야.

### Review 2

**G:** _____ you _____ _____ the new book, *Living in a Foreign Country*?

**B:** No, I didn't.

**G:** Look. It's _____ here. It's _____ _____ in New York.

**B:** Great. I'm _____ _____ _____ this book.

**G:** _____, _____.

**G:** 새 책인 "Living in a Foreign Country"에 대해 들어 봤니?
**B:** 아니, 못 들어 봤어.
**G:** 봐. 바로 여기 있어. 그것은 뉴욕에서의 삶에 관한 거야.
**B:** 멋지다. 이 책이 정말 궁금해.
**G:** 나도 그래.

※ 다음 우리말에 맞도록 대화를 영어로 쓰시오.

### Listen and Talk A-1

B: _____

G: _____

B: _____

G: _____

B: 너는 우주에 간 첫 번째 우주선에 대해 들어 봤니?
G: 아니, 못 들어 봤어. 궁금하다.
B: 이것이 그 우주선 포스터야.
G: 정말? 그것을 사고 싶다.

### Listen and Talk A-2

G: _____

B: _____

G: _____

B: _____

G: 너는 화성에 관한 새로운 책에 관해 들어 봤니?
B: 아니, 못 들어 봤어. 나는 화성에 관해 정말 궁금해.
G: 봐. 바로 여기 있어. 그것은 화성과 그것의 위성들에 관한 내용이야.
B: 멋지다. 이 책을 사야겠어.

### Listen and Talk A-3

G: _____

B: _____

G: _____

B: _____

G: 너는 우주 마라톤에 대해 들어 봤니?
B: 아니, 못 들어 봤어.
G: 그것은 우주 정거장에서 하는 마라톤이야. 이 비디오를 봐.
B: 알겠어. 정말 궁금하다.

### Listen and Talk A-4

G: _____

B: _____

G: _____

B: _____

G: 너는 새로운 우주 음식에 대해 들어 봤니?
B: 응, 들어 봤어. 그건 일종의 아이스크림이야.
G: 응, 여기 있어. 맛있어 보인다.
B: 그 맛이 참 궁금하다.

### Listen and Talk B

1. A: _____

   B: _____

   A: _____

2. A: _____

   B: _____

   A: _____

   B: _____

1. A: 이것 봐. 새 뮤지컬에 대해 들어 봤니?
   B: 응, 들어 봤어. 좋은 노래들이 나온다고 들었어.
   A: 오, 정말 궁금하다.

2. A: 이것 봐. 새 뮤지컬에 대해 들어 봤니?
   B: 아니, 못 들어 봤어.
   A: 좋은 노래들이 나온다고 들었어.
   B: 오, 정말 궁금하다.

## Listen and Talk C

B: _____

G: _____

B: _____

G: _____

B: _____

G: _____

B: _____

G: _____

B: _____

G: _____

B: _____

B: 수빈아, "달에서의 생활"이라는 새 영화에 대해서 들어 봤니?

G: 아니.

B: 굉장히 좋다고 들었거든.

G: 그 영화가 정말 궁금하네. 뭐에 관한 거야?

B: 달에서 살기 위해 노력하는 한 남자에 관한 영화래.

G: 그거 재미있겠다.

B: 봐. 그 영화가 여기 우주 극장에서 상영되고 있어.

G: 영화가 몇 시에 상영되는데?

B: 2시 30분에 시작해.

G: 우선 점심부터 먹고 영화를 보자.

B: 좋아. 나 배고파. 가자!

## Review 1

G: _____

B: _____

G: _____

B: _____

G: _____

G: Tony, 영화 My Hero에 대해 들어 봤니?

B: 아니, 못 들어 봤어.

G: 음, 정말 좋다고 들었어.

B: 그 영화에 대해 정말 궁금하다. 무엇에 대한 것이니?

G: 그것은 아들을 구하는 아빠에 관한 거야.

## Review 2

G: _____

B: _____

G: _____

B: _____

G: _____

G: 새 책인 "Living in a Foreign Country"에 대해 들어 봤니?

B: 아니, 못 들어 봤어.

G: 봐. 바로 여기 있어. 그것은 뉴욕에서의 삶에 관한 거야.

B: 멋지다. 이 책이 정말 궁금해.

G: 나도 그래.

※ 다음 우리말과 일치하도록 빈칸에 알맞은 것을 골라 쓰시오.

**1** The _____ New _____
A. Thing      B. Best

**2** Rada lived on a _____ world, _____ _____ in space.
A. out      B. little      C. far

**3** She _____ _____ her father, mother, and brother Jonny.
A. with      B. there      C. lived

**4** Rada's father and _____ people _____ _____ spaceships.
A. on      B. other      C. worked

**5** _____ Rada and Jonny were children, and they _____ _____ in space.
A. were      B. only      C. born

**6** _____ day, Dad told Rada and Jonny, "We're _____ _____ to Earth tomorrow."
A. going      B. one      C. back

**7** Rada and Jonny looked at Dad _____ _____ and _____ him.
A. towards      B. in      C. floated      D. surprise

**8** Rada asked Dad, "_____ _____ _____ on Earth?"
A. it      B. what's      C. like

**9** "_____ is _____ there.
A. different      B. everything

**10** _____ _____ , the sky is blue," _____ Dad.
A. answered      B. example      C. for

**11** "I've _____ _____ a blue sky," _____ Jonny.
A. seen      B. never      C. said

**12** "The sky _____ _____ _____ here," said Rada.
A. always      B. is      C. black

**13** "You _____ _____ to wear your big heavy space _____ because _____ is air everywhere.
A. have      B. there      C. don't      D. suits

**14** It's also _____ to jump there _____ Earth _____ you _____," said Dad.
A. pulls      B. hard      C. down      D. because

**15** "_____ _____?" asked Rada.
A. else      B. what

**16** "There are hills, and they are _____ _____ soft green _____.
A. with      B. grass      C. covered

1  최고의 새로운 것

2  Rada는 먼 우주의 작은 세계에 살고 있었다.

3  그녀는 아빠, 엄마 그리고 남동생 Jonny와 함께 그곳에서 살고 있었다.

4  Rada의 아빠와 다른 사람들은 우주선에서 일했다.

5  Rada와 Jonny만이 아이들이었고, 그들은 우주에서 태어났다.

6  어느 날, 아빠가 Rada와 Jonny에게, "우리는 내일 지구로 돌아갈 거야."라고 말했다.

7  Rada와 Jonny는 깜짝 놀라 아빠를 바라보았고, 그에게 둥둥 떠서 갔다.

8  Rada가 아빠에게, "지구는 어떤 곳인가요?"라고 물었다.

9  "그곳에선 모든 것이 다르단다.

10  예를 들어, 하늘은 파란색이지."라고 아빠가 대답했다.

11  "전 한 번도 파란 하늘을 본 적이 없어요."라고 Jonny가 말했다.

12  "여기는 하늘이 항상 검은색이잖아요."라고 Rada가 말했다.

13  "그곳에는 모든 곳에 공기가 있기 때문에 크고 무거운 우주복을 입을 필요가 없단다.

14  또한 지구가 너희들을 끌어당기기 때문에 거기에서는 점프하는 것도 어렵단다." 아빠가 말했다.

15  "그 밖에 또 뭐가 있어요?" Rada가 물었다.

16  "언덕들이 있는데 그것들은 부드러운 초록색의 잔디로 뒤덮여 있단다.

**17** You can _____ _____ the hills," _____ Mom.

A. down        B. roll        C. answered

**18** "Dad, _____ you _____ _____ _____ a hill?" asked Rada.

A. ever        B. down        C. have        D. rolled

**19** "Yes, it's really _____!" _____ Dad.

A. answered        B. amazing

**20** Jonny was _____, so he _____ a milk container and _____ it.

A. shook        B. thirsty        C. opened

**21** The milk _____ in the _____ and _____ balls.

A. formed        B. floated        C. air

**22** Jonny _____ the _____.

A. balls        B. swallowed

**23** "Jonny, _____ you drink milk that _____ on Earth, you'll _____ _____," said Mom.

A. way        B. wet        C. get        D. if

**24** _____ that night, Rada and Jonny _____ a _____ time about Earth.

A. long        B. talked        C. later

**25** It was _____ to think about _____ the new _____ they were _____ to see and do.

A. things        B. exciting        C. all        D. going

**26** There was _____ _____ _____ Rada and Jonny really wanted to do.

A. new        B. thing        C. one

**27** They _____ about it _____ _____ and didn't tell Mom and Dad _____ it.

A. night        B. thought        C. all        D. about

**28** It was _____ _____.

A. secret        B. their

**29** The _____ day, Rada's family _____ _____ a spaceship.

A. got        B. next        C. on

**30** "It's _____ to _____ a long _____," said Mom.

A. trip        B. going        C. be

**31** "That's _____. I'm _____ _____!" said Rada.

A. so        B. alright        C. excited

**32** The spaceship _____ _____.

A. landed        B. finally

---

**17** 언덕을 굴러 내려갈 수도 있어." 엄마가 대답했다.

**18** "아빠, 언덕을 굴러 내려가 본 적 있어요?" Rada가 물었다.

**19** "그럼, 정말 놀라워!" 아빠가 대답했다.

**20** Jonny는 목이 말라서 우유 용기를 열어 그것을 흔들었다.

**21** 우유가 공기 중으로 떠서 방울을 형성했다.

**22** Jonny는 그 우유 방울을 삼켰다.

**23** "Jonny, 만약 네가 지구에서 그런 식으로 우유를 마신다면, 다 젖을 거야." 엄마가 말했다.

**24** 그날 밤 늦게, Rada와 Jonny는 지구에 대해서 오랜 시간 이야기했다.

**25** 그들이 보고, 하게 될 모든 새로운 것들을 생각하는 것은 흥미로웠다.

**26** Rada와 Jonny가 정말로 하고 싶었던 한 가지 새로운 것이 있었다.

**27** 그들은 밤새 그것에 대해서 생각했고 엄마와 아빠에게는 그것을 말하지 않았다.

**28** 그것은 그들의 비밀이었다.

**29** 다음날, Rada의 가족은 우주선에 올랐다.

**30** "긴 여행이 될 거야." 엄마가 말했다.

**31** "괜찮아요. 정말 신나요!" Rada가 말했다.

**32** 우주선이 마침내 착륙했다.

**33** "Dad, it's _____ _____ _____ on Earth," said Rada.
  A. walk          B. to          C. difficult

**34** "I know. Earth is _____ _____ _____," said Dad.
  A. down          B. you          C. pulling

**35** Rada and Jonny _____ _____ _____.
  A. float          B. couldn't          C. anymore

**36** That was the _____ _____ _____.
  A. new          B. first          C. thing

**37** "_____ that _____?" asked Rada.
  A. sound          B. what's

**38** "A _____ is _____," said Mom.
  A. singing          B. bird

**39** "I've _____ _____ a bird _____," said Rada.
  A. heard          B. sing          C. never

**40** "And I've _____ _____ the _____," said Jonny.
  A. felt          B. wind          C. never

**41** _____ were _____ _____ things.
  A. new          B. these          C. all

**42** Rada and Jonny _____ _____ _____ _____ hill.
  A. ran          B. nearest          C. up          D. the

**43** At the _____, they looked at _____ _____ and _____.
  A. other          B. top          C. laughed          D. each

**44** Then they _____ _____ on the _____ green grass and _____ down the hill.
  A. rolled          B. down          C. lay          D. soft

**45** That was _____ _____!
  A. secret          B. their

**46** "This is the _____ _____ thing of all!" _____ Rada and Jonny.
  A. shouted          B. new          C. best

**47** And they _____ _____ the _____ of the hill again.
  A. top          B. up          C. ran          D. to

---

**33** "아빠, 지구에서는 걷는 것이 어려워요." Rada가 말했다.

**34** "그래. 지구가 너를 끌어당기고 있거든." 아빠가 말했다.

**35** Rada와 Jonny는 더 이상 떠다닐 수 없었다.

**36** 그것이 첫 번째 새로운 것이었다.

**37** "저건 무슨 소리죠?"라고 Rada가 물었다.

**38** "새가 노래하는 거야." 엄마가 말했다.

**39** "새가 노래하는 것을 들어 본 적이 없어요."라고 Rada가 말했다.

**40** "그리고 저는 바람을 느껴 본 적도 없어요."라고 Jonny가 말했다.

**41** 이러한 것들이 모두 새로운 것들이었다.

**42** Rada와 Jonny는 가장 가까운 언덕으로 뛰어 올라갔다.

**43** 꼭대기에서, 그들은 서로를 쳐다보고 웃었다.

**44** 그리고 나서 그들은 부드러운 초록 잔디에 누워서 언덕 아래로 굴러 내려갔다.

**45** 그것이 그들의 비밀이었다!

**46** "이것이 모든 것들 중에서 최고의 새로운 것이에요!" Rada와 Jonny는 외쳤다.

**47** 그리고 그들은 언덕 꼭대기로 다시 뛰어 올라갔다.

※ 다음 우리말과 일치하도록 빈칸에 알맞은 말을 쓰시오.

**1** The _____ New _____

**2** Rada lived on a little world, _____ _____ _____ _____.

**3** She _____ _____ _____ her father, mother, and _____ Jonny.

**4** Rada's father and _____ people _____ _____ spaceships.

**5** _____ Rada and Jonny were children, and they _____ _____ _____ _____.

**6** _____ _____, Dad told Rada and Jonny, "We're _____ _____ Earth tomorrow."

**7** Rada and Jonny looked at Dad _____ _____ and _____ him.

**8** Rada asked Dad, "_____ _____ _____ on Earth?"

**9** "_____ _____ _____ there.

**10** _____ _____, the sky is blue," answered Dad.

**11** "_____ _____ _____ a blue sky," said Jonny.

**12** "The sky _____ _____ _____ here," said Rada.

**13** "You _____ _____ _____ wear your big heavy space suits _____ _____ _____ _____ everywhere.

**14** It's also hard to _____ there because Earth _____ _____ _____," said Dad.

**15** "_____ _____?" asked Rada.

**16** "There are hills, and they _____ _____ _____ soft green grass.

**17** You can _____ _____ the hills," answered Mom.

**18** "Dad, _____ _____ _____ _____ _____ a hill?" asked Rada.

**19** "Yes, it's _____ _____!" answered Dad.

**20** Jonny was _____, _____ he _____ a milk container and _____ it.

**21** The milk _____ in the air and _____ balls.

**22** Jonny _____ the balls.

**23** "Jonny, _____ you drink milk _____ _____ on Earth, you'll _____ _____," said Mom.

**1** 최고의 새로운 것

**2** Rada는 먼 우주의 작은 세계에 살고 있었다.

**3** 그녀는 아빠, 엄마 그리고 남동생 Jonny와 함께 그곳에서 살고 있었다.

**4** Rada의 아빠와 다른 사람들은 우주선에서 일했다.

**5** Rada와 Jonny만이 아이들이었고, 그들은 우주에서 태어났다.

**6** 어느 날, 아빠가 Rada와 Jonny에게, "우리는 내일 지구로 돌아갈 거야."라고 말했다.

**7** Rada와 Jonny는 깜짝 놀라 아빠를 바라보았고, 그에게 둥둥 떠서 갔다.

**8** Rada가 아빠에게, "지구는 어떤 곳인가요?"라고 물었다.

**9** "그곳에선 모든 것이 다르단다.

**10** 예를 들어, 하늘은 파란색이지." 라고 아빠가 대답했다.

**11** "전 한 번도 파란 하늘을 본 적이 없어요."라고 Jonny가 말했다.

**12** "여기는 하늘이 항상 검은색이잖아요."라고 Rada가 말했다.

**13** "그곳에는 모든 곳에 공기가 있기 때문에 크고 무거운 우주복을 입을 필요가 없단다.

**14** 또한 지구가 너희들을 끌어당기기 때문에 거기에서는 점프하는 것도 어렵단다." 아빠가 말했다.

**15** "그 밖에 또 뭐가 있어요?" Rada가 물었다.

**16** "언덕들이 있는데 그것들은 부드러운 초록색의 잔디로 뒤덮여 있단다.

**17** 언덕을 굴러 내려갈 수도 있어." 엄마가 대답했다.

**18** "아빠, 언덕을 굴러 내려가 본 적 있어요?" Rada가 물었다.

**19** "그럼. 정말 놀라워!" 아빠가 대답했다.

**20** Jonny는 목이 말라서 우유 용기를 열어 그것을 흔들었다.

**21** 우유가 공기 중으로 떠서 방울을 형성했다.

**22** Jonny는 그 우유 방울을 삼켰다.

**23** "Jonny, 만약 네가 지구에서 그런 식으로 우유를 마신다면, 다 젖을 거야." 엄마가 말했다.

**24** _____ _____ _____, Rada and Jonny talked _____ _____ _____ about Earth.

**25** It was _____ to _____ about _____ _____ _____ they were _____ _____ see and do.

**26** There was _____ _____ _____ Rada and Jonny really _____ _____ _____.

**27** They thought about it _____ _____ and didn't tell Mom and Dad about it.

**28** It was _____ _____.

**29** The next day, Rada's family _____ _____ a spaceship.

**30** "_____ _____ _____ _____ a long trip," said Mom.

**31** "That's _____. I'm _____ _____!" said Rada.

**32** The spaceship _____ _____.

**33** "Dad, it's difficult _____ _____ on Earth," said Rada.

**34** "I know. Earth is _____ _____ _____," said Dad.

**35** Rada and Jonny _____ _____ _____.

**36** That was _____ _____ _____ _____.

**37** "_____ that _____?" asked Rada.

**38** "A bird _____ _____," said Mom.

**39** "_____ _____ _____ a bird _____," said Rada.

**40** "And _____ _____ _____ the wind," said Jonny.

**41** _____ were _____ _____ _____.

**42** Rada and Jonny _____ _____ _____ _____ _____ hill.

**43** At the top, they looked at _____ _____ and _____.

**44** Then they _____ _____ on the soft green grass and _____ _____ the hill.

**45** That was _____ _____!

**46** "This is the _____ _____ _____ of all!" shouted Rada and Jonny.

**47** And they ran _____ _____ _____ _____ of the hill again.

---

**24** 그날 밤 늦게, Rada와 Jonny는 지구에 대해서 오랜 시간 이야기했다.

**25** 그들이 보고, 하게 될 모든 새로운 것들을 생각하는 것은 흥미로웠다.

**26** Rada와 Jonny가 정말로 하고 싶었던 한 가지 새로운 것이 있었다.

**27** 그들은 밤새 그것에 대해서 생각했고 엄마와 아빠에게는 그것을 말하지 않았다.

**28** 그것은 그들의 비밀이었다.

**29** 다음날, Rada의 가족은 우주선에 올랐다.

**30** "긴 여행이 될 거야." 엄마가 말했다.

**31** "괜찮아요. 정말 신나요!" Rada가 말했다.

**32** 우주선이 마침내 착륙했다.

**33** "아빠, 지구에서는 걷는 것이 어려워요." Rada가 말했다.

**34** "그래. 지구가 너를 끌어당기고 있거든." 아빠가 말했다.

**35** Rada와 Jonny는 더 이상 떠다닐 수 없었다.

**36** 그것이 첫 번째 새로운 것이었다.

**37** "저건 무슨 소리죠?"라고 Rada가 물었다.

**38** "새가 노래하는 거야." 엄마가 말했다.

**39** "새가 노래하는 것을 들어 본 적이 없어요."라고 Rada가 말했다.

**40** "그리고 저는 바람을 느껴 본 적도 없어요."라고 Jonny가 말했다.

**41** 이러한 것들이 모두 새로운 것들이었다.

**42** Rada와 Jonny는 가장 가까운 언덕으로 뛰어 올라갔다.

**43** 꼭대기에서, 그들은 서로를 쳐다보고 웃었다.

**44** 그리고 나서 그들은 부드러운 초록 잔디에 누워서 언덕 아래로 굴러 내려갔다.

**45** 그것이 그들의 비밀이었다!

**46** "이것이 모든 것들 중에서 최고의 새로운 것이에요!" Rada와 Jonny는 외쳤다.

**47** 그리고 그들은 언덕 꼭대기로 다시 뛰어 올라갔다.

※ 다음 문장을 우리말로 쓰시오.

**1** The Best New Thing
➡ _____

**2** Rada lived on a little world, far out in space.
➡ _____

**3** She lived there with her father, mother, and brother Jonny.
➡ _____

**4** Rada's father and other people worked on spaceships.
➡ _____

**5** Only Rada and Jonny were children, and they were born in space.
➡ _____

**6** One day, Dad told Rada and Jonny, "We're going back to Earth tomorrow."
➡ _____

**7** Rada and Jonny looked at Dad in surprise and floated towards him.
➡ _____

**8** Rada asked Dad, "What's it like on Earth?"
➡ _____

**9** "Everything is different there.
➡ _____

**10** For example, the sky is blue," answered Dad.
➡ _____

**11** "I've never seen a blue sky," said Jonny.
➡ _____

**12** "The sky is always black here," said Rada.
➡ _____

**13** "You don't have to wear your big heavy space suits because there is air everywhere.
➡ _____

**14** It's also hard to jump there because Earth pulls you down," said Dad.
➡ _____

**15** "What else?" asked Rada.
➡ _____

**16** "There are hills, and they are covered with soft green grass.
➡ _____

**17** You can roll down the hills," answered Mom.
➡ _____

**18** "Dad, have you ever rolled down a hill?" asked Rada.
➡ _____

**19** "Yes, it's really amazing!" answered Dad.
➡ _____

**20** Jonny was thirsty, so he opened a milk container and shook it.
➡ _____

**21** The milk floated in the air and formed balls.
➡ _____

**22** Jonny swallowed the balls.
➡ _____

**23** "Jonny, if you drink milk that way on Earth, you'll get wet," said Mom.
➡ _____

**24** Later that night, Rada and Jonny talked a long time about Earth.
➡ _____

**25** It was exciting to think about all the new things they were going to see and do.
➡ _____

**26** There was one new thing Rada and Jonny really wanted to do.
➡ _____

**27** They thought about it all night and didn't tell Mom and Dad about it.
➡ _____

**28** It was their secret.
➡ _____

**29** The next day, Rada's family got on a spaceship.
➡ _____

**30** "It's going to be a long trip," said Mom.
➡ _____

**31** That's alright. I'm so excited!" said Rada.
➡ _____

**32** The spaceship finally landed.
➡ _____

**33** "Dad, it's difficult to walk on Earth," said Rada.
➡ _____

**34** "I know. Earth is pulling you down," said Dad.
➡ _____

**35** Rada and Jonny couldn't float anymore.
➡ _____

**36** That was the first new thing.
➡ _____

**37** "What's that sound?" asked Rada.
➡ _____

**38** "A bird is singing," said Mom.
➡ _____

**39** "I've never heard a bird sing," said Rada.
➡ _____

**40** "And I've never felt the wind," said Jonny.
➡ _____

**41** These were all new things.
➡ _____

**42** Rada and Jonny ran up the nearest hill.
➡ _____

**43** At the top, they looked at each other and laughed.
➡ _____

**44** Then they lay down on the soft green grass and rolled down the hill.
➡ _____

**45** That was their secret!
➡ _____

**46** "This is the best new thing of all!" shouted Rada and Jonny.
➡ _____

**47** And they ran up to the top of the hill again.
➡ _____

※ 다음 괄호 안의 단어들을 우리말에 맞도록 바르게 배열하시오.

**1** (Best / Thing / New / The)
➡ _____

**2** (lived / Rada / a / on / world, / little / out / far / space. / in)
➡ _____

**3** (there / lived / she / with / father, / her / and / mother, / Jonny. / brother)
➡ _____

**4** (father / Rada's / and / people / other / on / spaceships. / worked)
➡ _____

**5** (Rada / only / and / were / Jonny / children, / and / were / they / space. / in / born)
➡ _____

**6** (day, / one / told / Dad / Rada / Jonny, / and / "we're / back / going / to / tomorrow." / Earth)
➡ _____

**7** (Jonny / and / Rada / at / looked / Dad / surprise / in / and / him. / towards / floated)
➡ _____

**8** (asked / Rada / Dad, / it / "what's / on / Earth?" / like)
➡ _____

**9** (is / "everything / there. / different)
➡ _____

**10** (example, / for / sky / the / blue," / is / Dad. / answered)
➡ _____

**11** (never / "I've / seen / a / sky," / blue / Jonny. / said)
➡ _____

**12** (sky / "the / always / is / here," / black / Rada. / said)
➡ _____

**13** (don't / "you / to / wear / have / big / your / heavy / suits / space / because / is / there / everywhere. / air)
➡ _____

**14** (also / it's / to / hard / jump / there / Earth / because / pulls / down," / you / Dad. / said)
➡ _____

**15** (else?" / "what / Rada. / asked)
➡ _____

**16** (are / "there / hills, / and / are / they / with / covered / soft / grass. / green)
➡ _____

**1** 최고의 새로운 것

**2** Rada는 먼 우주의 작은 세계에 살고 있었다.

**3** 그녀는 아빠, 엄마 그리고 남동생 Jonny와 함께 그곳에서 살고 있었다.

**4** Rada의 아빠와 다른 사람들은 우주선에서 일했다.

**5** Rada와 Jonny만이 아이들이었고, 그들은 우주에서 태어났다.

**6** 어느 날, 아빠가 Rada와 Jonny에게, "우리는 내일 지구로 돌아갈 거야."라고 말했다.

**7** Rada와 Jonny는 깜짝 놀라 아빠를 바라보았고, 그에게 둥둥 떠서 갔다.

**8** Rada가 아빠에게, "지구는 어떤 곳인가요?"라고 물었다.

**9** "그곳에선 모든 것이 다르단다.

**10** 예를 들어, 하늘은 파란색이지"라고 아빠가 대답했다.

**11** "전 한 번도 파란 하늘을 본 적이 없어요."라고 Jonny가 말했다.

**12** "여기는 하늘이 항상 검은색이잖아요."라고 Rada가 말했다.

**13** "그곳에는 모든 곳에 공기가 있기 때문에 크고 무거운 우주복을 입을 필요가 없단다.

**14** 또한 지구가 너희들을 끌어당기기 때문에 거기에서는 점프하는 것도 어렵단다." 아빠가 말했다.

**15** "그 밖에 또 뭐가 있어요?" Rada가 물었다.

**16** "언덕들이 있는데 그것들은 부드러운 초록색의 잔디로 뒤덮여 있단다.

**17** (you / roll / can / down / hills," / the / Mom. / answered)
➡ _____

**18** (have / "Dad / ever / you / down / rolled / hill?" / a / Rada. / asked)
➡ _____

**19** ("yes, / really / it's / amazing!" Dad. / answered)
➡ _____

**20** (was / Jonny / thirsty, / he / so / opened / a / container / milk / and / it. / shook)
➡ _____

**21** (milk / the / in / floated / the / air / and / balls. / formed)
➡ _____

**22** (swallowed / Jonny / balls. / the)
➡ _____

**23** ("Jonny, / you / if / milk / drink / way / that / Earth, / on / get / you'll / wet," / Mom. / said)
➡ _____

**24** (that / later / night, / Jonny / and / Rada / talked / long / a / Earth. / about / time)
➡ _____

**25** (was / it / exciting / think / to / all / about / new / the / things / were / they / going / see / do. / and / to)
➡ _____
_____

**26** (was / there / new / one / Rada / thing / and / really / Jonny / do. / to / wanted)
➡ _____

**27** (thought / they / it / about / night / all / and / didn't / Mom / tell / and / it. / about / Dad)
➡ _____

**28** (was / it / secret. / their)
➡ _____

**29** (next / the / day, / family / Rada's / on / got / spaceship. / a)
➡ _____

**30** (going / "it's / be / to / long / a / trip," / Mom. / said)
➡ _____

**31** (alright. / "that's // so / I'm / excited!" Rada. / said)
➡ _____

**32** (spaceship / the / landed. / finally)
➡ _____

**17** 언덕을 굴러 내려갈 수도 있어." 엄마가 대답했다.

**18** "아빠, 언덕을 굴러 내려가 본 적 있어요?" Rada가 물었다.

**19** "그럼, 정말 놀라워!" 아빠가 대답했다.

**20** Jonny는 목이 말라서 우유 용기를 열어 그것을 흔들었다.

**21** 우유가 공기 중으로 떠서 방울을 형성했다.

**22** Jonny는 그 우유 방울을 삼켰다.

**23** "Jonny, 만약 네가 지구에서 그런 식으로 우유를 마신다면, 다 젖을 거야." 엄마가 말했다.

**24** 그날 밤 늦게, Rada와 Jonny는 지구에 대해서 오랜 시간 이야기했다.

**25** 그들이 보고, 하게 될 모든 새로운 것들을 생각하는 것은 흥미로웠다.

**26** Rada와 Jonny가 정말로 하고 싶었던 한 가지 새로운 것이 있었다.

**27** 그들은 밤새 그것에 대해서 생각했고 엄마와 아빠에게는 그것을 말하지 않았다.

**28** 그것은 그들의 비밀이었다.

**29** 다음날, Rada의 가족은 우주선에 올랐다.

**30** "긴 여행이 될 거야." 엄마가 말했다.

**31** "괜찮아요. 정말 신나요!" Rada가 말했다.

**32** 우주선이 마침내 착륙했다.

**33** ("Dad, / difficult / it's / walk / to / Eaeth," / on / Rada. / said)
➡ _____

**34** (know. / "I / is / Earth / you / pulling / down," / Dad. / said)
➡ _____

**35** (Jonny / and / Rada / couldn't / anymore. / float)
➡ _____

**36** (was / that / first / the / thing. / new)
➡ _____

**37** ("what's / sound?" / that / Rada. / asked)
➡ _____

**38** (bird / "a / singing," / is / Mom. / said)
➡ _____

**39** (never / "I've / heard / bird / a / sing," / Rada. / said)
➡ _____

**40** ("and / never / I've / felt / wind," / the / Jonny. / said)
➡ _____

**41** (were / these / new / things. / all)
➡ _____

**42** (Jonny / and / Rada / up / ran / nearest / the / hill.)
➡ _____

**43** (the / at / top, / looked / they / each / at / other / laughed. / and)
➡ _____

**44** (they / then / down / lay / the / on / green / soft / grass / and / down / rolled / hill. / the)
➡ _____

**45** (was / that / secret! / their)
➡ _____

**46** (is / "this / best / the / thing / new / all!" / of / Rada / shouted / Jonny. / and)
➡ _____

**47** (and / ran / they / up / the / to / top / of / hill / again. / the)
➡ _____

**33** "아빠, 지구에서는 걷는 것이 어려워요." Rada가 말했다.

**34** "그래. 지구가 너를 끌어당기고 있거든." 아빠가 말했다.

**35** Rada와 Jonny는 더 이상 떠다닐 수 없었다.

**36** 그것이 첫 번째 새로운 것이었다.

**37** "저건 무슨 소리죠?"라고 Rada가 물었다.

**38** "새가 노래하는 거야." 엄마가 말했다.

**39** "새가 노래하는 것을 들어 본 적이 없어요."라고 Rada가 말했다.

**40** "그리고 저는 바람을 느껴 본 적도 없어요."라고 Jonny가 말했다.

**41** 이러한 것들이 모두 새로운 것들이었다.

**42** Rada와 Jonny는 가장 가까운 언덕으로 뛰어 올라갔다.

**43** 꼭대기에서, 그들은 서로를 쳐다보고 웃었다.

**44** 그러고 나서 그들은 부드러운 초록 잔디에 누워서 언덕 아래로 굴러 내려갔다.

**45** 그것이 그들의 비밀이었다!

**46** "이것이 모든 것들 중에서 최고의 새로운 것이에요!" Rada와 Jonny는 외쳤다.

**47** 그리고 그들은 언덕 꼭대기로 다시 뛰어 올라갔다.

※ 다음 우리말을 영어로 쓰시오.

**1** 최고의 새로운 것
➡ _____

**2** Rada는 먼 우주의 작은 세계에 살고 있었다.
➡ _____

**3** 그녀는 아빠, 엄마 그리고 남동생 Jonny와 함께 그곳에서 살고 있었다.
➡ _____

**4** Rada의 아빠와 다른 사람들은 우주선에서 일했다.
➡ _____

**5** Rada와 Jonny만이 아이들이었고, 그들은 우주에서 태어났다.
➡ _____

**6** 어느 날, 아빠가 Rada와 Jonny에게, "우리는 내일 지구로 돌아갈 거야."라고 말했다.
➡ _____

**7** Rada와 Jonny는 깜짝 놀라 아빠를 바라보았고, 그에게 둥둥 떠서 갔다.
➡ _____

**8** Rada가 아빠에게, "지구는 어떤 곳인가요?"라고 물었다.
➡ _____

**9** "그곳에선 모든 것이 다르단다.
➡ _____

**10** 예를 들어, 하늘은 파란색이지."라고 아빠가 대답했다.
➡ _____

**11** "전 한 번도 파란 하늘을 본 적이 없어요."라고 Jonny가 말했다.
➡ _____

**12** "여기는 하늘이 항상 검은색이잖아요."라고 Rada가 말했다.
➡ _____

**13** "그곳에는 모든 곳에 공기가 있기 때문에 크고 무거운 우주복을 입을 필요가 없단다.
➡ _____

**14** 또한 지구가 너희들을 끌어당기기 때문에 거기에서는 점프하는 것도 어렵단다." 아빠가 말했다.
➡ _____

**15** "그 밖에 또 뭐가 있어요?" Rada가 물었다.
➡ _____

**16** "언덕들이 있는데 그것들은 부드러운 초록색의 잔디로 뒤덮여 있단다.
➡ _____

**17** 언덕을 굴러 내려갈 수도 있어." 엄마가 대답했다.
➡ _____

**18** "아빠, 언덕을 굴러 내려가 본 적 있어요?" Rada가 물었다.
➡ _____

**19** "그럼, 정말 놀라워!" 아빠가 대답했다.
➡ _____

**20** Jonny는 목이 말라서 우유 용기를 열어 그것을 흔들었다.
➡ _____

**21** 우유가 공기 중으로 떠서 방울을 형성했다.
➡ _____

**22** Jonny는 그 우유 방울을 삼켰다.
➡ _____

**23** "Jonny, 만약 네가 지구에서 그런 식으로 우유를 마신다면, 다 젖을 거야." 엄마가 말했다.
➡ _____

**24** 그날 밤 늦게, Rada와 Jonny는 지구에 대해서 오랜 시간 이야기했다.
➡ _____

**25** 그들이 보고, 하게 될 모든 새로운 것들을 생각하는 것은 흥미로웠다.
➡ _____

**26** Rada와 Jonny가 정말로 하고 싶었던 한 가지 새로운 것이 있었다.
➡ _____

**27** 그들은 밤새 그것에 대해서 생각했고 엄마와 아빠에게는 그것을 말하지 않았다.
➡ _____

**28** 그것은 그들의 비밀이었다.
➡ _____

**29** 다음날, Rada의 가족은 우주선에 올랐다.
➡ _____

**30** "긴 여행이 될 거야." 엄마가 말했다.
➡ _____

**31** "괜찮아요. 정말 신나요!" Rada가 말했다.
➡ _____

**32** 우주선이 마침내 착륙했다.
➡ _____

**33** "아빠, 지구에서는 걷는 것이 어려워요." Rada가 말했다.
➡ _____

**34** "그래. 지구가 너를 끌어당기고 있거든." 아빠가 말했다.
➡ _____

**35** Rada와 Jonny는 더 이상 떠다닐 수 없었다.
➡ _____

**36** 그것이 첫 번째 새로운 것이었다.
➡ _____

**37** "저건 무슨 소리죠?"라고 Rada가 물었다.
➡ _____

**38** "새가 노래하는 거야." 엄마가 말했다.
➡ _____

**39** "새가 노래하는 것을 들어 본 적이 없어요."라고 Rada가 말했다.
➡ _____

**40** "그리고 저는 바람을 느껴 본 적도 없어요."라고 Jonny가 말했다.
➡ _____

**41** 이러한 것들이 모두 새로운 것들이었다.
➡ _____

**42** Rada와 Jonny는 가장 가까운 언덕으로 뛰어 올라갔다.
➡ _____

**43** 꼭대기에서, 그들은 서로를 쳐다보고 웃었다.
➡ _____

**44** 그리고 나서 그들은 부드러운 초록 잔디에 누워서 언덕 아래로 굴러 내려갔다.
➡ _____

**45** 그것이 그들의 비밀이었다!
➡ _____

**46** "이것이 모든 것들 중에서 최고의 새로운 것이에요!" Rada와 Jonny는 외쳤다.
➡ _____

**47** 그리고 그들은 언덕 꼭대기로 다시 뛰어 올라갔다.
➡ _____

※ 다음 우리말과 일치하도록 빈칸에 알맞은 말을 쓰시오.

**One Minute Speech**

1. Did you _____ _____ the new book, *Dave's Adventures*?

2. This book _____ _____ Dave and his _____ in the _____.

3. The _____ _____ are Dave and a big bear. The story is fun.

4. _____ you _____ _____ the book?

5. Then you _____ _____ it!

1. 새 책인 Dave의 모험에 관해 들어 봤니?
2. 이 책은 Dave와 숲에서의 그의 모험에 관한 거야.
3. 주인공은 Dave와 큰 곰이야. 이야기가 재미있어.
4. 그 책에 관해 궁금하니?
5. 그러면 그것을 꼭 읽어 봐야 해!

**Read and Complete**

1. Rada's family lived in space. One day, they _____ _____ _____ _____ to Earth.

2. Rada's family talked about life on Earth. They talked about the blue sky and hills which _____ _____ _____ green grass.

3. The next day, Rada's family _____ _____ a spaceship. It was _____ _____ _____ to Earth.

4. When they _____ _____ Earth, Rada and Jonny _____ _____ the nearest hill and _____ _____ it. That was _____ _____ _____ to them.

1. Rada의 가족은 우주에서 살고 있었다. 어느 날, 그들은 지구로 돌아가기로 결정했다.
2. Rada의 가족은 지구의 생활에 대해 이야기했다. 그들은 파란 하늘과 초록색 잔디로 뒤덮인 언덕에 대해 이야기했다.
3. 다음날, Rada의 가족은 우주선에 올랐다. 그것은 지구로의 긴 여행이었다.
4. 그들이 지구에 도착했을 때, Rada와 Jonny는 가장 가까운 언덕으로 뛰어 올라가 아래로 굴러 내려갔다. 그것은 그들에게 최고의 새로운 것이었다.

**Around the World**

1. Russia _____ the first dog _____ _____. It was small, and _____ _____ was Laika.

2. Yuri Gagarin _____ _____ space _____ _____ _____ _____.

3. The USA _____ the _____ _____ _____ the moon. His name was Neil Armstrong.

4. Russia _____ the first space station. It _____ _____ the Earth _____ 3,000 times.

1. 러시아는 우주에 최초의 개를 보냈다. 그것은 작았고, 이름은 Laika였다.
2. Yuri Gagarin이 최초로 우주에 갔다.
3. 미국은 달에 최초의 인간을 보냈다. 그의 이름은 Neil Armstrong이었다.
4. 러시아가 최초의 우주정거장을 건설하였다. 그것은 거의 3천 번 지구 주변을 돌았다.

※ 다음 우리말을 영어로 쓰시오.

**One Minute Speech**

1. 새 책인 Dave의 모험에 관해 들어 봤니?

   ➡ _____

2. 이 책은 Dave와 숲에서의 그의 모험에 관한 거야.

   ➡ _____

3. 주인공은 Dave와 큰 곰이야. 이야기가 재미있어.

   ➡ _____

4. 그 책에 관해 궁금하니?

   ➡ _____

5. 그러면 그것을 꼭 읽어 봐야 해!

   ➡ _____

**Read and Complete**

1. Rada의 가족은 우주에서 살고 있었다. 어느 날, 그들은 지구로 돌아가기로 결정했다.

   ➡ _____

2. Rada의 가족은 지구의 생활에 대해 이야기했다. 그들은 파란 하늘과 초록색 잔디로 뒤덮인 언덕에
   대해 이야기했다.

   ➡ _____

   _____

3. 다음날, Rada의 가족은 우주선에 올랐다. 그것은 지구로의 긴 여행이었다.

   ➡ _____

4. 그들이 지구에 도착했을 때, Rada와 Jonny는 가장 가까운 언덕으로 뛰어 올라가 아래로 굴러 내려갔다.
   그것은 그들에게 최고의 새로운 것이었다.

   ➡ _____

   _____

**Around the World**

1. 러시아는 우주에 최초의 개를 보냈다. 그것은 작았고, 이름은 Laika였다.

   ➡ _____

2. Yuri Gagarin이 최초로 우주에 갔다.

   ➡ _____

3. 미국은 달에 최초의 인간을 보냈다. 그의 이름은 Neil Armstrong이었다.

   ➡ _____

4. 러시아가 최초의 우주정거장을 건설하였다. 그것은 거의 3천 번 지구 주변을 돌았다.

   ➡ _____

MEMO

적중100

2학기

# 정답 및 해설

동아 | 윤정미

중 2

적중100

# Lesson 5

# Living Healthily and Safely

사가 적절하므로 regularly가 적절하다. (3) 명사 problems 를 수식하는 형용사 형태가 적절하므로 동사 vary를 various 로 고친다. (4) 문자를 보내다는 의미로 동사 text를 현재분사인 texting으로 바꾸는 것이 적절하다.

## 시험대비 실력평가
p.08

01 instead of  02 ①  03 blink  04 ③
05 ③  06 ⑤  07 nervous  08 ④

01 한 가지가 또 다른 것을 대체하거나 다른 것을 할 때 사용하는. 식사나 회의 중에는 스마트폰을 꺼라. 문자를 보내는 대신에 사람들과 직접 대화를 나눌 수 있다.

02 take medicine: '약을 복용하다', take a rest: '휴식을 취하다'

04 스마트폰을 확인했을 때 아무런 문자 메시지가 없다면 슬픈 기분이 드는가? 만약 당신의 대답이 '그렇다'이면, 당신은 스마트폰 중독일지 모른다.

05 신체의 일부가 아플 때 가지는 느낌 – 고통

05 매일, 매주 등의 같은 시간에 – 규칙적으로

07 유의어 관계이다. 건강한 = 초조한, 불안한

08 '스마트폰을 현명하지 않게 또는 과도하게 사용하면 다양한 문제가 일어날 수 있다.', '스마트폰을 내려다볼 때, 목에 가해지는 압박이 증가한다.'

## 교과서 Conversation

### 핵심 Check
p.10~11

1 What's wrong  2 anything wrong
3 ⑤

## 서술형 시험대비
p.09

01 (1) has  (2) well  (3) smombie  (4) nervous
02 (1) prevent, 방지하다, 막다  (2) medicine, 약, 약물
(3) addiction, 중독  03 (t)ext / (c)ause
04 (1) without  (2) such  (3) From now on  (4) fall asleep  05 (1) addiction  (2) regularly
(3) various  (4) texting

01 (1) '머리가 아프다'는 표현으로 동사 have를 사용한다. (2) '건강해 보이다'는 look well을 사용한다. (3) 글의 흐름상 단어 '스몸비'가 적절하다. (4) 나는 스마트폰이 곁에 없을 때 초조해진다.

03 • 많은 사람들은 전화를 하기 보다는 문자 메시지를 보내기를 좋아한다. • 스마트폰을 과도하게 사용하면 눈이 건조해질 수 있다.

04 (1) without: ~ 없이 (2) such: 그러한 (3) from now on: 지금부터 (4) fall asleep: 잠들다

05 (1) 스마트폰 중독의 의미로 동사 addict를 명사 addiction으로 바꾸어야 한다. (2) 빈칸에는 동사 exercise를 수식하는 부

## 교과서 대화문 익히기

### Check(√) True or False
p.12

1 T  2 T  3 T  4 F

## 교과서 확인학습
p.14~15

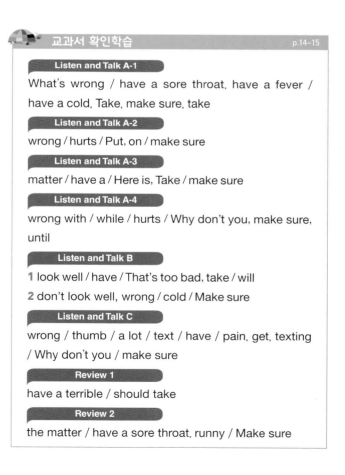

**Listen and Talk A-1**
What's wrong / have a sore throat, have a fever / have a cold, Take, make sure, take

**Listen and Talk A-2**
wrong / hurts / Put, on / make sure

**Listen and Talk A-3**
matter / have a / Here is, Take / make sure

**Listen and Talk A-4**
wrong with / while / hurts / Why don't you, make sure, until

**Listen and Talk B**
1 look well / have / That's too bad, take / will
2 don't look well, wrong / cold / Make sure

**Listen and Talk C**
wrong / thumb / a lot / text / have / pain, get, texting / Why don't you / make sure

**Review 1**
have a terrible / should take

**Review 2**
the matter / have a sore throat, runny / Make sure

01 Make sure　　02 ④　　03 ③　　04 have a

01 상대방에게 당부하는 표현으로 '반드시 ~하도록 해라, ~을 확실히 해라'라는 의미의 'make sure ~'를 사용한다.

02 빈칸에는 상대방이 어딘가 아파 보일 때 묻는 말이 적절하다..

03 감기에 걸린 것 같다는 말 다음에 이어질 말로 치과에 가라는 말은 어색하다.

04 '~가 아프다'는 표현은 'have a/an+명사' 형태로 쓴다. 명사 자리에 아픈 증상이나 병명을 써서 어디가 아픈지 표현한다.

01 ④　　02 ⑤　　03 ④　　04 ⑤
05 the [problem]matter, happened　　06 ⑤
07 ④　　08 pain　　09 Here is　　10 ③
11 What's the matter with you　　12 ④
13 ⑤　　14 ④

01 B의 대답으로 보아 빈칸에는 문제점이나 증상을 묻는 말이 오는 것이 적절하다.

02 빈칸 뒤의 this는 medicine을 가리키므로 '약을 먹다' 표현으로 동사 take를 사용한다.

03 (D) 상대방의 증상을 묻는 표현 → (A) 증상 말하기 → (B) 상대방에게 당부하는 표현 말하기 → (C) 알았다고 대답하기

04 '~가 아프다'는 표현은 'have a/an+명사' 형태로 쓴다.

06 (B)는 상대방에게 당부하는 표현이다.

07 '반드시 ~하도록 하다, ~을 확실히 하다'라는 의미의 'make sure ~'는 상대방에게 당부할 때 사용하는 표현이다.

08 toothache는 '치통'이기 때문에 '아픔, 통증'을 나타내는 pain이 적절하다.

09 '여기에 ~가 있다'는 표현으로 'Here is+단수 명사'를 사용한다.

10 이가 아프다고 했기 때문에 치과에 가라는 충고가 적절하다.

11 문제점이나 증상을 묻는 표현이다.

12 It은 texting thumb을 가리키는 대명사로 'What's texting thumb?'에 대한 대답으로 ④에 들어가는 것이 적절하다.

13 Ms. Kim이 문자 메시지를 많이 보내지 않는다는 것은 본문에 언급되어 있지 않다.

14 ④번은 '몸이 안 좋아 보여. 무슨 일 있니?'라는 물음에 '아무 문제없다.'는 대답 다음에 머리가 아프다고 말하는 것은 어색하다.

01 ⓐ wrong ⓑ have ⓒ have

02 Take this medicine and make sure you take a good rest.

03 (A) What's wrong with your leg
(B) while I was playing soccer
(C) make sure you don't play socce
04 pain, thumb　　　　05 make sure, don't text
06 I get tired easily.

01 ⓐ 아파 보인다는 말 다음에 상대방의 증상을 묻는 표현이 적절하다. ⓑ와 ⓒ는 '~가 아프다'는 의미로 동사 have를 사용한다.

02 '이 약을 먹어'라는 명령문으로 동사 Take로 문장을 시작한다. 그리고 '꼭 ~하도록 해라'는 당부의 표현으로 'make sure+주어+동사' 어순이 적절하다.

03 (B)의 while은 접속사로 '~하는 동안'의 의미를 가지고 뒤에는 '주어+동사'가 와야 한다. be동사와 함께 사용이 되어 축구를 하다는 표현은 진행형으로 나타내는 것이 적절하다. (C)는 상대방에게 당부하는 표현으로 'make sure+주어+동사'의 어순이 적절하다.

04 Andy가 엄지손가락이 아프다는 말을 한 것으로 보아 texting thumb은 엄지손가락에 있는 통증을 말한다는 것을 알 수 있다.

05 texting thumb은 문자 메시지를 너무 많이 보내서 생기는 통증이므로 Ms. Kim의 충고는 '문자 메시지를 너무 많이 보내지 말라'는 것이 적절하다.

06 get+형용사: ~하게 되다 / tire를 tired로 바꾸어 '피로한, 피곤하게 된'을 의미하도록 한다.

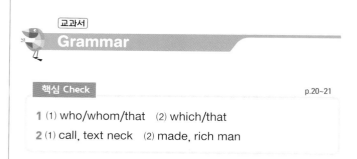

교과서
## Grammar

핵심 Check　　　　　　　　　　　　　　　p.20~21

1 (1) who/whom/that　　(2) which/that
2 (1) call, text neck　　(2) made, rich man

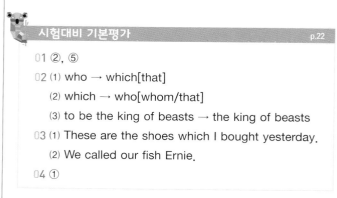
01 ②, ⑤

02 (1) who → which[that]
(2) which → who[whom/that]
(3) to be the king of beasts → the king of beasts

03 (1) These are the shoes which I bought yesterday.
(2) We called our fish Ernie.

04 ①

01 선행사가 The friend로 사람이며 met의 목적어 역할을 할 수 있는 목적격 관계대명사 who나 whom 또는 that이 적절하다.

02 (1) 선행사가 사물이므로 who를 which나 that으로 고쳐야 한

다. (2) 선행사가 사람이므로 which를 who나 whom 또는 that으로 고쳐야 한다. (3) call은 목적격 보어로 to부정사를 취하지 않는다.

03 (1) which는 관계대명사 목적격이다. (2) 'call+목적어+목적격 보어'의 어순을 취한다.

04 call A B: A를 B라고 부르다 the arrow on the screen: 화면의 화살표

01 ②　　　　02 ④　　　　03 ⑤
04 (1) that　(2) which　(3) which　(4) which
(5) consider　　05 I still remember the stories
(which[that]) my grandfather told me.　　06 ⑤
07 ④　　　　08 ①　　　　09 ③
10 (1) that　(2) whom　(3) who is　　11 ⑤
12 ②
13 (1) New York is a big city which[that] many people
　　　visit every year.
　　(2) My favorite subject is math which[that] I'm
　　　good at.
　　(3) The man who[whom/that] I saw at the mall was
　　　my math teacher.
　　(4) She is a famous movie star who[whom/that]
　　　many people like.
　　(5) I was surprised at the speed with which he
　　　learned to speak. 또는 I was surprised at the
　　　speed which[that] he learned to speak with.
　　(6) Do you know the girl to whom Anne is
　　　talking? 또는 Do you know the girl who[whom/
　　　that] Anne is talking to?
14 ①　　　　15 ④
16 (1) We call Shakespeare England's national poet.
　　(2) I consider him to be a coward.
17 ②, ④

01 <보기>와 나머지는 목적격 관계대명사이지만, ②번은 주격 관계대명사이다.

02 모두 주격이나 목적격으로 사용된 관계대명사 that이 들어갈 수 있지만 ④번은 소유격 관계대명사 whose가 들어가야 한다.

03 take는 보통 to부정사나 as와 함께 쓰이며 take A(명사) B(명사)의 형태로 쓰이지 않는다.

04 (1) 선행사가 사람이므로 that, (2) 선행사가 사물이므로 which, (3) 전치사 in이 있으므로 that은 쓸 수 없다. (4) 선행사가 사물이므로 which, (5) to부정사를 목적격 보어로 쓸 수 있는 것은 consider이다.

05 '이야기들을 아직 기억한다'에서 목적격 관계대명사를 이용하여

'이야기들'을 '할아버지께서 내게 해 주신'이 수식하는 구조로 만들어 준다.

06 call은 동사 다음에 두 개의 명사(구)가 목적어, 목적격 보어로 쓰이므로 'as hip hop'이 아니라 as 없이 'hip hop'이 되어야 한다.

07 관계대명사의 선행사가 사람이면 who, whom이나 that을 쓰고 사물이면 which나 that을 쓴다. ③ This is the house which she lives in.

08 ①번은 접속사이지만 나머지는 모두 관계대명사이다.

09 ③번은 4형식이지만 <보기>와 나머지는 모두 목적어와 목적격 보어가 있는 5형식이다. call A B는 목적격 보어 자리에 to부정사나 형용사를 쓰지 않지만 to부정사나 형용사를 목적격 보어로 취하는 많은 동사들이 있다.

10 목적격 관계대명사와 '주격 관계대명사+be 동사'는 생략할 수 있다.

11 선행사가 사람이므로 who, whom이나 that을 이용하고 목적격이므로 목적어로 쓰인 him은 쓰지 말아야 한다.

12 call은 동사 다음에 두 개의 명사(구)가 목적어와 목적격 보어로 쓰인다. 형용사나 to부정사가 목적격 보어로 올 수 없다. call A B: A를 B라고 부르다

13 목적격 관계대명사는 수식하는 선행사가 사람이면 who나 whom, that을, 사람이 아니면 which나 that을 쓴다. 일반적으로 목적격 관계대명사는 생략될 수 있다. 목적격 관계대명사가 전치사의 목적어인 경우 전치사는 관계대명사절의 끝에 오거나 관계대명사 앞에 올 수 있다. 전치사가 관계대명사절의 끝에 올 경우에는 관계대명사를 생략할 수 있다. 전치사가 관계대명사 앞에 올 경우에는 관계대명사 that을 쓸 수 없으며, 관계대명사를 생략하지 않는다.

14 call은 동사 다음에 두 개의 명사(구)가 목적어와 목적격 보어로 쓰인다. regard가 'A를 B로 여기다'의 뜻으로 쓰이는 경우 보통 'regard A as B'의 형태를 취한다.

15 ④ 관계대명사 that은 전치사 다음에는 쓸 수 없다. that → whom

16 call A B: A를 B라고 부르다 (2) consider는 call과는 다르게 목적격 보어로 to부정사를 취할 수 있다.

17 주어진 문장과 ②, ④번은 목적격 관계대명사이다. ① 동격절을 이끄는 접속사, ③번은 의문사, ⑤번은 주격 관계대명사이다.
swallow: 제비

01 (1) I bought the snack which[that] everyone likes.
　　(2) Romeo and Juliet is the movie which[that]
　　　Helen saw.
　　(3) The person who[whom/that] I love the most is
　　　my sister.
　　(4) The author who[whom/that] I like the most is
　　　C.S. Lewis.

(5) Look at the boy to whom Mary is talking. 또는 Look at the boy who[whom/that] Mary is talking to.

(6) Look at Chris and his dog that Bella is playing with.

02 (1) People call New York City the Big Apple.

(2) Some people may not consider him as a hero.

(3) They named her the Boxer of the Year.

(4) His ability made him a famous person.

(5) We elected him to be a leader.

(6) His followers believed him to be a genius.

(7) They regard Mike as a fool.

03 call the rooftop the park in the sky

04 (1) Andy is the boy (who/whom/that) Hajun met in Canada.

(2) The table (which/that) my dad made for me is sturdy.

(3) Hemingway is the author whom I like the most.

(4) The book which he wrote is fun.

(5) Can I borrow the book (which/that) you told me about? 또는 Can I borrow the book about which you told me?

05 (1) My grandmother made the chocolate cake.

(2) We met the people on the plane.

(3) He wants to rent a car.

(4) Do you have a friend?

06 (1) They called him Mr. Long.

(2) They regarded him as their leader.

07 (1) We call Chicago the Windy City because it is very windy there.

(2) I like the cookies (which/that) my mother made for me.

(3) The country (which/that) I want to visit the most is France.

(4) Harry was the partner that I worked with last year.

01 (1), (2) 선행사가 사물이므로 관계대명사 which나 that, (3), (4) 선행사가 사람이므로 관계대명사 who, whom이나 that, (5) 목적격 관계대명사가 전치사의 목적어인 경우 전치사는 관계대명사절의 끝에 오거나 관계대명사 앞에 올 수 있으며 전치사가 관계대명사절의 끝에 올 경우에는 관계대명사를 생략할 수 있다. 전치사가 관계대명사 앞에 올 경우에는 관계대명사 that을 쓸 수 없다. (6) 선행사가 '사람+동물'이므로 관계대명사 that을 써야 한다. 목적격 관계대명사는 생략될 수 있다.

02 (1) call A B: A를 B라고 부르다 (2) consider는 consider A as B의 형태로도 쓰인다. (3) name A B: A를 B라고 이름 짓다 (4) make A B: A를 B로 만들다 (5) elect는 to부정사를

목적격 보어로 취할 수 있다. (6) believe는 to부정사를 목적격 보어로 취한다. (7) regard A as B: A를 B로 여기다

03 call A B: A를 B라고 부르다 rooftop: 지붕[옥상] / 우리는 그 옥상을 하늘의 공원이라고 부른다.

04 (1) 선행사가 사람이므로 who, whom이나 that, (2) 선행사가 사물이므로 which나 that, (3) 관계대명사가 접속사와 대명사의 역할을 하므로 him을 삭제해야 한다. (4) 관계대명사가 접속사와 대명사의 역할을 하므로 it을 삭제해야 한다. (5) 전치사가 관계대명사 앞에 올 경우에는 관계대명사 that을 쓸 수 없으며, 관계대명사를 생략하지 않는다. sturdy: 억센, 튼튼한

05 목적격 관계대명사는 선행사가 사람이면 who나 whom, that, 사물이나 동물이면 which나 that을 쓰고 관계대명사절에서 목적어 역할을 한다. 목적격 관계대명사절에는 동사 뒤에 목적어가 없다는 것에 주의한다.

06 (1) call A B는 목적격 보어 자리에 to부정사나 형용사를 쓰지 않는다. (2) regard는 'regard A as B(A를 B로 여기다)' 형태로 쓰인다.

07 선행사가 사물이면 which나 that, 사람이면 who, whom이나 that을 쓴다. (4) 함께 일한 파트너이므로 전치사 with를 빠뜨리면 안 된다. 또한 that을 사용해야 하므로 전치사 with를 관계대명사절의 마지막에 위치시켜야 한다.

## Reading

확인문제     p.28

1 T   2 F   3 F   4 T

확인문제     p.29

1 F   2 F   3 T   4 T   5 F   6 T

### 교과서 확인학습 A     p.30~31

01 Be Smart with    02 Living without smartphones

03 unwise or too much use    04 a smombie

05 like zombies    06 on their smartphones

07 such people    08 various safety problems

09 may not see, so    10 get into    11 to prevent

12 simple    13 while, walking

14 dry eyes, text neck    15 health problems

16 dry eyes    17 look at, blink

18 feel dry    19 Another problem

20 look down at, on

21 Too much use, too much texting

22 text neck　　23 some tips

24 try to blink　　25 up to your eye level

26 neck stretching exercises

27 How do you fee　28 feel nervous, around

29 feel sad, no text message

30 smartphone addiction　　　31 to prevent this

32 turn off, during　33 instead of texting

1 Be Smart with Your Smartphones!

2 Living without smartphones is difficult for many of us these days.

3 However, unwise or too much use of smartphones can cause various problems.

4 Are you a smombie?

5 All over the world, people are walking around like zombies.

6 Their heads are down, and their eyes are on their smartphones.

7 We call such people smombies, smartphone zombies.

8 If you are a smombie, you can have various safety problems.

9 You may not see a hole in the street, so you may fall and get hurt.

10 You may get into a car accident, too.

11 So what can you do to prevent these problems?

12 It's simple.

13 Do not look at your smartphone while you are walking!

14 Do you have dry eyes or text neck?

15 Smartphones can cause various health problems.

16 One example is dry eyes.

17 When you look at your smartphone, you do not blink often.

18 Then your eyes will feel dry.

19 Another problem you can have is neck pain.

20 When you look down at your smartphone, the stress on your neck increases.

21 Too much use of your smartphone, for example, too much texting, can cause neck pain.

22 We call this text neck.

23 Here are some tips for these problems.

24 For dry eyes, try to blink often.

25 For text neck, move your smartphone up to your eye level.

26 You can also do some neck stretching exercises.

27 How do you feel when you don't have your smartphone with you?

28 Do you feel nervous when your smartphone is not around?

29 Do you feel sad when you check your smartphone and there is no text message?

30 If your answers are "yes," you may have smartphone addiction.

31 There are various things you can do to prevent this.

32 For example, turn off your smartphone during meals or meetings.

33 You can talk to people instead of texting them.

01 ②　　02 ①, ④　　03 ⑤　　04 ③

05 Other → Another　　06 ④　　07 ②

08 (A) nervous　(B) sad　(C) to prevent　09

addiction　10 people　11 ③, ④　12 ②

13 (A)smartphone　(B) safety　14 ⑤

15 ②　　　16 Another problem that[which] you

can have is neck pain.　17 ③

18 is around → is not around

19 smartphone addiction

20 (1) I can turn off my smartphone during meals or meetings.

(2) I can talk to people instead of texting them.

21 ④　　22 he was texting and (he) didn't see a

hole　23 ①, ③　24 ④　25 ③

26 ①　　27 (A) addiction　(B) off　(C) instead of

28 ④　　29 ③　　30 ⑤

01 ② 앞에 나오는 내용과 상반되는 내용이 뒤에 이어지므로 However가 가장 적절하다. ① 그러므로, ③ 게다가, ⑤ 즉, 다시 말해

02 ⓑ와 ①, ④번은 5형식, call A B는 'A를 B라고 부르다'라는 의미이며, smombies와 smartphone zombies는 동격이다. call A B와 유사하게 목적격 보어 자리에 명사가 올 수 있는 동사로는 make, name, elect, consider 등이 있다. ② 3형식, ③, ⑤ 4형식

03 안전 관련 문제들을 예방하는 것은 '간단하다.'

04 주어진 문장의 these problems에 주목한다. ③번 앞 문장의 내용들을 받고 있으므로 ③번이 적절하다.

05 other 뒤에는 복수명사, another 뒤에는 단수명사가 온다.

06 ② 부사적 용법(목적), ⓑ와 나머지는 명사적 용법

07 ② 위 글은 '스마트폰으로 인한 건강상의 문제들과 이런 문제들을 방지하기 위한 몇 가지 조언'에 관한 글이다.

08 (A) feel은 감각동사로 '형용사'를 보어로 써야 하므로 nervous가 적절하다. (B) feel은 감각동사로 '형용사'를 보어로 써야 하므로 sad가 적절하다. (C) 이것을 '예방하기 위해' 할 수 있는 일이라고 해야 하므로 to prevent가 적절하다.

09 addiction: 중독, 1. 해로운 약을 복용하거나 그것의 복용을 중단할 수 없는 상태, 2. 어떤 것에 대한 매우 강한 소망이나 그것에 대한 욕구

10 '사람들'을 가리킨다.

11 ⓐ와 ③, ④번은 동명사, 나머지는 모두 현재분사

12 위 글은 스몸비들이 스마트폰을 보며 걷다가 일어날 수 있는 안전 관련 문제들에 관한 글이므로, '당신은 스몸비인가요?'가 적절하다. ⑤ troublemaker: 말썽꾸러기

13 다양한 '안전' 관련 문제들을 예방하기 위해 걷고 있는 동안에는 '스마트폰'을 보지 말아야 한다.

14 ⑤ 스몸비들이 가질 수 있는 가장 위험한 문제가 무엇인지는 대답할 수 없다. ① No. ② Yes. ③ It means a smartphone zombie. ④ They can have various safety problems.

15 ⓐ look at: ~을 보다, look down at: ~을 내려다보다 ⓑ For dry eyes[text neck]: 안구 건조증[거북목 증후군]에는

16 목적격 관계대명사 'that'이나 'which'가 생략되어 있다.

17 ⓓ와 ③번: (특정한 수·정도)까지, up to your eye level: 당신의 눈높이까지, ① (육체적·정신적으로) ~할 수 있는, ② ~에게 달려 있는, ~의 의무[책임]인, ④ (특히 나쁜 짓을) 하고 있는, ⑤ look up to: ~을 우러러보다, 존경하다

18 스마트폰이 주위에 '없을' 때 당신은 초조한 기분이 드는가?라고 하는 것이 흐름상 적절하다.

19 '스마트폰 중독'을 가리킨다.

20 (1) 식사나 회의 중에는 스마트폰을 끌 수 있다. (2) 문자를 보내는 대신에 사람들과 이야기를 할 수 있다.

21 이 글은 '스마트폰 중독과 예방'에 관한 글이다.

22 '문자를 보내고 있었고 구덩이를 보지 못했기 때문'이다.

23 ⓐ와 ①, ③번은 접속사(때), ②, ④, ⑤번은 의문부사(언제)

24 ④ 스마트폰을 눈높이까지 들고, 목 스트레칭 운동을 해야 하는 사람은 '수지'이다.

25 주어진 문장의 this에 주목한다. ③번 앞 문장의 smartphone addiction을 받고 있으므로 ③번이 적절하다.

26 앞의 내용의 예가 나오고 있으므로 For example이 가장 적절하다. ② 그러므로, ③ 게다가, 더욱이, ④ 그러나, ⑤ 다른 한편으로는, 반면에

27 (A) 스마트폰 '중독'이라고 해야 하므로 addiction이 적절하다. addition: 덧셈, 추가(된 것), (B) 식사나 회의 중에는 스마트폰을 '끄'라고 해야 하므로 off가 적절하다. turn on: 켜다, (C) 문자를 보내는 '대신에'라고 해야 하므로 instead of가 적절하다.

28 빈칸 뒤에 이어지는 예들(거리에 있는 구덩이를 보지 못해서 넘어져서 다칠지도 모르고, 또한 교통사고를 당할지도 모르는 것)은 다양한 '안전' 관련 문제들에 해당한다. ② 정신적인, ③ 경제적인, ⑤ 신체적인

29 ⓐ와 ①, ④: 현재분사, ②, ③, ⑤: 동명사

30 이 글은 '현명하지 않은 스마트폰 사용으로 인한 다양한 안전 관련 문제들'에 관한 글이다.

---

### 🦉 서술형 시험대비
p.40~41

01 (A) is (B) like (C) It's
02 (A) zombies (B) heads (C) eyes
03 (1) 당신은 거리에 있는 구덩이를 보지 못할 수도 있고, 그래서 넘어져서 다칠지도 모른다.
　 (2) 당신은 또한 교통사고를 당할지도 모른다.
04 blink
05 When you look down at your smartphone, the stress on your neck increases.
06 (A) too much use (B) texting
07 머리는 아래를 향하고 눈은 스마트폰을 향한 채로 스마트폰을 보며 걷는 것
08 We call such people smombies, smartphone zombies.　　09 As[Because]
10 원인: 스마트폰을 볼 때, 눈을 자주 깜박거리지 않기 때문이다.
　 원인: 눈을 자주 깜박이려고 노력해라.
11 for instance

---

01 (A) 동명사 'Living'이 주어이므로 is가 적절하다. (B) 좀비'처럼'이라고 해야 하므로 like가 적절하다. alike는 명사 앞에는 쓸 수 없다. (C) '주어+동사'가 와야 하므로 소유격 Its가 아니라 It's가 적절하다.

02 그들은 '머리'를 숙이고, 그들의 '눈'은 스마트폰을 향한 채로 '좀비'처럼 걸어다니고 있는 사람들이다. walk with one's head hanging down: 머리를 숙이고 걷다

03 스마트폰을 보며 걷다가 일어날 수 있는 안전 관련 문제들이 ⓐ번 뒤에 설명되어 있다.

04 blink: 눈을[눈이] 깜박이다, 눈을 감고 아주 빨리 다시 눈을 뜨다

05 'on'을 보충하면 된다.

06 너무 많이 '문자'를 하는 것과 같이 스마트폰을 '너무 많이 사용하는 것'으로 인해 생기는 목 통증을 의미한다.

07 스몸비의 모습이 스마트폰을 현명하지 않게 사용하거나 너무 과도하게 사용하는 것의 예에 해당한다.

08 smombies와 smartphone zombies는 동격이므로 사이에 콤마를 찍는 것이 적절하다.

09 'so' 대신에, 이유를 나타내는 접속사 'As'나 'Because'를 맨 앞에 쓰는 것이 적절하다.

10 '스마트폰을 볼 때, 당신은 눈을 자주 깜박거리지 않기 때문에' 눈이 건조하다고 느낄 것이라고 했다. 안구 건조증에는, '눈을 자주 깜박이려고 노력하라'는 조언을 하고 있다.

11 for example = for instance: 예를 들어

**영역별 핵심문제**       p.42~47

01 (i)ntelligent      02 ④      03 ③

04 ①      05 cause      06 ③      07 ④

08 ③      09 문자를 너무 많이 하면 texting thumb 이 생길 수 있다는 것      10 ⑤      11 ⑤

12 ④      13 ③      14 ⑤      15 ③

16 ④      17 ①      18 ④

19 (1) Jane Eyre is the book (which) Yumi read yesterday

    (2) The jacket (which) I'm wearing is a present from my grandmother.

    (3) People call such food fajitas.

    (4) The festival made the city a popular place to visit.

20 ①      21 ③      22 ②, ⑤      23 ④

24 ②      25 (A) Another   (B) increases   (C) tips

26 Do you feel nervous when your smartphone is not around?      27 while → during

28 ④      29 Emma / feel dry

30 (1) 스마트폰이 주위에 없을 때 초조한 기분이 드는 경우

    (2) 스마트폰을 확인했을 때 아무런 문자 메시지가 없으면 슬픈 기분이 드는 경우

31 texting

01 반의어 관계이다. 비싼 : 싼 = 어리석은 : 똑똑한

02 스마트폰 없이 사는 것은 요즘 많은 사람들에게 어려울 수 있다. 하지만 스마트폰을 현명하지 않게 또는 과도하게 사용하면 다양한 문제를 야기할 수 있다.

03 팔, 다리, 몸을 가능한 멀리 펴다. '뻗다, 기지개를 켜다'

04 잠이 든; 자고 있는

05 • 그 사고의 원인은 분명하지 않다. 경찰은 여전히 그것을 조사 중이다. • 스마트폰을 과도하게 사용하는 것은 건조한 눈을 야기할 수 있다. look into: 조사하다

06 blink는 '눈을 깜박거리다'는 뜻이다.

07 상대방의 증상을 묻는 표현이 아닌 것을 찾는다.

08 texting thumb이 무엇이냐는 물음에 'It's pain in your thumb.'이라고 답하는 것이 적절하다.

09 that은 앞의 문장을 가리키는 대명사로 사용되었다.

10 Texting thumb은 문자를 너무 많이 해서 생길 수 있는 아픔이기 때문에 마지막 문장은 'you don't text too much'가 되어야 적절하다.

11 make sure는 뒤에 '주어+동사'가 나와야 한다. 그래서 'make sure you don't play soccer'로 바꾸는 것이 적절하다.

12 ④ A의 '축구하다 넘어져 다쳤다'는 말에 B가 '그거 좋겠다'고 답하는 것은 적절하지 않다.

13 ⓒ의 take는 '먹다, 복용하다'는 의미로 사용되었다.    this는 'some medicine'을 가리킨다.

14 call A B는 목적격 보어 자리에 to부정사나 형용사를 쓰지 않는다.

15 ③ The card (which/that) I bought yesterday was sent to Sue..

16 ④번은 주격 관계대명사이고 나머지는 모두 목적격 관계대명사이다.

17 call을 제외하고 모두 to be를 목적격 보어로 받을 수 있는 동사들이다. call은 동사 다음에 두 개의 명사(구)가 목적어와 목적격 보어로 쓰인다.

18 ④번은 목적격 관계대명사로 생략할 수 있다. ① 주격 관계대명사, ② 지시형용사, ③ 접속사, ⑤ 지시대명사이다.

19 (1) Jane Eyre는 책이름으로 사물이므로 which를 사용한다. (2) '입고 있는'은 진행형으로 나타내는 것이 적절하다. (3) call A B: A를 B라고 부르다 (4) The festival made the city to visit이 a popular place를 수식하도록 만든다.

20 주어진 문장의 various safety problems에 주목한다. ①번 뒤 문장에서 안전 관련 문제들의 예가 나오고 있으므로 ①번이 적절하다.

21 ⓐ their eyes are on their smartphones: 그들의 눈은 스마트폰을 향하고 있다, ⓑ get into a car accident: 교통사고를 당하다

22 ⓒ와 ①, ③, ④는 부사적 용법, ② 형용사적 용법, ⑤ 명사적 용법

23 위 글은 스마트폰이 일으킬 수 있는 건강상의 문제들 중에서 안구 건조증과 목 통증에 대해 설명하는 글이므로, '당신은 안구 건조증이나 거북목 증후군이 있나요?'가 적절하다.

24 앞의 내용의 예가 나오고 있으므로 for example이 가장 적절하다. ① 게다가, ④ 사실은, ⑤ 그 결과

25 (A) various health problems 중에서 일어날 수 있는 '또 다른 문제'이므로 Another가 적절하다. another: 셋 이상 중에서 두 번째, the other: 둘 중에서 나머지 하나, (B) 스마트폰을 내려다볼 때, 목에 가해지는 압박이 '증가한다'고 해야 하므로 increases가 적절하다. decrease: 줄다[감소하다], (C) advice는 셀 수 없는 명사이므로 복수 형태로 쓸 수 없다. some pieces of advice로 쓸 수 있다.

26 when 이하는 시간의 부사절로 '~할 때'라는 의미이다. around는 부사로 쓰였다.

27 during+특정한 때를 나타내는 명사, while+주어+동사

28 식사나 회의 중에는 스마트폰을 끄고 '문자를 보내는 대신에' 사람들과 이야기하라고 하는 것이 적절하다.

29 Q1: 'Emma'가 눈을 자주 깜박이도록 노력해야 한다. Q2: 스마트폰을 사용할 때 눈이 '건조하다고 느끼기' 때문이다.

30 본문 앞부분의 질문에 대한 대답이 '그렇다'이면, 당신은 스마트폰 중독일지도 모른다고 했다.

31 전치사 다음에 동명사로 쓰는 것이 적절하다.

## 단원별 예상문제　　p.48~51

01 various　　02 ③　　03 (A) Here are
(B) (n)ervous　04 look well　05 ②, ④　　06 ④
07 ④　　　　08 (A) What's wrong　(B) It's pain in
your thumb　(C) make sure you don't text too much
09 Why don't you do some finger stretching
exercises?　　　　10 ③
11 (1) The pizza (which/that) my dad made was really
delicious.
(2) I know the girl (whom/who/that) you are talking
about.
(3) We elected Chris class president.
(4) The game that we saw was very boring.
(5) He called me Queen.
12 ①, ③, ⑤　13 ④
14 (1) We call such a dance Salsa.
(2) Nobody liked the spaghetti which Nicole made.
(3) We elected Alex president of our club.
(4) She is the singer who[whom] I like most.
15 ②　　　　16 ③
17 various safety problems　　　　18 ⑤
19 ③　　　20 healthier
21 (1) 운동을 많이 하지 않는다.
→ 매일 30분 동안 걸으려고 노력할 것이다.
(2) 너무 많은 패스트푸드를 먹는다.
→ 일주일에 한 번만 패스트푸드를 먹을 것이다.
(3) 종종 밤에 먹는다.
→ 10시 이후에 먹지 않을 것이다.
22 ②

01 유의어 관계이다. 아픈 = 다양한

02 유명한 사람: 유명 인사

03 '여기에 ~가 있다'는 표현은 Here is[are] ~를 사용한다. some
tips라는 복수명사가 있으므로 Here are가 적절하다.

04 'look+형용사'를 이용하여 '~처럼 보이다'를 쓰고, well은 형용
사로 '건강한'의 의미를 가지고 있다.

05 머리가 아프다는 말에 '안 됐구나'라는 표현이 적절하다.

06 스마트폰이 야기할 수 있는 여러 문제를 언급하고 있기 때문에
(A)는 various가 적절하고, (B)는 눈을 자주 깜박거리지 않기
때문에 눈이 건조해진다는 dry가 적절하고, (C)는 목에 가해지
는 압박이 증가한다는 increases가 적절하다.

07 ⓓ 'have + a/an+병명/증상' 형태로 '어디가 아프다'는 표현이
다. have cold → have a cold

08 (A)는 상대방의 증상을 묻는 표현이 적절하다. (B)는 texting
thumb이 무엇이냐는 물음에 대한 답으로 적절한 것을 고르면
된다. (C)는 texting thumb을 예방하기 위한 조언으로 적절한
표현을 찾는다.

09 'Why don't you+동사원형 ~?' 형태를 이용하여 영작한다.

10 등이 아프다는 증상에 대해 스트레칭 운동을 하라는 조언이 적
절하다.

11 (1) 선행사가 사물이므로 which나 that, (2) 선행사가 사람이
므로 who, whom이나 that, (3) '목적어+목적격 보어'의 어순
이 되어야 한다. (4) 관계대명사가 접속사와 대명사의 역할을 하
므로 it을 삭제해야 한다. (5) call은 동사 다음에 두 개의 명사
(구)가 목적어와 목적격 보어로 쓰인다. as를 삭제해야 한다.

12 선행사가 사람이므로 목적격 관계대명사로 who나 whom 또는
that을 써야 한다.

13 ④ They called the ship Titanic. call은 동사 다음에 두 개
의 명사(구)가 목적어와 목적격 보어로 쓰인다. 목적격 보어 자
리에 to부정사나 형용사를 쓰지 않는다는 것에 주의한다.

14 (1) call A B: A를 B라고 부르다 (2) 선행사가 사물이므로 목
적격 관계대명사로 which를 쓴다. (3) elect A B: A를 B로
선출하다 (4) 선행사가 사람이므로 목적격 관계대명사로 who
나 whom을 쓴다.

15 these problems는 스마트폰을 보며 '걷다가' 일어날 수 있는
안전 관련 문제들이므로, '걷고 있는' 동안에는 스마트폰을 보지
마라고 하는 것이 적절하다.

16 ③번: 비슷한(형용사), ⓐ와 나머지: ~와 같이[마찬가지로], ~
처럼(전치사)

17 these problems는 'various safety problems'를 가리킨다.

18 글의 흐름으로 보아 '건강' 문제가 알맞다.

19 스마트폰을 내려다볼 때, 목에 가해지는 압박이 '증가한다'.

20 healthy-healthier-healthiest

21 First, Second, Third 다음의 내용을 쓰면 된다.

22 ⓑ는 부사적 용법(목적), ① 부사적 용법(형용사 수식), ④ 부
사적 용법(원인), ⑤ 부사적 용법(이유), ② 형용사적 용법, ③
명사적 용법(진목적어), persuade: 설득하다

## 서술형 실전문제　　p.52~53

01 wrong / have a, headache / should take / will
02 texting thumb, pain / (1) finger stretching
exercises　(2) tex
03 (A) What's the matter　(B) have a sore throat
(C) Make sure you get some rest
04 (1) The book which/that I'm reading is about
nature.

9

(2) Kenya is the country which/that John wants to visit.

(3) J. K. Rowling is a famous novelist who/whom/that many people like.

(4) I want to know the name of the girl who/whom/that I met at the party.

(5) Start by identifying the people with whom you want to work. 또는 Start by identifying the people that/who/whom you want to work with.

(6) The rate at which hair grows can be very slow. 또는 The rate which/that hair grows at can be very slow.

05 (A) without   (B) hole   (C) prevent

06 Their heads are down, and their eyes are on their smartphones.

07 (A) smartphones   (B) hole

08 (A) dry eyes   (B) neck pain        09 up → down

10 원인: 스마트폰을 너무 많이 사용하는 것, 예를 들어 너무 많이 문자를 하는 것

조언: (1) 당신의 눈높이까지 스마트폰을 위로 올려라.
(2) 목 스트레칭 운동을 할 수 있다.

01 그림으로 보아 Mike는 두통이 심하다.

03 (A)는 B의 대답으로 보아 어디가 아파 보일 때 증상을 묻는 표현이 적절하다. (B)는 아픈 증상을 이야기하는 표현으로 동사 have를 이용한다. (C)는 Mina에게 당부를 하는 표현으로 'make sure+주어+동사'의 어순을 이용한다.

04 목적격 관계대명사는 선행사가 사람이면 who나 whom, that을, 사람이 아니면 which나 that을 쓴다. 보통 목적격 관계대명사는 생략할 수 있다. 목적격 관계대명사가 전치사의 목적어일 때 전치사는 관계사절의 끝에 오거나 관계대명사 앞에 올 수 있다. 전치사가 관계사절의 끝에 올 경우에는 관계대명사를 생략할 수 있다. 전치사가 관계대명사 앞에 올 경우에는 관계대명사 that을 쓸 수 없으며, 관계대명사를 생략하지 않는다.

05 (A) 글의 흐름상 스마트폰 '없이' 사는 것이 어렵다고 하는 것이 적절하다. (B) 거리에 있는 '구덩이'를 보지 못할 수도 있다고 해야 하므로 hole이 적절하다. whole: 전체[전부]의, (C) 이런 문제들을 '예방하기' 위해라고 해야 하므로 prevent가 적절하다. protect: 보호하다

06 'down'을 보충하면 된다.

07 그들은 걷고 있는 동안에 '스마트폰'을 보고 거리에 있는 '구덩이'를 보지 못할 수도 있기 때문이다.

08 스마트폰이 일으킬 수 있는 건강상의 문제들 중의 하나가 '안구 건조증'이고 또 다른 문제는 '목 통증'이다.

09 거북목 증후군에는 당신의 눈높이까지 스마트폰을 위로 올리라고 조언하고 있기 때문에 스마트폰을 '내려다'볼 때, 목에 가해지는 압박이 증가한다고 하는 것이 적절하다.

10 스마트폰을 내려다볼 때, 목에 가해지는 압박이 증가하므로 '스마트폰을 너무 많이 사용하는 것'이 목 통증을 일으킬 수 있다. text neck에는 '당신의 눈높이까지 스마트폰을 위로 올리고 목 스트레칭 운동 또한 할 수 있다'는 조언을 하고 있다.

### 창의사고력 서술형 문제                             p.54

|모범답안|

01 (1) A: You don't look well. What's wrong? B: I have a toothache.
A: That's too bad. Make sure you go to the dentist. B: OK, I will.

(2) A: You don't look well. What's wrong? B: I have a sore throat.
A: That's too bad. Make sure you drink a lot of water. B: OK, I will.

02 call the clock tower Big Ben

03 (A) to change   (B) From now on
(C) once a week   (D) after   (E) my best

02 call A B: A를 B라고 부르다 the clock tower: 시계탑

### 단원별 모의고사                                    p.55~58

| 01 ③ | 02 pain | 03 ① | 04 ⑤ |
|------|---------|------|------|
| 05 ④ | 06 ② | 07 ⑤ | |
| 08 your back | | 09 ① | 10 ④ |
| 11 ② | 12 texting thumb | | |

13 (1) Cameron is the director (who/whom/that) Gillian likes best.

(2) We liked the story Jason told us.

(3) His business made him a millionaire.

(4) We call Bali the Island of Gods.

14 ②

15 (1) Every student respects him.

(2) You can do various things to prevent this.

16 ⑤

17 (1) He is a gentleman (who/whom/that) I built a good trust on.

(2) These are the pants (which/that) I bought yesterday.

(3) She doesn't consider him an artist.

(4) This is the issue about which we need to express our opinion. 또는 This is the issue (which/that) we need to express our opinion about.

(5) Ella received some flowers that her boy friend had sent to her.

(6) They call it 'Non La.'

01  ③의 prevent는 '예방하다, 막다'는 의미로 'to stop something from happening, or stop someone from doing'이 되어야 한다.

02  유의어 관계이다. 건강한 = 고통

03  빨리 배우고 이해할 수 있는: 똑똑한

04  빈칸에는 모두 아픈 증상을 나타내는 표현으로 'have a+증상/병명' 형태가 적절하다.

05  (D)의 증상을 묻는 질문에 (A)의 답이 적절하고, 이어서 (C)의 걸을 수 있는지에 대한 물음에 (B)가 적절하다.

06  ② A의 몸이 안 좋아 보인다는 말에 노래 경연대회에서 일등을 했다는 말은 어색하다.

07  ⑤ 문제점을 묻는 질문에 대해 상대에게 당부하는 표현은 자연스럽지 않다.

08  Peter의 등이 아픈 것에 대해 처방을 해주는 문장으로 it은 Peter의 등을 가리킨다.

10  ④ 콧물이 난다는 말에 치과에 가라는 말은 어색하다.

11  ② Andy가 Ms. Kim을 찾아간 이유는 오른손 엄지손가락이 아파서이다.

13  선행사가 사람이면 who나 whom, that을 쓰고, 사물이나 동물이면 which나 that을 쓴다. 보통 목적격 관계대명사는 생략될 수 있다. call A B: A를 B라고 부르다 make A B: A를 B로 만들다

14  목적격 보어로 명사와 동사원형을 취할 수 있는 동사로는 make가 적절하다.

15  선행사가 사람이면 who나 that을 쓰고, 사물이나 동물이면 which나 that을 쓴다.

16  call은 동사 다음에 두 개의 명사(구)가 목적어, 목적격 보어로 쓰이므로 'as Cookie Eater'가 아니라 as 없이 'Cookie Eater'가 되어야 한다.

17  (1) 선행사가 사람이므로 who, whom이나 that, (2) 선행사가 사물이므로 which나 that, (3) '목적어+목적격 보어'의 어순이 되어야 한다. (4) 전치사가 관계대명사 앞에 올 경우에는 관계대명사 that을 쓸 수 없으며, 관계대명사를 생략하지 않는다. (5) 관계대명사가 접속사와 대명사의 역할을 하므로 them을 삭제해야 한다. (6) call은 동사 다음에 두 개의 명사(구)가 목적어와 목적격 보어로 쓰인다. as를 삭제해야 한다.

18  (A) feel은 감각동사로 '형용사'를 보어로 써야 하므로 dry가 적절하다. (B) Another problem이 주어이므로 is가 적절하다. (C) '목 스트레칭' 운동 또한 할 수 있다고 해야 하므로 stretching이 적절하다.

19  ②번과 ⑤번은 4형식, ③번은 3형식, ⓐ와 ①, ④번은 5형식이다.

20  스마트폰을 볼 때, 당신은 눈을 자주 '깜박거리지 않기' 때문에 눈이 건조하다고 느낄 것이라고 했기 때문에 눈을 자주 깜박거리는 것은 스마트폰으로 인한 다양한 건강상의 문제에 해당하지 않는다.

21  목적격 관계대명사 which 또는 that이 생략되어 있다.

22  ③ 스마트폰 중독을 예방하기 위해 할 수 있는 일은 '여러 가지가 있다.'

# Different People, Different Views

시험대비 실력평가                           p.62

01 ④        02 myth        03 ③        04 ⑤
05 deal with   06 ②                   07 gather   08 ④

01 '한 예가 Henri Matisse가 그린 "The Flight of Icarus (이카로스의 비행)"와 Marc Chagall이 그린 "The Fall of Icarus(이카로스의 추락)"이다'고 했으므로, 같은 (same) 주제를 가진 다른 그림이라는 것을 알 수 있다.

02 '신이나 용감한 사람들, 마법의 생물 등에 관한 오래된 이야기'로 신화(myth)가 적절하다.

03 '새의 몸을 덮고 있는 가볍고 부드러운 것 중 하나'는 '깃털'이다.

04 '매우 크게 무언가를 말하다'는 '외치다'이다.

05 deal with ~: ~을 다루다

06 in contrast는 '그에 반해서, 반면에'라는 뜻으로, 앞 문장 과 대조의 관계를 나타낼 때 쓰는 연결어구이다.

07 유의어 관계이다. 소리치다 : 모으다

08 • 접속사 but이 있기 때문에 앞 문장과 대조를 이루는 내용이 적절하다. 'Matisse의 그림은 매우 단순하지만, Chagall의 그림에는 세부적인 것들이 많다. • 태양에 너무 가까이 날지 마라. 밀랍이 녹을 거야(melt).

서술형 시험대비                              p.63

01 (1) warned   (2) gathered, wax
   (3) simple    (4) adventurous
02 (1) foolish, 어리석은   (2) skip, 빼먹다, 거르다
   (3) adventurous, 모험심이 강한   (4) glue, 붙이다
03 (1) details   (2) Furthermore
   (3) outline   (4) in addition to
04 (1) escape   (2) warning

01 (1) 날개가 준비되었을 때, 그는 아들에게 경고했다. "태양에 너무 가까이 날지 마라." (2) 그 다음에 Daedalus는 새의 깃털을 모아 그것들을 밀랍으로 붙였다. (3) Matisse의 그림은 매우 단순하다. 그의 그림에서, Icarus의 몸은 단지 단순한 윤곽만으로 되어 있다. (4) Matisse는 Icarus가 용감하고 모험심이 강하다고 생각했다. 반면에 Chagall은 Icarus가 어리석다고 생각했다.

02 (1) 어리석거나 현명하지 않은 (2) 무언가를 피하거나 하지 않

다 (3) 새롭고 흥미로운 일을 기꺼이 시도하려고 하는 (4) 풀을 사용하여 물건을 결합하다

03 (1) Matisse의 그림이 단순하다고 했으므로 but 뒤에는 대조되는 단어가 적절하다. many 뒤에는 복수 명사가 와야 한다. (2) Matisse의 그림에 대한 추가적인 설명이 오기 때문에 furthermore가 적절하다. (3) Matisse의 그림을 보면 Icarus의 몸은 윤곽만으로 되어 있다. (4) Chagall의 그림은 Icarus 이외에도(in addition to) 사람들과 집을 그렸다.

교과서
## Conversation

핵심 Check                                p.64~65

1 ③    2 ⑤

교과서 대화문 익히기

Check(√) True or False                    p.66

1 T   2 F   3 T   4 T

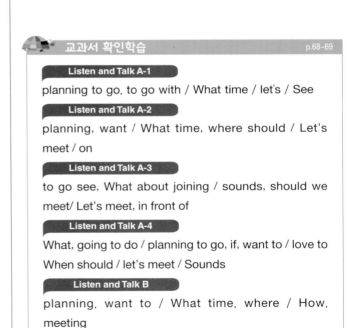

교과서 확인학습                            p.68~69

**Listen and Talk A-1**
planning to go, to go with / What time / let's / See

**Listen and Talk A-2**
planning, want / What time, where should / Let's meet / on

**Listen and Talk A-3**
to go see, What about joining / sounds, should we meet/ Let's meet, in front of

**Listen and Talk A-4**
What, going to do / planning to go, if, want to / love to When should / let's meet / Sounds

**Listen and Talk B**
planning, want to / What time, where / How, meeting

**Listen and Talk C**
going to do / special / planning to go / love to, What time should / How about / Where should / Let's, of

## 시험대비 기본평가      p.70

01 planning to see     02 ④     03 ⑤

04 ③

01 'be planning to+동사원형'은 '~할 계획이다'라는 의미로 미래의 계획을 말할 때 쓴다.

02 (A)에는 B의 대답으로 보아 A가 몇 시에 만날지 시간 약속을 정하고 있고, (B)는 B가 '도서관 앞 에서 만나자'고 했기 때문에 어디서 만날지 약속 장소를 정하는 것을 알 수 있다.

03 B의 대답으로 보아 미래의 계획에 대해 물어보는 말이 적절하다.

04 대화에서 A의 대답으로 보아 시간 약속을 정하고 있다는 것을 알 수 있다.

## 시험대비 실력평가      p.71~72

01 ②        02 What time should we meet?

03 (B)—(C)—(A)—(D)

04 I'm planning to go hiking this Sunday.    05 ⑤

06 ①        07 to meet at 9 at the subway station

08 How about meeting at 2:30 in front of Star Movie Theater?

09 ③     10 ⑤     11 ③

12 What time should we meet?

13 don't we meet in front of the library /
we meet in front of the library

01 Jenny가 Kevin에게 피아노 콘서트에 함께 하자고 제안하는 말이다. ②는 '2시경에 만날까?'라는 시간 약속을 정하는 말이다.

03 함께 가자는 제안에 (B)가 승낙하고, 시간 약속을 묻는 말에 (C) 10시 30분에 만나자고 제안하고, (A)의 찬성하는 말과 약속 장소를 정하는 질문에 (D)의 버스 정류장에서 만나자는 말이 적절하다.

04 'be planning to+동사원형(~할 계획이다)'이라는 표현을 이용한다. '하이킹을 가다'는 go hiking을 사용한다.

05 'be planning to+동사원형'은 '~할 계획이다'라는 의미로 계획을 말할 때 사용한다.

06 여자의 마지막 말에 9시에 만나자고 했기 때문에 약속 시간을 묻는 When이 적절하다.

07 여자의 마지막 말에 지하철역에서 9시에 만나자고 했다.

08 '~하는 게 어때?'는 How about+-ing ~? 형태를 이용한다. '~ 앞에서'는 in front of를 쓴다.

09 'I'd love to!'는 '그러고 싶다!'라는 의미로 '함께 갈래?'라는 제안에 대한 답으로 적절하다.

10 Kate가 전시회에 가자고 Minho를 초대했으나, 그 이유는 대화에 언급되어 있지 않다.

11 전치사 about 뒤에는 동명사 meeting이 적절하다.

12 약속 시간을 정하는 표현으로 의문사 what을 이용한 'What time should we meet?'이 적절하다.

13 제안을 할 때 'Let's+동사원형, Why don't we+동사원형?, Shall we+동사원형?' 등을 사용한다.

## 서술형 시험대비      p.73

01 I'm planning to go to a piano concert this Friday.

02 Do you want to go with me. /
Where should we meet?

03 (A) What are you going to do this Sunday?

(B) You can go with us if you want to.

(C) When should we meet?

04 What time and where should we meet?

01 'be planning to+동사원형(~할 계획이다)'이라는 표현을 이용한다.

02 (A) 함께 하자고 제안하는 표현은 'Do you want to go with ~?'를 사용한다. (B) 약속 장소를 정하는 표현은 의문사 Where와 조동사 should를 이용하여 'Where should we meet?'으로 쓴다.

04 밑줄 친 문장에서 Dream 아트 홀에서 2시에 만나자고 했기 때문에 만날 시간과 장소를 묻는 말이 적절하다.

교과서

## Grammar

### 핵심 Check      p.74~75

1 (1) saw, do[doing]    (2) heard, do[doing]    (3) cleaned

2 (1) Emma was so bored that she started singing by herself.

(2) Our team practiced hard so that we could win the game.

(3) I was so tired that I couldn't work.

**01** (1) sang → sing(또는 singing)

(2) to fly → fly(또는 flying)

(3) very → so

(4) what → that

**02** (1) cry(또는 crying)    (2) thrown

(3) burn(또는 burning)    (4) fall(또는 falling)

**03** ④

**04** He arrived so late that he missed his plane.

**01** (1), (2) 지각동사의 목적격보어는 목적어와의 관계가 능동일 경우 원형부정사나 현재분사가 쓰인 다. (3), (4) 'so+형용사[부사]+that+주어+동사'의 형태로 '매우 ~해서 …하다'라는 의미를 나타 낸다.

**02** (1) 지각동사의 목적격보어는 목적어와의 관계가 능동일 경우 원형부정사나 현재분사가 쓰인다. (2) 지각동사의 목적격보어는 목적어와의 관계가 수동일 경우 과거분사가 쓰인다. (3) 집이 타는 것이므로 burnt가 아닌 burn 또는 burning이 적절하다. (4) 비가 떨어지는 것이므로 능동의 의 미를 나타내는 fall 또는 falling이 적절하다.

**03** 'so+형용사[부사]+that+주어+동사'의 형태로 '너무 ~해서 … 하다'

**04** so를 추가하여 'so+형용사[부사]+that+주어+동사(매우 ~해 서 …하다)' 구문으로 쓴다.

**01** ⑤      **02** ②      **03** ①

**04** The fish is so fast that I can't catch it.   **05** ④

**06** (1) touching   (2) sing   (3) repeated   (4) clean

     (5) so   (6) that   (7) too

**07** ③      **08** thirsty so that → so thirsty that

**09** ③, ④      **10** ③, ⑤

**11** her open[opening] the window      **12** ②, ⑤

**13** ③      **14** ②      **15** ③

**16** (1) My sister was so tired that she went to bed early.

     (2) It rained so hard that we had to stay at home.

**17** (1) When I was reading a book in the garden, I heard a rabbit talk[talking] to himself.

     (2) I could feel him pull[pulling] my hair.

     (3) Somin saw Minji ride[riding] a bike.

     (4) She walked so slowly that everybody passed by her.

     (5) I'm so full that I can't eat anymore.

**18** (1) to download → download(또는 downloading)

     (2) very → so

     (3) surprised enough → too surprised

**01** 목적어와의 관계가 능동이므로 지각동사의 목적격보어로 원형부정사 혹은 현재분사가 적절하고 원인과 결과를 나타내는 'so+형용사[부사]+that+주어+동사' 구문이 적절하다.

**02** hear는 지각동사이므로 목적격보어로 원형부정사 혹은 현재분사, 과거분사를 취한다. someone이 내 이름을 부르는 주체가 되므로 call 또는 calling이 적절하다.

**03** 원인과 결과를 나타내는 'so ~ that ...' 구문이 적절하다.

**04** 원인과 결과를 나타내는 'so ~ that ...' 구문이 적절하다.

**05** 지각동사 watch의 목적격보어로 원형부정사 혹은 현재분사가 적절하다. I watched him sing[singing] in his first performance.

**06** (1) 지각동사 see의 목적격보어로 현재분사가 적절하다. (2) 지각동사 hear의 목적격보어로 원형부정사가 적절하다. (3) 노래가 반복되는 것이므로 목적격보어로 수동의 의미를 갖는 과거분사가 적절하다 (4) make는 사역동사이므로 목적격보어로 원형부정사가 적절하다. (5), (6) 'so+형용사[부사]+that+주어+동사' 구문이 다. (7) 'so+형용사[부 사]+that+주어+can't ~'는 'too+형용사[부사]+to 동사원형'으로 바꿔 쓸 수 있다.

**07** 이웃에 의해 내 이름이 불린 것이므로 지각동사 heard의 목적격보어로 과거분사 called를 쓰는 것이 적절하다.

**08** 'so+형용사[부사]+that+주어+동사'는 원인과 결과를 나타내지만 'so that+주어+동사'는 목적을 나타낸다.

**09** 목적어와의 관계가 능동이므로 지각동사의 목적격보어로 원형부정사 혹은 현재분사가 적절하다.

**10** 'so+형용사[부사]+that+주어+can ~'은 '형용사[부사]+enough+to 동사원형'으로 바꿔 쓸 수 있다.

**11** Mina가 창문을 여는 소리를 들었다는 의미이다. 목적어와 목적격보어의 관계가 능동이므로 원형부정사 또는 현재분사로 써야 한다.

**12** ① I heard Somi talking[talk] with Yubin. ③ He was so busy that he skipped lunch. ④ It was such a nice day that we went on a picnic.

**13** (A) 지각동사의 목적어와 목적격보어의 관계가 능동이므로 현재분사가 적절하다. (B) 지각동사의 목적어와 목적격보어의 관계가 능동이므로 원형부정사가 적절하다. (C) 지각동사의 목적어와 목적격보어의 관계가 수동이므로 과거분사가 적절하다.

**14** 'so that+주어+동사'는 목적을 나타내어 '~하기 위해서' 또는 '~하도록'이라는 의미로 to부정사의 부사적 용법의 '목적'과 바꿔 쓸 수 있다. 원인과 결과를 나타내는 'so ~ that ...'과 혼동하지 않도록 유의한다.

**15** 주어진 문장과 ③번은 목적격보어로 쓰인 현재분사이다. ① 분사구문 ② 진행형을 만드는 현재분사 ④, ⑤ 동명사

**16** (1) 결과를 나타내는 so와 (2) 이유를 나타내는 because절이므로 'so+형용사[부사]+that+주어+동사' 구문으로 원인과 결과를 나타낼 수 있다.

**17** (1)~(3) 지각동사의 목적격보어로 원형부정사나 현재분사를 이용한다. (4), (5) 'so+형용사[부사]+that+주어+동사'의 형태로 '매우 ~해서 …하다'라는 의미를 나타낸다.

**18** (1) 지각동사의 목적격보어로 원형부정사나 현재분사가 적절하다. (2) 'so+형용사[부사]+that+주어+동사(너무 ~ 해서 …하다)' 구문으로 원인과 결과를 나타낸다. (3) 내용상 '너무 ~ 해서 …할 수 없다'는 'too+형용사[부사]+to 동사원형' 구문이 적절하다. so+형용사[부사]+that+주어+can … = 형용사[부사]+enough+to 동사원형, so+형용사[부사]+that+주어+can't … = too+형용사[부사]+to 동사원형

---

**01** (1) Eric heard Mina play[playing] the guitar.

(2) I saw Mike swim[swimming] in the lake.

(3) She felt her heart beat[beating] fast.

(4) Simpson won the Trophy in 2008 but saw it stolen 10 years ago.

(5) She got up so late that she had to run all the way to school.

(6) She speaks too quietly for me to understand.

(7) I left early enough to arrive on time.

**02** I heard Maryline singing a song at the concert.

**03** (1) Dad was too busy to play with us.

(2) The dog was small enough to go through the hole.

(3) The coffee is too hot for her to drink.

(4) The math problem was easy enough for Laura to solve.

**04** Pandora was so foolish that she opened the box which Zeus had given to her.

**05** (1) It rained so hard that he couldn't play soccer.

(2) Last night I was so tired that I went to bed early.

(3) The box was so heavy that I couldn't carry it.

(4) There were so many people that we didn't get into the sea.

(5) It rained so heavily that they had to cancel the game.

**06** (1) to carry    (2) arrested

(3) open[opening]    (4) take

**07** (1) It was so dark that we couldn't see anything.

(2) I want to live so long that I can see you rise in the world.

**08** (1) He looked at the violinist dancing.

(2) The teacher heard Somin playing the piano.

**09** (1) fall(또는 falling)

---

**01** (1)~(3) 지각동사의 목적어와 목적격보어의 관계가 능동이므로 목적격보어로 원형부정사 혹은 현재분사가 적절하다 (4) 지각동사의 목적어와 목적격보어의 관계가 수동이므로 과거 분사가 적절하다. (5) 'so+형용사[부사]+that+주어+동사 (너무 ~ 해서 …하다)' 구문으로 원인과 결과를 나타낸다. (6) so+형용사[부사]+that+주어+can't … = too+형용사[부사]+to 동사원형 (7) so+형용사[부사]+that+주어+can … = 형용사[부사]+enough+to 동사원형

**02** 진행형의 문장이므로 목적격보어로 현재분사가 적절하다.

**03** (1) so ~ that 주어 can't … = too ~ to … (2) so ~ that 주어 can … = ~ enough to … (3), (4) 'so ~ that …' 구문에서 주절의 주어와 that절의 주어가 서로 다를 경우 'too ~ to …'나 '~ enough to …'로 바꿔 쓸 때 'for+ 목적격'으로 주어를 나타낸다. drink와 solve의 목적어가 문장의 주어와 같으므로 목적어를 쓰지 않음에 주의한다.

**04** '매우 ~해서 …하다'라는 의미를 나타내는 'so+형용사[부사]+that+주어+동사' 구문을 이용한다.

**05** 'so+형용사[부사]+that+주어+동사'의 형태로 '매우 ~해서 …하다'라는 의미를 나타낸다. so 뒤의 형용사[부사]는 원인을, that 뒤에 나오는 내용은 그에 따른 결과를 나타낸다.

**06** (1) want는 to부정사를 목적격보어로 받는다. (2) 지각동사의 목적어와 목적격보어의 관계가 수동일 때 목적격보어로 과거분사가 적절하다. (3) 목적어와 목적격보어의 관계가 능동일 때 목적격보어로 원형부정사나 현재분사가 적절하다. (4) 사역동사 make는 원형부정사를 목적격보어로 받는다.

**07** (1) too ~ to … = so ~ that 주어 can't … (2) ~ enough to … = so ~ that 주어 can …, rise in the world: 출세하다

**08** 지각동사의 목적어와 목적격보어의 관계가 능동이며, 진행형으로 쓰이고 있으므로 현재분사를 이용한다.

**09** 지각동사 see의 목적어 Icarus와 목적격보어의 관계가 능동이므로 목적격보어로 원형부정사나 현재분사가 적절하다.

---

교과서
## Reading

🖊️ **확인문제**      p.82

1 T    2 F    3 F    4 T    5 T    6 F

🖊️ **확인문제**      p.83

1 T    2 F    3 F    4 T    5 T    6 F

01 Same, Different
02 different paintings, the same subject
03 example, by, by
04 the same Greek myth    05 Greek Myth
06 a great inventor
07 so, that, keep, forever
08 however, to leave, kept
09 to escape    10 flying    11 I need wings
12 glued them together
13 Don't fly too close    14 melt
15 to fly    16 so, that, warning
17 higher and higher    18 cried out
19 fell into    20 Different
21 deal with, same subject, different
22 flying, falling    23 comes from, different ideas
24 brave, adventurous    25 In contrast
26 very simple, many details
27 only Icarus, some stars
28 Furthermore, outline
29 In contrast, in addition to
30 difference, different painting styles
31 Whose painting
32 same thing in different ways

1 Same Story, Different Paintings
2 We often find different paintings with the same subject.
3 An example is The Flight of Icarus by Henri Matisse and The Fall of Icarus by Marc Chagall.
4 They are both about the same Greek myth.
5 The Greek Myth of Icarus
6 Daedalus was a great inventor.
7 King Minos liked Daedalus' work so much that he wanted to keep Daedalus with him forever.
8 Daedalus, however, tried to leave, so the King kept him and his son, Icarus, in a tall tower.
9 Daedalus wanted to escape.
10 One day, Daedalus saw birds flying.
11 "Wings! I need wings!" he shouted.
12 Daedalus then gathered bird feathers and glued them together with wax.
13 When the wings were ready, he warned his son, "Don't fly too close to the sun.
14 The wax will melt."

15 Daedalus and Icarus began to fly.
16 Icarus was so excited that he forgot his father's warning.
17 He flew higher and higher, and the wax began to melt.
18 "Oh, no! I'm falling," Icarus cried out.
19 Icarus fell into the sea and died.
20 Two Different Paintings
21 Matisse and Chagall both deal with the same subject in their paintings, but they are different.
22 First, in Matisse's painting, you can see Icarus flying, but in Chagall's painting, the boy is falling.
23 This difference comes from the different ideas that the two painters had.
24 Matisse thought that Icarus was brave and adventurous.
25 In contrast, Chagall thought that Icarus was foolish.
26 Second, Matisse's painting is very simple, but Chagall's painting has many details.
27 In Matisse's painting, there are only Icarus and some stars.
28 Furthermore, Icarus' body has just a simple outline.
29 In contrast, Chagall painted many people and houses in addition to Icarus.
30 This difference comes from the different painting styles of the two painters.
31 Whose painting do you like more?
32 People will have different answers because they may see the same thing in different ways.

01 ②    02 ②, ⑤    03 ③    04 ③
05 their paintings    06 careful → foolish 또는 stupid    07 ②     08 ④
09 the different subject → the same subject the same ways → different ways
10 ④    11 ⑤    12 ③
13 difference 14 ④    15 ⓐ ③, ⑤   ⓑ ①, ②, ④
16 (A) simple   (B) the same   (C) different 17 ②
18 ③
19 (A) playing 또는 play   (B) dancing 또는 dance (C) standing 또는 stand
20 (1) Chagall의 그림에서는 바이올린 연주자의 얼굴을 볼 수 있지만 Matisse의 그림에서는 바이올린 연주자의 얼굴을 볼 수 없다.

(2) Chagall의 그림에서 바이올린 연주자가 춤추고 있는 것을 볼 수 있지만, Matisse의 그림에서는 그가 가만히 서 있는 것을 볼 수 있다.

(3) Chagall의 그림은 더 역동적이다.　　　　21 ①

22 than Matisse's　　　　23 Matisse의 그림에는 Icarus와 몇 개의 별들만 있고, 게다가 Icarus의 몸은 단지 단순한 윤곽만으로 되어 있기 때문이다.　　　　24 outline

25 (A) simple　(B) many details

26 (A) flying　(B) falling　　　27 ③　　　28 ④

29 ⑤　　　　30 ②

31 (A) different  painting styles　(B) subject

32 1. ④　2. ⑤　3. ⑦　4. ②　5. ①　6. ③　7. ⑥

01 바로 뒤에 같은 그리스 신화에 관한 두 화가의 다른 그림에 대한 설명이 이어지고 있으므로, '같은' 주제의 '다른' 그림 들을 발견한다고 하는 것이 적절하다. ① usual: 흔히 하는[있는], 평상시의, 보통의, unusual: 특이한, 흔치 않은, 드문, ③ equal: 동일한[같은], unequal: 불공평한

02 ⓒ와 ②, ⑤번: 신화, legend: 전설, ①, ③, ④: (근거 없는) 이야기, 사회적 통념[미신]

03 ③ 'Icarus'가 아니라 'Daedalus'가 새의 깃털을 모아 그 것들을 밀랍으로 붙였다.

04 위 글은 '화가들이 갖고 있던 서로 다른 생각들이 같은 주제를 다르게 그리도록 만드는 것'에 관한 글이다.

05 'Matisse와 Chagall의 그림'을 가리킨다.

06 Chagall의 그림에서 Icarus가 추락하고 있는 것은 Chagall이 Icarus를 '어리석다'고 생각했기 때문이라고 하는 것이 적절하다.

07 ② 십인십색(十人十色), 취향도 가지가지다, 사람들은 같은 것을 다른 방식들로 볼 수 있기 때문에, 누구의 그림이 더 좋은가에 대해 서로 다른 대답을 할 것이라고 했으므로 어울리는 속담으 로는 '십인십색'이 적절하다.

08 A in addition to B = A besides B = not only A but also B = B as well as A: A뿐만 아니라 B도, not A but B: A가 아니라 B

09 화풍이 달랐기 '때문에' Matisse와 Chagall은 '같은' 주제 를 '다른' 방법으로 그렸다.

10 ⓐ 같은 주제를 '가진' 다른 그림들이라고 하는 것이 적절하다. ⓑ 저자 이름 앞의 'by': …가 그린[쓴/만든]

11 글의 도입부에서 '우리는 종종 같은 주제의 다른 그림들 을 발견한다.'고 말한 뒤에 같은 주제의 예로 Icarus에 관 한 그리스 신화를 설명하는 내용의 글이므로, 제목으로는 'Icarus에 관한 그리스 신화'가 적절하다.

12 주어진 문장의 gathered bird feathers에 주목한다. ③ 번 앞 문장에서 필요하다고 말한 날개를 만들기 위해서 새의 깃털을 모은 것이므로 ③번이 적절하다.

13 주어 자리이므로 different의 명사형인 'difference'를 쓰는 것이 적절하다.

14 앞에 나오는 내용과 상반되는 내용이 뒤에 이어지므로 In contrast가 가장 적절하다. in contrast: 그에 반해서, 반면에, ① 그러므로, ② 즉, 다시 말해, ③ 게다가, ⑤ 게다가, 더욱이

15 ⓐthat: 목적격 관계대명사, ⓑthat: 접속사

16 (A) Matisse의 그림은 매우 '단순하다'고 해야 하므로 simple 이 적절하다. complex: 복잡한, (B), (C) 사람들은 '같은' 것을 '다른' 방식들로 볼 수 있다고 해야 하므로 (B)는 the same이, (C)는 different가 적절하다.

17 위 글은 '비교와 대조'의 방식으로 쓰인 글이다.

18 왜 Matisse와 Chagall이 Icarus를 그렸는지는 대답할 수 없다. ① Matisse's. ② We can see only Icarus and some stars. ④ We can see many people and houses. ⑤ Because their painting styles were different.

19 지각동사 see의 목적격보어 자리이므로 동사원형이나 현재분사로 쓰는 것이 적절하다.

20 뒤에 나오는 문장들을 쓰는 것이 적절하다.

21 (B)와 ①번: 가만히 있는, ②, ⑤: 아직(도) (계속해서), ③ (비교급을 강조하여) 훨씬[더욱], ④ 그런데도, 그럼에도 불구하고

22 Chagall의 그림은 'Matisse의 그림(Matisse의 것)보다' 더 역동적이다.

23 바로 다음 문장의 내용을 쓰는 것이 적절하다.

24 outline: 윤곽 / 세부가 없는 사물의 주된 형태나 가장자리

25 Matisse는 매우 '단순하게' 그렸지만, Chagall은 그의 그림에 많은 세부적인 것들'을 그렸다.

26 Matisse의 그림에서 Icarus는 '날고' 있지만, Chagall의 그림에서 그는 '추락하고'있다.

27 in contrast: 그에 반해서

28 Matisse가 왜 Icarus를 용감하고 모험심이 강하다고 생각 했는지는 대답할 수 없다. ① Yes. ② He is flying. ③ He is falling. ⑤ No.=

29 but 이하의 has many details와 대조되는 simple이 적절하다.

30 ⓑ: 앞에 나오는 내용에 추가하는 내용이 뒤에 이어지므로 Furthermore가 가장 적절하다. ⓒ: 앞에 나오는 내용과 상반 되는 내용이 뒤에 이어지므로 In contrast가 가장 적 절하다. ① Therefore: 그러므로, On the other hand: 한편, 반면에, ③ Likewise: 마찬가지로, ④ In other words: 즉, 다시 말해, ⑤ Moreover = In addition: 게 다가, 더욱이

31 화풍이 달랐기' 때문에 Matisse와 Chagall은 같은 '주제' 를 다른 방법으로 그렸다.

32 Matisse: ④ 용감하고 모험심이 강한, ⑤ 매우 단순한, ⑦ 날고 있다, 주제: ② Icarus, Chagall: ① 많은 세부적인 것들, ③ 추락하고 있다, ⑥ 어리석은

01 warning

02 ⓐ The Flight of Icarus by Henri Matisse and The Fall of Icarus by Marc Chagall

   ⓑ bird feathers

03 (A) subject   (B) forever   (C) excited

04 Icarus

05 painters had them → painters had

06 (A) brave and adventurous   (B) flying

   (C) foolish(또는 stupid)   (D) falling

07 has many details → is very simple / is very simple → has many details 또는 Matisse's painting → Chagall's painting / Chagall's painting → Matisse's painting

08 because they may see the same thing in different ways

09 (A) Icarus   (B) some stars

   (C) a simple outline   (D) Icarus

10 (A) so   (B) that

11 to fly → flying 또는 fly

12 different subject → same subject

---

01 Icarus는 "태양에 너무 가까이 날지 마라. 밀랍이 녹을 거야."라는 아버지의 '경고'를 잊은 것이다. warn의 명사형인 'warning'이 적절하다.

02 ⓐ Henri Matisse가 그린 "The Flight of Icarus"와 Marc Chagall이 그린 "The Fall of Icarus", ⓑ '새의 깃털'을 가리킨다.

03 (A) 같은 '주제'의 다른 그림들이라고 해야 하므로 subject가 적절하다. object: 물건, 목적, subject: (논의 등의) 주제[대상/화제], (그림·사진 등의) 대상[소재], (B) Minos왕은 Daedalus의 작품을 매우 좋아해서 Daedalus를 그의 곁에 '영원히' 두고 싶어 했다고 해야 하므로 forever가 적절하다. temporarily: 일시적으로, 임시로, (C) 감정을 나타내는 동사는 수식받는 명사가 감정을 느끼게 되는 경우에 과거분사를 써야 하므로 excited가 적절하다.

04 Matisse와 Chagall의 그림에서 같은 주제는 'Icarus'이다.

05 that이 목적격 관계대명사이므로, 맨 끝의 목적어 them을 삭제하는 것이 적절하다.

06 Matisse는 Icarus가 '용감하고 모험심이 강하다'고 생각했기 때문에 그의 그림에서 Icarus가 '날고 있지만', Chagall은 Icarus가 '어리석다'고 생각했기 때문에 그의 그림에서 여러분은 Icarus가 '추락하고 있는 것'을 볼 수 있다.

07 Matisse의 그림은 '매우 단순하지만', Chagall의 그림은 '세부적인 것들이 많다'로 고치는 것이 적절하다.

08 in different ways: 다른 방식들로

09 Matisse의 그림에서 여러분들은 'Icarus'와 '몇 개의 별들'

---

만 볼 수 있다. 게다가 Icarus의 몸은 단지 '단순한 윤곽'만으로 되어 있다. 반면에 Chagall의 그림에서 여러분들은 단지 'Icarus'뿐만 아니라 많은 사람들과 집들도 볼 수 있다.

10 so+형용사/부사+that+주어+동사: 매우 ~해서 …하다

11 지각동사 saw의 목적격보어이므로 현재분사나 원형부정사로 고치는 것이 적절하다.

12 The Flight of Icarus 와 The Fall of Icarus 는 다른 그림들이지만 '같은' 주제를 가지고 있다.

01 (f)urthermore     02 ④     03 ③

04 ①     05 deal with     06 ⑤

07 (C)–(B)–(A)–(D)     08 ⑤

09 They are going to go to the Van Gogh exhibition.

10 ②     11 (1) I'm planning to go swimming

(2) How about meeting   (3) Where should we meet?

12 ⑤     13 ⑤     14 (1) play(또는 playing)

(2) carry(또는 carrying)   (3) paint(또는 painting)

15 ②     16 ④

17 (1) I heard someone repeat[repeating] my name.

(2) A girl saw a boy feed[feeding] fish.

(3) Did you listen to him tell[telling] the news?

(4) He was so hungry that he ate three pieces of pizza.

(5) The food was so awful that we didn't eat it.

(6) This box is too heavy for me to carry.

18 ⓐ Flight   ⓑ flying 또는 fly   ⓒ fly

   ⓓ to fly 또는 flying   ⓔ flew

19 ②     20 ⑤     21 ③     22 ②, ⑤

23 Matisse의 그림에서, 여러분은 Icarus가 날고 있는 것을 볼 수 있지만, Chagall의 그림에서는 그가 추락하고 있다.

24 ③     25 ⑤     26 ④     27 ④

---

01 유의어 관계이다. 녹다 : 게다가

02 ⓐ furthermore는 '게다가, 더욱이'라는 뜻으로 앞 문장에 또 다른 정보를 덧붙여 제시할 때 쓰는 연결어이다. ⓑ in contrast는 '그에 반해서, 반면에'라는 뜻으로, 앞 문장과 대조 관계를 나타낼 때 쓰는 연결어구이다.

03 말린 잎에 끓는 물을 부어 만든 뜨거운 음료

04 공중을 나는 행위, 즉 '비행'을 나타낸다.

05 • 이번 주에, 여러분의 분노를 어떻게 다뤄야 하는지에 대해 배워 보도록 합시다. • 그 책은 사랑이라는 주제를 다루고 있다. • A: 이 상황을 혼자 다룰 수 있니? B: 물론, 할 수 있어. 어떤 도움 없이 그것을 다룰 수 있어.

06 in addition to는 '~에 더하여, ~ 이외에도'의 뜻이고, '게다가'는 furthermore, in addition이다.

07 (C) 계획을 말하고 함께 하자고 제안함 → (B) 승낙의 답과 함께 만 날 시간을 제안한다. → (A) 약속 시간과 장소를 정하고 → (D) 마지 막으로 그때 보자는 말로 대화를 마친다.

08 만날 장소를 물어보는 말은 Kate의 마지막 말(Let's meet in front of the ticket office.) 앞에 오는 것이 적절하다.

09 그들은 Van Gogh 전시회에 갈 예정이다.

10 ② Minho는 이번 주 토요일에 특별한 일이 없다고 했기 때문에 바쁘지 않다는 것을 알 수 있다.

12 ⑤의 'Do you want to go with me?'는 함께 가자고 제안하는 표현이다.

13 첫 문장의 smell은 목적격 보어로 현재분사가 나와야 한다. 두 번째 문장 에서 see는 목적격보어로 동사원형이나 현재분사가 나와야 한다. (엄마가 만드 는 것이므로 능동)

14 (1)~(3) 지각동사의 목적어가 목적격보어의 행위의 주체가 될 경우 목적격보어로 원형부정사나 현재분사를 쓴다.

15 ② I was so hungry that I ate a whole pizza.

16 the man이 개를 산책시키는 것이므로(능동) walk나 walking 이 적절하다.

17 (1)~(3) 지각동사의 목적어와 목적격보어의 관계가 능동일 경 우 목적격보어로 동사원형이나 현재분사가 적절하다. (4)~(6) 'so+형용사[부사]+that+주어+동사(너무 ~해서 …하다)' 구 문으로 원인과 결과를 나타낸다. so+형용사[부사]+that+주어 +can't … = too+형용사[부사]+to 동사원형

18 ⓐ 이카로스의 '비행'이라고 해야 하므로 Flight 가 적절하다. ⓑ 지각동사 saw의 목적격보어이므로 현재분사나 원형부정사가 적 절하다. ⓒ 부정명령문이므로 동사원형이 적절하다. ⓓ begin은 목적어로 to부정사와 동명사를 둘 다 쓸 수 있다. ⓔ 과거시제로 쓰는 것이 적절하다.

19 새의 깃털을 모아 그것들을 밀랍으로 붙였기 때문에, 태양에 너 무 가 까이 날면 '밀랍이 녹을 것'이라고 하는 것이 적절하다.

20 (A)와 ⑤: (그림·사진 등의) 주제[소재], ① 학과, 과목, ② 지 배를 받는, 복종하는(형용사), ③ 연구[실험] 대상, 피험자, ④ 주어

21 Icarus는 매우 흥분해서 아버지의 경고를 잊고 점점 더 높이 날 아 밀랍이 녹아 바다로 떨어져서 죽었기 때문에, '부주 의한' 성 격이라고 하는 것이 적절하다. ② patient: 인내심 있는, ③ careless: 부주의한, ④ reasonable: 사리를 아 는, 합리적인, ⑤ 호기심 많은

22 ⓐ와 ②, ⑤: (주제·소재로) ~을 다루다, ① 제어하다, 통제하 다, ③ 거래하다, ④ 준비하다

23 they는 Matisse와 Chagall의 그림을 가리키므로, 두 그 림의 차 이를 설명하는 것이 적절하다.

24 두 그림의 차이는 '두 화가들이 갖고 있던 서로 다른 생각'에 서 기인한다.

25 주어진 문장의 This difference에 주목한다. ⑤번 앞 문장 의 내용을 받고 있으므로 ⑤번이 적절하다.

26 '둘째'라고 하면서 Matisse와 Chagall이 Icarus를 다르게 그 린 것에 대한 설명을 하고 있으므로, 앞에는 '두 화가가 같은 주 제(Icarus)를 다르게 다룬 것에 대한 첫 번째 설명'이 나왔을 것이라고 하는 것이 적절하다.

27 ④ Matisse와 Chagall은 서로 '다른' 화풍을 가지고 있어서, '같은' 주제를 '다르게' 그렸다.

### 단원별 예상문제 p.102~105

| | | | |
|---|---|---|---|
| 01 (f)oolish | 02 ③ | 03 ⑤ | 04 ⑤ |
| 05 ③ | 06 planning to go to | | 07 ② |
| 08 ③ | 09 What are you going to do this Saturday? | | 10 I'd love to go with you! 11 ② |
| 12 ①, ⑤ | 13 ③, ④ | 14 ④ | 15 ② |
| 16 ①, ④ | 17 ④ | 18 Matisse and Chagall both deal with the same subject in their paintings, but they are different. | 19 falling → flying / flying → falling |
| 20 ③, ⑤ | 21 Matisse는 Icarus가 용감하고 모험심이 강하다고 생각 했다. 반면에 Chagall은 Icarus가 어리석다고 생각했다. | 22 different | 23 ③ |
| 24 (A) a simple outline  (B) many details | | | |

01 유의어 관계이다. 소리치다 : 어리석은

02 '그 혹은 그녀가 그것을 피할 수 있도록 누군가에게 나쁜일 이 일어날 수 있다고 말하다'라는 의미로 '경고하다'가 적절 하다.

03 (A) Daedalus는 달아나기를 원했기 때문에 날개가 필요하다고 '외쳤다'가 적절하다. (B) 새 깃털을 '모아서' 왁스로 붙 였다가 적절하다. (C) 태양에 너무 가까이 가면 '밀랍'이 녹는다가 적절 하다.

04 let's 뒤에 동사원형을 취한다.

05 (C)의 in contrast는 '반면에'란 뜻이다.

06 '~할 계획이다'는 'be planning to+동사원형'을 쓴다.

07 G의 마지막 말에 10시 30분에 만나자고 했기 때문에 약속 시간 을 정하는 말이 적절하다.

08 ⓐ에는 시간을 정하는 When이나 What time이 적절하고, ⓑ 에는 '~하는 게 어때?'라는 How about ~?이나 What about ~?가 적절하다. ⓒ는 장소를 정하는 표현으로 의문 사 where 가 적절하다.

09 의문사 what으로 문장을 시작하고 'be going to+동사원형' 구 문을 이용한다.

10 '너와 함께 가고 싶다'는 의미로 중복되는 말인 'go with you'가 생략되어 있다.

11 첫 번째 문장에서는 지각동사의 목적격보어로 원형부정사나 현재 분사가 적절하다. 두 번째 문장에서는 '형용사[부사]+enough+to 동사원형 (= so+형용사[부사]+that+주어+can ...)' 구문이 적절 하다.

12 ② The teacher saw Hoyeong dance[dancing]. ③ I felt

somebody watch[watching] me. ④ He was looking at the monkey eat[eating] bananas.

13 ① It was so sad that I cried a lot ② The cake was so delicious that I ate it all. ⑤ The man is so rich that he can buy anything he wants.

14 ⓑ We heard her play[playing] the piano. ⓓ Jocelyn felt him hold[holding] her hand. ⓕ The dog ran too quickly for me to catch. catch의 목적어와 문장의 주어가 같으므로 it을 쓰지 않는 것이 적절하다. ⑧ The sky was clear enough to see stars very well.

15 앞에 나오는 내용과 상반되는 내용이 뒤에 이어지므로 however 가 가장 적절하다. ① 그러므로, ③ 게다가, ⑤ 그 결과

16 ⓑ와 ②, ③, ⑤: 명사적 용법, ① 형용사적 용법, ④ 부사적 용법

17 Daedalus가 새의 깃털을 어떻게 모았는지는 대답할 수 없다. ① No. ② It's the Greek Myth of Icarus. ③ Because Daedalus tried to leave. ⑤ Because he was so excited that he forgot his father's warning.

18 with를 보충하면 된다. deal with: (주제·소재로) ~을 다루다

19 Matisse는 Icarus가 용감하고 모험심이 강하다고 생각했던 반면에 Chagall은 Icarus가 어리석다고 생각했기 때문에, Matisse의 그림에서, 여러분은 Icarus가 '날고 있는 것'을 볼 수 있지만, Chagall의 그림에서는 그 소년이 '추락하고 있다'고 하는 것이 적절하다.

20 ⓒ와 ①, ②, ④: ~에서 기인하다, ③ is caused by로 고치는 것이 적절하다. ⑤ 원인 results in 결과

21 Matisse는 Icarus가 날고 있는 것을 그렸고 Chagall은 그 소년이 추락하고 있는 것을 그린 원인을 설명하면 된다.

22 'difference'의 형용사형인 'different'를 쓰는 것이 적절하다.

23 furthermore = additionally = moreover = in addition = besides: 게다가, 더욱이, ③ beside: 옆에

24 Matisse는 몸이 단지 '단순한 윤곽'만으로 되어 있는 Icarus와 몇 개의 별들만 그렸지만, Chagall은 Icarus뿐 만 아니라 많은 사람들과 집들과 같은 '많은 세부적인 것들' 도 그렸다.

(2) Did you hear Sophia open[opening] the window?

(3) Did you feel your mom touch[touching] you on the shoulder?

06 Orpheus was such a great musician that Hades returned his wife to him.

07 We often find different paintings with the same subject.

08 ⓑ The Greek Myth of Icarus
ⓓ Don't fly too close to the sun. The wax will melt.

09 because

02 함께 가자고 제안하는 표현으로 Do you ~로 시작하는 일반동사 의문문을 이용한다.

03 (1) 이번 주 월요일에 도서관에 갈 계획이다. (2) 5시 30분에 만나기로 했다.

04 'so+형용사[부사]+that+주어+can't ...' = 'too+형용사 [부사]+to동사원형', 'so+형용사[부사]+that+주어+can ...' = '형용사[부사]+enough+to 동사원형' 의미상의 주어 for us와 for me를 빠뜨리지 않도록 주의한다. 의미상의 주어 for anyone은 일반인을 말하므로 생략할 수 있다. 또 한 that절의 목적어와 문장의 주어가 같으므로 her나 it을 쓰지 않는 것이 적절하다.

05 (1)~(3) 지각동사의 목적어와 목적격보어의 관계가 능동이므로 목적격보어로 원형부정사나 현재분사가 적절하다.

06 'so ... that' 구문에서 that 앞에 형용사나 부사 대신 명사가 오면 so 대신 such를 쓴다.

07 빈도부사 'often'을 일반동사 앞에 쓰는 것이 적절하다.

08 ⓑ 'Icarus에 관한 그리스 신화'를 가리킨다. ⓓ '태양에 너무 가까이 날지 마라. 밀랍이 녹을 거야.'를 가리킨다.

09 so+부사+that+주어+동사: '매우 ~해서 …하다'라는 의미이므로 because, as, since 등의 이유를 나타내는 접속사를 사용하여 고치는 것이 적절하다.

01 (A) You can go with us if you want to.
(B) let's meet at 9 at the subway station.

02 Do you want to go with me

03 (1) They are going to go to the library.
(2) They are going to meet at 5:30.

04 (1) The room was too noisy for us to hear him speak.
(2) She speaks too fast for me to understand.
(3) The math problem is easy enough to solve.

05 (1) Did you see Minsu play[playing] soccer?

|모범답안|

01 I'm planning to go / What time should we meet / about meeting

02 (1) Tom was so nervous that he couldn't play well.
(2) I was so happy that I danced.
(3) The boy was so tired that he fell asleep on the floor.
(4) The movie was so sad that everybody cried.

03 (A) a violinist (B) can see (C) dancing
(D) standing still (E) more dynamic

01 ④　　　　02 simple　　　　03 ③　　　　04 ⑤
05 ①　　　　06 ⑤　　　　07 ②
08 They are going to meet in front of the ticket office.
09 plan, in front of, ticket office
10 (1) F　(2) T　11 ③　　　12 (C) → (B) → (A) → (D)
13 (1) I heard my uncle play[playing] the guitar.
　(2) I saw them wear[wearing] their sneakers in the house.
　(3) I saw a queen smell[smelling] a rose.
　(4) The movie was so good that they watched it twice.
　(5) The weather was so bad that they stayed home.
　(6) John is too sick to go to school.
14 (1) This problem is so easy that everybody can solve it.
　(2) The meal was so good that we decided to have dinner at the restaurant once again.
15 ①　　　　16 ②
17 (1) ran → run[running]　(2) to beat → beat[beating]
　(3) burns → burning　(4) too → so
　(5) slippery so that → so slippery that
　(6) carry it → carry
18 ③　　　　19 ⑤
20 (A) same subject　(B) warning
21 He flew higher and higher, and the wax began to melt.

01 ④번은 'escape'에 대한 설명이다. skip은 'to avoid something or not to do something(무언가를 피하거 나 하지 않다)'가 적절하다.

02 반의어 관계이다. 다른 : 같은 = 복잡한 : 단순한

03 약속 시간을 정하는 물음에 대한 답은 ③이 적절하다.

04 G의 대답으로 보아 약속 시간을 정하는 표현이 적절하다.

05 '사소한 사실, 특징 또는 정보'는 detail(세부 사항)을 의미 한다.

06 '언제 어디서 만날까?'라는 물음에 '좋아. 그때 보자.'라는 말은 자 연스럽지 못하다.

07 Kate가 '11시에 만나는 게 어때?'라고 말하는 것으로 보아 약속 시간을 정하는 말이 적절하다.

09 Kate는 Minho와 이번 주 토요일에 대한 계획을 말하고 있고, 11시 국립미술관 매표소 앞에서 만나기로 했다.

10 (1) Minho는 Jenny와 함께 쇼핑을 갈 계획이다. (2) Minho 와 Sumi는 12시 30분에 쇼핑몰 앞에서 만나기로 했 다.

11 대화의 마지막 말에 그때 보자고 했기 때문에 시간을 정하는 말 이 오는 것이 적절하다.

12 (C) 이번 주 토요일의 계획을 말하며, 함께 가자고 제안한 다음 → (B)에서 승낙의 표현과 함께 만날 시간과 장소를 정하는 질문

을 하고 → (A) 2시에 Dream 아트 홀에서 만나자는 말이 오고 → 마지막으로 (D) 토요일에 보자는 말이 자연 스럽다.

13 (1)~(3) 지각동사의 목적어와 목적격보어가 능동의 관계일 경 우 목적격보어로 원형부정사나 현재분사를 쓴다. (4), (5) 'so+ 형용사[부사]+that+주어+동사' 구문을 이용하여 원인과 결과 를 나타낸다. (6) so+형용사[부사]+that+주어 +can't ... = too+형용사[부사]+to 동사원형

14 (1), (2) 'so+형용사[부사]+that+주어+동사' 구문을 이용하 여 원인과 결과를 나타낸다.

15 지각동사의 목적어와 목적격보어가 능동의 관계일 경우 목적격 보어로 원형부정사나 현재분사를 쓴다.

16 ② 첫 번째 문장은 'so+형용사[부사]+that+주어+동사' 구문 으로 원인과 결과를 나타내지만, 두 번째 문장은 'so that+주어 +동사' 구문으로 목적을 나타낸다.

17 (1)~(2) 지각동사의 목적어와 목적격보어가 능동의 관계에 있을 경우 목적격보어로 원형부정사나 현재분사를 쓴다. (3) smell은 목적격보어로 현재분사를 취한다. (4) 'so+형용사[부 사]+that+주어+동사(너무 ~해서 …하다)' 구문으로 원인과 결 과를 나타낸다. (5) 'so+형용사[부사]+that+ 주어+동사'는 원 인과 결과를 나타내지만 'so that+주어+동사'는 목적을 나타낸 다. (6) 'so+형용사[부사]+that+주어+can ...' 구문을 '형용사 [부사]+enough+to 동사원형' 구문으로 바꿀 때, that절 내의 동사의 목적어 와 문장의 주어가 같으면 목적어를 쓰지 않는 것 이 적절하다.

18 (A)와 ①, ②, ④: 현재분사, ③, ⑤: 동명사

19 ⓐ: King Minos, ⓑ와 ⓒ: Daedalus, ⓓ와 ⓔ: Icarus 를 가리킨다.

20 Matisse와 Chagall은 'Icarus에 관한 그리스 신화'라는 '같은 주제'의 다른 그림들을 그렸는데, Icarus는 아버지의 '경고'를 잊었기 때문에 바다로 떨어져서 죽었다.

21 higher and higher(비교급＋and＋비교급): 점점 더 ~하 게

# Life in Space

## 시험대비 실력평가     p.116

01 secret    02 ①    03 ④    04 ⑤
05 are covered with    06 ③    07 recently
08 ④

01 한 사람이나 몇 사람만 알고 다른 사람에게는 말하지 말아야 하는 정보: secret(비밀)

02 Jonny가 우유 용기를 열고는 흔들었다. 우유가 공기 중으로 떠서 공 모양이 되었다.

03 손을 이용하여 무언가를 아래로 옮기다: pull down(아래로 끌어내리다)

04 물이나 다른 액체로 덮여 있거나 가득 차 있는: wet(젖은)

05 be covered with: ~로 덮여 있다

06 동사로 '삼키다'라는 의미와 명사로 '제비'의 뜻을 가지고 있는 swallow가 적절하다. 두 번째 문장은 '제비 한 마리가 왔다고 해서 여름이 온 것은 아니다.'라는 뜻으로 작은 조짐 하나를 너무 확대 해석하지 말라는 의미이다.

07 유의어 관계이다. 놀라운 = 최근의

08 • 그들은 서로(each other)를 쳐다보고 웃었다. • Rada 와 Jonny는 부드러운 초록색의 잔디 위에 누워서(lay down) 언덕 아래로 굴러갔다.

## 서술형 시험대비     p.117

01 (1) pulls   (2) covered   (3) exciting   (4) curious
02 (1) shaking   (2) rolling down   (3) landing
03 (1) (f)orm   (2) (l)and
04 (1) were born   (2) surprise
    (3) don't have to, space suit, everywhere
05 (1) air: 공기   (2) secret: 비밀   (3) space suit: 우주복

01 (1) 또한 그곳에서는 지구가 끌어당기고 있기 때문에 뛰어오르는 것이 어렵지. (2) 언덕들은 초록색의 잔디로 덮여 있지. (3) 그들이 보고, 그리고 하게 될 새로운 모든 것들에 대해서 생각하는 것은 흥미로웠다. (4) 나는 우주 마라톤에 대해 정말 궁금하다.

02 be동사와 함께 현재진행형(be+동사-ing) 형태를 사용한다.

03 (1) form: 양식; 형성하다, 만들다 (2) land: 육지; 착륙하다

04 (1) be born: 태어나다 (2) in surprise: 놀라서 (3) space suit: 우주복

---

05 (1) 당신이 숨을 쉬는 당신 주위에 있는 기체 (2) 한 사람 또는 몇 사람 들에 의해서만 알려진, 그리고 다른 사람들에게 말해져서는 안 되는 정보 (3) 우주비행사들이 우주에서 입는 특별한 옷

## 교과서 Conversation

### 핵심 Check     p.118~119

1 ③    2 Have, heard about    3 ⑤    4 ①, ②, ⑤

## 교과서 대화문 익히기

### Check(√) True or False     p.120

1 T    2 T    3 F    4 T

## 교과서 확인학습     p.122~123

**Listen and Talk A-1**
hear about, that / curious about / to buy

**Listen and Talk A-2**
Did, hear about / I'm really curious about / right here, about

**Listen and Talk A-3**
Did you hear about / I didn't / Look at / I'm really curious about

**Listen and Talk A-4**
about / a type / hear it is / curious about

**Listen and Talk B**
1 about / heard / curious about
2 Look at, hear about / it has great songs/ curious

**Listen and Talk C**
about / good / curious about, about / about, who, to live / interesting / is plaing / What time / begins / Let's, and then / hungry

**Review 1**
did you / heard / curious, about / about, who

**Review 2**
about / right, living / curious about

**시험대비 기본평가**                                                    p.124

01 curious about          02 ④          03 ①, ③
04 hear about

01 궁금증을 표현하거나 보다 많은 정보를 알고 싶을 때 사용하는 표현으로 be curious about을 쓴다.

02 B의 No, I didn't.와 어울리는 질문은 ④번이 적절하다. ④번은 새로운 정보를 알고 있는지 물어 보는 말이다.

03 새로운 정보에 대하여 궁금증을 표현하는 것으로 'I want to know ~. I'd like to know ~, I'm curious about ~' 등을 사용할 수 있다.

04 '~에 대해서 들어 봤니?'라는 표현으로 'Did you hear about ~?'을 사용한다.

**시험대비 실력평가**                                                   p.125~126

01 ④          02 ④, ⑤          03 ⑤          04 ②
05 here it is          06 ④
07 It's about a father who saves his son.          08 ①
09 ③          10 ⑤          11 ②
12 (c)urious

01 G가 No, I didn't.로 과거시제로 답하고 있기 때문에 과거 시제 의문문이 적절하다. 그리고 G의 마지막 말에 I want to buy it.이라고 관심을 가지고 있다는 것을 알 수 있으므로 ⑤는 적절하지 않다.

02 새로운 정보에 대해 궁금증을 나타내는 표현이 적절하다.

03 (D) 우주 마라톤에 대해 들어 봤니?'에 대한 답으로 (C) 부정의 답이 오고 → (B) 우주 마라톤에 대한 설명과 비디오를 보라는 말에 → (A) 동의의 답과 함께 궁금증을 나타내는 표현이 적절하다.

04 '~에 관해 듣다'는 hear about, '~이 궁금하다'는 be curious about을 사용한다.

06 ④ 새로운 뮤지컬에 대해 들어본 적이 없다고 답하고 나서 좋은 노래들이 나온다고 들었다고 말하는 것은 어색하다.

07 '~에 관한 것이다'는 be about이고, a father를 수식하는 관계대명사절을 이용한다. 선행사가 단수 명사 a father이므로 save는 단수 형태 saves로 쓴다.

08 Did you hear about ~?은 상대방이 어떤 정보를 알고 있는지 묻는 표현이다.

09 선행사가 단수 명사 a man이므로 주격 관계대명사 뒤의 동사도 단수인 is가 적절하다.

10 영화를 본 후에 그들이 무엇을 할 것인지는 대화에서 언급되어 있지 않다.

11 '그건 일종의 아이스크림이야'라고 말하고 있으므로 알고 있다는 것을 알 수 있다.

12 어떤 것을 알고 싶거나 세상에 대해 배우고 싶어 하는: 궁금한, 호기심 많은

**서술형 시험대비**                                                     p.127

01 Did you hear about the new book, Living in a Foreign Country ?
02 I'm really curious about this book.
03 (A) Did you hear about the new running shoes, Speed ?
   (B) What about them?
   (C) I'm curious about them.
04 about a father who[that] saves his son
05 That sounds interesting.

01 '~에 관해 들어 봤니?'라는 표현은 Did you hear about ~?으로 시작한다. 그리고 the new book과 Living in a Foreign Country는 동격 관계로 동격의 comma를 사용한다.

02 형용사 curious는 be curious about 형태로 '~에 관해 궁금해하다'는 의미다.

04 '~에 관한 것이다'는 be about을 사용하고, 사람을 선행사로 하는 관계대명사 who나 that을 사용한다. 주격 관계대명사의 동사는 단수 동사인 saves를 쓴다.

05 (B) 새로운 영화에 대해 알고 있는지 묻고 → (F) 알지 못한다는 대답을 하고 → (A) 정말 좋다고 들었다고 이야기 해주고 → (C) 정말로 궁금해진다는 말로 관심을 표현하고 무엇에 관한 내용인지 묻는다. → (D) 영화 내용을 말해준다 → (E) 마지막으로 그거 재미있겠다는 문장이 오는 것이 자연스럽다.

[교과서]
# Grammar

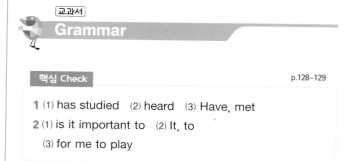

**핵심 Check**                                                         p.128~129

1 (1) has studied   (2) heard   (3) Have, met
2 (1) is it important to   (2) It, to
  (3) for me to play

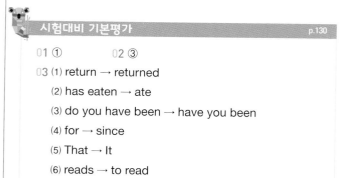

**시험대비 기본평가**                                                    p.130

01 ①          02 ③
03 (1) return → returned
   (2) has eaten → ate
   (3) do you have been → have you been
   (4) for → since
   (5) That → It
   (6) reads → to read

01 it을 가주어로 하고 to부정사를 진주어로 쓸 수 있는 ①번이 적절하다.

02 ③ 'have gone to'는 '~에 가고 없다'는 결과를 나타내는 것으로 3인칭만 주어로 쓸 수 있다. I have been to Hong Kong.으로 고쳐야 한다.

03 (1) 현재완료는 'have[has]+과거분사'의 형태이다. (2) 현재완료는 과거를 나타내는 어구와 함께 쓸 수 없다. (3) 현재완료의 의문문은 have 동사를 주어 앞으로 보낸다. (4) 현재완료에서 'since+시간 명사', 'for+기간 명사'를 쓴다. (5) 가주어로는 That이 아니라 It을 쓴다. (6) 진주어로 to부정사가 적절하다.

시험대비 실력평가    p.131~133

01 ④    02 ⑤    03 ③    04 ①

05 ③    06 (1) has   (2) haven't   (3) gone

(4) went   (5) to sleep   (6) for 07 ④    08 ②

09 ①    10 It is necessary to take a break

regularly.    11 ⑤    12 ②    13 ①

14 (1) It is difficult for me to guess the ending of story.

(2) It is boring to read a science book.

(3) It is important to read for an hour every day.

(4) I worked in the hospital snack bar then.

(5) Jim has had a cat for three years.

(6) Garry has gone to New York on business and he stays there now.

15 (1) Josh has lost his smartphone.

(2) Sophia has lived in Georgia for five years.

16 ⑤    17 ③    18 ②, ④

01 ④ 언제 영화를 봤는지 묻는 문장으로 특정한 과거의 한 시점을 묻는 것이므로 현재완료가 아니라 과거시제가 되어야 한다. when은 현재완료와 쓰이지 않는다.

02 '가주어(It) ~ 진주어(to부정사) …' 구문이 적절하다. ②번은 It is so kind of you to lend me the book.이 적절하다.

03 현재완료의 의문문은 'Have[Has]+주어+과거분사 ~?'이다. It이 나와 있으므로 It을 가주어로 하고 빈칸에는 진주어로 이용할 수 있는 to부정사가 나와야 한다. 그러므로 ③번이 적절하다.

04 가주어로 It이 적절하다.

05 부정문이므로 yet이 적절하다.

06 (1) 주어가 3인칭 단수이므로 has가 적절하다. (2) 현재완료의 부정문은 'have[has]+not[never]+과거분사'로 나타낸다. (3) have[has] gone to는 '~에 가고 없다'는 결과를 나타낸다. (4) 현재완료는 과거를 나타내는 어구와 함께 쓸 수 없다. (5) 진주어로 to부정사가 적절하다. (6) to부정사의 의미상 주어는 to부정사 바로 앞에 'for+명사의 목적격'의 형태로 쓴다.

07 ① Angie bought a new smartphone yesterday. ② Has she told you the good news yet? ③ I have been to England once. ⑤ I've been learning English for ten years.

08 ②번은 인칭대명사로 '그것'이라고 해석 가능하지만 나머지는 모두 가주어로 쓰인 it이다.

09 현재완료형의 질문에 대한 답은 have[has]를 이용하여 답한다.

10 '규칙적으로 휴식을 취하는 것(to take a break regularly)'을 진주어로 하고 가주어 It을 이용하여 'It ~ to …' 형식으로 쓴다.

11 현재완료의 결과적 용법(…해서 (그 결과) 지금 ~하다)을 이용하여 과거에 집으로 가서 지금 여기에 없다는 결과를 나타내도록 한다.

12 가주어로 it을 쓰고 진주어로 to부정사를 쓰는 것이 적절하다.

13 ①과 <보기>는 계속 용법이다. ②, ⑤ 결과 용법 ③ 경험 용법 ④ 완료 용법

14 (1) 진주어로 to guess를 쓴다. (2) 가주어로는 This가 아니라 It을 쓴다. (3) 진주어로 to부정사를 쓴다. (4) 현재완료 는 과거를 나타내는 어구와 함께 쓸 수 없다. then은 '그때, 그 당시'라는 뜻으로 과거를 나타내는 말이다. (5) 현재완료 에서 'since+시간 명사', 'for+기간 명사' (6) have[has] been to는 '~에 가 본 적이 있다'는 경험을 나타내고, have[has] gone to는 '~에 가고 없다'는 결과를 나타내므 로 have gone to로 고쳐야 한다.

15 (1) 스마트폰을 잃어버려서 지금 가지고 있지 않으므로 현재완료의 '결과' 용법으로 나타낸다. (2) 5년 전에 살기 시작해서 아직도 살고 있으므로 현재완료의 '계속' 용법으로 나타 낸다.

16 현재완료는 과거를 나타내는 어구와 함께 쓸 수 없으며, 현재완료에서는 'since+시간 명사', 'for+기간 명사'를 쓴다.

17 '가주어(It) ~ 진주어(to부정사: to hang out with my friends after finals) …' 구문으로 쓴 ③번이 적절하다.

18 문장에 쓰인 형용사가 사람의 성향, 성격을 나타내는 말일 때는 to부정사의 의미상의 주어로 'of+목적격'을 쓴다. 현재완료는 과거의 특정 시점을 나타내는 의문사 when과는 함께 쓰이지 않는다.

서술형 시험대비    p.134~135

01 (1) Kelly has lived in LA since she was 10 years old.

(2) The government has become more interested in education.

(3) He has heard about the rumor.

(4) It is wonderful to travel to other countries.

(5) Is it possible for him to get tickets for the game?

02 (1) To drive at night is dangerous.

(2) It is dangerous to drive at night.

(1) To steal things is wrong.

(2) It's wrong to steal things.

03 (1) |모범답안| I have eaten nacho several times.

I have never eaten nacho.

(2) |모범답안| I have never been to Jeju-do before.

I have been to Jeju-do two times.

04 (1) Sonya has visited New York three times.

(2) I have eaten dinner.

05 (1) It was exciting to think about all the new things.

(2) It was great to swim in the cool blue sea.

(3) It's good to eat a lot of vegetables.

(4) It is true that the pen is mightier than the sword.

06 (1) I have never seen a sunrise.

(2) He has taught English for 20 years.

(3) Is it safe to drink this water?

(4) It's lucky for me to play soccer on the team.

(5) It is important to brush your teeth every day.

07 (1) When did you hear from Susan?

(2) Mr. Brown has lived in Jeju-do since 2010.

(3) Have you been to Canada before?

(4) To use a ticket machine in the theater is easy.

또는 It is easy to use a ticket machine in the theater.

(5) It's important for her to understand him.

08 They haven't finished their project yet. /
Have they finished their project yet?

09 (1) has rained since[has been raining since]

(2) has gone

01 (1)~(3) 현재완료를 이용하여 배열한다. (4)~(5) '가주어(it) ~ 진주어(to부정사) …' 구문을 이용한다. (5)번에서 to부정사의 의미상의 주어로 for him을 써야 하는 것에 주의한다.

02 to부정사가 문장의 주어로 쓰일 때 주어 자리에 가주어 It을 두고 to부정사 부분(진주어)을 문장 뒤로 보낸다.

03 현재완료의 '경험' 용법을 이용하여 쓴다.

04 (1) 현재완료의 '경험' 용법을 이용한다. (2) 현재완료의 '결과' 용법을 이용한다.

05 (1)~(3) 문장의 주어로 쓰인 to부정사를 뒤로 보내고 대신 주어 자리에 가주어 it을 쓴다. (4) 주어로 쓰인 that절의 경우에도 긴 that절을 뒤로 보내고 주어 자리에 가주어 it을 쓴다.

06 (1) 현재완료의 '경험' 용법을 이용한다. (2) 현재완료의 '계속' 용법을 이용한다. (3)~(5) '가주어(It) ~ 진주어(to부정사) …' 구문을 이용한다. (4) 내가 축구를 하는 것이므로 의미상의 주어 for me를 써 주어야 한다.

07 (1) 현재완료는 과거의 특정 시점을 나타내는 어구와 함께 쓸 수 없다. (2) 현재완료에서 'since+시간 명사', 'for+기간 명사' (3) have[has] been to는 '~에 가본 적이 있다'는 경험을 나타

내고, have[has] gone to는 '~에 가고 없다'는 결과를 나타내므로 3인칭만 주어가 될 수 있다. 주어가 you이므로 been to로 고쳐야 한다. (4) to부정사를 주어로 하거나 전체 문장을 '가주어(It) ~ 진주어(to부정사) …' 구문으로 고쳐 쓴다. (5) for her가 to understand의 의미상의 주어가 되도록 고쳐야 한다.

08 현재완료의 부정문은 'have[has]+not[never]+과거분사' 로, 의문문은 'Have[Has]+주어+과거분사 ~?'로 나타낸다. already는 부정문이나 의문문에서 yet이 되어야 함에 주의한다.

09 (1) 현재완료의 '계속' 용법을 이용한다. (2) 현재완료의 '결과' 용법을 이용한다.

교과서
**Reading**

확인문제      p.136

1 T   2 T   3 F   4 T

확인문제      p.137

1 T   2 F   3 F   4 T

교과서 확인학습 A      p.138~139

01 Best    02 far out in space

03 lived there with    04 worked on

05 Only, were born    06 going back to

07 in surprise    08 What's it like    09 is different

10 For example    11 I I've never seen

12 is always black

13 don't have to, there is air    14 pulls you down

15 What else    16 are covered with

17 roll down    18 have you ever rolled down

19 amazing    20 opened, shook

21 floated, formed    22 swallowed

23 get wet    24 Later that night

25 exciting, all the new things    26 one new thing

27 all night    28 their secret    29 got on

30 It's going to be    31 so excited

32 finally    33 to walk

34 pulling you down

35 couldn't float anymore

36 the first new thing    37 What's

38 is singing    39 I've never heard

40 I've never felt   41 These    42 the nearest

43 each other    44 lay down, rolled down

45 their secret    46 best new thing
47 up to the top

1 The Best New Thing

2 Rada lived on a little world, far out in space.

3 She lived there with her father, mother, and brother Jonny.

4 Rada's father and other people worked on spaceships

5 Only Rada and Jonny were children, and they were born in space.

6 One day, Dad told Rada and Jonny, "We're going back to Earth tomorrow."

7 Rada and Jonny looked at Dad in surprise and floated towards him.

8 Rada asked Dad, "What's it like on Earth?"

9 "Everything is different there.

10 For example, the sky is blue," answered Dad.

11 "I've never seen a blue sky," said Jonny.

12 "The sky is always black here," said Rada.

13 "You don't have to wear your big heavy space suits because there is air everywhere.

14 It's also hard to jump there because Earth pulls you down," said Dad.

15 "What else?" asked Rada.

16 "There are hills, and they are covered with soft green grass.

17 You can roll down the hills," answered Mom.

18 "Dad, have you ever rolled down a hill?" asked Rada.

19 "Yes, it's really amazing!" answered Dad.

20 Jonny was thirsty, so he opened a milk container and shook it.

21 The milk floated in the air and formed balls.

22 Jonny swallowed the balls.

23 "Jonny, if you drink milk that way on Earth, you'll get wet," said Mom.

24 Later that night, Rada and Jonny talked a long time about Earth.

25 It was exciting to think about all the new things they were going to see and do.

26 There was one new thing Rada and Jonny really wanted to do.

27 They thought about it all night and didn't tell Mom and Dad about it.

28 It was their secret.

29 The next day, Rada's family got on a spaceship.

30 "It's going to be a long trip," said Mom.

31 That's alright. I'm so excited!" said Rada.

32 The spaceship finally landed.

33 "Dad, it's difficult to walk on Earth," said Rada.

34 "I know. Earth is pulling you down," said Dad.

35 Rada and Jonny couldn't float anymore.

36 That was the first new thing.

37 "What's that sound?" asked Rada.

38 "A bird is singing," said Mom.

39 "I've never heard a bird sing," said Rada.

40 "And I've never felt the wind," said Jonny.

41 These were all new things.

42 Rada and Jonny ran up the nearest hill.

43 At the top, they looked at each other and laughed.

44 Then they lay down on the soft green grass and rolled down the hill.

45 That was their secret!

46 "This is the best new thing of all!" shouted Rada and Jonny.

47 And they ran up to the top of the hill again.

01 ③          02 ②, ⑤          03 ⑤          04 ③
05 shook      06 ②             07 if you drink milk that way on Earth, you'll get wet  08 ②
09 (A) to think about all the new things they were going to see and do
   (B) one new thing Rada and Jonny really wanted to do
   (C) one new thing Rada and Jonny really wanted to do
10 (A) exciting   (B) night   (C) on          11 ⑤
12 (A) landed   (B) pulling   (C) new
13 lie → lay   14 ④          15 ③          16 ②
17 (A) shake   (B) balls   (C) swallow        18 ④
19 Rada and Jonny couldn't float anymore
20 familiar → new          21 they lay down on the soft green grass and rolled down the hill.
22 ⓐ ridden   ⓑ ride   ⓒ rode
23 오전: 공원에서 자전거를 탔다.
   오후: 해변으로 가서 수영을 했다.
   밤: 지구에서 사는 것에 대해 Rada와 Jonny
24 Rada thought it was wonderful to live on Earth and Jonny thought it was great to be on Earth.

25 ②　　26 do them → do　　27 one
new thing they really wanted to do　　28 ②
29 to sing → sing 또는 singing　　30 ⑤

01 ⓐ in space: 우주에서, ⓑ on Earth: 지구(상)에서

02 (A)와 ②, ⑤번: 막연한 상황을 나타내는 비인칭 주어, As it happened: 공교롭게도, ① 가목적어, ③ It is[was] ... that 의 구문으로 문장의 어떤 부분을 강조할 때 씀, ④ 가주어

03 위 글은 '공상 과학 소설(SF)'이다. ① 독후감, ② (신문, 잡지 의) 글, 기사, ③ 전기, ④ 수필

04 ③ 'space'를 'Earth'로 고치는 것이 적절하다.

05 opened와 병렬구문을 이루도록 shook이라고 쓰는 것이 적절 하다.

06 ⓑ와 ②, ⑤: 경험 용법, ① 결과 용법 ③ 계속 용법 ④ 완료 용법

07 조건의 부사절에서는 현재시제가 미래를 대신하므로, 'if you drink'라고 하는 것이 적절하다.

08 지구에서는 점프하는 것이 '어렵다'고 했다.

09 ⓐ It은 가주어로서 진주어인 to think about all the new things they were going to see and do를 대신한다. ⓑ와 ⓒ: Rada와 Jonny가 정말로 하고 싶었던 한 가지 새로운 것을 가리 킨다.

10 (A) 모든 새로운 것들을 생각하는 것이 '흥미로웠던' 것이므로 exciting이 적절하다. (감정을 나타내는 동사는 감정을 유발할 때 현재분사를 쓰는 것이 적절하다.) (B) all+단수 명사는 그 기간 내내 어떤 일이 계속 됨을 나타내므로 night가 적절하다. (C) 우주선에 '오르는' 것이므로 on이 적절하다. get on: 타다, 오르다, get off: 내리다

11 ⑤ (특히 좋거나 신나는 일을) 기대하는, Rada와 Jonny는 지 구 여행을 기대하고 있다. ① 속상한, ② 혼란스러워 하는, ③ 걱정[우려]하는, ④ 실망한

12 (A) 우주선이 마침내 '착륙했다'고 해야 하므로 landed가 적절 하다. take off: 이륙하다, (B) 지구가 너를 '끌어당기고' 있다 고 해야 하므로 pulling이 적절하다. push: 밀다, (C) 지구에 서 겪 는 모든 새로운 것들에 대해 이야기하고 있으므로 new를 써서 최고의 '새로운 것'이라고 하는 것이 적절하다. familiar: 친숙한

13 과거시제로 써야 하므로 lay로 고치는 것이 적절하다. lie-lay-lain: 눕다

14 이 글은 지구에서 겪는 모든 새로운 것들에 대해 이야기하는 글 이므로, 제목으로는 '그들이 지구에서 겪은 새로운 것들'이 적절 하다.

15 Rada는 새가 노래하는 것을 들어 본 적이 '없다'.

16 주어진 문장의 else에 주목한다. ②번 앞 문장에서 우주 와 지구 의 다른 점을 설명한 것 외에 "그 밖에 또 뭐가 있어요?"라고 묻 는 것이므로 ②번이 적절하다.

17 우주에서는 지구에서 사람들이 하는 방식으로 우유를 마실 수

없다. 먼저, 당신은 우유 용기를 열어 그것을 '흔든다'. 그 다음, 우유가 공기 중으로 떠서 '방울'을 형성한다. 마지막으로 그 우유 방울을 '삼킨다.'

18 아빠가 언제 언덕을 굴러 내려갔는지는 대답할 수 없다. ① Because there is air everywhere. ② Because Earth pulls you down. ③ You can roll down the hills. ⑤ He swallowed the balls of milk.

19 'Rada와 Jonny가 더 이상 떠다닐 수 없었던 것'이 첫 번째 새 로운 것이었다.

20 These가 앞에서 말한 새로운 것들을 받은 것이기 때문에, 이러 한 것들이 모두 '새로운' 것들이었다라고 고치는 것이 적절하다. familiar: 익숙한

21 'lie'의 과거 'lay'를 사용하여 영작하는 것이 적절하다.

22 ⓐ 현재완료 시제이므로 과거분사로 쓰는 것이 적절하다. ⓑ Let's 다음에 동사원형으로 쓰는 것이 적절하다. ⓒ 과거에 일 어난 일이므로 과거시제로 쓰는 것이 적절하다.

23 오전에는 자전거를 탔고, 오후에는 수영을 했고, 밤에는 지구에서 사는 것에 대해 Rada와 Jonny가 이야기를 했다.

24 Rada와 Jonny는 지구에서 사는 것이 '멋있다'고 생각했다.

25 ⓐ와 ②, ④: 가주어, ① 비인칭주어, ③ 인칭대명사, 그것(앞에 이미 언급되었거나 현재 이야기되고 있는 사물·동물을 가리킴), ⑤ 가목적어

26 all the new things와 they 사이에 see and do의 목적어에 해당하는 목적격 관계대명사 which/that이 생략되어 있는데, 목적어 them을 또 쓰는 것은 옳지 않다.

27 Rada와 Jonny의 비밀은 '그들이 정말로 하고 싶었던 한 가지 새 로운 것'이다.

28 이 글은 Rada와 Jonny가 지구에서 겪는 새로운 것들에 대해 이 야기하는 글이다.

29 hear는 지각동사로서 'hear+목적어+동사원형/-ing'의 형태로 쓰인다.

30 Rada와 Jonny가 언덕 꼭대기로 몇 번 뛰어올라갔는지는 대답할 수 없다. ① Because Earth is pulling you down. ② No. ③ No. ④ They lay down on the soft green grass and rolled down the hill.

### 서술형 시험대비　　p.148~149

01 (A) children　(B) who[that]

02 Rada and Jonny looked at Dad in surprise and floated towards him.

03 color

04 (A) must(또는 have to)　(B) hard(또는 difficult) (C)balls

05 I have

06 will drink → drink

07 never

08 no more

09 lay down, rolled down

10 (A) other   (B) What   (C) different

11 ran → floated

12 ⓑ on Earth   ⓒ in space

21 ③, ⑤         22 What's it like on Earth?

23 (A) because   (B) What   (C) if         24 ⑤

25 ①, ③, ④   26 There was one new thing which(또는 that) Rada and Jonny really wanted to do.

27 It's going to be a long trip         28 ①

29 has ever heard → has never heard

has ever felt → has never felt

30 best new thing

---

01 우주에는 그곳에서 태어난 Rada와 Jonny를 제외하고는 '아이들'이 없었다. (B)에는 주격 관계대명사 who[that]를 쓰는 것이 적절하다.

02 'in'을 보충하면 된다.

03 지구의 하늘은 파란색이고, 우주의 하늘은 항상 검은색이라고 했으므로 하늘의 '색깔'이 서로 다르다.

04 (A) 우주에서는 크고 무거운 우주복을 입을 '필요가 있다.' have to = must (B) 지구에서는 점프하는 것이 '어렵다.' (C) 우주에서는 '우유 '방울'을' 삼킨다.

05 현재완료로 물었기 때문에 Yes, I 'do'가 아니라 Yes, I 'have'로 답하는 것이 적절하다.

06 조건의 부사절에서는 현재시제가 미래를 대신하므로, 'if you drink'라고 하는 것이 적절하다.

07 (A) 이번이 새가 노래하는 것을 처음 들어 본 때이다. = 나는 새가 노래하는 것을 들어 본 적이 없다. (B) 이번이 내가 바람을 처음 느껴 본 때이다. = 나는 바람을 느껴 본 적이 없다.

08 not ~ anymore = no more: 더 이상 … 아닌[하지 않는], no longer도 가능하다.

09 부드러운 초록 잔디에 '누워서' 언덕 '아래로 굴러 내려간' 것이 그들의 비밀이었다.

10 (A) 뒤에 복수명사가 나오므로 other가 적절하다. another+단수 명사, (B) is like의 목적어가 와야 하므로 What이 적절하다. (C) 바로 뒤에 하늘의 색이 다른 예가 나오고 있으므로, 그곳에선 모든 것이 '다르다'고 하는 것이 적절하다. similar: 비슷한, 유사한

11 우주에서 일어나고 있는 일이므로, 그에게 '달려서' 가는 것이 아니라 '둥둥 떠서 갔다'로 고치는 것이 적절하다.

12 ⓑ는 '지구(상)에서', ⓒ는 '우주에서'를 가리킨다.

### 영역별 핵심문제
p.151~155

01 land        02 ④        03 ③        04 ①

05 space       06 ⑤        07 ④        08 ②

09 It's about a man who is trying to live on the moon.

10 ①        11 (1) Did you hear about   (2) I'm really curious about it.   (3) What's it about?        12 ②

13 ②        14 ①        15 ⑤

16 (1) for Tony to hand in his report by tomorrow

(2) for you to be careful when you cross the street

17 ③        18 ④        19 ⑤        20 ④

---

01 반의어 관계이다. 신난 : 지루한 = 이륙하다 : 착륙하다

02 모든 곳에 공기가 있기 때문에 크고 무거운 우주복을 입을 필요가 없다(don't have[need] to). 또한 그곳에서는 지구가 너희를 끌어당기고 있기(pulls you down) 때문에 뛰어 오르는 것이 어렵다. pull down은 이어 동사(동사+부사)로 대명사 you는 동사와 부사 사이에 위치한다.

03 엄마의 몸에서 나오다: 태어나다(be born)

04 공중에서 아래로 이동한 후 땅이나 다른 표면에 도착하다

05 • 저 책상은 너무 많은 공간을 차지한다. • 이 주차장에는 90대의 주차 공간이 있다. • 6월 18일, 중국은 첫 여성우주 비행사를 우주로 보냈다.

06 lie down은 '눕다'라는 뜻이다

07 (C) 새로운 우주 음식에 대해 들어 봤는지 묻고 → (B) 긍정의 답과 함께 우주 음식이 일종의 아이스크림이라고 말한다. → (A) 그 말에 동의하고 그 음식을 가리키며 맛있어 보인다고 말한다. → (D) 마지막으로 맛이 궁금하다고 말한다.

08 영화 내용을 설명하는 말 앞인 ②가 적절하다.

09 영화 'Life on the Moon'은 무엇에 관한 것인가?

10 ① 새 영화가 정말로 좋다는 말을 들은 사람은 Subin이 아니라 B다.

12 ⓑ의 'right'은 부사로 '바로'의 의미이다.

13 ②에는 사람의 성격이나 성질을 나타내는 형용사(foolish)가 왔으므로 의미상의 주어 앞에 of가 들어가야 한다. 나머지는 모두 for가 들어간다.

14 since(~한 이래로)는 보통 현재완료와 함께 많이 쓰인다. 이때 since절에는 과거 시제가 많이 쓰인다.

15 ⑤번은 '계속' 용법이지만 나머지는 '경험' 용법이다.

16 '~해야 한다'는 의미를 가주어 it을 이용하여 '~할 필요가 있다'라고 쓰려면 진주어로 to부정사를 이용한다. 이때 의미상의 주어를 빠뜨리지 않도록 주의한다.

17 ⓐ Has Daniel found → Did Daniel find ⓒ gone → been ⓔ since → for ⓕ follows → to follow ⓖ That → It

18 ④번은 to부정사의 부사적 용법이지만 나머지는 모두 진주어로 쓰인 명사적 용법으로 쓰였다.

19 ⑤ 현재완료는 과거를 나타내는 어구와 함께 쓸 수 없다.

20 앞의 내용의 예가 나오고 있으므로 For example이 가장 적절하

다.① 그러나, ② 그러므로, ③ 게다가, ⑤ 즉

21 ⓐ와 ③, ⑤번: 미래를 나타내는 부사(구)와 함께 쓰여 현재진행되는 의미가 아니라 가까운 미래를 나타낸다. 나머지는 다 현재 진행되는 의미를 나타낸다.

22 be like: ~와 같다

23 (A) 크고 무거운 우주복을 입을 필요가 없는 이유를 말해야 하므로 because가 적절하다. though: 비록 ~이지만(양보), (B) 그 밖에 또 '뭐가' 있냐고 물어야 하므로 What이 적절하다. (C) '만약' 그런 식으로라고 해야 하므로 if가 적절하다. unless = if ~ not

24 Jonny는 우유 용기를 열어 흔들었을 때 우유가 공기 중으로 떠서 형성된 '우유 방울을 삼켰다.'

25 ⓐ와 ②, ⑤: 명사적 용법, ①, ④ 부사적 용법, ③ 형용사적 용법

26 'ne new thing과 Rada and Jonny 사이에 do의 목적어에 해당하는 목적격 관계대명사 which/that이 생략되어 있다.

27 "긴 여행이 될 거야."라는 엄마의 말을 가리킨다.

28 주어진 문장의 These에 주목한다. ①번 앞 문장의 내용들을 받고 있으므로 ①번이 적절하다.

29 Rada는 새가 노래하는 것을 들어 본 적이 '없고', Jonny는 바람을 느껴 본 적이 '없다.'

30 Rada와 Jonny에게 모든 것들 중에서 '최고의 새로운 것'은 부드러운 초록 잔디에 누워서 언덕 아래로 굴러 내려간 것이었다.

## 단원별 예상문제 p.156~159

01 smooth  02 ③  03 I'm interested in it.
04 ③  05 ⑤  06 hear about, that, into
07 ②  08 who is trying to live on the moon
09 have you heard about the new movie
10 I'm really curious about the movie.  11 ③
12 (1) He has slept for thirty minutes.
   (2) The celebrity has just arrived at the airport.
   (3) Sue has never been to France before.
   (4) I have forgotten the new student's name.
   (5) It is important to share various opinions.
   (6) It is nice of you to remember my birthday.
13 ⑤  14 ②  15 ⑤  16 ③
17 ②  18 ③  19 ②, ⑤
20 ⓒ the hills  ⓓ to roll[rolling] down the hills
   ⓔ the milk container
21 ④  22 ①, ③  23 ④  24 ②
25 (1) Rada와 Jonny가 더 이상 떠다닐 수 없었던 것.
   (2) Rada가 새가 노래하는 것을 들어 본 것.
   (3) Jonny가 바람을 느껴 본 것.

01 반의어 관계이다. 똑똑한 : 어리석은 = 거친 : 부드러운

02 누군가나 어떤 것의 방향으로 또는 더 가까이: '~을 향해'

03 새로운 정보에 관심이 있다는 표현으로 be curious about, be

04 전치사 about 뒤에 있는 부정사 to live를 동명사 living으로 바꾸는 적절하다.

05 get on은 '~을 타다, 탑승하다'라는 의미로 '우주선에 올랐다'가 맞다.

06 'hear about ~'은 '~에 관해 듣다'는 뜻이고, 선행사에 the first(서수)가 있을 때는 보통 관계대명사 that을 사용하는 것이 적절하다.

07 G의 첫 번째 말에 우주선에 대해 궁금하다고 했으므로 빈칸에는 긍정의 대답이 오는 것이 적절하다. ⑤번은 대화와 관련이 없는 말이다.

08 관계대명사 who 뒤에 동사 is를 사용하고 be동사 뒤에 현재분사 trying이 오는 것이 적절하다. 그 다음 'trying to+ 동사원형' 형태가 온다.

09 현재완료를 사용해 'Have you heard about ~?'이라고 들어 본 적이 있는지 물을 수 있다.

10 부사 really는 be동사 뒤에 오고 be curious about을 사용하여 문장을 완성한다.

11 현재완료에서 'since+시간 명사', 'for+기간 명사'

12 (1) 현재완료의 '계속' 용법을 이용한다. (2) 현재완료의 '완료' 용법을 이용한다. (3) 'have[has] been to'는 '~에 가본 적이 있다'는 경험을 나타낸다. (4) 현재완료의 '결과' 용법을 이용한다. (5) '가주어(it) ~ 진주어(to부정사) …' 구문을 이용한다. (6) 문장에 쓰인 형용사가 사람의 성향, 성격을 나타내는 말일 때는 to부정사의 의미상의 주어로 'of+목적격'을 쓴다.

13 ① It's great to be here. ② It's fun to play with friends. ③ It is boring to fish in the lake. ④ It's exciting for us to have you here

14 ② Have you been to London before?

15 가주어 it을 이용하여 바꿔 쓰는 것으로 원래 문장의 to부정사를 진주어로 쓴다.

16 ⓒ in

17 (A)와 ②번: (외관·내용 등이) …을 닮아, 유사하여; …일 것 같아, …과 다름없이(전치사), be like: ~와 같다, ①, ③, ⑤: ~을 좋아하다(동사), ④ [외관·형태·성질 등이] 같은 (same)(형용사)

18 '그곳에는 모든 곳에 공기가 있기 때문에' 크고 무거운 우주복을 입을 필요가 없다고 하는 것이 적절하다.

19 It은 가주어로서 진주어인 to jump there를 대신한 것이므로 to jump there나 jumping there를 가주어 It 자리에 쓸 수 있고, 의미상의 주어인 for you를 써도 된다.

20 ⓒ 언덕들, ⓓ 언덕을 굴러 내려가는 것, ⓔ 우유 용기를 가리킨다.

21 Rada는 지구 여행을 기대하고 있으므로 "괜찮아요. 정말 신나요!"라고 하는 것이 적절하다. ② 감정을 나타내는 동사는 사람을 수식할 때 보통 과거분사를 써야 하므로 interested가 적절하다. ③ pleasant는 '상냥한'이라는 뜻일 때를 제외하고는 사

람을 주어로 해서 쓸 수 없다. pleased로 쓰는 것이 적절하다.

22 all the new things와 they 사이에 see and do의 목적어에 해당하는 목적격 관계대명사 which/that이 생략되어 있다.

23 Rada와 Jonny는 정말로 하고 싶었던 한 가지 새로운 것에 대해서 엄마와 아빠에게 말하지 않았다.

24 consequently: 그 결과, 따라서, finally와 나머지는 다 '마침내'

25 앞의 세 문장들의 내용을 가리킨다.

서술형 실전문제　　　　　　　　　p.160~161

01 (A) Did you hear about the new snack?
  (B) I'm curious about it.
02 You can choose a player who you like and play.
03 (1) for　(2) before　(3) since
04 (1) They are talking about the new movie.
  (2) They will eat[have] lunch.
05 (1) It was easy to answer his questions.
  (2) It is easy to cook camping food.
  (3) It is safe and comfortable to live in Seoul.
  (4) It was very wise of her to say so.
06 (1) has live, since　(2) have read, three times
  (3) has taken
07 (A) don't have to　(B) hard　(C) amazing
08 pulls down you → pulls you down
09 (A) get wet　(B) shake

02 조동사 can 뒤에 동사원형 choose를 쓰고 관계대명사절 'who you like'가 선행사인 목적어 'a player'를 꾸며주고 and 뒤에 play가 choose와 병렬구조로 문장을 완성한다.

03 (1), (3) 현재완료에서 'since+시간 명사', 'for+ 기간 명사' (2) ago는 현재완료와 함께 사용할 수 없으나 before는 사용할 수 있다.

04 (1) Subin과 Andy는 새 영화에 관해 이야기하고 있다. (2) 영화를 보기 전에 점심을 먹을 것이다.

05 (1) It을 가주어로 하고 to부정사를 진주어로 쓴다. (2) It을 가주어로 하고 진주어 to cook의 목적어로 camping food를 쓴다. (3) 전치사 in의 목적어로 Seoul을 쓴다. (4) to say의 주어가 she이므로 of her로 의미상의 주어를 나타내야 한다.

06 (1) 현재완료의 '계속' 용법을 이용한다. (2) 현재완료의 '경험' 용법을 이용한다. (3) 현재완료의 '결과' 용법을 이용한다.

07 (A) 그곳에는 모든 곳에 공기가 있기 때문에 크고 무거운 우주복을 입을 '필요가 없다'고 해야 하므로 don't have to가 적절하다. (B) 지구가 너희들을 끌어당기기 때문에 거기에서는 점프하는 것도 '어렵다'고 해야 하므로 hard가 적절하다. (C) 언덕을 굴러 내려가는 것이 '놀라운' 것이므로 amazing이 적절하다. (감정을 나타내는 동사는 감정을 일으킬 때 현재분사를 쓰는 것이 적

절하다.)

08 목적어가 인칭대명사일 때는 타동사와 부사 사이에 목적어를 쓰는 것이 적절하다.

09 지구에서 우유 용기를 열어 그것을 '흔들면' 우유가 용기에서 쏟아져 나와서 당신을 '젖게' 만들 것이기 때문이다.

창의사고력 서술형 문제　　　　　　　p.162

|모범답안|

01 (1) It is exciting to learn a new language.
  (2) It's necessary for me to see a doctor.
  (3) It is important to exercise regularly.
  (4) It's difficult to learn Chinese.
  (5) It's fun to go to the beach.
02 (A) ridden a bike　(B) rode bikes
  (C) swum before　(D) to swim　(E) living on Earth

단원별 모의고사　　　　　　　　　p.163~166

01 ④　　　02 arrive / reach　　　03 ①
04 ④　　　05 ③　　06 ⑤　　　07 ②
08 They are going to eat lunch.
09 about, who　　　10 (1) F　(2) T　11 ⑤
12 ④　　　13 ②　　　14 ③
15 (1) Have you found → Did you find
  (2) played the piano since → have played the piano for
  (3) gone → been
  (4) Search → To search[Searching]또는 Search information using the Internet is easy. → It is easy to search information using the Internet.
  (5) of → for
16 (1) He has known her since he was ten years old.
  (2) He hasn't finished his homework yet.
  (3) They have seen the movie four times.
  (4) She has gone to Paris.
  (5) It was helpful to visit this web site.
  (6) It is hard for a child to wash a big dog.
17 (A) different　(B) blue　　18 ①, ②, ④　　19 (e)lse
20 have you ever rolled down a hill?　　　21 ④

01 ④번은 'pull down'에 대한 설명이다. roll down은 'to move downward by turning over and over(반복해서 돌면서 아래로 내려오다)'가 적절하다.

02 반의어 관계이다. 다른 : 같은 = 도착하다 : 출발하다

03 '액체의 표면에 머무르고 가라앉지 않다'는 float '뜨다'가 적절하다.

04 '새 노래에 대해 들어 봤느냐'는 A의 물음에 '아니, 못 들어 봤다'

고 말하고는 새 노래에 대한 설명을 하는 건 자연스럽지 않다.

05 대화는 화성에 관한 책에 대한 이야기다.

06 G의 답으로 보아 영화의 내용을 묻는 말이 적절하다.

07 빈칸 다음의 말이 영화의 내용이 무엇인지 묻고 있으므로 그 영화에 관심이 있다는 것을 알 수 있다.

10 (1) 두 사람은 새로운 책에 대해 이야기 중이다. (2) 소년은 새 책에 대해 궁금해 하기 때문에 관심이 있다는 것을 알 수 있다.

11 B가 그 영화가 정말 궁금하다고 말하는 것으로 보아 G는 영화에 대해 좋은 평가를 내리고 있다고 추측할 수 있다.

12 (D)에서 새 책에 대한 정보를 알고 있는지 묻고, (A)에서 부정의 답이 오고 이어서 (C)에서 책에 관한 내용을 이야기해 주고 나서 (B)에서 이 책이 궁금하다고 말하는 것이 자연스럽다.

13 현재완료는 과거의 특정 시점을 나타내는 의문사 when과 함께 쓸 수 없다. When did you visit Italy?

14 주어진 문장과 ③번은 가주어로 쓰이고 있다. ①, ⑤ 비인칭 주어 ② It ~ that 강조구문 ④ 인칭대명사

15 (1) 현재완료는 과거를 나타내는 ~ ago와는 함께 쓰이지 않는다. (2) 오래전에 시작해서 아직도 즐기고 있다고 했으므로 현재완료의 '계속' 용법으로 나타내는 것이 적절하다. 'since+시간 명사', 'for+ 기간 명사'임에 유의한다. (3) have[has] been to는 '~에 가 본 적이 있다'는 경험을 나타내고, have[has] gone to 는 '~에 가고 없다'는 결과를 나타내므로 have been to로 고쳐야 한다. (4) to부정사나 동명사가 주어가 되도록 하거나 가주어 it을 사용하고 진주어로 to부정사를 쓴다. (5) to부정사의 의미상 주어는 to부정사 바로 앞에 'for+명사의 목적격'의 형태로 쓴다.

16 (1) 현재완료의 '계속' 용법을 이용한다. (2) 현재완료의 '완료' 용법 을 이용한다. 부정문이므로 yet을 쓰는 것에 주의한다. (3) 현재완료의 '경험' 용법을 이용한다. (4) 현재완료의 '결과' 용법을 이용한다. have[has] been to는 '~에 가 본 적이 있다'는 경험을 나타내고, have[has] gone to 는 '~에 가고 없다'는 결과를 나타낸다. (5) '가주어(it) ~ 진주어(to부정사) …' 구문을 이용한다. (6) '가주어(it) ~ 진주어(to부정사) …' 구문을 이용하고 to 부정사의 의미상의 주어로 'for+목적격'을 쓴다

17 지구에서 하늘의 색깔은 우주의 그것과는 다르다. 그것은 검은 색이 아니라 '파란색'이다.

18 ⓐ와 ③, ⑤번: 경험 용법, ①, ④: 계속 용법, ② 완료 용법

19 else: 그 밖에

20 'down'을 보충하면 된다. roll down: 굴러 내려가다

21 지구가 끌어당기기 때문에 지구에서 점프하는 것이 어려운 것이므로, 우주복을 입는 것과 점프하는 것은 상관이 없다.

# 교과서 파헤치기

Lesson 5

## 단어 TEST Step 1                                      p.02

| | | |
|---|---|---|
| 01 충고 | 02 유명인사, 유명인 | 03 ~ 동안 |
| 04 현명하지 않은 | 05 아픈, 쓰린 | 06 열, 열병 |
| 07 단순한 | 08 눈을 깜박이다 | 09 엄지손가락 |
| 10 막다, 예방하다 | 11 목구멍 | 12 건강 |
| 13 피부 | 14 초조한, 불안한 | 15 다양한 |
| 16 구덩이, 구멍 | 17 과목 | 18 건조한, 마른 |
| 19 식사 | 20 약 | 21 규칙적으로 |
| 22 똑똑한, 지적인 | 23 어려운 | 24 다치다 |
| 25 약속 | 26 사고 | 27 안전 |
| 28 예, 사례 | 29 증가하다 | 30 작가, 저자 |
| 31 끔찍한, 무서운 | 32 중독 | 33 야기하다 |
| 34 아픔, 고통 | 35 지금부터 | 36 전 세계적으로 |
| 37 잠들다 | 38 ~ 대신에 | 39 (~한 상태에) 처하다 |
| 40 휴식을 취하다, 쉬다 | | 41 목이 아프다 |
| 42 예를 들어 | 43 건강해 보이다 | |

## 단어 TEST Step 2                                      p.03

| | | |
|---|---|---|
| 01 thumb | 02 hole | 03 health |
| 04 difficult | 05 promise | 06 regularly |
| 07 simple | 08 nervous | 09 advice |
| 10 prevent | 11 hurt | 12 during |
| 13 skin | 14 blink | 15 various |
| 16 celebrity | 17 sore | 18 unwise |
| 19 subject | 20 medicine | 21 fever |
| 22 dry | 23 intelligent | 24 throat |
| 25 meal | 26 increase | 27 dentist |
| 28 smart | 29 exercise | 30 addiction |
| 31 without | 32 toothache | 33 safety |
| 34 author | 35 instead of ~ | 36 a few |
| 37 these days | 38 have a runny nose | |
| 39 for example | 40 take a rest | 41 try to+동사원형 |
| 42 fall asleep | 43 from now on | |

## 단어 TEST Step 3                                      p.04

1 rest, 휴식   2 pad, 패드   3 cause, 야기하다
4 hole, 구덩이   5 blink, 눈을 깜박이다
6 regularly, 규칙적으로   7 pain, 고통
8 text, 문자를 보내다 9 throat, 목구멍

10 increase, 증가하다   11 medicine, 약, 약물
12 prevent, 막다, 예방하다   13 safety, 안전
14 thumb, 엄지손가락   15 exercise, 운동
16 addiction, 중독

## 대화문 TEST Step 1                                      p.05~06

**Listen and Talk A-1**

look sick, What's wrong / have a sore throat, have a fever / have a cold, Take, medicine, make sure, take, rest / Thank you

**Listen and Talk A-2**

wrong / back hurts a lot / Put, on / I will / make sure, stretching exercises

**Listen and Talk A-3**

matter / have a, toothache / Here is, medicine, Take / make sure, dentist / I will

**Listen and Talk A-4**

wrong with / fell, hurt, while / Can, walk / hurts / Why don't you, make sure, don't play, until

**Listen and Talk B**

1 don't look well, wrong / have a headache / That's too bad, Make sure, take / will

2 don't look well, wrong / have a cold / Make sure, doctor / I will

**Listen and Talk C**

wrong / thumb hurts / use, a lot / text a lot / have texting thumb / pain, your thumb, get, from texting / didn't know / Why don't you / make sure you don't text

**Review 1**

wrong / have a terrible headache / should take some medicine / I will

**Review 2**

the matter / have a sore throat, have a runny nose / cold, Make sure, get some rest / I will

## 대화문 TEST Step 2                                      p.07~08

**Listen and Talk A-1**

W: You look sick. What's wrong, Inho?
B: I have a sore throat. I have a fever, too.
W: I think you have a cold. Take this medicine and make sure you take a good rest.
B: OK. Thank you.

W: What's wrong, Peter?

B: I don't know, Ms. Kim, but my back hurts a lot.

W: Put a heating pad on it.

B: OK, I will.

W: And make sure you do some stretching exercises.

W: What's the matter, Chris?

B: I have a terrible toothache.

W: Here is some medicine. Take this.

B: Thank you.

W: And make sure you go to the dentist. B: OK, I will.

W: What's wrong with your leg, Sam?

B: I fell and hurt my foot while I was playing soccer.

W: Can you walk?

B: Yes, but it hurts a lot.

W: Why don't you put some ice on it? And make sure you don't play soccer until next week.

1 A: You don't look well. What's wrong?

　B: I have a headache.

　A: That's too bad. Make sure you take some medicine.

　B: OK, I will.

2 A: You don't look well. What's wrong?

　B: I have a cold.

　A: That's too bad. Make sure you go see a doctor.

　B: OK, I will.

W: What's wrong, Andy?

B: Hello, Ms. Kim. My right thumb hurts.

W: Hmm. Do you use your smartphone a lot?

B: Yes, I text a lot. Why?

W: I think you have texting thumb.

B: Texting thumb? What's texting thumb?

W: It's pain in your thumb. You can get it from texting too much.

B: Oh, I didn't know that.

W: Why don't you do some finger stretching exercises?

B: OK, I will. W: And make sure you don't text too much.

G: What's wrong, Mike?

B: I have a terrible headache.

G: I think you should take some medicine.

B: OK, I will.

M: What's the matter, Mina?

G: I have a sore throat. I also have a runny nose.

M: I think you have a cold. Make sure you get some rest.

G: OK, I will.

---

01 Be Smart with　02 Living without, difficult, days

03 unwise, use, cause　　　04 Are, smombie

05 over, around like　　　06 down, eyes, on

07 call such people

08 If, various safety

09 may, so, fall, hurt　　　10 get into, too

11 what, to prevent　　　12 It's simple

13 at, while, walking　　　14 dry, text neck

15 cause, health problems

16 example, dry eyes

17 When, look at, blink　　　18 your, feel dry

19 Another, have, pain

20 down at, on, increases

21 use, for, texting, cause

22 call, text　　23 Here, tips, problems

24 dry, try, blink　25 move, up, level

26 also, stretching exercises

27 How, feel, don't

28 feel nervous, around

29 feel sad, check, text

30 answers, may, addiction

31 There, various, prevent　　　32 turn off, during

33 instead of texting

---

01 Be Smart with

02 Living without smartphones, these days

03 unwise or too much use, can cause

04 Are, a smombie

05 All over the world, walking around like zombies

06 down, on their smartphones

07 call such people smombies

08 various safety problems

09 may not see, so, may fall, get hurt

10 may get into, too

11 to prevent these problems　　　12 simple

13 Do not look at, while, walking

14 dry eyes, text neck

15 various health problems

16 One example, dry eyes

17 look at, blink often        18 will feel dry

19 Another problem, is neck pain

20 look down at, stress on, increases

21 Too much use, too much texting, neck pain

22 call, text neck   23 Here are some tips

24 dry eyes, try to blink

25 move, up to, your eye level

26 can also, neck stretching exercises

27 How do you feel

28 feel nervous, around

29 feel sad, no text message

30 answers, smartphone addiction  31 to prevent this

32 For example, turn off, during

33 can, instead of texting

1 스마트폰을 현명하게 사용하라!

2 스마트폰 없이 사는 것은 요즘 많은 사람들에게 어렵다.

3 하지만 스마트폰을 현명하지 않게 사용하거나 너무 과도하게 사용하는 것은 다양한 문제를 야기할 수 있다.

4 당신은 스몸비인가요?

5 전 세계적으로 사람들이 좀비처럼 걸어다니고 있다.

6 그들의 머리는 아래를 향하고, 그들의 눈은 스마트폰을 향하고 있다.

7 우리는 그런 사람들을 스몸비, 즉 스마트폰 좀비라고 부른다.

8 만약 당신이 스몸비라면, 당신은 다양한 안전 관련 문제들을 겪을 수 있다.

9 당신은 거리에 있는 구덩이를 보지 못할 수도 있고, 그래서 넘어져서 다칠지도 모른다.

10 당신은 또한 교통사고를 당할지도 모른다.

11 그렇다면 이런 문제들을 방지하기 위해 무엇을 할 수 있을까?

12 간단하다.

13 걷고 있는 동안에는 스마트폰을 보지 마라!

14 당신은 안구 건조증이나 거북목 증후군이 있나요?

15 스마트폰은 다양한 건강상의 문제를 일으킬 수 있다.

16 한 가지 예가 안구 건조증이다.

17 스마트폰을 볼 때, 당신은 눈을 자주 깜박거리지 않는다.

18 그러면 눈이 건조하다고 느낄 것이다.

19 일어날 수 있는 또 다른 문제는 목 통증이다.

20 스마트폰을 내려다볼 때, 목에 가해지는 압박이 증가한다.

21 스마트폰을 너무 많이 사용하는 것은, 예를 들어, 너무 많이 문자를 하는 것은 목 통증을 일으킬 수 있다.

22 이런 증상을 거북목 증후군이라고 부른다.

23 여기에 이런 문제들을 위한 몇 가지 조언이 있다.

24 안구 건조증에는, 눈을 자주 깜박이려고 노력해라.

25 거북목 증후군에는 당신의 눈높이까지 스마트폰을 위로 올려라.

26 목 스트레칭 운동 또한 할 수 있다.

27 스마트폰이 없을 때 어떤 기분이 드나요?

28 스마트폰이 주위에 없을 때 당신은 초조한 기분이 드는가?

29 스마트폰을 확인했을 때 아무런 문자 메시지가 없으면 슬픈 기분이 드는가?

30 만약 당신의 대답이 '그렇다'이면, 당신은 스마트폰 중독일지도 모른다.

31 이것을 방지하기 위해 할 수 있는 일은 여러 가지가 있다.

32 예를 들어, 식사나 회의 중에는 스마트폰을 꺼라.

33 문자를 보내는 대신에 사람들과 이야기를 할 수 있다.

1 Be Smart with Your Smartphones!

2 Living without smartphones is difficult for many of us these days.

3 However, unwise or too much use of smartphones can cause various problems.

4 Are you a smombie?

5 All over the world, people are walking around like zombies.

6 Their heads are down, and their eyes are on their smartphones.

7 We call such people smombies, smartphone zombies.

8 If you are a smombie, you can have various safety problems.

9 You may not see a hole in the street, so you may fall and get hurt.

10 You may get into a car accident, too.

11 So what can you do to prevent these problems?

12 It's simple.

13 Do not look at your smartphone while you are walking!

14 Do you have dry eyes or text neck?

15 Smartphones can cause various health problems.

16 One example is dry eyes.

17 When you look at your smartphone, you do not blink often.

18 Then your eyes will feel dry.

19 Another problem you can have is neck pain.

20 When you look down at your smartphone, the

stress on your neck increases.

21 Too much use of your smartphone, for example, too much texting, can cause neck pain.

22 We call this text neck.

23 Here are some tips for these problems.

24 For dry eyes, try to blink often.

25 For text neck, move your smartphone up to your eye level.

26 You can also do some neck stretching exercises.

27 How do you feel when you don't have your smartphone with you?

28 Do you feel nervous when your smartphone is not around?

29 Do you feel sad when you check your smartphone and there is no text message?

30 If your answers are "yes," you may have smartphone addiction.

31 There are various things you can do to prevent this.

32 For example, turn off your smartphone during meals or meetings.

33 You can talk to people instead of texting them.

**Talk and Play**

1. wrong

2. have a fever

3. Make sure, some rest

4. I will

**After You Read B**

1. Be Smart with

2. fell, got hurt

3. was texting, didn't see

4. Do not, while, are walking

5. feel dry

6. Try to blink

7. when, text a lot

8. up to, eye level, stretching exercises

9. have smartphone addiction

10. Turn off, during, instead of texting

**Around the World**

1. Be careful, using, while

2. There are, so, while, are using

3. means, side, who are texting

**Talk and Play**

1. A: What's wrong?

2. B: I have a fever.

3. A: That's too bad. Make sure you get some rest.

4. B: OK, I will.

**After You Read B**

1. Be Smart with Your Smartphones!

2. Minho: Yesterday, I fell on the street and got hurt.

3. I was texting and I didn't see a hole.

4. Reply: Do not use your smartphone while you are walking.

5. Emma: My eyes feel dry when I use my smartphone.

6. Reply: Try to blink often.

7. Suji: I have neck pain when I text a lot.

8. Reply: Move your smartphone up to your eye level and do some neck stretching exercises .

9. Eric: I think I have smartphone addiction.

10. Reply: Turn off your smartphone during meals or meetings and talk to people instead of texting them.

**Around the World**

1. This sign says, "Be careful of using your smartphone while you are walking."

2. There are traffic lights on the ground, so people can see them while they are using their smartphones.

3. This sign on the ground means, "This side of the street is for people who are texting."

**9** adventurous, 모험심이 강한  **10** outline, 윤곽, 외형
**11** skip, 빼먹다, 거르다  **12** feather, 깃털
**13** wing, 날개  **14** furthermore, 게다가
**15** myth, 신화  **16** warn, 경고하다

## 단어 TEST Step 1  p.21

| | | |
|---|---|---|
| 01 특별한 | 02 용감한 | 03 창의적인 |
| 04 단순한 | 05 세부 사항 | 06 모험심이 강한 |
| 07 전부의, 전체의 | 08 아름다움, 미 | 09 주제 |
| 10 경고, 주의 | 11 녹다 | 12 역동적인 |
| 13 달아나다, 탈출하다 | | 14 비행, 날기 |
| 15 전시회 | 16 로맨틱한, 낭만적인 | |
| 17 차이 | 18 빼먹다, 거르다 | 19 영원히 |
| 20 모으다 | 21 붙이다 | 22 상상력이 풍부한 |
| 23 (새의) 털, 깃털 | 24 다른 | 25 문장 |
| 26 잊어버리다, 잊다 | 27 발명가 | 28 예, 사례 |
| 29 어리석은 | 30 윤곽, 외형 | 31 게다가, 더욱이 |
| 32 준비된 | 33 신화 | 34 경고하다 |
| 35 ~와 사랑에 빠지다 | | 36 ~에 관심이 있다 |
| 37 ~을 다루다 | 38 ~에 더하여, ~일 뿐 아니라 | |
| 39 ~을 자랑스러워하다 | | 40 그에 반해서 |
| 41 ~에 초점을 맞추다 | | 42 ~하는 게 어때? |
| 43 ~하려고 시도하다 | | |

## 단어 TEST Step 2  p.22

| | | |
|---|---|---|
| 01 subject | 02 whole | 03 dynamic |
| 04 warn | 05 escape | 06 exhibition |
| 07 simple | 08 myth | 09 beauty |
| 10 special | 11 gather | 12 romantic |
| 13 sci-fi movie | 14 adventurous | 15 feather |
| 16 difference | 17 brave | 18 melt |
| 19 creative | 20 flight | 21 outline |
| 22 different | 23 foolish | 24 sentence |
| 25 forever | 26 imaginative | 27 forget |
| 28 inventor | 29 ready | 30 furthermore |
| 31 example | 32 detail | 33 skip |
| 34 warning | 35 deal with | |
| 36 higher and higher | | 37 fall in love with ~ |
| 38 in front of ~ | 39 in addition to | 40 try to+동사원형 |
| 41 be interested in ~ | | 42 be proud of ~ |
| 43 focus on ~ | | |

## 단어 TEST Step 3  p.23

**1** exhibition, 전시회  **2** shout, 소리치다
**3** foolish, 어리석은  **4** flight, 비행  **5** romantic, 낭만적인
**6** escape, 달아나다  **7** gather, 모으다  **8** detail, 세부 사항

## 대화문 TEST Step 1  p.24~25

**Listen and Talk A-1**

planning to go, to go with / What time should, meet / begins at, let's meet / See, then

**Listen and Talk A-2**

planning to go see, want to go / What time, where should / at 3 o'clock, Let's meet / See, on Saturday

**Listen and Talk A-3**

planning to go see, What about joining / sounds, should we meet / Let's meet, in front of

**Listen and Talk A-4**

What, going to do / planning to go, if, want to / love to When should / let's meet / Sounds

**Listen and Talk B**

planning to see, want to / What time, where, meet / How, meeting / See you then

**Listen and Talk C**

up / going to do / Nothing special / planning to go, want to go / love to, What time should, meet / How about meeting / Where should / Let's, in front of / see you there

**Review 1**

planning to, Why don't you join / should we meet / Let's meet, at the bus stop / then

**Review 2**

planning to go, Do you want / What time should, meet / let's meet, in front of

**Review 3**

I'm planning to go shopping, join / What, meet / about meeting / Where should, meet / meet in front of

## 대화문 TEST Step 2  p.26~27

**Listen and Talk A-1**

G: I'm planning to go to a piano concert tomorrow. Do you want to go with me, Kevin?

B: Sure. What time should we meet?

G: The concert begins at 7 o'clock, so let's meet at 6 at the bus stop.

B: OK. See you then.

G: I'm planning to go see Cats this Saturday. Do you want to go with me?

B: Sure. What time and where should we meet?

G: The musical starts at 3 o'clock. Let's meet at 2 at Dream Art Hall.

B: Great. See you on Saturday.

**Listen and Talk A-3**

G: I'm planning to go see a soccer game next Friday. What about joining me, Jinho?

B: That sounds great. What time should we meet?

G: Let's meet at 10:30 in front of Green Stadium.

B: OK. See you then.

**Listen and Talk A-4**

B: What are you going to do this Sunday?

G: I'm planning to go to Dream Amusement Park with my brother. You can go with us if you want to.

B: I'd love to. When should we meet?

G: I want to go early, so let's meet at 9 at the subway station.

B: Sounds good. I'll see you then.

**Listen and Talk B**

A: I'm planning to see a movie this Saturday. Do you want to go with me?

B: Sure. What time and where should we meet?

A: How about meeting at 2:30 in front of Star Movie Theater?

B: OK. See you then.

**Listen and Talk C**

B: Hi, Kate. What's up?

G: Hi, Minho. What are you going to do this Saturday?

B: Nothing special. Why?

G: I'm planning to go to the Van Gogh exhibition at the National Art Museum. Do you want to go with me?

B: I'd love to! He's my favorite painter. What time should we meet?

G: How about meeting at 11?

B: OK. Where should we meet?

G: Let's meet in front of the ticket office.

B: Sounds good. I'll see you there at 11.

**Review 1**

G: I'm planning to go to a piano concert this Friday. Why don't you join me, Kevin?

B: Sure. What time should we meet?

G: Let's meet at 10:30 at the bus stop.

B: OK. See you then.

**Review 2**

B: I'm planning to go to a soccer game tomorrow. Do you want to go with me, Susan?

G: Sure. What time should we meet?

B: The game begins at 7, so let's meet at 6 in front of Dream Stadium.

G: OK. See you then.

**Review 3**

B: Sumi, I'm planning to go shopping with Jenny this Saturday. Will you join us?

G: Sounds great. What time should we meet?

B: How about meeting at 12:30?

G: OK. Where should we meet?

B: Let's meet in front of the shopping mall.

본문 **TEST** Step 1                                          p.28~29

01 Same, Different

02 different paintings, same subject

03 example, and, by

04 both, same, myth          05 Greek Myth

06 a great inventor

07 so, that, keep, forever

08 however, tired, so, kept

09 wanted to escape

10 One, saw, flying

11 need wings, shouted

12 gathered, feathers, glued, wax

13 ready, warned, Don't, close     14 wax, melt

15 began to fly    16 so, that, forgot, warning

17 flew, higher, melt

18 falling, cried out          19 fell into, died

20 Different Paintings

21 deal with, subject, different

22 painting, see, flying, falling

23 comes from, different ideas

24 thought, brave, adventurous

25 contrast, thought, foolish

26 simple, but, details

27 there, only, some stars

28 Furthermore, just, outline

29 In contrast, addition to

30 difference, different, styles

31 Whose painting, more

32 because, same, different ways

본문 **TEST** Step 2                                          p.30~31

01 Same, Different Paintings

02 different paintings, the same subject

03 example, by, by

04 both, the same Greek myth     05 Greek Myth

06 a great inventor

07 work so, that, wanted to keep, forever

08 however, tired to leave, so, kept

09 wanted to escape

10 saw birds flying

11 I need wings, shouted

12 gathered, glued them together with wax

13 ready, warned, Don't fly too close

14 will melt     15 began to fly

16 so, that, warning

17 higher and higher

18 falling, cried out     19 fell into, died

20 Different Paintings

21 both deal with, same subject, different

22 see Icarus flying, falling

23 comes from, different ideas

24 thought, brave, adventurous

25 In contrast, foolish

26 very simple, many details

27 only Icarus, some stars

28 Furthermore, simple outline

29 In contrast, in addition to

30 difference comes from, different painting styles

31 Whose painting, like more

32 because, same thing in different ways

가까이 날지 마라.

14 밀랍이 녹을 거야."

15 Daedalus와 Icarus는 날기 시작했다.

16 Icarus는 매우 흥분해서 아버지의 경고를 잊었다.

17 그는 점점 더 높이 날았고, 밀랍은 녹기 시작했다.

18 "오, 안 돼! 추락하고 있어." Icarus는 비명을 질렀다.

19 Icarus는 바다로 떨어져서 죽었다.

20 다른 두 그림

21 Matisse와 Chagall 둘 다 그들의 그림에서 같은 주제를 다루었지만, 그것들은 다르다.

22 첫째, Matisse의 그림에서, 여러분은 Icarus가 날고 있는 것을 볼 수 있지만, Chagall의 그림에서는 그 소년이 추락하고 있다.

23 이러한 차이는 두 화가들이 갖고 있던 서로 다른 생각에서 기인한다.

24 Matisse는 Icarus가 용감하고 모험심이 강하다고 생각했다.

25 반면에 Chagall은 Icarus가 어리석다고 생각했다.

26 둘째, Matisse의 그림은 매우 단순하지만, Chagall의 그림에는 세부적인 것들이 많다.

27 Matisse의 그림에는 Icarus와 몇 개의 별들만 있다.

28 게다가 Icarus의 몸은 단지 단순한 윤곽만으로 되어 있다.

29 반면에 Chagall은 Icarus뿐만 아니라 많은 사람들과 집들을 그렸다.

30 이러한 차이는 두 화가의 서로 다른 화풍에서 기인한다.

31 여러분은 누구의 그림이 더 좋은가?

32 사람들은 같은 것을 다른 방식들로 볼 수도 있기 때문에 서로 다른 대답을 할 것이다.

---

**본문 TEST** Step 3      p.32~33

1 같은 이야기, 다른 그림

2 우리는 종종 같은 주제의 다른 그림들을 발견한다.

3 한 예가 Henri Matisse가 그린 "The Flight of Icarus (이카로스의 비행)"와 Marc Chagall이 그린 "The Fall of Icarus (이카로스의 추락)"이다.

4 그것들은 둘 다 모두 같은 그리스 신화에 관한 것이다.

5 Icarus에 관한 그리스 신화

6 Daedalus는 훌륭한 발명가였다.

7 Minos왕은 Daedalus의 작품을 매우 좋아해서 Daedalus를 그의 곁에 영원히 두고 싶어 했다.

8 그러나 Daedalus는 떠나려고 했고, 그러자 왕은 그와 그의 아들인 Icarus를 높은 탑에 가두었다.

9 Daedalus는 탈출하고 싶었다.

10 어느 날, Daedalus는 새가 날고 있는 것을 보았다.

11 "날개! 날개가 필요해!" 그가 외쳤다.

12 그 다음에 Daedalus는 새의 깃털을 모아 그것들을 밀랍으로 붙였다.

13 날개가 준비되었을 때, 그는 아들에게 경고했다. "태양에 너무

---

**본문 TEST** Step 4~Step 5      p.34~37

1 Same Story, Different Paintings

2 We often find different paintings with the same subject.

3 An example is The Flight of Icarus by Henri Matisse and The Fall of Icarus by Marc Chagall.

4 They are both about the same Greek myth.

5 The Greek Myth of Icarus

6 Daedalus was a great inventor.

7 King Minos liked Daedalus' work so much that he wanted to keep Daedalus with him forever.

8 Daedalus, however, tried to leave, so the King kept him and his son, Icarus, in a tall tower.

9 Daedalus wanted to escape.

10 One day, Daedalus saw birds flying.

11 "Wings! I need wings!" he shouted.

12 Daedalus then gathered bird feathers and glued them together with wax.

13 When the wings were ready, he warned his son,

"Don't fly too close to the sun.

14 The wax will melt."

15 Daedalus and Icarus began to fly.

16 Icarus was so excited that he forgot his father's warning.

17 He flew higher and higher, and the wax began to melt.

18 "Oh, no! I'm falling," Icarus cried out.

19 Icarus fell into the sea and died.

20 Two Different Paintings

21 Matisse and Chagall both deal with the same subject in their paintings, but they are different.

22 First, in Matisse's painting, you can see Icarus flying, but in Chagall's painting, the boy is falling.

23 This difference comes from the different ideas that the two painters had.

24 Matisse thought that Icarus was brave and adventurous.

25 In contrast, Chagall thought that Icarus was foolish.

26 Second, Matisse's painting is very simple, but Chagall's painting has many details.

27 In Matisse's painting, there are only Icarus and some stars.

28 Furthermore, Icarus' body has just a simple outline.

29 In contrast, Chagall painted many people and houses in addition to Icarus.

30 This difference comes from the different painting styles of the two painters.

31 Whose painting do you like more?

32 People will have different answers because they may see the same thing in different ways.

**Talk and Play**

1. I'm planning to, want to go with
2. What time, meet
3. How about meeting
4. Where, meet
5. Let's meet in front of
6. Sounds, See, than

**Around the World**

1. was proud of
2. One day, fell in love with himself
3. that, all the bad things
4. they all came out
5. a great musician

6. met, return my wife

**After You Read D Reading Project**

1. Title
2. Painter
3. In, painting, is flying
4. thought, brave, adventurous
5. simple, drew only, some stars
6. Title
7. Painter
8. is falling, thought, was foolish
9. many details, in addition to

**Talk and Play**

1. A: I'm planning to go to the library this Monday. Do you want to go with me, Jiho?
2. B: Sure. What time should we meet?
3. A: How about meeting at 5:30?
4. B: OK. Where should we meet?
5. A: Let's meet in front of the library.
6. B: Sounds good. See you then.

**Around the World**

1. Narcissus: Narcissus was proud of his beauty.
2. One day , he saw his face in the water and fell in love with himself.
3. Pandora: There was a box that had all the bad things in the world inside.
4. Pandora opened it, and they all came out.
5. Orpheus: Orpheus was a great musician.
6. When his wife died, he met Hades and told him, "Please return my wife to me."

**After You Read D Reading Project**

1. Title : The Flight of Icarus
2. Painter : Henri Matisse
3. In Matisse's painting , Icarus is flying .
4. He thought Icarus was brave and adventurous.
5. His painting is very simple . He drew only Icarus and some stars .
6. Title : The Fall of Icarus
7. Painter : Marc Chagall
8. In Chagall's painting, Icarus is falling . He thought Icarus was foolish .
9. His painting has many details . He painted many people and houses in addition to Icarus.

11 towards, ~을 향해  12 space station, 우주 정거장
13 adventure, 모험  14 swallow, 삼키다
15 land, 착륙하다  16 secret, 비밀

## 단어 TEST Step 1  p.40

| | | |
|---|---|---|
| 01 도착하다 | 02 모험 | 03 맛 |
| 04 놀라운 | 05 어려운 | 06 뜨다, 떠가다 |
| 07 외치다 | 08 풍선 | 09 그릇, 용기 |
| 10 다른 | 11 궁금한, 호기심이 많은 | |
| 12 목마른 | 13 모든 곳에 | 14 우주 정거장 |
| 15 탐험, 탐사 | 16 마침내 | 17 ~한 이래로 |
| 18 외국의 | 19 신난, 흥분한 | 20 눕다 |
| 21 삼키다 | 22 흔들다 | |
| 23 ~쪽으로, ~을 향하여 | | 24 우주선 |
| 25 고치다 | 26 젖은 | 27 웃다 |
| 28 구하다 | 29 최근에 | 30 우주복 |
| 31 형성하다, 만들어 내다 | | 32 비밀, 기밀 |
| 33 부드러운 | 34 아주 신나는 | 35 ~할 필요 없다 |
| 36 (둘 사이의) 서로 | 37 ~으로 뒤덮이다 | 38 아래로 끌어내리다 |
| 39 눕다 | 40 예를 들어 | |
| 41 ~에 관해 궁금해 하다 | | 42 ~으로 달려가다 |
| 43 더 이상 ~ 않다 | | |

## 단어 TEST Step 2  p.41

| | | |
|---|---|---|
| 01 dventure | 02 balloon | 03 difficult |
| 04 float | 05 excited | 06 different |
| 07 exploration | 08 soft | 09 amazing |
| 10 finally | 11 since | 12 fix |
| 13 foreign | 14 spaceship | 15 secret |
| 16 everywhere | 17 wind | 18 shout |
| 19 shake | 20 curious | 21 towards |
| 22 space suit | 23 thirsty | 24 container |
| 25 swallow | 26 hill | 27 lie |
| 28 thrilling | 29 laugh | 30 wet |
| 31 grass | 32 recently | 33 save |
| 34 taste | 35 be curious about ~ | |
| 36 try to+동사원형 | 37 in surprise | 38 not ~ anymore |
| 39 be covered with | | 40 get on |
| 41 for example | 42 each other | 43 roll down |

## 단어 TEST Step 3  p.42

1 amazing, 놀라운  2 float, 뜨다  3 spaceship, 우주선
4 form, 형성하다, 만들다  5 arrive , 도착하다
6 save, 구하다  7 curious, 호기심 많은  8 wet, 젖은
9 exploration, 탐험, 탐사  10 foreign, 외국의

## 대화문 TEST Step 1  p.43~44

**Listen and Talk A-1**

hear about, that went into space / curious about /
spaceship / want to buy

**Listen and Talk A-2**

Did, hear about / I'm really curious about / right here,
about / buy

**Listen and Talk A-3**

Did you hear about / I didn't / space station, Look at /
I'm really curious about

**Listen and Talk A-4**

about, space food / a type of / hear it is, looks good /
curious about the taste

**Listen and Talk B**

1 about / heard / curious about
2 Look at, hear about / No, didn't / it has great
  songs/ realy curious about

**Listen and Talk C**

hear about / didn't / heard good / curious about,
about / about, who, trying to live / sounds interesting
/ is playing / What time / begins at / Let's eat lunch,
and then / hungry, Let's go

**Review 1**

did you hear about / No, didn't / heard / curious
about, about / about, who saves his son

**Review 2**

Did, hear about / right, about living / really curious
about / Me, too

## 대화문 TEST Step 2  p.45~46

**Listen and Talk A-1**

B: Did you hear about the first spaceship that went
   into space?
G: No, I didn't. I'm curious about it.
B: This is a poster of the spaceship.
G: Really? I want to buy it.

**Listen and Talk A-2**

G: Did you hear about the new book about Mars?
B: No, I didn't. I'm really curious about Mars.
G: Look. It's right here. It's about Mars and its moons.
B: Great. I think I'll buy the book.

G: Did you hear about the space marathon?

B: No, I didn't.

G: It's a marathon on a space station. Look at this video.

B: OK. I'm really curious about it.

G: Did you hear about the new space food?

B: Yes, I did. It's a type of ice cream.

G: Yes, and here it is. It looks good.

B: I'm really curious about the taste.

1 A: Look at this. Did you hear about the new musical?

　 B: Yes, I did. I heard it has great songs.

　 A: Oh, I'm really curious about it.

2 A: Look at this. Did you hear about the new musical?

　 B: No, I didn't.

　 A: I heard it has great songs.

　 B: Oh, I'm really curious about it.

B: Subin, did you hear about the new movie, Life on the Moon?

G: No, I didn't.

B: I heard it's really good.

G: I'm really curious about the movie. What's it about?

B: It's about a man who is trying to live on the moon.

G: That sounds interesting.

B: Look. The movie is playing at the Space Theater here.

G: What time is the movie?

B: It begins at 2:30.

G: Let's eat lunch first and then see the movie.

B: OK. I'm hungry. Let's go!

G: Tony, did you hear about the movie, My Hero ?

B: No, I didn't.

G: Well, I heard it's really good.

B: I'm really curious about the movie. What's it about ?

G: It's about a father who saves his son.

G: Did you hear about the new book, Living in a Foreign Country ?

B: No, I didn't.

G: Look. It's right here. It's about living in New York. B: Great. I'm really curious about this book.

G: Me, too.

01 Best, Thing　　02 like, far out　　03 lived there with

04 other, worked on　　　　05 Only, were born

06 One, going back

07 in surprise, floated towards　　08 What's it like

09 Everything, different

10 For example, answered

11 never seen, said

12 is always black

13 don't have, suits, there

14 hard, because, pulls, down

15 What else　　16 covered with, grass

17 roll down, answered

18 have, ever rolled down

19 amazing, answered

20 thirsty, opened, shook

21 floated, air, formed

22 swallowed, balls

23 if, way, get wet

24 Later, talked, long

25 exciting, all, things, going　　26 one new thing

27 thought, all night, about　　28 their secret

29 next, got on　　30 going, be, trip

31 alright, so excited　　32 finally landed

33 difficult to walk

34 pulling you down

35 couldn't float anymore　　36 first new thing

37 What's, sound　　38 bird singing

39 never heard, sing

40 never felt, wind　　41 These, all new

42 ran up the nearest

43 top, each other, laughed

44 lay down, soft, rolled　　45 their secret

46 best new, shouted　　47 ran up to, top

01 Best, Thing　　02 far out in space

03 lived there with, brother

04 other, worked on

05 Only, were born in space

06 One day, going back to

07 in surprise, floated towards　　08 What's it like

09 Everything is different　　10 For example

11 I've never seen　　12 is always black

13 don't have to, because there is air

14 jump, pulls you down　　15 What else

16 are covered with

17 roll down     18 have you ever rolled down

19 really amazing 20 thirsty, so, opened, shook

21 floated, formed        22 swallowed

23 if, that way, get wet

24 Later that night, a long time

25 exciting, think, all the new things, going to

26 one new thing, wanted to do

27 all night     28 their secret     29 got on

30 It's going to be

31 alright, so excited

32 finally landed   33 to walk

34 pulling you down

35 couldn't float anymore

36 the first new thing        37 What's, sound

38 is singing     39 I've never heard, sing

40 I've never felt   41 These, all new things

42 ran up the nearest

43 each other, laughed

44 lay down, rolled down

45 their secret    46 best new thing

47 up to the top

1 최고의 새로운 것

2 Rada는 먼 우주의 작은 세계에 살고 있었다.

3 그녀는 아빠, 엄마 그리고 남동생 Jonny와 함께 그곳에서 살고 있었다.

4 Rada의 아빠와 다른 사람들은 우주선에서 일했다.

5 Rada와 Jonny만이 아이들이었고, 그들은 우주에서 태어났다.

6 어느 날, 아빠가 Rada와 Jonny에게, "우리는 내일 지구로 돌아갈 거야."라고 말했다.

7 Rada와 Jonny는 깜짝 놀라 아빠를 바라보았고, 그에게 둥둥 떠서 갔다.

8 Rada가 아빠에게, "지구는 어떤 곳인가요?"라고 물었다.

9 "그곳에선 모든 것이 다르단다.

10 예를 들어, 하늘은 파란색이지."라고 아빠가 대답했다.

11 "전 한 번도 파란 하늘을 본 적이 없어요."라고 Jonny가 말했다.

12 "여기는 하늘이 항상 검은색이잖아요."라고 Rada가 말했다.

13 "그곳에는 모든 곳에 공기가 있기 때문에 크고 무거운 우주복을 입을 필요가 없단다.

14 또한 지구가 너희들을 끌어당기기 때문에 거기에서는 점프하는 것도 어렵단다." 아빠가 말했다.

15 "그 밖에 또 뭐가 있어요?" Rada가 물었다.

16 "언덕들이 있는데 그것들은 부드러운 초록색의 잔디로 뒤덮여 있단다.

17 언덕을 굴러 내려갈 수도 있어." 엄마가 대답했다.

18 "아빠, 언덕을 굴러 내려가 본 적 있어요?" Rada가 물었다.

19 "그럼, 정말 놀라워!" 아빠가 대답했다.

20 Jonny는 목이 말라서 우유 용기를 열어 그것을 흔들었다.

21 우유가 공기 중으로 떠서 방울을 형성했다.

22 Jonny는 그 우유 방울을 삼켰다.

23 "Jonny, 만약 네가 지구에서 그런 식으로 우유를 마신다면, 다 젖을 거야." 엄마가 말했다.

24 그날 밤 늦게, Rada와 Jonny는 지구에 대해서 오랜 시간 이야기했다.

25 그들이 보고, 하게 될 모든 새로운 것들을 생각하는 것은 흥미로웠다.

26 Rada와 Jonny가 정말로 하고 싶었던 한 가지 새로운 것이 있었다.

27 그들은 밤새 그것에 대해서 생각했고 엄마와 아빠에게 그것을 말하지 않았다.

28 그것은 그들의 비밀이었다.

29 다음날, Rada의 가족은 우주선에 올랐다.

30 "긴 여행이 될 거야." 엄마가 말했다.

31 "괜찮아요. 정말 신나요!" Rada가 말했다.

32 우주선이 마침내 착륙했다.

33 "아빠, 지구에서는 걷는 것이 어려워요." Rada가 말했다.

34 "그래. 지구가 너를 끌어당기고 있거든." 아빠가 말했다.

35 Rada와 Jonny는 더 이상 떠다닐 수 없었다.

36 그것이 첫 번째 새로운 것이었다.

37 "저건 무슨 소리죠?"라고 Rada가 물었다.

38 "새가 노래하는 거야." 엄마가 말했다.

39 "새가 노래하는 것을 들어 본 적이 없어요."라고 Rada가 말했다.

40 "그리고 저는 바람을 느껴 본 적도 없어요."라고 Jonny가 말했다.

41 이러한 것들이 모두 새로운 것들이었다.

42 Rada와 Jonny는 가장 가까운 언덕으로 뛰어 올라갔다.

43 꼭대기에서, 그들은 서로를 쳐다보고 웃었다.

44 그러고 나서 그들은 부드러운 초록 잔디에 누워서 언덕 아래로 굴러 내려갔다.

45 그것이 그들의 비밀이었다!

46 "이것이 모든 것들 중에서 최고의 새로운 것이에요!" Rada와 Jonny는 외쳤다.

47 그리고 그들은 언덕 꼭대기로 다시 뛰어 올라갔다.

1 The Best New Thing

2 Rada lived on a little world, far out in space.

3 She lived there with her father, mother, and brother Jonny.

4 Rada's father and other people worked on spaceships

5 Only Rada and Jonny were children, and they were born in space.

6 One day, Dad told Rada and Jonny, "We're going back to Earth tomorrow."

7 Rada and Jonny looked at Dad in surprise and floated towards him.

8 Rada asked Dad, "What's it like on Earth?"

9 "Everything is different there.

10 For example, the sky is blue," answered Dad.

11 "I've never seen a blue sky," said Jonny.

12 "The sky is always black here," said Rada.

13 "You don't have to wear your big heavy space suits because there is air everywhere.

14 It's also hard to jump there because Earth pulls you down," said Dad.

15 "What else?" asked Rada.

16 "There are hills, and they are covered with soft green grass.

17 You can roll down the hills," answered Mom.

18 "Dad, have you ever rolled down a hill?" asked Rada.

19 "Yes, it's really amazing!" answered Dad.

20 Jonny was thirsty, so he opened a milk container and shook it.

21 The milk floated in the air and formed balls.

22 Jonny swallowed the balls.

23 "Jonny, if you drink milk that way on Earth, you'll get wet," said Mom.

24 Later that night, Rada and Jonny talked a long time about Earth.

25 It was exciting to think about all the new things they were going to see and do.

26 There was one new thing Rada and Jonny really wanted to do.

27 They thought about it all night and didn't tell Mom and Dad about it.

28 It was their secret.

29 The next day, Rada's family got on a spaceship.

30 "It's going to be a long trip," said Mom.

31 That's alright. I'm so excited!" said Rada.

32 The spaceship finally landed.

33 "Dad, it's difficult to walk on Earth," said Rada.

34 "I know. Earth is pulling you down," said Dad.

35 Rada and Jonny couldn't float anymore.

36 That was the first new thing.

37 "What's that sound?" asked Rada.

38 "A bird is singing," said Mom.

39 "I've never heard a bird sing," said Rada.

40 "And I've never felt the wind," said Jonny.

41 These were all new things.

42 Rada and Jonny ran up the nearest hill.

43 At the top, they looked at each other and laughed.

44 Then they lay down on the soft green grass and rolled down the hill.

45 That was their secret!

46 "This is the best new thing of all!" shouted Rada and Jonny.

47 And they ran up to the top of the hill again.

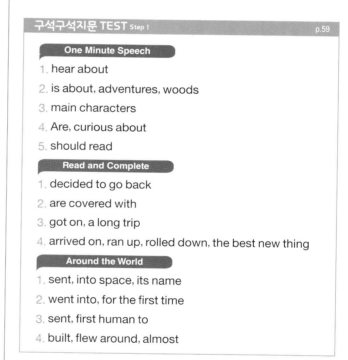

구석구석지문 TEST Step 1     p.59

**One Minute Speech**

1. hear about
2. is about, adventures, woods
3. main characters
4. Are, curious about
5. should read

**Read and Complete**

1. decided to go back
2. are covered with
3. got on, a long trip
4. arrived on, ran up, rolled down, the best new thing

**Around the World**

1. sent, into space, its name
2. went into, for the first time
3. sent, first human to
4. built, flew around, almost

구석구석지문 TEST Step 2     p.60

**One Minute Speech**

1. Did you hear about the new book, Dave's Adventures?
2. This book is about Dave and his adventures in the woods .
3. The main characters are Dave and a big bear. The story is fun.
4. Are you curious about the book? 5. Then you should read it!

43

1. Rada's family lived in space. One day, they decided to go back to Earth.

2. Rada's family talked about life on Earth. They talked about the blue sky and hills which are covered with green grass.

3. The next day, Rada's family got on a spaceship. It was a long trip to Earth.

4. When they arrived on Earth, Rada and Jonny ran up the nearest hill and rolled down it. That was the best new thing to them.

## Around the World

1. Russia sent the first dog into space . It was small, and its name was Laika.

2. Yuri Gagarin went into space for the first time .

3. The USA sent the first human to the moon. His name was Neil Armstrong.

4. Russia built the first space station. It flew around the Earth almost 3,000 times.

# 적중100

영어 기출 문제집

## 정답 및 해설

동아 | 윤정미